Consciousness, Performing Arts and Literature

Consciousness, Performing Arts and Literature:

Trajectories, 2014-2018

Edited by

Daniel Meyer-Dinkgräfe

**Cambridge
Scholars**
Publishing

Consciousness, Performing Arts and Literature: Trajectories, 2014-2018

Edited by Daniel Meyer-Dinkgräfe

This book first published 2018

Cambridge Scholars Publishing

Lady Stephenson Library, Newcastle upon Tyne, NE6 2PA, UK

British Library Cataloguing in Publication Data
A catalogue record for this book is available from the British Library

ISBN (10): 1-5275-1360-2
ISBN (13): 978-1-5275-1360-0

CONTENTS

INTRODUCTION

My retirement at the end of February 2017 gave me the opportunity of reflecting on my research, in the higher education context, since 1994. This personal trajectory interlinks closely with that of the discipline(s) I have been involved with: first and foremost, theatre studies, more recently extending to dance studies and opera studies in my own research and publications, combined with a keen interest and editorial activity in the developments of fine arts, music, film and television, and literature.

Over the years, in my own research, what I have been doing since I embarked on my PhD dissertation is to interrogate and explore phenomena of theatre in the context of consciousness studies, to seek explanations for experiences described by theatre artists, dancers and artists involved in opera, across the world. My research is thus anchored in consciousness studies, defined as the "study of how we think, feel and act, why we think, feel and act as we do, and what it feels like to think, feel and act as we do" (Meyer-Dinkgräfe 2013a, 11). Within consciousness studies, I focus further on positions of spirituality to provide explanatory contexts for phenomena of theatre and performance. I understand spirituality in a non-religious way, with the implication that "spirituality culminates in the full development of mind," and "any move in the direction of this fullness can be called spirituality" (Malekin and Yarrow 1997). My approach has been eclectic in so far as I have gone with the aspects of consciousness studies that had, for me, the highest explanatory value, independent of where any specific aspect might have come from. I have found much value in Vedanta philosophy, much of that in the form of Vedic Science as developed on the basis of Vedanta philosophy by the late Maharishi Mahesh Yogi.

In 1991, when I had made my decision to pursue a doctorate in theatre studies and had decided to apply for a place at the then Royal Holloway and Bedford New College, I submitted two different thesis proposals, one around a conventional topic relating to contemporary British drama, and one on the actor's emotional involvement reconsidered from the perspective of Vedic Science. In due course I received a response directly from a prospective supervisor with the clear indication that were I to want to proceed with the British drama topic, he was not interested, but he would be very keen to supervise my consciousness studies topic. I completed my PhD in 1994 and was appointed to a Lectureship in Drama at the University of Wales Aberystwyth a few weeks later.

This particular, Vedic Science-oriented approach was based on my familiarity with the Transcendental Meditation movement--I learnt this meditation technique in my early teens, later trained to be a teacher of TM and spent several months teaching at Maharishi International University (MIU, later renamed Maharishi University of Management, MUM). I was invited to develop my own syllabus for a one-month block module relating contemporary drama to consciousness studies. While the syllabus was approved by the head of department, I was later asked to remove Beckett's *Waiting for Godot* from the syllabus at the request of the university's President. This incident alerted me to the essential necessity of differentiating between unadulterated knowledge derived directly from Maharishi Mahesh Yogi, and its institutional mediation. This relative openness also enabled me, in due course, to extend my knowledge base beyond that available from Maharishi Mahesh Yogi to, for example, Maharishi's former disciple Sri Sri Ravi Shankar, and, most recently, German geobiologist Hans Binder. In my 2013 book *Observing Theatre: Spirituality and Subjectivity in the Performing Arts*, I introduced Binder's philosophy as the basis for discussions of aspects of theatre as varied as *nostalgia* in theatre, intuitive collaboration, praise of acting in theatre criticism, practice as research, digital performance, theatre and philosophy, the canon, applied theatre and aspects of acting including helping actors cope with stage fright.

When I started my higher education career, consciousness studies as a disciplinary area was in its infancy, as was the interrogation of the arts from a consciousness studies perspective. I vividly recall my first participation in a national conference in the UK where I presented my position, and a well-established senior figure in the British higher education drama scene told me that if I meant what I said he would certainly not send his children to be taught by me. Two years later, at an international conference, I presented on the topic of universality from the consciousness studies perspective and a colleague stormed out shouting that he had hoped never to have to encounter such ideas about universality ever again. My work was published, and in 2000 I was able to found the peer review journal, *Consciousness, Literature and the Arts* (http://www.dmd27.org/CLA.html) with the support of my department--over the years, I even had the privilege of the services of a PhD student to help with the administrative work on the journal. In institutional terms, however, it took a long while for my work to be accepted and acknowledged to the extent that it was considered of sufficient merit for an internal promotion. With the support of the department, an extensive outside evaluative report was commissioned on whether consciousness studies was considered, in the academic world of social sciences and sciences, as a serious subject, or a New-Age-like niche. In 2007, a newly appointed head of department summoned me to his office a month after taking up his role and told me: "I do not wish my department to be associated nationally or internationally with *Theatre and Consciousness*". He proceeded to offer me a sabbatical, "to realign your research interests to the established strengths of the department". The previous year I had edited a Festschrift for German theatre director and politician Heinz-Uwe Haus (2007), who had worked at the forefront of theatre in the so-called German Democratic Republic and had been a member of the political organisation that was instrumental in bringing about the end of that regime.

From this work I realised that in my department I was witnessing the beginning of a totalitarian regime in miniature, with the whole range of responses, from real or feigned not noticing anything amiss, via a conscious accepting a role in the opposition but without the option of leaving, all the way to seeking immediate escape. I escaped, to a professorship at the University of Lincoln, signing my contract only three months after that memorable meeting with the new head of department. In Lincoln, the journal could continue, as well as the two book-series I had launched in 2005, *Theatre and Consciousness* with Intellect and *Consciousness, Literature and the Arts* with Rodopi--any "re-alignment" of my profile in Aberystwyth would have included discontinuing the journal and the two book-series.

In the social sciences and sciences, it has been notoriously difficult, even impossible, to argue any causality—correlation is as close as these approaches get. It is against this background that I point to the following broad development, which overlaps with my own. In 1991, I began with my research into the relationship between insights in consciousness studies and theatre. In 1994, the Center for Consciousness Studies at the University of Arizona in Tucson launched the first of the ongoing bi-annual conferences, Towards a Science of Consciousness. In 1994, the *Journal of Consciousness Studies* was launched, 1996 saw the launch of the Association for the Scientific Study of Consciousness with its annual conferences and its journal, *Consciousness and Cognition*. 1996 also saw the publication of my doctoral thesis. The British Psychological Society founded its sections on *Consciousness and Experiential Psychology* and *Transpersonal Psychology* in 1997. It is also in these years that other publications began to emerge in the field of theatre, literature and consciousness, for example with Peter Malekin and Ralph Yarrow's *Consciousness, Literature and Theatre: Theory and Beyond* (1997). In 1999 I edited, "Performance and Consciousness" as a themed issue of *Performing Arts International*, in 2000 I launched the peer reviewed journal *Consciousness, Literature and the Arts*, in 2001 followed an issue on "Consciousness and Drama" in *Studies in the Literary Imagination*. The Intellect and Rodopi book series were launched in 2005, as well as a bi-annual conference series, *Consciousness, Theatre, Literature and the Arts*, which I hosted in Aberystwyth (2005, 2007), Lincoln (2009, 2011, 2013) and New York (with Gregory Tague at St Francis College, 2015). In 2006, Jade Rosina McCutcheon and I launched the working group *Performance and Consciousness* at the International Federation for Theatre Research. In the Lincoln School of Performing Arts at the University of Lincoln, an MA Theatre and Consciousness ran from 2008/9 to 2010/11, with a total of ten graduates, and the subsequent MA Drama in the Lincoln School of Fine and Performing Arts had a pathway "Theatre and Consciousness" with five graduates.

The editorial policy for both the CLA journal and for the two book-series was intentionally wide open, not geared towards any specific ideology or methodological approach. In particular, the editorial boards of the journal and the book series embraced new ideas, no matter how radical, as long as they were presented in a robust way. Rodopi in particular supported this policy by allowing decisions about accepting a proposal or, based on the accepted proposal, accepting the completed manuscript, to be taken solely by the members of the editorial board, who engaged in thorough peer review. When Rodopi was taken over by Brill quite recently, their new requirement for peer review outside of the editorial board would have been problematic in the earlier phase when the consciousness, literature and the arts field was in its infancy. However, the field has become sufficiently established in the meantime, and such concerns are no longer needed. Those still active in Higher Education will need to consider carefully whether explicit rules and implicit expectations or fears regarding research audit procedures, such as the Research Excellence Framework (REF) in the United Kingdom, may have a debilitating impact on the opportunities they allow researchers to develop and present genuinely new insights, as they have been presented in the CLA journal and the Rodopi/Brill and Intellect book-series, and as I am presenting them in this book. It stands to reason that it is in principle impossible, or at least very difficult, to predict anything genuinely new—if it is predictable, it cannot be new to the extent that it is being predicted. The danger is that structures such as the REF limit what is acceptable as research, or what scores highly, to predictable contexts, because in that way the chance for new insights is at best limited. REF-procedures might serve to consolidate and perpetuate the status quo and managers afraid of losing funding that depends on the outcomes of such audits might award work that plays it safe.

Approximately the same time that the conference series, and the two book-series were launched marks the beginning of the "cognitive turn" in performance and literary studies—insights specifically from cognitive science were used to further understand phenomena of performance, including theatre, and literature. A few years later, spirituality, anchored in religions and religious studies/theology entered the formalised scene, with a *Performance, Religion and Spirituality* working group within the International Federation for Theatre Research, which also launched its own journal. The open nature of the initial Consciousness, Literature and the Arts development separated into those two more formalised, but also by the very nature of that formalisation, more limited branches. At the University of Huddersfield, UK, the Centre for Psychophysical Performance Research, founded by Franc Chamberlain and Deborah Middleton, focuses on Mindfulness and performance, with a new journal on that topic launched in 2017/18. It is even possible to refer to the Performance Philosophy area in this context, which may well have been first formalised through the foundation, by Dan Watt and myself, of the working group *Performance and Philosophy* within TaPRA (Theatre and Performance Research Association) in 2005, still continuing, and the immensely popular Performance Philosophy network formally launched in 2013 with an international conference of which Watt was a co-organiser—it now has its own book series and journal (the journal co-edited by Watt).

Against this background of trajectories, personal, institutional and cultural, I present work I published and wrote (unpublished) between 2014 and today. I begin with three forays into the discussion of dance from a consciousness studies perspective. This section starts with a professorial reflection on the nature of dance, a conversation with Barbara Sellers-Young. This is followed by two articles about German dancer/philosopher Aurelia Baumgartner, considering her approach to spirituality and its expression in her dance performances in general, and specifically in her work with horses.

From there I move on to opera, with a reassessment of the apparent clash between Regieoper and Werktreue—director's opera and productions that seek to be true to the composer/librettists' intentions, and an introduction to the spiritual nature of the work of International Opera Theater. In shorter contributions, I comment on the alleged crisis in opera that critics note at regular intervals, and I expand my work on conducting beyond my 2013 insights.

Eight chapters follow on theatre and consciousness. Here I offer a new perspective on liveness and livecasts (chapter 6), revisit, with Anita S. Hammer, the concept of a universal language of the theatre (chapter 7), discuss two productions of new plays (with Yana Meerzon, Wajdi Mouawad's *Scorched*, chapter 8), and with Gregory F. Tague, Stoppard's *The Hard Problem*, chapter 9), and the use of science in Prebble's *The Effect* (chapter 10). I add a new dimension to debates of ethical issues in relation to theatre in my consideration of the ethical implications of children playing characters in plays with "adult themes" (chapter 11). I introduce the concept of *theatre of the heart* in chapter 12, bringing a 2017 publication up to date with more recent material. With Tanatchaporn Kittikong I discuss the concept of beauty, comparing Western and Thai positions (chapter 13).

In the final part of the book I develop the concept of "practice as research". In chapter 14, I tackle the question of whether theatre needs conflict to be successful. The final chapter is taken up with my first novel, which launches the genre of spiritual romance—I make use of a number of the issues I raise in my 2013 books and in the preceding chapters of the current book, integrating them in the narrative.

Each chapter begins with a general statement that places the chapter within the context of the book overall. For previously published work, the contextualisation also charts the publication history. I do not change the text itself of previously published work—rather, I identify any additional, later thoughts as such in the contextualisation and they usually follow after the previously published text. In this way, development of thinking over time is always transparent.

PART ONE:

DANCE AND CONSCIOUSNESS

CHAPTER ONE

PROFESSORIAL REFLECTIONS:
INFORMAL DISCUSSIONS AND REFLECTIONS

BARBARA SELLERS-YOUNG
AND DANIEL MEYER-DINKGRÄFE

[First published in *Dance, Movement and Spiritualities*, 1:2 (2014), 241-250;
reprinted here with permission from Intellect Publishing]

Contextualisation

The launch of *Dance, Movement and Spiritualities* with Intellect Publishing in 2014 is one stone in the mosaic of the expanding development of seeking further understanding of phenomena, particularly subjective experiences, of fictional characters, and of artists and spectators across the disciplines of literature, film and TV, fine arts, dance, music, and theatre. I was invited by the founding editor, Dr Amanda Williamson, to join the editorial board. For issue 1:2, I was invited to contribute the first of an ongoing series of "professorial reflections", on open format of conversation between two established colleagues. Having become confident with collaboration via skype for previous publications, I approached Barbara Sellers-Young, whom I had met many years ago at a conference of the International Federation for Theatre Research—I was aware that she had extended her research within the field of theatre and performance studies to dance, and she was interested in the consciousness studies / spirituality context—she contributed to the *Consciousness, Literature and the Arts* journal as early as 2002. In 2009, I chaired a session at an IFTR conference to which she contributed a paper on "Rationality, neuroplasticity and contemplative practice". In 2013, she co-edited, with Jade Rosina McCutcheon, a book on *Embodied Consciousness: Performance Technologies* for Palgrave MacMillan, to which I contributed a chapter. We talked over skype for a number of occasions for this reflection and edited the transcript into five sections, starting with increasing acceptance for the topic of spirituality in relation to the arts, and the emphasis on the body that is necessary particularly in an art form that involves the body to the extent that dance does. We discuss social aspects of dance and spirituality in terms of ritual and consider the personal dimension of spirituality and dance in the contexts of choices that the dancer has to make, and the dancer's age.

Introduction

Sellers-Young
One of the things that emerges from some of the articles published in *Dance, Movement & Spiritualities* is an attempt to define spirituality as separate from religious belief. This seems a very comfortable place to work from.

Meyer-Dinkgräfe
I met neuroscientist Vilayanur S. Ramachandran at the 2002 'Towards a Science of Consciousness' conference in Tucson, Arizona, and I asked him "from your background, you were brought up in India, aren't you aware that there is more to life than what science can deal with at the moment?". He said, "Yes of course I am". He was very lively and passionate, as he always is, about that as well: "but I am a scientist. As a scientist I can talk only in terms of what science can achieve at any point in time, but I am also trying to push the boundaries of science for science to be able to grasp a little bit more of what is still out there, and which I am aware of".

Increasing acceptance

Meyer-Dinkgräfe
If I look back over the last twenty years that I have been working in this area, you get a completely different response at conferences to the idea of spirituality. In the past, colleagues' responses could range from mild irritation to major concern; nowadays they take up ideas and develop them further.

Sellers-Young
That idea of spirituality in dance seems very popular at the present moment as the discipline considers the phenomenon of perception of wholeness with self and the universe that is an integral part of a dancer's experience. For example, there is a conference that is going to take place next March called 'Law and the Curated Body'. It is going to have a

significant section that includes contemplative practice as in North America there is an increased inclusion of contemplative practice in programmes/academic environments. Simon Fraser University in British Columbia has actually started a two-year M.A. in Contemplative Practice in Higher Education.

The body and somatics

Sellers-Young
Spirituality is also strongly linked to somatics, which has a long history in dance, beginning with Mabel Todd's book *The Thinking Body*. The body/mind methodologies integrated with somatics include Alexander, Feldenkrais, Yoga, T'ai Chi and Pilates. Each of these has, as part of its history, a relationship to Asian physical disciplines either directly as in the case of Yoga, T'ai chi, chi gong, or indirectly in the approaches evolved by the founders of the specific somatic approach. Inherent in each of these is a form of contemplation in which the breath, imagery and the exploration of the dancer's somatic landscape play an integral role in expanding the dancer's proprioceptive and kinaesthetic awareness. This allows them a level of self-understanding that can be incorporated into learning the technical vocabulary of a specific dance form. Also inherent in somatic training that is integrated within contemplative practice is an opportunity for stillness in which the body's neurological structures experience moments of deep calm. Anthony Damasio discusses these moments as opportunities for the dissolution of previous neurological organizations in order to allow for new neurological arrangements. Thus, moments of contemplative relaxation promote the opportunity to release muscular tensions and to allow for new pathways of creativity. The experience of creative expression is another area of deep connection that is a spiritual state for dancers.

Meyer-Dinkgräfe
It is always interesting to observe how especially in dance it is necessary to talk about spirituality in terms of the body, because more than many other people, dancers are, by definition of their art and in what they are doing on a daily basis, more aware of their bodies than other people. So, anything that will be related to spirituality for the dancer will have to be experienced also in the body. It is in the body anyway, but the dancer is probably most likely able to pinpoint also a spiritual experience in relation to the body: if they have a specific spiritual experience, they are able to say where it is located in their bodies.

When I think about dance and body, what I am thinking about, especially from my knowledge and experience of having seen many South Asian performances, is that I find that I can often detect without much effort any non-South Asian dancer in a group of South Asian dancers.

Sellers-Young
When you say, "non-South Asian", do you mean in training or in authenticity?

Meyer-Dinkgräfe
In authenticity, even if they have trained obviously in the South Asian dance form. In some ways there is a difference and that is probably not just limited to the South Asian context; I would also say that, in very broad terms, if African dance is performed by dancers from Africa it is different to when it is danced by Caucasians who have trained in that particular dance form. There is a different physicality there.

Sellers-Young
I just gave a paper at the Congress on Research in Dance core conference on Edward Said and his homage to a very famous Egyptian dancer called Tahia Carioca and though he does not use necessarily the language of Egyptian aesthetics he is trying to make an argument for an Egyptian aesthetic in relation to what they call *raqs al sharqi* in Egypt, which is what we call belly dancing. His underlying comment was that if you did not learn the dance in Egypt you did not know how to dance because you would not understand the implicit nature of the aesthetic that is embedded within the ritual formations of Egypt. So, you are right, that is true, so how is that related then to spirituality, particularly from a trans-national or cross-cultural standpoint? Do you create a new kind of spirituality in relationship to the body or can you say that you really never embody the deeper levels of the original form so therefore your spirituality is defunct? It raises many questions that are often part of contemporary theorizing about performance, spirituality and the body.

Meyer-Dinkgräfe
What could be the reasons for an apparent difference between a dancer of South Asian origin and a dancer not of South Asian origin when they perform in a dance or drama form originating in South Asia? I discussed this a few months ago with my colleagues Arya Madhavan and Sreenath Nair – they had this to say:

The kinds of differences that can be observed may relate to the ways in which movements characteristic of the individual dance and drama styles are being executed by the dancers. For example, a movement may need to come across and be executed in a very gentle and flowing manner, which may be difficult for a non-South Asian performer due to the ways in which their bodies were conditioned within the culture in which they grew up. Their execution of such movements might be sharper. The same applies for martial arts.

Much depends thus on the way the bodies are cultured. In Chinese martial arts, for example, much emphasis is placed on a sitting position, and young and old can sit in that posture with apparent ease, because they will have learnt it and practiced it from a very young age. The level of experience is important as well. A dancer with less training will be less proficient in their dance, and this will show. Although this applies to both South Asian and non-South Asian performers, there has been a tendency for non-South Asian performers to embark on their training later in life than South Asian performers.

There are clear differences in the structure of the bodies: South Asian performers have a shorter torso in relation to their legs, while non-South Asian performers, in particular Caucasians, tend to have a longer torso, which tends to be similar in length to their lower bodies. Some non-South Asian performers compensate for this by bending lower for some positions, but the difference is obvious. Despite this physical difference, on rare occasions non-Indian dancers can achieve near-Indianness. Perhaps this has to do, in individual cases, with an upbringing close to Indian philosophy, for example as members of the Hare Krishna movement.

The inner cultural context is equally important, and this is exemplified by the lighting of the lamp at the beginning of a South Indian dance performance. They begin a process of transformation that brings them closer to their tradition, leads to concentration and to submission of the ego to the higher purpose. (Nair and Madhavan 2014)

From my own perspective, I added that the South Asian dancers enter the energy field of their tradition and are thus supported. It stands to reason that someone to whom this tradition is new, and who is thus not part of this energy field, will not have access to it at all, or to a much lower degree.

Social dimension: Ritual

Sellers-Young
So, the question is: do religious tradition and ritual inspire some form of spiritual experience in the performative dimension of the dancer?

Meyer-Dinkgräfe
Also, the rituals that go with performance. My daughter Myfanwy was taught for several years in Kudiyattam by Arya Madhavan, and even at the age of eight, Myfanwy said that there was a difference if she did the rituals at the beginning of the training and at the end of the training. Recently we had a conference on women in Asian performance and Arya did a brief Kudiyattam performance. I noticed that she had forgotten to do the ritual at the end and I reminded her. She said, "Thank you so much" and immediately went back to the performance space and did that particular part of completing the performance. It was something that was very important to her.

Sellers-Young
Dance is a part of rituals to celebrate a variety of occasions from personal life cycles to community and national events. Ethnography provides an opportunity to understand how dance and the moving body are organized as a medium of expression integrated into the ritual and social ethos of the community through a particular aesthetic. As some of the most deeply held beliefs are related to a community's ritual foundations, an understanding of how dance functions within ritual and related spiritual frameworks helps us to understand the implications of dance in secular environments.

For example, traditional ritual forms taught in a dance programme provide an opportunity to understand the latter through an embodiment of the form. For example, this is a description of an African dance class at the University Oregon:

> Dance and music are integral to African ceremonies and rituals that relate to many aspects of daily life – welcome, harvest, healing, initiation, possession, and more. Explore African spirituality and the way indigenous spiritual concepts are given form. Learn dances from a variety of cultural groups, while becoming familiar with the ideological and historical contexts that ground such forms of expression through readings, videos, and discussion. This class places a very heavy emphasis on student engagement with the course material. You will attend the performance of *Dance Africa* on campus, and also create and perform an original dance piece with your classmates.

The personal dimension

Meyer-Dinkgräfe
In addition to these social aspects, spirituality is eminently personal.

Sellers-Young

One of the dance forms I have been completely fascinated with is belly dance. I have just done a second edited volume and I am using my sabbatical year to actually do a single authored book on the form. It looks at the dance form in two ways: on the one hand it looks at its inclusion as part of the second wave of the feminist movement, and on the other hand in terms of the incorporation of a whole mythic dimension of the concept of the goddess. Dancers from the 1970s write about a desire to create a new religion that celebrates a woman's body and negates the patriarchal conception. This attitude has continued to exist, but even more fundamentally, belly dance has become a real place of spiritual development for women from around the world.

Studying belly dance has caused me to contemplate the possibility that we do not respect enough the possibilities of being us, the range of levels of conscious realization that are encompassed in those possibilities: spirituality is about how you conduct your life as an individual or how you conduct your life with a group. You can look at it from many different directions and as far as I am concerned there is not a god out there being beyond who we are as individuals. For me, spirituality is just completely devoid of religious tradition but at the same time I can see how ritual traditions actually inflect and impact your experience. My spirituality has evolved from the fact that I have been a member of various meditation groups for years and I love the combination of reducing experience to a moment of stillness.

In addition to ritual, which we discussed earlier, the whole area of somatic and spiritual studies stands out for me as a teacher and impacts even on courses not directly related to it. I am teaching two courses, an undergraduate and a graduate course in ethnography and this is where in dance studies, you really see the incorporation of spirituality either directly or indirectly. Certainly, all of the studies that come out on African dance on the continent or in the diaspora, including by people that are very theoretical in their approach, people like Barbara Browning, who still actually begins in the language that she uses to discuss, incorporate an attitude of the potential spirituality or the extreme presence of the moment, which is another way I would describe spirituality.

Personal dimension: Choices

Meyer-Dinkgräfe

Going back to the observation that spirituality has become an interesting topic for discussion in many contexts over the past few years, including dance, we must realize that it has become almost an industry, with many approaches to it on offer, including for sale, in bookshops or workshops or courses. While that is exciting and interesting, it also points to a dimension of spirituality that several traditions actually emphasize: the need to be both open and ready, and to differentiate between approaches that are conducive for spiritual development, and approaches that claim to be beneficial for spiritual development but are in fact not, and decide, on the basis of such differentiation, for oneself (not for others) on which approaches to take further.

For example, I recently received a video from German dancer/philosopher Aurelia Baumgartner of her horses, Arab Grey, Pegasus, and chestnut mare, Mabrouka, performing with a Butoh dancer. The dancer's movements came across as compacted, strained, a kind of hunched movement possibly deriving from Noh in terms of that form's concentration and the slowness. I am wondering whether much of the energy in Butoh is created in the solar plexus because Pegasus in particular was very interested in that region of the dancer, always having its nostrils near there and on one occasion accidentally touching the dancer's skin and shying back a little, but immediately going back. The themes of Butoh are intentionally dark, "negative", and in my experience this is reflected in the kind of energy that Butoh generates.

Sellers-Young

They are trying to challenge your conceptions of beauty and I might be a little outside of my knowledge base here because it is something that I have read about and seen performances of, but not immediately practiced. One of the influences is Mary Wigman and German expressionism, so if you think about expressionism, one of its explicit roles was trying to get you to re-see the world around you. For example, at the time expressionists sought to challenge a view of the landscape that did not see light or did not see relationships between elements. Butoh is actually also trying to have you see things differently and very definitely in terms of the social political elements, not necessarily returning to a concept of the beautiful that is related to the traditional forms of Japanese past. It's not trying to be Kabuki, because that would be how in Japan you would have defined the beautiful, but they are actually trying to get you to rethink beauty and its implication. Particularly after the bombing of Hiroshima and Nagasaki you have to ask: how do you then redefine the beautiful when you have had such historically destructive things happen within the context of your society where people's bodies are literally challenged?

I remember the Butoh performance of Kazuo Ohno. I saw him perform at the age of 85. It was in a theatre that held about 2,500 people – so it was a pretty good-sized space. I was mid-way back in the theatre. With minimal gestures you could literally feel the man performing. It was almost like he would move a hand this way and the energy of that movement would reverberate out to the audience. This is one of the things Zeami, the founder of Noh, talks about: you come onstage and learn to breathe with your audience and by breathing with the audience and integrating your breath with that of the audience, you transform the space.

Meyer-Dinkgräfe
When Baumgartner took Pegasus and Mabrouka out of the arena into the paddock [after their encounter with the Butoh dancer], the horses galloped at full speed for a very long time, back and forth, until they were breathing and sweating very heavily, as if they wanted to get rid of the energy they may have picked up from the dancer. Taking several aspects of this encounter with Butoh into account, the dark nature of the energy, the focus of energy on the solar plexus (which as one of the chakras, in the context of Indian philosophy, is a highly sensitive area of the mind/body), and the response of the horses to the Butoh dancer, I come to the conclusion, for myself, that I would rather not encounter more performances, live or recorded, of Butoh, because I'd rather have different kinds of energies circulating in my body that I experience as more conducive to spiritual development. Such a personal choice, which is part of the development of spirituality for everyone, can of course come across as controversial in wider discussion.

Age

Meyer-Dinkgräfe
You mentioned already another point that I find very interesting and worth discussing further and that is age in relation to dance, the body, expectations and possibly then taking it further to wisdom and experience and in that sense, spirituality. I remember that in 1993 in Toronto I saw a performance of Chandralekha (1928–2006) who was then 65 years old; her age did not matter in the performance. I also then remembered that I had been at the last performance of the Düsseldorf Prima Ballerina, Tilly Söffing, in the late 1970s. Because my mother is an actress and other actors were there as well, and some of them knew this dancer, we went backstage afterwards and Söffing, who was in her early 30s at that point, said that her whole body had been in excruciating pain throughout the

performance, and that she would now look forward to a long time recuperating in a sanatorium. In the second half of that performance we saw her successor as Prima Ballerina; I think Tilly Söffing had done the fire bird and the new one was the dying swan. She was younger, though not quite young as she had already been in a number of other places for a few years, so there was talk among these acting colleagues of my mother's about how long she would have until her body wouldn't make it anymore, five or six years, and that would be it, and they also talked about what those dancers would be doing when their active careers ended: would they go into a sanatorium for a year and when they got out of there what would they do then, would they become choreographers and artistic directors of ballet companies? When I saw Chandralekha dancing at the age of 65, I realized that there were quite a number of Indian performers who were way beyond that age of western classical ballet dancers and still active and performing well.

Some years ago, I attended the performance of a Cardiff-based Bharata Natyam company in Aberystwyth, in the company of Mohiniattam performer Kalamandalam Radhika. She commented that the leading dancer and artistic director of the company was a very good teacher, explaining that judgment with reference to the observation that this dancer's students were better than she was herself, but she and they were appearing onstage together. I asked her whether she could give me examples because I can't see the difference because I am not trained. She said the hands should be bent backwards to a certain level of flexibility and her hands were just not that flexible anymore, so she could not normally bend them to the extent her students could. The students learnt from her and she taught them properly and allowed them to show the better technique, as it were, or execution of the technique onstage next to her.

Sellers-Young
I do think that age is pivotal, particularly in ballet and to a certain extent modern dance, as both are about the body conquering the space.

Some forms I think are more comfortable with the body as they are working with gravity and the earth rather than trying to conqueror the earth. In Japan, I attended a celebration of older dancers; nobody was below the age of 70. They were making a real point that you can age and dance in Japan and not have the same kinds of issues that you find in the West in general. What is the relationship between the wisdom/spirituality that the body would have because of its practice for years and years that they are then passing on something spiritual or something aesthetic?

You and I have both had a range of experiences in terms of performance and a range of experiences globally. As you were talking about India I was thinking about my experience of being at a performance in southern Sudan and age is just not an issue. You participate according to your age and there is a real acceptance that it will be different if you are 20 or if you are 70 and everywhere in between, or if you are pregnant or not pregnant, or if you are male or female, but the group is all moving together in a generalized pattern in relationship to the instrumentations in the centre.

Meyer-Dinkgräfe
So, it is considered as something "normal", and probably in that context nobody would be surprised to see an older person dance and would possibly also not admire an older person because they are dancing because it is something that an older person otherwise does not do?

Sellers-Young
Older people dance, there is no expectation, no critique of it actually fulfilling a certain kind of specific aesthetic.

Meyer-Dinkgräfe
I am saying this because there is a television series in the UK called *Britain's Got Talent* (2014) where otherwise unknown people will perform and are selected by the panel and audience; the winner will receive £100,000 and they perform at the Royal Variety Show in front of the Queen. During the 2014 series they had a 79-year-old woman in one of the preliminaries who danced some Latin dance with her dance teacher and everybody was amazed that she could move in that way at her age. There was surprise, praise, astonishment and appreciation because she is so old and so I wonder whether in Sudan there would not be this wonder and this combination of wonderment that she is so old and can still dance like that?

Sellers-Young
No, I don't think it operates in the same way. I think it has to do with the function of the form. Everything I saw that takes place in Sudan was really in original format, and rituals serve a different purpose in society and so in a ritual format it was the position of yourself and the community and being with that community in the performance. One ritual in particular is called a Pumbo, in and around the family coming to the point where they can actually cover the graves with cement and the family can take off the white clothes of mourning and go back to normal life. It was a primary ritual that was taking place. There were some things that took place at

other points of time, but this was the big one that united the community. The dance itself is part of a celebration of being alive and the difference between their lives and our lives is great. They get up with the light and go to bed with the light, they have one set of food to eat in the dry season and another set of food in the wet season, so their relationship to each other and the land is fundamental. There is not this other layer that gets built upon, they operate on a fundamentally different level.

Meyer-Dinkgräfe
Maybe the link might be that with increasing age, performers become more at home, familiar, confident with, feel independent in relation to their own tradition and that will have an impact directly, not mediated, on their ability to express any spiritual content that the form has or that the contents they are presenting has. They might be independent even of their own intellectual knowledge of it: they might not be able to tell you about it, they might not be able to give you a lecture about it, but because it has become embodied to such an extent without the intellectual interference of thinking about it – especially in academic terms – their connection with the spiritual is stronger. That might then explain, or could be related to, this experience that you talked about earlier with this 85-year-old in the large auditorium where every movement, and especially in the Butoh form, reverberates in the whole auditorium and you felt it sitting a good way back.

Sellers-Young
I think that is a good possibility. As you were talking I couldn't help but contemplate my own ageing. There is a deeper realization of the preciousness of being able to move and its impact on others, whether it is playing with my grandchildren or doing T'ai chi in the morning. There is an impact that is constantly on-going, this recognition that as you get older you think a lot about how long you are going to live. All of those factors come together with the way you age, and for me the spiritual component of it is that it is not about me, there is a generosity that I think comes through you in some cases. In terms of what people would tell you about acting, it's the way that you approach the subtext of your character that actually creates the characteristics: it's not the words, it's the subtext that is important, and as you get older your personal subtext changes. In that changing, particularly if you follow any kind of spiritual path in life, I meditate daily and I think it actually transforms how I experience things: only now I am realizing things that my T'ai chi teacher said to me ten to fifteen years ago because you get deeper into a place within your body that

is not about how big the gesture or how strong or dynamic it is, it is really about how subtle and integrated it is within the framework of your entire being and your sense of relationship to the world. I feel like I actually sink into the world's energy and for me that is the most profound spiritual component that ageing has given. I had a kind of energy when I was younger and using up all that energy I felt I couldn't have that deeper love or focus but ageing has given me that.

CHAPTER TWO

SPIRITUALITY IN AURELIA BAUMGARTNER'S TANZPHILOSOPHIE

[First published in *Dance, Movement and Spiritualities*, 1:3 (2014), 393-412; reprinted here with permission from Intellect Publishing]

Contextualisation

In April 2013, the newly launched network *Performance Philosophy* organised its first conference, held at Surrey University. Many presentations at many conferences have been characterised by sharing knowledge and insights that are "safe and sound", of the kind that would elicit a few polite factual questions in the time allocated to post-presentation discussion. At the Surrey conference, there was an unusual spirit of innovation and originality that led to genuine excitement and lively debate at the prospect of the genuine marriage of performance and philosophy. Sadly, almost at the end of the conference, much of that free spirit was at best dampened, in many cases killed off entirely, by the voice of the establishment: the Harvard University-based keynote speaker argued, categorically and very eloquently, that such a marriage was impossible in principle. The performance philosophy debate has not quite yet recovered the liveliness and rigour of innovation pre-Harvard-keynote. At that conference, I first encountered German dancer/philosopher Aurelia Baumgartner, and was intrigued by her work, particularly her 2012 performance involving horses. An extensive email communication after the conference led to my attending a performance of her work in December 2013 near her home and dance studio on the shore of Lake Starnberg near Munich, Germany, followed by a wide-ranging three-hour interview. Since 2013, Baumgartner has presented both theoretical papers and her dance practice at academic conferences, such as the 2004 World Congress of the International Conference for Theatre Research, the 2015 6th International Conference on Consciousness, Theatre, Literature and the Arts (New York) and the 2015 annual conference of the Theatre and Performance Research Association (TaPRA) in Worcester. In the first of two articles I wrote about and with Baumgartner, I address her spirituality in general, in the second one I focus specifically on her work with horses in *Tanzende Pferde—Spiegelungen im Raum / Dancing Horses: Reflections in Space*.

Spirituality

From the earliest history, the arts have been associated with a beneficial impact on those exposed to it as makers or receivers. In the West, Aristotle in his *Poetics* wrote about the cathartic impact of theatre, while in the East, the *Natyashastra*, the ancient Indian text about drama and theatre, which also includes music and dance, relates how dance/drama were created by Brahma, the creator, in response to the request of the Gods for him to create an art form accessible to all human beings and with the explicit purpose of restoring the golden age to humankind. The use of the arts in therapy (dramatherapy, dance therapy and so on) confirms the validity of such early claims of the beneficial impact of the arts on humans in terms of increased well-being, as does research into that impact.

This role of the arts in improving our lives has been contextualized further in the fields of religion, philosophy and consciousness studies. The high currency of contextualizing the arts in these fields is reflected in academia in the emergence and continuing success of the "Theatre, Performance and Philosophy" working group within the Theatre and Performance Research Association (TaPRA), the working groups "Performance and Consciousness" and "Religion and Performance" within the International Federation for Theatre Research (IFTR), the "Performance Philosophy" working group within Performance Studies International (PSI), the network "Performance Philosophy", the Institute of Performance and Spirituality with its associated journal, and the recently founded journal *Dance, Movement and Spiritualities*, as well as, in the context of consciousness studies, *Consciousness, Literature and the Arts* (refereed online journal, book series with Intellect and Rodopi, and biannual conferences since 2005).

For most of these contexts, spirituality, explicitly or implicitly, is central, and in many, the term and concept of *spirituality* has been understood in a non-religious way. It is this understanding that forms the basis of my article, with the implication that "spirituality culminates in the full development of mind", and "any move in the direction of this fullness can be called spirituality" (Malekin and Yarrow 1997: 90).

Aurelia Baumgartner

It is against this understanding of spirituality that I discuss the performative practice of German Aurelia Baumgartner (www.tanzphilosophie.de). The discussion is drawn from a personal, three-hour conversation I held with Baumgartner in one of the studios of her dance school, within a few feet of Lake Starnberg near Munich, in December 2013. The tranquillity of the studio and its surroundings provided an ideal environment to allow the physical and emotional memories of Baumgartner's performance of *Nomad's Rhythm* on the evening before that interview to inform the conversation.

Figure 1: Aurelia Baumgartner in *Human without Cerebrum: Attempts* (photographer: Dorothee Elfring).

Following many years of training in a wide range of classical and contemporary approaches to dance, she founded the School for Contemporary Dance, housed in a pavilion within a few feet of the shore of Lake Starnberg in Berg, near Munich in Germany, where she has developed a student base of around 120. Her studio also serves as the basis for her own dance projects, which she launched in 2004 under the umbrella of "Aureliana Contemporary Dance Project". Her website provides documentation of her projects, including video clips of some, and complete video recordings of others of her productions. Most of the video material has been edited from recordings of live performances, only some is artwork created specifically for the video medium.

I would like to present my discussion of Baumgartner's work in terms of concentric circles around a core. The circles are:

1. *Inspiration* (how she gets ideas and how she develops them into the performances open to the public);
2. *Intuitive collaboration* (details of the way she works with the dancers, musicians and other artists she involves in her productions);
3. *Femininity, beauty and non-linearity* (overarching characteristics of her approach and performances);
4. *Biography* (her training, a pivotal, life-changing crossroads she encountered at the age of 14, and her heritage);
5. *Cultural and philosophical contextualization* (training in a wide range of approaches with related dance vocabularies that she now has at her disposal in creating her choreographies, and studies to M.A. level in western philosophy, in addition to further reading and practice of eastern philosophies).

It is possible to describe and analyse Baumgartner's work in terms of these circles. They constitute an approximation of the core, which can be understood as the communal experience of Baumgartner's performances, arising in the spaces she shares with her spectators: the physical spaces of the venues she performs in, and, much more intangibly, the spaces of consciousness, where the contents and characteristics of those concentric circles merge with the sensitivities and existential orientations of Baumgartner and each spectator at any moment of any performance. This approach must thus be understood as a heuristic tool to capture a holistic practice leading to a holistic experience.

Figure 2: Aurelia Baumgartner in *Asturias* (photographer: Dorothee Elfring).

Inspiration

The question of artistic inspiration has been fascinating across centuries – each era develops its own ideas (Meyer-Dinkgräfe 2005: 15–19). Baumgartner realizes that "altogether I can say I go through life with an artist's eye at all times. Whatever I feel might be an inspiration. I might be inspired by anything I see, which I then try to capture with my camera" (2013). If she is interested in a theme or subject, she will first of all try to digest this within herself to allow it to grow and develop in a tacit way.

Once Baumgartner has settled on a theme or subject, she tries to find material from her rich reservoir of impressions that fits and matches with that theme or subject. Thus, her work emerges tacitly, from within. An example is the production of *Mensch ohne Großhirn/Human without Cerebrum*, which she eventually presented first at the conference Soundcheck Philosophie in May 2013 in Naumburg, Germany, and which she revived as part of *Nomad Rhythms* in late 2013. The performance of this revival in Starnberg on 13 December 2013 is at the centre of the argument in this article. Baumgartner had an overall idea for this performance piece first and then she got in touch with the musicians, Markus Wagner (bass, composition, arrangement), Ken Weinzierl (guitar) and Franz Schledorn (trombone) and asked them whether they might be interested in working on this project with her to take it further. At that stage she found dialogue very important also because within herself she works with relations and relationships in the triad of impulse, resistance and structure. In that process the poem by Durs Grünbein, which she had read some time ago, came back to memory. She allowed all these associations to come freely from her subconscious. Then she thought that the production might be an interesting project for a specific event, the Soundcheck Philosophie event in Naumburg, which had *alienation* as its main subject.

> With the poem I had text, then I thought I would like to have a dialogic structure for the whole piece, allowing myself to enter a dialogue with the poem, and in the end at the beginning the first and the second part enter a dialogue with each other in so far as one element of the first part appears on the screen while I mention and recite the second part and *vice versa*. I might pick up something here, discard there and build the discarded material into the process somewhere else, or not, as the case maybe. (2013)

Baumgartner has thus developed, and implicitly trusts, an intuitive way of responding to intuitions and working with them. This applies not only to her creative work on productions, but also to her writing as a philosopher:

> I wrote my MA thesis about philosopher Immanuel Kant's *Critique of Judgement*. The basic idea for this subject and the argument came in a dream to me. Immediately after I finished dreaming, I got up, sat down at my desk and wrote down the ideas because otherwise I might have forgotten them again. In this way I had the whole structure and the argument in front of me. (2013)

Realizing this is the way she works means, practically speaking, that she keeps a pen and paper next to her bed so that if necessary she can write something down very quickly also in the middle of the night.

> When I have got ideas for choreography in the middle of the night I might be found to go down into the basement where I have a very small studio space and then do some dance movements in my night gown which I capture with a camera so that I can be assured that it will be there the next day. (2013)

Baumgartner thus acknowledges the tacit functioning of her consciousness; she makes full use of it in her creative and philosophical thinking, and she contextualizes it as well, arguing that many ego- and self-boundaries are lifted in the state of sleep, which makes it possible for people to perceive, on that level, basic structures of life which our soul is aware of but which are overshadowed by the intellect during the waking state. These are overshadowed by schemata that we have developed in order to allow us to orientate ourselves in life. All those schemata exist in order to help us overcome a fear of the unknown: "the artistic process, as well as deep sleep, allow us to let go to some extent at least of those schemata and safety mechanisms" (Baumgartner 2013).

To summarize: Baumgartner's inspiration and her resulting way of working are predominantly intuitive and thus spiritual. She has realized this and the implications for her life and her work and trusts it.

Figure 3: Aurelia Baumgartner in *Wicked (Siguirija)*
(photographer: Dorothee Elfring).

Intuitive collaboration

Baumgartner's contextualization of the production of *Nomad Rhythms* in Starnberg on 13 December 2013 for the programme notes indicates the ways in which Baumgartner works with her fellow-artists on her productions. This section takes up the discussion of Baumgartner's intuitive approach to her work, extending it from her inspiration to the way she works with other artists she involves in her productions. A good example is the element of contact improvisation that was part of one of the dialogues or duos with the Spanish *flamenco puro*/pure flamenco dancer, Jairo Amaya in the *Nomad Rhythms* production. It must be noted that the level of physical contact characteristic of contact improvisation was not easy for Amaya, because *flamenco puro*, the dance form that he is used to and has been trained in, is predominately a solo form and any contact is symbolized rather than expressed directly. For example, to infold the other dancer and to move in such a way that one rolls off the back of the other is unusual for Amaya, and it did not work out perfectly at the performance on 13 December simply because Amaya had not developed the level of trust needed for this to work out properly.

Figure 4: Jairo Amaya and Aurelia Baumgartner in *Wicked (Siguirija)*
(photographer: Dorothee Elfring).

So, this is work in progress: he tries to work with me in the more
contemporary contact improvisation way while at the same time I pick up
material from him which I then put into practice in my way that is not
necessarily precisely as done in the Spanish tradition but amalgamated and
fused with what I am able to perform. This way of collaboration gives rise
to very interesting dimensions that are no longer purely one's own.
(Baumgartner 2013)

In working with others, Baumgartner does not think that there is a
hierarchy as such, or at least it is not intended. What is true, however, is
that she is the engine, the person who has the ideas and wants to put them
into action. She then works with painters, module artists, film-makers,
photographers, actors and musicians. She works with dancers from
different artistic backgrounds, such as classical ballet or, as in the
production of *Nomad Rhythms*, *flamenco puro*. Baumgartner feels very
honoured to be able to work with Jairo Amaya, because from experience
not many *Gitanos* (Romani people in Spain, colloquially referred to as
gypsies) are open to collaboration. They tend to be very reserved, and one
of the reasons for this is that flamenco is considered almost like a fashion
in some circles, as the "Spanish fire" that becomes an industry for export
of Spanish exotica. As such it is overly stylized, and the essence of
flamenco puro is almost ruined in the process. Some of this fashionable
flamenco may still be virtuosic and extraordinary, but it loses its purity.

Amaya comes from the School of *flamenco puro*/pure flamenco, untouched by those elements of export fashion.

In some of the pieces that form part of *Nomad Rhythms*, Amaya dances while Baumgartner stands at the back of the stage, level with the musicians, and accompanies his dance with clapping of her hands. She explains this aspect of live collaboration, as opposed to that in rehearsal, as follows:

It is one of the highest possible levels of concentration in working with him when he is performing with his rhythm, which is then expressed in my different ways of clapping. This is quite unlike following the rhythm provided by the metronome: instead it becomes faster, slower, louder, or softer. All this is improvised and requires an enormous level of concentration. A particular level of difficulty comes through the contretemps, the interim tempi that are created by interchange and interplay between him clicking his fingers and the rhythm provided by his feet. In such situations it is essential to maintain the rhythm in such a way that it remains in between rather than fitting in and becoming one with either the rhythm of the feet or the rhythm of the hands. There are no time and space left for thought: it is a case of me living the rhythm in those situations. While it might appear that only my hands are doing something, it is in fact the whole body that is fully involved, and I think that is also quite visible in the performance that I am sometimes almost tempted to run up and join him on the floor.

It is an exchange of question and answer almost between myself and the dancer and leads to a unity of some sort. However, this functions through some opposition between tiempo and contra-tiempo through syncopes about the basic rhythm in a sort of playing with the rhythm. This intricate exchange of rhythms then has to be balanced with the rhythms provided by the musicians. They are excellent musicians, but it is a hard training and learning process for them as well because we don't live in the Spanish culture. When it comes to my clapping of my hands, it is important to know that there are differences in that as well: there are hollow and muffled sounds by having more of a hollow space between the hands while clapping, compared to different sounds when the palms of the hands come together straight. It is especially challenging after having danced for a while to engage in this clapping with sweaty palms because that influences the sound quality. The clapping of the hands thus becomes an instrument in its own right and has to sound like one. (2013)

Figure 5: Aurelia Baumgartner and Jairo Amaya, with Franz Schledorn, trombone, in *Farucca* (photographer: Dorothee Elfring).

Baumgartner also explains why in the Spanish material in *Nomad Rhythms*, the live singing that is normally part of flamenco, was replaced by the trombone: many Spanish song lyrics are not comprehensible to a modern audience because they are written in *gitano* Spanish. Many of the song texts in this flamenco music are originally about the persecution that the *gitano*, the gypsies, had to suffer from Christian rulers. On the other hand, they are texts from folklore, usually singing of the admiration of female beauty or stories of the daily life and the joy and struggle between friendship or loves. If we have difficulties understanding the meaning of the lyrics then it becomes like fashionable folklore, which is fascinating and interesting in itself but lacks depth or the possibility to achieve depth.

> As a result of these observations and thoughts, I tried to find a way for improved authenticity in putting this on stage myself. How can I find a way of being able to empathise, to feel what they might be feeling when they presented it in the way that is typical and characteristic for themselves? I get to this point of understanding by talking to Jairo by discussing things with him, by asking him what is meant here, how this comes across and so on. It is a very strong and intensive learning process because he still teaches me repeatedly. (Baumgartner 2013)

In the daily rehearsal process, Baumgartner films the improvisation so that she can then look at the material later and edit critically. This allows her the highest level of flexibility and freedom in improvisation. She has come to dislike giving set steps to others, which they then have to perform as instructed. Her work thus develops as a free interplay between imagination and reason, according to Immanuel Kant. Imagination does not run wild because structure is present. However, structure does not restrict: the imagination is given the amount of space it needs to make use of this structure.

To summarize: grounded in her own past and current experience, and always open to new experience regarding herself and others, Baumgartner is able to work with others in a genuinely collaborative manner, accepting what the other artists bring to the work, assimilating, adapting and responding to this intuitively, in the moment, in conjunction with ideas that may arise not out of the moment of rehearsal, but from intuitive and holistic reflection of it.

Femininity, beauty and non-linearity

According to Saint Germain, one of the Ascended Masters in theosophy and other esoteric traditions, the purpose for souls to be incarnated as humans on the planet earth is for them to be able to develop the feminine side of their nature, irrespective of whether they are born as man or woman (2004). Against this background, femininity gains a very important role in the context of spirituality. According to Baumgartner, conceptual thinking is patriarchal – it allows us to classify or categorize the world. This forms the basis for ideologies, which in turn always form the basis for strife, struggle, estrangement, enemies and wars and ultimately exclusion. In one way she considers herself as a fairly masculine kind of person in so far as she takes initiative and seeks achievement. However, in her work she tries not to express this masculine side: "I find that this expresses itself in a desire to receive and to let go and allowing things to develop that I would consider predominately feminine in nature" (2013). In practice, this combination of masculine impulse and drive, and the feminine ability of letting go, may take the shape of Baumgartner being inspired by a concept, and then allowing the initial concept to encounter, and interact with, a different concept. The result is that her work is not linear and logical – it is not straightforward from A to B in a narrative way. "I have to qualify this: in some cases, in some areas I am narrative from A to B but at the same time by overlaying several layers of my work, networks come into existence" (Baumgartner 2013). Thus, the linear structure which seeks to understand and thus dominate the world is broken up through these additional layers; the result is "a more modest ego where humans no longer need to consider themselves as the crown of creation in order not to experience fear. This would then be a state of existence where one feels more integrated into and supported by the earth" (Baumgartner 2013).

Integration is a feminine principle, and it is at the heart of Baumgartner's art. The relationship of *yin* and *yang* is reflected in this approach: both need each other mutually, neither dominates the other, and both are allowed to exist in their own right and in relation to each other. Thus, mind and body are not separated, one cannot exist without the other, and each needs the other. And this is also the area where concepts and experiences such as play, playfulness and vulnerability become relevant. Letting go of concepts on the stage is related to the fear of going out and just doing something without knowing precisely what is going to happen. In preparing for the performance on 13 December, she noticed that the floor of the venue was concrete, covered with the dance mat, and in the dress rehearsal she decided not to use her feet with full force because otherwise her joints would not be able to support her in the performance properly. In the performance itself, during the first half she noticed that she was not able to feel the earth through the concrete. Without that grounding, without that feeling of the earth it was not possible to get across to her audience what she would have wanted to get across, and what she would have been able to get across if that feeling of the earth had been present. Grounding the body and feeling the earth are essential in spiritual development.

Figure 6: Aurelia Baumgartner in *Wicked (Siguirija)*
(photographer: Dorothee Elfring).

The experience reflected here is one of having to let go again and go out on the stage and performing under those difficult circumstances. In this way the space is integrated into the performance experience and this on a different level again becomes a form of play and becomes playful because Baumgartner has to improvise – she has to do things differently:

> I have to do certain steps in a different way because I just can't do them in the way I intended to on this particular ground. So much happens spontaneously and that is again something that musicians have to respond to and react to in the moment. (2013)

As key attitudes and experiences in the context of spirituality, femininity and related concepts and experiences of play, playfulness, vulnerability and letting go, are central to Baumgartner's life and art. She is aware of the apparent opposition of this to masculinity, but seeks to integrate both, arguing, specifically in view of the concept of the male gaze that it would of course be possible to neutralize one's appearance as a woman, to come in training gear and to cut one's hair short. However, such an attitude in turn would also be a response and the question then arises why women are expected only to react:

> why shouldn't it be possible and allowed for female performers to relish the feminine form and to be able to express one's femininity in and through the body without at the same time seeking to conform with some outwardly superimposed ideal of beauty by cosmetic surgery and all other kinds of rather artificial approaches which again would only be a way of responding. (Baumgartner 2013)

Response is not independent; response is either in the negative (making yourself ugly), or a positive (making yourself beautiful). "What I am aiming at is a lived femininity which allows you to enjoy the way we really are rather than any kind of response or ideal" (Baumgartner 2013).

These views, arguments and experiences find their way into her work, for example in the use of the pointe shoes in *Human without Cerebrum*. She used them as a sign for the romantic concept of dance because the female dancer with these pointe shoes has been performing the roles of nymphs, of princesses and other creatures beyond the human who are by their very nature unobtainable, and who cannot be reached by conventional humans. This kind of supernatural female creature is a very strongly male idea, just as today's supermodels are male ideas – they are unreachable because of the extremely slim nature of that ideal, "almost starved, almost dead" (Baumgartner 2013). The pointe shoe in ballet lifts the body off the ground into a romantic state of obedience or suspense, leaving the image of a woman that does not really exist. In a similar way *High Gloss Magazines* show images that are airbrushed to the extreme even in the cases of the women who are already the most beautiful around. Thus, an extreme form of femininity is created artificially. Bordo analysed this phenomenon in her ground-breaking 1993 study *Unbearable Weight: Feminism, Western Culture and the Body*, and in the new preface for the tenth anniversary edition in 2003, she considers the digital modification of images of celebrity women as "perceptual pedagogy, How to Interpret Your Body 101 [...] Digital creations, visual cyborgs, teaching us what to expect from flesh and blood" (2003: xviii). Baumgartner is aware of this dimension, and argues:

> [...] if we only react to it by saying we present women in a different way, then that is only a position of opposition – not one where women actually know who and where they are. What I am trying to do is to find out and experience and sense in myself what femininity is in the first place. I would then be interested in the response this kind of approach has among my audience. (2013)

Baumgartner argues that this approach is reflected in the costumes she wears in her performances – not only dresses but sometimes also trousers. In her last piece in the *Nomad Rhythms* production she wore stylized trousers based on the trousers worn by the gypsy smiths. On other occasions she does not have specialist costumes like that, and on those occasions, she performs in what looks more like training gear. In the context of the Spanish gypsies she tried to create her costumes in such a way that they reflected some of the cultural context without being tacky or cheesy but still related to the context that she wanted to demonstrate.

Eclectic background video, lighting in soft pastel colours and imaginative soundscapes are characteristic of Baumgartner's productions. Although on their own many such components may not be beautiful as such, they combine to an impression of beauty for the spectator. This in turn is related to femininity, because it is the aspects of femininity permeating her work that make the work as a whole, in a holistic sense, beautiful. Baumgartner is ambiguous about that impression her work creates on the spectator, given that the concept of beauty, or beauty as an ideal of art, have been abolished, almost.

> Just like love, beauty is part of a growing marketing dimension, it has become an industry and so in some cases not jumping that bandwagon might actually be an indication of people trying to avoid being accused of

jumping the bandwagon. The accusation here would be that one is not critical enough, just swimming with the flow. (2013)

On the other hand, eminent German actor and director Gustaf Gründgens (1899–1963) argued that it is incredibly easy to direct a scandal but to create real beauty onstage is so much more difficult (1963). There is a striking difference between any airbrushed ideal of beauty and the one that we encounter in Baumgartner's work. The individual artists contributing to those images and the background, and the music and the dance develop, and bring in their own understanding and experience of beauty. Overall, Baumgartner's work expands the concept, the idea and the experience of beauty. It allows it to transcend those material values of the airbrush and is more than that because it comes from deeply within. This is what is fascinating about performance in theatre and dance: objects and contents of everyday life gain a different, larger dimension when they are presented on the stage. The challenge then is to say, with some precision at least, what causes this additional dimension, this larger dimension to grow, to develop, to come into existence in the first place. The performance leads to a holistic experience and this holistic experience is not limited to understanding, which is a faculty of the intellect. The holistic experience is beautiful because of the joy of being holistic.

To summarize: femininity is a major aspect of spirituality; Baumgartner has developed a clear position in relation to this concept and experience, and related issues of vulnerability and fear, letting go, non-linearity and beauty. In performance, what comes across to the spectator as the performer's vulnerability is in fact the performer revealing their innermost essence onstage; however, that essence is in fact not vulnerable at all because it emerges from the invincible level of the platonic form of beauty.

Figure 7: Aurelia Baumgartner, with Franz Schledorn, trombone, in *Human without Cerebrum: Attempts* (photographer: Dorothee Elfring).

Aspects of biography

Training and Crossroads

Baumgartner trained in classical ballet from an early age, as well as in ice skating, which became her passion. According to a number of different spiritual traditions, all humans are in the process of spiritual development, at different stages according to the Divine Plan (Saint Germain 2004). For all humans, their individual paths include the necessity to make decisions, major or minor, at many junctions and crossroads. For Baumgartner, the most influential crossroads came when at the age of 14 she injured her knee and was declared an invalid by the specialist who saw her in hospital. After a year of treatment, without any success, she made her first decision at those crossroads by asking her parents to arrange for her to attend a boarding school in France, thus giving her the opportunity of leaving Germany altogether. In the meantime, the condition of her knee deteriorated because in the course of her growth the cartilage in the knee did not grow with the bones, a condition exacerbated through having always jumped on to the hard ice during her years of ice skating. She developed a condition called *osteochondrosis dissecans*. Later, she had to have the piece of cartilage that was stuck in the knee joint operated out, which left her with an almost stiff leg. This was the trigger for the second major decision in relation to the injury crossroads:

> If the doctor told me not to do any exercise any more and still the cartilage ended up in the knee joint where it had to be operated on, then I might as well do everything again because there the doctor might get it wrong as well. I lost trust in conventional medicine at that point. (Baumgartner 2013)

She was 17 years old at that time and started with yoga. This proved an essential decision on her path. At that time yoga was not as popular and available everywhere as it is today, but she came across a self-help book by Kareen Zebroff and started exercising on the basis of that book "and suddenly I was able to move my knee joint" (2013). Yoga, together with breathing exercises and an enhanced awareness of her nutrition opened up a completely new path that brought her back to dance. She shifted from working with dance on ice to working with dance on snow, from ice skating to ski ballet – since her accident in ice skating she has never been on the ice again, never put on skates again because the size of the shock at the time: "It had been such an enormous dream of mine, which had been erased from one moment to the next when this diagnosis was given to me" (2013). Baumgartner's involvement with ski ballet was very successful:

she became part of the German national team for ski ballet. It is in this context that she also met the partner of leading German dance teacher Jessica Iwanson and through this connection she learnt Iwanson's approach to dance. At the same time, she studied philosophy at the University of Munich, emphasizing that she needed the balance of thinking and physical engagement "I always had to move. Having to think only felt like having myself cut off from the head down" (2013). Baumgartner also trained in other approaches to dance apart from Iwanson, such as Graham and Cunningham, which were to become influential in her own practice.

Heritage

Baumgartner presents herself as a dancing philosopher, and her work as dance philosophy. She wants to convey ideas of philosophy through her work and understands it as embodied philosophy. Baumgartner's interest in philosophy, and the interweaving of philosophy and dance characteristic of her life, may well have been inherited: her father, Hans Michael Baumgartner (1933–1999) was a disciple of eminent philosopher Hermann Krings (1913–2004) and became Professor of Philosophy in Giessen and Bonn. In addition to inheritance, which one can assume but not empirically prove, there were life influences (nurture versus nature). Baumgartner developed an interest in her father's world. She had many questions about, or even of life, and asked questions beginning with "why", also triggered by insecurities that arose in the wake of the injury and the diagnosis: "I left the hospital on that day totally destroyed" (2013). Insecurity as the basis for asking questions may have been caused as well by the absence of her father for much of her childhood: "I didn't see my father much as a child" (2013). Her father had to be away from home a lot due to his profession, with his home in Starnberg near Munich and his work in Giessen and Bonn, respectively. Because her mother was highly respectful of her father's work, she arranged the home in such a way that she did not involve him in any activity she could take care of herself. As a result, both Baumgartner and her sister did not spend much time with their father.

> In those days, so many years ago, it was different anyway, the father was a bit more distant. My mother is quite an emancipated woman. Over a lot of the time of my childhood and that of my sister, she was almost a single parent as far as parenting was concerned because in addition to taking care of us she was the carer for her mother, so she could not accompany her husband when he went away. (2013)

To summarize: the crossroads of the injury led to major decisions in the path of Baumgartner's spiritual development, first that of seeking a major change in her life by going to France, and second that of seeking out yoga to heal herself. The depth of her relation to philosophy can be understood through her heritage: she is likely to have inherited a tendency to ask questions of life from her philosopher father, while the tendency was enhanced by life experiences: the crisis of the injury and the perceived injustice of it, and the discrepancy of a growing interest in her father's world and work, and the fact that her father was often away and she rarely spent time with him. These are the innermost contexts, implicit and tacit rather than explicit, but informing the contents of all the other circles.

Figure 8: Aurelia Baumgartner in *Human without Cerebrum: Attempts* (photographer: Dorothee Elfring).

Cultural and philosophical contextualization

Baumgartner's work has been influenced by a wide range of material from across different cultures. Her work with Jairo Amaya reflects a major interest in Spanish dance traditions, and her training encompasses pakua and taiji. An overarching aim of Baumgartner's performance work has become to express philosophical ideas, to embody them in her dance, and thus to develop a mode of thinking through the body rather than merely in the rational mind. A philosopher will see something different in the performances than a non-philosopher. It is very important to undertake every possible attempt to get away from pure intellectual thinking – to allow a holistic approach and perspective and experience in which the intellectual, the judgemental is one but not the exclusive component. This tendency is evident in her emphasis on inspiration, from her ways of intuitive collaboration, and her emphasis on femininity. It is also an important development in the overall trend towards considering the world in terms of embodiment. Then it becomes interesting how to understand this kind of embodiment in practical terms, what it means precisely.

Figure 9: Aurelia Baumgartner with Franz Schledorn (trombone) in *Human without Cerebrum: Attempts* (photographer: Dorothee Elfring).

The case study to exemplify thinking through the body is provided by the performance of *Nomad Rhythms* on 13 December 2013. Baumgartner's own contextualization of this production reveals those overarching aspects very clearly. First of all, she comments on the influence from Spanish *flamenco*, and how this interweaves with philosophy, in this case Nietzsche, and aspects of femininity in the first section of the production, *Cartucha*:

> In the first part I tried to recreate the path of the Spanish gypsies, *gitanos* in the various different dance forms that are represented in that part, *rumba*, *fandango*, *tango*, *farucca* and *siguirija*. I tried to do this both on a more traditional level but then also to break up this tradition by use for example of an excerpt by Nietzsche which I spoke into the microphone at some point in this first part. It is interesting to note that in the first piece, *Cartucha*, in the dance form of rumba, I had on the video female faces behind bars to show the restriction of femininity. (2013)

Her comments on the second piece, *Asturias*, the *flamenco* dimension combines with material on her inspiration and her way of collaborating with Amaya.

> With regard to the second piece, *Asturias*, this was a choreography that I had done in the past and which I had revived for this production. I re-choreographed it as a *pas de deux* with Jairo Amaya and it took a long time for him to be open to my approach, coming from his own very specialist one. At first initially he told me that this *Asturias* was not actually a proper flamenco piece. Later, however, he observed me in the pieces where this was a component part, and, in the end, he said: 'what you are doing here is actually flamenco after all because what you are doing is pure. You are expressing the rhythm in a pure way as you experience it in your body. Your body language is different from the Spanish one, but it is not superimposed', and this is something that he would like to learn from me, to become more familiar with my body language, to understand my body language just as I tried to understand his body language, where understanding is again not merely an intellectual process but is embodied itself. It was after about four years of working with him that he said: 'let's do this together', so that is why I reintegrated this *Asturias* into the piece. This whole episode was a very interesting one in my own development as an artist because at first this *gitano* says what I am doing is not proper flamenco, so I was left with the impression that he doesn't understand me in this respect. Then he came and said, 'I now understand what you are doing', so it is a mutual process of understanding over the years. What I have put on stage in this first part of this programme is the path of the *gitanos* encountering different things again and again and picking them up and integrating them into their own form. (Baumgartner 2013)

Central to her philosophy of the thinking body was the piece *Human without Cerebrum*, and two related questions: (1) to what extent is rationality the only form of perceiving and grasping the world and (2) is this way of perceiving and grasping the world rated too highly? In response to those questions, Baumgartner started developing both the concept and the related practice of *body thinking* – to grasp it theoretically, to put it into practice in her pedagogical work, in her teaching, and to make it visible practically in her performances without becoming illustrative.

> My performances are structured as body-thinking, the impulse to thematise the body as a comprehensive form of thinking – with reference to Immanuel Kant as a thinking-in-motion with enhanced perception. This approach was inspired by my choreographic and pedagogical work with bodies in dance, as well as my encounter of Asian body and consciousness

techniques (pakua, taiji, martial arts, yoga, cien chiqua and others) and it has been influenced further by the study of oriental and occidental philosophies.

I thus try to conventionalise body thinking as a process of forming structures caused by impulses and resistance as opposites of the other. The process I am talking about here is one of creating structure that deconstructs and reconstructs precoded structures in this interaction with the 'other' and does so without demand of a final interpretant. This process thus remains open in the sense of Eco's 'open work of art'. (Baumgartner 2013)

To summarize: Baumgartner's work has been influenced by many approaches to dance and dance forms, as well as many ideas from western and eastern philosophy. She considers her productions as stages in an attempt to develop ways of expressing thinking and philosophy through the body, as a form of embodied thinking. She exposes herself on a daily basis to a wide range of potential influences, but does not get lost in that whirlpool, but forges her own distinctive pathway. This expression of strength suggests that she is firmly rooted and grounded (hence her ability to notice when she is unable to feel the earth on occasions when she performs on concrete). The experience of being grounded, and the mode of life resulting from it are further indications of true spirituality, which is not lifted off the ground of reality as the characters portrayed by female dancers in classical ballet, represented by the pointe shoes (see above). Spirituality is not mood-making, but a very real characteristic of life.

Figure 10: Aurelia Baumgartner, Raphaela Baumgartner and Arab Grey Pegasus in *Tanzende Pferde: Spiegelungen in Raum/Dancing Horses: Reflections in Space* (photographer: Herbert Hoffmann). Image edited by Roman Luyken (see Meyer-Dinkgräfe 2014).

Outlook

The concentric circles of Baumgartner's art that I have discussed in this article allow an insight into individual layers of spirituality of the holistic nature of this artist's exciting work. The crossroads of injury led to major decisions in the path of Baumgartner's spiritual development. The depth of her relation to philosophy can be understood through her heritage. Baumgartner's inspiration and her resulting way of working are predominantly intuitive and thus spiritual. She has realized this and implications for her life and her work and trusts it. Femininity is a major aspect of spirituality; Baumgartner has developed a clear position in relation to this concept and experience, and related issues of vulnerability and fear, letting go, non-linearity and beauty. Baumgartner's work is influenced by many approaches to dance and dance forms, as well as many ideas from western and eastern philosophy. She considers her productions as stages in an attempt to develop ways of expressing thinking and philosophy through the body, as a form of embodied thinking. Grounded in her own existing experience, and always open to new experience regarding herself and others, Baumgartner is able to work with others in a genuinely collaborative manner, accepting what the other artists bring to the work, assimilating, adapting and responding to this intuitively, in the moment, in conjunction with ideas that may arise not out of the moment of rehearsal, but from intuitive and holistic reflection of it. Not only Baumgartner and her collaborators are thus able to relish and enjoy their creative work, but all those aspects of their work will have their conscious or unconscious impact on each spectator.

All these aspects come together in Baumgartner's work in a holistic manner, such that no one single aspect can be considered to be dominating the other. In performance, these aspects become engaging and demanding for spectators, who are invited to partake in the holistic nature of the performance. What happens between performer and spectators in Baumgartner's performances is comparable to Indian performance aesthetics, where performers and spectators together create, in performance, the aesthetic experience of *rasa*. "Many things in my performances are such that people will not understand them in a narrative way. If you want a story and if you wanted to hear and see a story being told, then this is not what you get in my performances" (Baumgartner 2013). The multidimensional nature of her performances, productions and choreographies develop and require different or new modes of reception on the part of the audience, in so far as the impressions might break up predetermined ideas. Not being able to fit what one perceives onstage with an appreciated and predeveloped, predetermined pattern of reception means that new patterns of reception need to be developed to be able to make sense of what is happening onstage.

> You will find narrative in the case of classical ballet: a story is being told, people go home satisfied and contented because they have seen something, they know what they have seen. That is less demanding than an encounter with my performances, where spectators will be thinking, "what was this about, what happened here?" so that they ask questions. (Baumgartner 2013)

Spirituality thus travels and multiplies.

CHAPTER THREE

DANCING HORSES AND REFLECTING HUMANS

[First published in *Choreographic Practices*, 5:2 (2015), 241-257, reprinted here with permission from Intellect Publishing]

Contextualisation

While Chapter Two provides a general overview of Baumgartner's dance philosophy, in this chapter I discuss her 2012 *Tanzende Pferde: Spiegelungen im Raum/Dancing Horses: Reflections in Space* in depth. Both there and here I give much space to Baumgartner's position in her own words, quoting her extensively, to place my interpretation within a solid frame. Since the article first appeared in 2015, Baumgartner has extended her work with Pegasus and Mabrouka to include explorations of the extent to which the human encounter with the animal may bring improved well-being. Anecdotally, such enhanced well-being was one of the results of the interaction between Pegasus and an autistic teenager, Christos Tsaoussidis, which Baumgartner initiated and oversaw for her 2016 performance of *Dancing Horses-Different Others*.

Introduction

In October 2012, German dancer and philosopher Aurelia Baumgartner presented two performances of her 90-minute production *Tanzende Pferde: Spiegelungen im Raum/Dancing Horses: Reflections in Space* in an arena, with a raised stage and a projection screen in the background. The production set out to show a performed anthology of the relationship between human and horse. The scope of that anthology was provided by ten distinct scenes, each with its specific contents, performers, presentation style and title. In the resulting panorama of impressions, unity was provided by the performance space and the ever-present combination of projected film and live presence of humans and horses.

The article about this work of art is based on a specific perspective on it: Meyer-Dinkgräfe's viewing of a 40-minute DVD edited by Baumgartner, based on footage from two cameras recorded during the two 90-minute performances. This particular perspective, a video of a choreography created by the original choreographer, was available for viewing as often as desired, in comparison with a performance that is much more short-lived and, in that sense, unique. The article focuses predominantly on the visual impression, leaving a discussion of the live music provided by bass, guitar and trombone to a separate discussion. The aim of the article is to provide a useful, honest and to the point testimony of this particular piece, and to add analytic force by contextualizing the insights gained from that predominantly descriptive testimony. The contexts are on the one hand the choreographer's perspective on selected aspects and scenes of the production, and on the other hand the critical literature exploring the relation of performance and animals that has emerged over the past fifteen to twenty years. A comparison of this production with other productions, past and present, that have used horses onstage (e.g., Joanna Haigood's *Equus Project*; see also Poppiti (2005) and Shook (2008)) is beyond the scope of this article.

Meyer-Dinkgräfe: descriptive testimony

Scene one of *Tanzende Pferde: Spiegelungen im Raum/Dancing Horses: Reflections in Space* encompasses a wide range of the horse–human interactions covered by, and the range of modes of presentation characteristic of the production. We become aware of the performance areas: the arena, the stage and the screen. The performers become visible: horses and humans, in the shade, in brighter light, in silhouettes from behind the screen, sometimes lit to appear as centaurs, half human, half horse, blurring boundaries – an effect enhanced by the blurring of projected images of buildings and structures, examples of built environment, human-created architecture, giving way to a red-lit area with sparkling fireworks in the background. The title of the scene is "Traumwelt" / "Dream World", in which everything is possible.

The first scene does not only provide the framework of contents and range of visual contexts, but also demonstrates and at the same time questions the status quo of horse—human interaction—two humans lead their horses through the arena, representing perhaps the most common association between horse and human, the human as guide and the horse as obediently following the human guide. This has been, for millennia, a relationship that has been widely accepted and not much questioned in ethical terms. Only after a few moments of the performance are the two humans guiding the horses revealed as female, however. This casting challenges the assumed status quo, insofar as at least historically it may well have been men who are more closely associated with animals than women.

It is striking to note that the production ends with the status quo in its more expected form, insofar as in scene ten, which makes use of the entire arena area, it is two men who are guiding two work horses around performing various chores, pulling, for example, a log behind them on a harness, or pulling a sheet of cloth. At the end of the scene and with it the performance, the two men and their horses are joined by many other performers dressed as peasants: male and female, adults and children. However, this last scene comes after we have watched the eight scenes in between, which have at least sought to develop the questions launched by the choice of having two women lead their horses into the arena in the first scene – hence scene ten is entitled: "Viele Fragen: Module im Loop" / "Many Questions: Modules in a Loop".

The eight scenes in between the frame provided by scenes one and scene ten pulsate as contractions and expansions of the relationship between humans and the horses, combining, separating, and blurring tradition and innovation in the process. They are expressions of Baumgartner's aim to investigate through her practice, through the performance, the question of whether it is possible that horse and human communicate through dance and whether it is thus possible that they find a common language of movement through what can be defined as free artistic play.

Scene two expands the relationship of female guide and their horses from the general context of scene one to a more playful, colourful dimension: six German women dressed in Arab garments walk in, their movement stylized and ceremonial. They walk in pairs, hand in hand, in a row. Two horses are led in behind them, one by a woman, the other possibly by a man. Both those humans also move in rhythm to the music. The background image changes colour to silver, with a central light source emanating sparkles, which is reminiscent of Peter Brook's film version of the *Mahabharata*, when Kunti invokes the gods to create her children. The movement of the women on the arena floor gets more lively and rhythmical, while the horses are being led faster as well. Then the women begin to engage in dance movements, presumably of the style relating to the garments they are wearing. Their movement is feminine, circular, free flowing, free moving and engaging. Earth, the red floor of the arena, is the ground, the basis, the provider, the source, and the security of humans and animals, of their lives, their bodies, their ambitions, their abilities, their play and playfulness, and their expression in colours, in music and in rhythm. The scene is entitled "Die Erde lebt" / "Earth Lives". This part of the scene relates to expansion, encompassing a wide range, freedom and community. The scenario narrows and contracts to reveal one female solo dancer performing a dance with a large veil, which she holds in both hands and moves in elegant waves around her body. Another woman, meanwhile, leads a horse in the background. It is not clear whether the horse in the background with the woman guiding that horse are projections or really in the space.

Scenes three and five work with projections of text on to the screen – these are further examples of the exploration of performative interrogation of established roles and assumptions, raising, for example, the question of whether the working horse might be in fact superior to their human guides. Baumgartner adapted the text from Swift's *Gulliver's Travels* (1726) and Kafka's *Ein Bericht für eine Akademie / A Report for an Academy*. In scene three, entitled "Auf der Suche" / "In Search Of", a horse with a load on its back (signifying the horse's assumed inferiority) is led in by one person who also carries a small lantern that creates intriguing light effects, immediately followed by a second horse without load led by two people. The text that accompanies this is translated from German: "Once Upon a Time / That's how all fairy tales begin / And most of the time they lead us into a forest. / A fairy tale of Yahoos and Houyhnhnms". The fairy tale scenario is thus evoked by the text, and the relationship between humans as superior and horses as inferior is questioned with reference to the role of humans and horses in Swift's *Gulliver's Travels*. In the scene "Wer *bist Du*" / "Who Are You", this ambiguity of inferiority and superiority is developed further in its juxtaposition of a conventional circus-style dressage and text from Kafka's text, which features a creature who was an ape once, who delivers a lecture about his turning into a human. In the scene, Christina Valle presents her Haflinger gelding Stromboli walking around the perimeter of the arena and walking in different steps. The horse is made to put his front legs up on a platform and to move its legs in the direction of its reigns, then is made to come down to the arena ground again, made to lie down on its side and get up again and walk around the arena.

Figure 2: Christina Valle presents her Haflinger gelding Stromboli. In the background: projection of text from Kafka's *Reden für eine Akademie / Lectures for an Academy*. Photo: Joerk Henkel

Thus, the performance juxtaposes the aesthetic contexts of horses in scene one ("Traumwelt") and scene two ("Die Erde lebt") with more mundane contexts for the existence of horses as working for humans (signified by the load carried by one of the horses) in scene three and performing for humans (dressage in scene five). At the same time, the binary opposites of human–animal; inferior–superior; master–servant; aesthetic–work; and real life–fairy tale are put into question in terms of the themes or titles of the scenes, "Dreamworld", "Earth Lives", "In Search Of" and "Who Are You", which hint at the possibility, or at least the aim of unification of binaries, in a more holistic perspective.

The seemingly conventional, but in fact much more ambiguous dressage in scene five was preceded, in scene four, entitled "Fnarp", by exclusive focus on humans in what comes across as reminiscent of much of what is going on in the contemporary performance art/dance scene, with a range of noises made by the performers (one male, one female), onstage and backstage. Some of the movement vocabulary is from classical ballet, but most is from modern dance material on the verge of acrobatics. The scene focuses the attention and concomitant thinking on humans, their sometimes strange, playful, straightforward or twisted interactions that do not need words.

Once the production has exposed the ambiguity in the roles of horses, it takes the spectator into the realm of Spanish flamenco dance in scenes six and seven, entitled "Cantes Jondos" and "Der Rhythmus der Pferde in den Beinen der Menschen" / "The Rhythm of the Horses in the Legs of the Humans", respectively. In scene six, Baumgartner dances in flamenco

style against projections of images from New York's Broadway and
London's West End, with boards on theatres advertising the musicals
Wicked and *Mamma Mia*.

Figure 3: *Flamenco puro* dancer Jairo Amaya with shadow of Frisian Filou.
Photo: Joerk Henkel.

In relation to the preceding scenes, "Cantes Jondos" takes us from the all-
encompassing first scene ("Traumwelt") via the exotic oriental context of
"Die Erde lebt" and the contraction within it from several women to the
focus on one woman, via the launch of the performative interrogation of
established roles and assumptions in "Auf der Suche", via an exploration
of human relationships in "Fnarp", via further expansion of the perspective
through further interrogation of the relationship between horses and
humans in "Wer bist Du", to the perspective of one person, with an
emphasis on the performing body's rhythm on its own.

The link to horses is quickly re-established in scene seven insofar as
the performer, Spanish flamenco dancer Jairo Amaya, engages further in
flamenco dance, but this time accompanied by impressive shadows of a
horse in the background. The bright light from the background into the
space, on to the stage, reveals shadows, silhouettes of the horse. From
watching the video, it is not certain that the horse is actually moving
somewhere behind the light and the screen, which is the area behind the
stage. Amaya cuts a different figure compared with Baumgartner in the
previous piece. The projections in scene six against the filmed background
of architectural elements are different from this one, where some material
is projected as well, but not as much, but equally monumental in size and
always intercut and over-layered by the horse in silhouette. The kind of
movements engaged in by Amaya leads to a feel of the whole scene that is

different to the previous one. The previous one was more playful and, in a way, more conventional in the sense of contemporary dance elements combined with the flamenco footwork. The movements of the horse and the movements of Amaya in relation to each other are unpredictable. Further adjectives that come to mind are powerful and energetic, but at the same time still of a feminine as opposed to a masculine quality. Whereas the previous section was more in line with taking, this one is more related to giving.

Scene Eight, entitled "Menschenkinder – Tierkinder" / "Human Children – Animal Children", expands the frame to encompass children for the first time in the performance. The screen is lit with light that starts as a small circle which becomes a large circle covering the entire backdrop. It changes from circle to oval. The colour that is projected is a lilac rose colour with a bright white circular light in the background. This is for the stage area. In between the light source and the screen, children are seen in silhouette, playing. The arena is lit with several reddish lights and two ponies are being led around by one person each, each an adult. The children then emerge from behind the screen, they are dressed as typical children learning to dance ballet with tutu and relevant dresses, and they are now taking turns, three of them each leading one of the ponies.

Figure 4: Aurelia Baumgartner with Arab Grey Pegasus, Raphaela Baumgartner in the background. Photo: Joerk Henkel.

With scene nine, "Körperbegegnungen" / "Body Encounters", we come to the focal point of the whole performance and the centre of this article, demonstrating the range of the potential of the relation between horse and human already hinted at in earlier sections, in particular the opening

"Traumwelt" and the third scene, "Auf der Suche". "Körperbegegnungen" starts off with a greenish light in the background. On the stage a young female performer with black hair and white outfit dances in a mix of contemporary and ballet styles, while on the arena floor Baumgartner engages in her main performance with the Arab Grey Pegasus. This is no longer a circus act as in an earlier scene "Wer bist Du?", but something quite different and of its own kind. Holding the horse on a more or less long lead, Baumgartner engages in her own dance. She leads the horse to move with her and allows the horse to move on its own. The performer is always moving in relation to the movement of the horse, sometimes allowing the horse a little bit of space of its own, which it then uses to inspect the floor; then Baumgartner moves fast towards the horse again. The horse notices and reacts to that fast movement, moving backwards but obviously not afraid, but in line with the movement that is coming towards it. It looks different from a horse that is frightened and shies away. There is much physical contact between Baumgartner and the horse, insofar as the dancer moves with her arms and body against the body of the horse. Meanwhile, the female dark-haired dancer is continuing her performance in the background on the stage. Sometimes the movement of the female on the stage and Baumgartner seems synchronized, sometimes less so. Sometimes the movements of the horse and dancer are slow and relaxed, elegant and calm. On other occasions there is more liveliness in there, and on some occasions where the horse and Baumgartner are livelier, the dancer onstage is in a calmer and settled position. As in Baumgartner's earlier scene six without horses, "Cantes Jondos", her body is predominantly upright and moving around with the horse, moving with the horse, moving against the horse, but it is also on occasion on the floor and enticing the horse to change its body posture accordingly.

At this point in the article, we bring in the voice of the choreographer, Aurelia Baumgartner, herself, to add her own perspective to the discussion above. She provides the background to and development of her relationship with her horse, Pegasus, including reference to the characteristics that he brings with him as an Arab Grey, his behaviour in general and in rehearsals for the production.

Figure 5: Aurelia Baumgartner with Arab Grey Pegasus. Photo: Fenny Rosemann.

Baumgartner – the choreographer's perspective

The processes with the horses began half a year before the performance when I found a suitable stable and held an information evening that presented the idea of the performance. I asked those people who had their horses in that stable which of them might be interested in joining the production. In August 2012 I gave some of the participants parts of the music so that they could get their horses used to the music, but that was not yet the music that was seen in the performance in the end. Only in September did I give Christina the piece of the music for the circus number in scene five. However, the music was only set in some parts and particularly the length of its duration was not yet fixed. In this case (as far as the length was concerned) the musicians worked alongside with and according to the abilities and indications of the horses. This was also the case during the performance itself. The same was true for the music for the work horses. The ponies had exercised and trained with classical music; all other music was only distributed on the first day of rehearsals of the ten days' worth of rehearsal.

I danced with Pegasus sometimes without music, sometimes with different kinds of music. The music in the performance itself for my scene with Pegasus had not been composed but was improvised apart from the basic rhythm of the Spanish tango, a four-beat rhythm. However, the length was my choice and decision. Also, the dancer on the stage behind me, my daughter, had firmly choreographed parts that could be put together in different ways. In the end I orientated myself in relation to my daughter, when she had come to an end; similarly, the musicians orientated themselves with both of us dancers.

I bought the Arab Grey Pegasus when he was three years old. I believe that it is important to work with one's own horse because of the level of trust that will have developed between horse and owner and horse and human, but I could imagine dancing with other horses. I gave him a lot of opportunity to walk and run on his own and freely. Initially I rode him a lot but found that it does not work well with my dancing, as different kinds of muscles of the legs are being tasked in riding a horse and dancing and the two did not go together well. I played a lot with Pegasus and later also with the mare that joined, Mabrouka, a chestnut. I noticed some behaviour especially in Pegasus that made sense when I read Monty Roberts's work on joined-up horsemanship. Within this context it seems likely that Pegasus developed the idea of me as the dominant mare within a herd of horses. For example, when I allow him to run freely he suddenly comes towards me and walks and runs behind and follows me in every step whenever I choose to move.

This is what is evident and essential to our performance together: the horse considers me as the dominant mare and at the same time maintains his freedom in relation to the human being and is not trained in the sense of a circus number. Thus, the movements between horse and human and in particular the horse itself are not conventional in the sense of dressage or movement to rhythm or music, and it is the question then whether the scientific approach may be more along the lines of the kind of interaction between this horse and this owner. Does he regard me as the dominant mare according to the ideas of Monty Roberts, and are some aspects of the horse's behaviour, which come across to me as invitations to play or dance, related to the stallion's patterns of seeking to impress? All of this goes beyond conventional drives of food or sex or fear, but becomes a cultural act, a decision to want to engage in this playful dance as that is what the horse wants to do at that moment.

All this applies in the context of the arena. It would be interesting to see how this works in the open field – possibly there the food drive, especially in the case of Pegasus, might prevail. It is interesting to note that different kinds of horses will probably be behaving and acting in different ways in relation to humans. Arabs in particular are very interested in humans, always want to be in contact with them – when they are standing in their boxes they look and see what people are doing. They demand respect from humans, otherwise they will not develop the friendship or will end friendships. They want communication and it seems that they are interested in understanding human language. In many cases the way that people behave with animals is characterized by a high and inappropriate level of presumptuousness as to what one can do with animals and what they are like. I think that especially Arab horses, despite, or possibly because of their very high level of sensitivity, enjoy particularly to communicate with humans and to dance with them. These horses are the only pure-bred race of horse; they go back to the prophet Mohammed. They have lived since early days with the *Bedouins* in their tents and the foals grow up with the *Bedouin* children. They have in those cultural contexts the status of a member of the family. This is the same with Pegasus: while he does not live with me and my daughter at our home, he is a wonderful friend.

During the rehearsal period, Pegasus did not want to be without his mare Mabrouka in the hall and was very agitated without her; therefore, I could not dance with him under those circumstances. Only when Mabrouka was present in the hall, even if only standing in a corner, was he comforted and calm and interested in dancing. He is very dominant with regard to his mare and is the same in the stables where he is normally living. Mabrouka danced during the rehearsals alone with the Egyptian women and was so happy during this process that she entered into the circle with the women on her own and when in the circle lay down and turned over. Again and again she wanted to join the circle of these women and integrate her own activities with theirs.

I started dancing with Pegasus after I started planning for this production, but with some interruptions and periods without dancing because last year from the middle of July to beginning of August I was in New York, and before that I was busy working on a different piece in Halle in Germany. In the middle of August 2012, I had a Flamenco production and after that we danced when we felt like it. It is something that cannot be enforced. If it is very cold in the stables it does not work for either of us, even when Pegasus wants to. On those occasions I only played with the horse, but on many occasions he tried and provoked me to actually dance.

In scene nine of the production, the contact improvisation between me and Pegasus, it is important to note that Pegasus was only initially led in on a lead rope, but after a while, quite early on in the scene, I released this lead and from then on, the animal was free in the arena and was allowed to engage in the dance or not as he liked. I only had two riding crops to help me guide the horse as my kinds of elongated arms without wanting to hurt him or without wanting to frighten, only to allow me to keep direct body contact through touching him with them when I was further away from him. On one occasion I did, however, frighten him with the riding crop: he galloped away from me but then he returned to the dance by moving in a curve in which I followed him.

The standard movement of an invitation to dance for Pegasus is to come towards me with raised front legs. He then likes it if I run away from him with pirouettes and he then follows me and when I then turn around and move again with my dance movements towards him, he reacts with a high level of attention and when I then turn around him, he turns in tune with that. He likes it when I touch him, and in the sense of contact improvisation, pass my weight onto him. He is very attentive in those situations and speaks with his front legs. He might, for example, lift a leg and then he likes it when I put my arm under his leg and support it, or if I move his leg with my movement. In this way, steps with raised front legs, a kind of Spanish step, Pegasus turns around his own axis and moves in physical contact with me – these are the fundamental patterns of movement in these encounters. Sometimes the mare comes and wants to join; initially Pegasus wanted to shoo her away in order to dance only with me, but sometimes I do not agree to this and now sometimes I try to involve both horses in the dance with me. Sometimes, therefore, I let Pegasus have his will to dance alone with me, or sometimes we dance all three of us. When we dance all three, the mare moves backwards, and I move at her side. Pegasus then moves towards the mare as if the two were a pair or I lean against Mabrouka and begin a contact improvisation with her. However, the mare is more sensitive and tender than Pegasus and needs a bit more time to feel herself into the situation and into the human movements and this works best when the mare is alone with me. Otherwise she is distracted by her attention that she needs to pay to Pegasus and he then tends to go in between us again to be alone with me.

With Pegasus I feel that he can express fear and love at the same time. For example, on the second day of the performance, at the second performance of the piece, I put a blanket over him in order not to have to completely wash him anymore because it is his highest delight to roll around in mud pits. One of the other performers helped to clean him and Pegasus stood outside with a blanket over and not on a lead, free. The other performer, Christian, pulled the blanket down without loosening the berth around his belly and thus the blanket was stuck around Pegasus's hind legs. Pegasus hates blankets anyway, his adrenalin level was very high and with that fear of having his hind legs not free he could easily have overrun me, but he did not move from the spot, possibly in order not to hurt me. He only neighed and hopped slightly up and down with hind and front legs in order to get rid of the blanket, which we then removed from him. This is an example that points to something else, which is that possibly there is an energy exchange of human and animal (and horse in this case) that is based on a mirror effect in the sense that during the performance there was a moment where I did not know whether I was a human or horse and I can only assume that Pegasus would have understood or experienced it in a similar way.

Dancing horses and reflecting humans

On the basis of a descriptive testimony (to allow a readership access to the production that did not see it, supported by a few representative images), and the choreographer's own perspective (which adds to the understanding of the production's creation and intention), it is now possible to provide further critical context for the production. There has been much exploration of the context of performance and animals over the past ten to fifteen years, with special issues in *Performance Research* (2000) and *The Drama Review* (2007), and most recently the *Theatre & Animals* contribution to the *Theatre &* series (Orozco 2013). Where does Baumgartner's production of *Tanzende Pferde: Spiegelungen im Raum* sit within this context?

The above two sections of this article suggest that both authors have seen the horses that appear in this performance, in particular Pegasus, in terms that are anthropomorphic, attributing human qualities, especially human emotions, to the horse, perceiving behaviour of the horse in terms of human emotions. This is nothing new, as Putnam explains: in 1798, scientists in Paris had music played to two elephants (originally presents from the East India Company to the Dutch but confiscated by the French in 1796 and transported to Paris) to establish the effect of music on them. The scientists observed what they referred to as "curiosity, surprise, and worry" (Putnam 2007: 156). Writing about training of big cats for the circus, Tait observes that "An analysis of discourse about training big cats [...] reveals that for all their obedience and clever execution of tricks over years, animal wildness is collapsed into an idea of emotional wildness" (2009: 67). While the big cat trainer seeks to show behaviour that allows the cats to trust him or her, the big cats are deemed "to be emotionally volatile, unpredictable and untrustworthy" in principle, by nature, and "the trainer cannot trust the wild animal, who might betray a trainer's affections at any moment" (2009: 72). Other historical explorations (Poppiti 2005) and analyses of specific performances (Shook 2008; Carlson 2007; Williams 2007; Dombek 2007) provide further examples of this kind. Current consensus in science suggests that from the behaviour of animals we can conclude that they are likely to have positive and negative emotions, but it is impossible for us to know with any certainty how the animals experience those emotions in relation to how we as humans experience them (Mills 2013).

Ethical issues in the relation of humans and animals in a performance context have featured prominently in the literature. Most take extreme human–animal encounters as their focus, in which a human performer subjects an animal directly and intentionally to suffering and even death. Performance artist Rachel Rosenthal, who has worked successfully with animals in many of her performances in ways she considers appropriate, writes:

> I hope that artists can display humaneness where perhaps other people can't. If artists don't, they are doubly guilty. I assume artists to be capable of empathy, compassion, understanding, respect, and intelligent behavior. If they knowingly hurt or demean animals, forcing them to "perform" against their nature, that is a punishable sin. (2007: 7)

Marjanic raises the questions of where the motto of freedom or artistic creativity comes into the debate, and how we can justify the pursuit of ethical accountability of artists in their work with animals in view of the daily mass slaughter of animals for other purposes (2010: 78).

In terms of the ethics of *Tanzende Pferde: Spiegelungen im Raum*, here is Baumgartner's position:

> I agree with Mangelsdorf (2013), who is referring to Brandt (2004) that it would be useful to create a 'third language' as an emphatic dialogue based on body language including movement and emotions. The only question is how this dialogue might be held and who will be the leader of this dialogue, so that in this dialogue horses might not mutually be considered again as inferior to humans by acting only out of their instincts, and their tribe and constitution-based attitude. Based on the experience of dancing with Pegasus, I think that horses have the capacity to choose their role. For example, when I was dancing with Pegasus sometimes he came with these carnivorous frontal movements towards me while I was trying to synchronize my movements with him. Then there is the experience I had with him expressing love and fear at the same time. Accidentally I came across an abscess with a hoof pick; it hurt so much that Pegasus promptly wanted to kick against the pain with his hoof but stopped in mid-air as otherwise he would have kicked me in the belly, which would have hurt and injured me severely. He chose not to hit me, maybe thus expressing a direct form of love towards me. He did not 'want' to hurt me, and I add: he did not want to hurt the human he loves. And this can only happen by his capacity to get a distance from his own pain and to put himself in my role as the one who would be hurt by his kick, thus by distancing himself from his own pain as a sort of 'self-reflection' and by compassion towards me as

an expression of love on its highest level (not because of sexuality, but through a capacity of feeling with another body).

In my opinion to create this beautiful creative exchange with horses, humans have to get this peripheral view by using other brain parts as described by movement and breathing practices of several oriental practices like Taiji or Yoga. By grounding the body, opening the energy ways and filling all body cells with Prana or Chi, you get into another state of mind and body consciousness caused by a lower tension of the brain cells because of the oxygen provided by constant deep breath. Thus, a human–animal encounter may be created by body language, body thinking that is body-based, centred on the body, mind and the soul, holistic, and not limited to only the human kind of 'thinking'. The human–animal encounter may be created by structuring the 'world' in a different way, maybe a new way, shown in the performative act of the dance between the human and the horse. A different relationship of human and animal (horse) may be built up in the way of a respectful, non-authoritarian, affectionate and playful encounter. To conclude, it may be worth considering whether animals might be understood to exist in a *zen-consciousness* of here and now, and thus do not have a blunt mind but heightened perception, which might bring them closer to the numinous than humans.

PART TWO:

OPERA AND CONSCIOUSNESS

CHAPTER FOUR

WERKTREUE AND REGIEOPER

[First published in in Fiona Schopf (ed), *Music on Stage*. Newcastle: Cambridge Scholars Publishing, 2015, 8-27, reprinted here with permission from the publisher, Cambridge Scholars Publishing]

Contextualisation

The formative years for my exposure to opera were from the mid-1970s to the late 1980s with performances at the Deutsche Oper am Rhein, Düsseldorf. The artistic director was Grischa Barfuss, from 1986 Kurt Horres. Peter Schneider was Erster Kapellmeister from 1968-1978, and General Music Director in Bremen from 1978-1985. Until the end of the Barfuss-era in 1986, Schneider carried on appearing in Düsseldorf as guest conductor, for some Verdi, but mainly Mozart, Strauss and particularly Wagner, esp. since his 1981 Bayreuth debut, because general music director Wakasugi was only beginning to develop his Wagner repertory.

Tickets came on sale on the Sunday before the next month, with the box office opening at 10am. Brochures with the full schedule including cast became available about a week before those Sundays. As I always decided which performances to attend depending on the cast, in the years before mailing lists had been introduced, I would phone the opera's general office every day from two weeks before the ticket sale started, and had a brochure sent to me in the post. For the Sundays of the ticket sale, I would turn up between 8 and 9am, depending on the likelihood of demand, and would usually be able to get the tickets I wanted (third tier, last seat on the side closest to the stage).

The house ensemble consisted of many excellent singers, such as tenors William Holley, Georgi Tscholakov, Janos B. Nagy, and a young Peter Seiffert. The major Verdi baritone was Eugene Holmes, and Mileva (Milica) Buljubasic the leading lyric soprano after Cilla Zentai had followed Schneider to Bremen. For Wagner, the opera worked with members of the ensemble and guests. In the early 1980s, for example, Simon Estes made his debut as Wotan in a Düsseldorf Ring cycle, with Gwendoylyn Killebrew who sang Fricka in many of the cycles. Manfred Jung sang the heroic tenor parts, Siegmund, Siegfried, Tristan, and

Florestan in Beethoven's *Fidelio*. Berit Lindholm was Brünhilde, Isolde, Elektra and Salome. Other singers for Wotan were Leif Roar, Norman Bailey, and Donald McIntyre. Carla Pohl and Sabine Hass were Sieglinde, an on one occasion Hildegard Behrens took over that part at very short notice from the scheduled soprano who had been taken ill. Peter Meven, Malcolm Smith and Hans Tschammer were the company's principal bass singers, sometimes supported by Karl Ridderbusch as a guest (Rocco in *Fidelio*, Hunding in *Walküre*, Gurnemanz in *Parsifal*). Other conductors were Friedemann Layer, Jiri Kout, Christian Thielemann, Alberto Erede, Arnold Quennet, and Yoram David.

With two or three ring cycles per year, those attending them regularly would recognise and acknowledge each other, sometimes also talk. One year, regulars of two cycles began to comment, towards the end of the second cycle, about one spectator who had been attending both cycles. He aroused curiosity and comments. He looked strikingly out of place in an opera house, as if it was an excruciatingly painful and boring experience for him. So why did he bother turning up? A year or so later I was at home flicking through TV channels and suddenly saw this opera spectator on the screen. It was a report, in a popular and highly acclaimed investigative journalism programme, about male escorts. The strange opera spectator was a male escort by profession, a more mature escort (late 40s, thinning hair) for more mature female clients. In the interview on TV he said that he was keen on attracting, and did attract, female clients from the more sophisticated levels of society. He was successful, he felt, in this endeavour not only because of his physical / sexual profile but because of his engagement with culture: he read the latest novels, watched the latest films and also (he said with a slight wince) went to opera performances.

Memorable moments from those years include a performance of *Siegfried*. Manfred Jung is about to find the piece of wood on stage from which he crafts the flute. Only he does not find it—and leaves the stage mid-scene. Peter Schneider had to stop the orchestra, just broadly shrugging his shoulders in surprise. After a few minutes, Jung returned, piece of wood in hand, and proceeded as if nothing had happened. Jung's singing was ever-reliable, but the voice could be throaty and the higher register of the voice narrow. After he re-emerged with the flute, however, for whatever reason, until the end of the scene (unfortunately all too soon), his voice was clear, fresh, radiant and open as never before (or, sadly, after).

It was at the opening night of the first new production under the artistic directorship of Kurt Horres, in 1986 that I encountered the one and only scandal I experienced in my theatre- and opera-going. The audience had become accustomed to profound, beautiful and in that best sense conservative productions in the long era under Barfuss. Horres set his agenda by inviting a representative of Regietheater for his first new production, of Verdi's *Macbeth*. New music director Hans Wallat conducted, and the part of Lady Macbeth was cast with Gabriele Schnaut. For the scene in which Macbeth is shown to suffer a nightmare, the curtain opened to reveal a vagina the size of the entire height of the stage, and little people specially hired for this scene crawled out of that vagina. Within seconds the audience erupted into tumultuous booing and shouting, which ended only when, some fifteen to twenty minutes into the protest, Wallat came on to the stage and pleaded with the audience to allow the performance to proceed. The director decided not to take a curtain call at the end of the performance.

A full season of Royal Opera Covent Garden, 1979/80, while I was Assistant Teacher of German at Beverley School, New Malden, as well as much opera in the old opera house in Oslo (1988-90), more Covent Garden since 1991, as well as one-offs in Geneva, Stockholm, the new opera house in Oslo, Staatsoper Munich, Deutsche Oper and Staatsoper Berlin, as well as opera houses in Hamburg, Bremen, Minden, Vienna, Hannover, Cologne, Barcelona, Arena di Verona, and the Bolshoi Theatre in Moscow have added to my range of experience. It was interesting to observe, over the years, the type of spectators that attend opera productions, and that also attended, for example, the 2017/18 exhibition *Opera: Passion, Power and Politics* at the Victoria and Albert Museum, London, UK, the immediacy of conversations among "opera lovers" who have never met before, and the lack of understanding that attending opera in particular, even more than attending dance or theatre, triggers in people who are simply not interested in these art forms—I still vividly recall when my enthusiasm of talking about my cultural adventure of the 1979/80 year in London was met by one interlocutor with a hilarious attempt at making a joke, because what she said was so obviously combined with contempt, disdain and envy, epitomised by the statement: "Oh, dann sind Sie ja jetzt gebüldet". The telling word in this German sentence is "gebüldet", which suggests a ridiculously pompous pronunciation of "gebildet". "Gebildet" means "erudite, well-educated". "Gebüldet" is usually used by two or more people talking about a person who is not present, to ridicule him/her and to cut someone down to size. It can signify either the ignorance of the person thus described, or the ignorance of those using the term, or both.

I was not discouraged by this comment, and over the past decade added research into and writing about opera to my profile. I published a number of articles and dedicated chapters of my two 2013 books to opera. The first chapter on opera in this book was indirectly inspired by my experience of the Düsseldorf *Macbeth* scandal and considers the binary opposite of productions that are truthful to the composer's intentions and those that apparently focus on the director's ideas, the wilder the better.

Terms

The debate regarding the role of the director in the context of an opera production has focused on the alleged binary opposite of *Werktreue* and *Regieoper* (applied to opera from the term coined in conjunction with theatre as *Regietheater*). *Werktreue* can be understood as the director's commitment to do as much justice as possible to the perceived intentions of the composer and librettist in the process of translating the libretto from page to stage in conjunction with the conductor who is in charge of the score. The director becomes the servant of the art form, in the service of the librettist, as much as the conductor is in the service of the composer. Related terms are *traditional*, *conventional* and *orthodox*. *Regieoper*, in contrast, places emphasis on the ideas that the director develops inspired by, and in relation to the combination of libretto and score. The director is no longer anyone's servant and develops an idea, often referred to as a concept, for the production and puts that idea or concept into practice over the rehearsal period. The historical development in opera is one from *Werktreue* to *Regieoper*, in parallel to the development within theatre: initially, the role of the director was to ensure singers or actors knew when to enter and exit the stage, leaving the activity of actors in theatre predominantly to improvisation, and not expecting from singers more than predominantly stationary delivery as close as possible to the ramp. According to Heeg, any binary is inappropriate that sets the work of art as it was originally intended, against the director's personal arbitrariness (2008: 30). Semiotics defines the play text or libretto as a text in its own right; equally, the performance is a text in itself, following its own rules, and thus independent of the play text or libretto. The binary of *Werktreue* and *Regieoper* disappears in the context of these definitions (Balme 2008: 47-8).

The opposition between the two comes into play if we consider results of the *Werktreue* approach as old-fashioned, lifeless, boring, and "fundamentalist in nature even if necessary for the discussion of opera and theatre" (Balme 2008: 43) and *Regieoper* as dynamic, associated with ideas, provocation and confrontation (Balme 2008: 43). The opposition can be found equally between the view of *Regieoper* as the apparent disregard for the original work, with traditionalists unable to see directorial decisions as resulting from, or as intrinsic to the work, but as superimposed arbitrarily on the work and thus artificial, an expression of decadence. In contrast to that view of *Regieoper*, *Werktreue* represents the view that the director's role is to express for the audience the author's perceived intentions without any conceptual superimposition of their own. As Heather MacDonald put it, productions following the *Werktreue* approach "allow the beauty of some of the most powerful music ever written to shine forth". MacDonald, writing in 2007, associates many European, in particular German, directors with *Regieoper* and sets up the Metropolitan Opera House in New York as a bastion of the *Werktreue* approach.

Problems with *Regieoper*

What is so problematic about *Regieoper*? Allegedly, if directors engage in this mode of directing, much of the original is lost. MacDonald, for example, argues that *Regieoper* denies its audiences the "unimpeded experience of an art form of unparalleled sublimity". She locates the origins of opera in the seventeenth-century as an attempt by the Florentines "to recover the power of Greek tragedy, which united drama and song. Since then, opera has expressed a limitless range of human emotions, set to music of sometimes unbearable exquisiteness" (2007). Here is a longer passage from MacDonald to demonstrate the passion of the argument:

> Without Mozart or Verdi, the Regietheater director is nothing; he cannot even hope for third-rate avant-garde status. In a world where displaying bodily fluids in jars, performing sex acts in public, or trampling religious symbols will land you a gig at the Venice Biennale and a government grant, the only source of outrage still available to the would-be scourge of propriety is to desecrate great works of art. (2007)

In general terms, this "depressing" phenomenon of *Regieoper*, MacDonald argues, "suggests a culture that cannot tolerate its own legacy of beauty and nobility" (2007). According to Klonovsky, *Regieoper* is characterised by an egalitarian view of history and people, epitomised by the word "downwards": nothing is great, nothing is beautiful, nothing has turned out well, in particular no human being. The only acceptable perspective on important people is that of the valet (who does not understand or accept anything beyond his sphere), and great deeds are the results of addictions, vanity and inhibitions. The lowest common denominator is that all people have sex, and that needs to be presented on stage as a result. The existence of high culture is considered by leftist intellectuals, among whom Klonovsky counts representatives of *Regieoper*, as suspect and scandalous (n.d.).

Rather than remaining general, some critics provide details as to where libretto and score do not match directors' choices: MacDonald, for example, writes about the 2011 Salzburg Festival production of Mozart's *Le nozze di Figaro* by Claus Guth:

> Lost, too, is the humor. The recognition scene, in which Figaro and Marcellina improbably discover their mother-son relationship, embodied Guth's cluelessness about comic tradition. The repeated "Sua madre's!" and "Tuo padre's!" of the startled participants should be a moment of ebullient silliness, as indicated by the music's mounting pitches, unbroken major harmonies, and accelerating tempo; instead, the characters stood around woodenly, looking uncomfortable, alienated, and glum. Figaro nervously cleaned his glasses rather than joyfully embrace his long-lost mother. The delightful fillip dissing the Count which ends the episode fell hollowly among this unhappy new family. Not surprisingly, the scene elicited not a chuckle from the audience on the night I saw it, nor was it apparently meant to—contrary to the patent intentions of Mozart and Da Ponte. (2011)

How do the singers and conductors respond to *Regieoper*? Writers opposed to this approach to opera directing in principle tend towards sweeping statements such as "singers, orchestra members, and conductors know how shameful the most self-indulgent opera productions are, and yet they are powerless to stop them" (MacDonald 2007). In fact, however, they seem not to have problems listing incidents where artists went on record with their dissatisfaction. Thus, MacDonald refers to baritone Sherrill Milnes and his appearance as Iago in a German production of Verdi's *Otello*: the director asked him to come on stage during the third-act duet between Otello and Desdemona, crawl across the stage on his belly and engage in obvious masturbation.

Milnes was astounded. "I won't do it, it's wrong on every front," he remembers responding. "At the very least, it's rude to interrupt the focal point of the scene between Desdemona and Otello. It's not about Iago's reaction." (In fact, Iago is not even supposed to be onstage.) "No way I'll put my hand on my crotch; it's embarrassing for Sherrill Milnes and it's embarrassing for Sherrill Milnes as Iago." But Milnes gave ground: "I came on the stage, but not as long as the director wanted, breathed a little hard and exited." (2007)

MacDonald also refers to soprano Diana Damrau and her involvement in the infamous Bavarian State Opera *Rigoletto*, set on the Planet of the Apes.

"I fulfilled my contract," she says scornfully. "This was superficial rubbish. You try to prepare yourself for a production, you read secondary literature and mythology. Here, we had to watch *Star Wars* movies and different versions of *The Planet of the Apes*...This was just...noise." (2007).

In 2010, Carl St Clair resigned from his post as general music director of the Komische Oper Berlin in protest against the *Regieoper* approach prevalent at the house. He had been critical of the *Regieoper* approach for some time, but the last straw came with Benedikt von Peter's production of *Fidelio*. St Clair commented: "In this particular production I experienced what I would consider the darkest side of Regietheater, where the back of Beethoven was used for a concept. ... This concept used and abused Beethoven's greatness in a way that was very disturbing to me" (Mangan 2010).

In defence of *Regieoper*

Regieoper finds many voices in its defence, which tend to be as sophisticated as those defending violence on screen or extreme body art among performance installations. A closer look at alleged analysis in favour, or even in defence of *Regieoper* tends to reveal much detailed description of offending productions, which is equally present in texts against *Regieoper*, in addition to phrases that reveal hermetically sealed jargon: Steier's comment on Bieito's 2003 production of Mozart's *Die Entführung aus dem Serail* is a suitable example.

> Setting the piece in a glittery, violent, vaguely eastern European whorehouse, peppered with guns, drugs, and all varieties of bodily fluid and physical assault, Bieito cut through any sentimental/contextual membrane protecting the opera from the stomach-churning brutality of such modern phenomena as human trafficking and snuff-films. In addition to the unswervingly committed cast, the Komische Oper hired 15 professional adult entertainers to fill out the sordid aesthetic texture of Bieito's vision. (2004)

What precisely is a membrane of any further description (here: "sentimental/contextual") in relation to an opera? What does the specific descriptor "sentimental / contextual" mean, precisely? What is the relationship between this particular opera and modern phenomena such as "human trafficking and snuff films", precisely? What is the purpose of the employment of "professional adult entertainers", precisely? In each case, the argument lacks precision and does not hold up to scrutiny.

It is not necessary to hide behind such jargon. In her introduction to a collection of interviews with opera directors, many of them in the *Regieoper* category, Beyer considers the question important as to what the director wants to achieve with his or her production, and differentiates between intended provocation of the spectator, conscious irritation of habits of thinking, seeing and hearing, and consensus. On the basis of interviews with fourteen opera directors, first published in 2005, Beyer concludes that there is agreement that the directors' task is to prove, again and with commitment, that, and how, music theatre can have a meaningful impact on its audience (2007: 15). Beyer emphasises that all the directors that feature in her book share their serious dedication to the operas they work on, their belief in the dialogue, and their love for and of opera (2007: 19).

In line with this argument, directors associated by the critics with *Regieoper* refuse to be categorised in this way. They insist that they work predominantly intuitively with their teams of singers and designers during, and not before, the rehearsal process, and do not superimpose a concept on to the opera in question but develop their ideas in relation to the libretto and music, even if in contrast. Peter Konwitschny is an example. He says:

> I do not consider myself a representative of the *Regietheater*. Often, these directors present one single idea, such as for example staging Rigoletto in an empty swimming pool or in a slaughterhouse. These ideas are not consequentially followed through and explored, and in most cases, the singers stand next to each other on stage just as unconnected as in conventional productions. My stagings, on the other hand, aim to return to the roots: to get to the core of the pieces, through the jungle of interpretative traditions, which in most cases, have distorted the pieces. The accusation that this is "too intellectual for the average viewer" is absurd and exposes the enemies of such theatre as opposing new insights. (2009)

Katharina Wagner, too, claims that she does not direct in order to provoke. She directs from within the piece, to bring out what she sees in it, and what it has to say today in relation to changes across its reception history. It is then left to each spectator to select any specific aspect they want to talk about in discussions of the production—there are many aspects on offer in her production, not limited to the role of the work in the Third Reich. In addition, there is the thought of the general discourse on art:

what is art in the first place? Who defines what art is, and what can art achieve in the spectator? (Steinbach 2011)

Many representatives of *Regieoper* thus claim not to be provocative intentionally. However, what *Regietheater* does, according to Heeg, (and this applies to *Regieoper* as well), is to challenge the great canonical works of theatre and opera by confronting them with the demands of the present and limited life, searching for the aspects in those works that have been left incomplete, or have not been thought through to their ends, due to the different times they were created in (2008: 31). He locates the advantage or strength of *Regieoper* in its examination of the past, its new interpretation and new definition of cultural self-image, in order to create cultural identity in times of crisis (33).

This approach may come across as provocative to an audience. In terms of audiences, Beyer differentiates between spectators for whom opera continues to be a hideaway from reality, an expression of their yearning for a feeling of security, and a place where feelings appear genuine, honest and strong and can be acted out without existential hazard. For others, opera is a means to ascertain the continuation of traditional values (2007: 18-19). Briegleb takes this argument in terms of audiences further, assuming that the yearning for theatre and opera that is "decent" is equivalent to the desire for comprehensible and stringent narrative. Against that background he argues that the difference between what he calls *alive* and *lethargic intellectualism* lies in the readiness, or unwillingness, to accept the stress caused by being confronted with theatre that is not easily understood, in the sense of the statement of theatre director Frank Baumbauer that theatre has to be straining (2008: 83). In turn, stringent narratives invite recognition and identification, and spectators stop thinking on their own. The cinema, Briegleb muses, is much more suitable to serve this mode of reception. (2008: 85). This argument seems to imply that it is the fault of the spectator if they dislike what they see in the opera house, because such dislike is characteristic of *intellectual lethargy*. Anders, too, takes up the perspective of the spectator, proposing that *Regieoper* plays with the spectator's expectations, provokes through new forms and cannot be digested easily by the spectator (2008: 117). Walburg places himself in the position of a spectator: "If I see *Macbeth* and it is set in the job centre, then I do not understand it. Someone tries to garner attention with something that does not make sense" (Kaiser et al. 2010: 33-34). Khuon, finally, insists that his theatre wants to avoid an audience leaving with the feeling that they have understood everything, and it was somehow great, but unable to remember even the contents after only two days (2008: 63).

Schmidt proposes avoiding the dead end of quarrel implied by the conventional, negative association of *Regieoper* by considering what we might hope and expect from *Regieoper* (2008: 71). One is the expectation that art opens up new spaces for experience. The director needs to be prepared to have his / her certainties shattered by getting in touch with the essence of the opera. If that were the case, we would not only question opera, but we would allow those operas to question us (2008: 77-78). Briegleb takes this consideration of the expectations regarding *Regieoper* further by suggesting how *Regieoper* could work best: he is in favour of complex narration, and sees two obstacles to its success: first, access to opera cannot be assumed any longer to be enabled by a common canon of signs and education. Secondly, directors sometimes confuse the foreign with the private (2008: 86).

The overall argument that emerges from these multiple positions is that self-indulgent work, and concepts that do not make sense because they do not relate to the spectator but are private to the director are not what *Regieoper* should be all about. Rather, *Regieoper* should be understood as the director's attempt to enable the audience, through their work, to think about the issues presented in the opera for themselves in a contemporary context. Gutjahr sums this up in her comment that *Regieoper* implies a new role for the director, close to that of an author; rather than reconstructing and interpreting an opera that claims sacrosanct status, directors develop a new conceptualisation of the stage experience, in which the opera hypertext is exposed to multiple exchanges with discourses, arts and media (2008: 22).

Werktreue

Opposition against, and justifications and explanations of *Regieoper* are frequently contextualised in relation to the concept of *Werktreue*. In that set of binary opposites, the call for *Werktreue* has been presented as a yearning for an irretrievable past, with its traditional understanding of art and culture, in which opera becomes the location of everything true, good and beautiful. Heeg understands such yearning not so much as a left-over of the "eternally of yesterday", but as a reaction of fear of and escape from the loss of a collective cultural identity in view of current trends of fragmentation (2008: 29-30). Balme takes this argument further and identifies the understanding of *Werktreue* as the inappropriate yearning for an irretrievable past as essentially fundamentalist in nature. *Werktreue*, (mis-)understood as a desire for unrestricted obedience, implies a disposition towards absolutes, which is in opposition to freedom of the arts and is close to fundamentalism (Balme 2008: 43). Linguistic studies reveal that the term *Werktreue* was first used in the Nazi newspaper *Völkischer Beobachter* in 1935 with reference to Furtwängler conducting Beethoven (Balme 2008: 45).

The views by eminent German theatre actor and director Gustaf Gründgens (1899-1963) are of particular interest in this context as he is widely considered a major proponent and representative of the *Werktreue* approach in the very early days of the debate. A statement of 1930, in which actor Gründgens writes about director Gründgens, provides evidence that the spectator is at the centre of Gründgens's theatre aesthetics: spectators should be able to understand what the actors say; for actors to say the words of the text in such a way that the spectators are able to understand them, the actors in turn need to understand what the dramatist is saying. The purpose of the director for Gründgens is to get out of the play and the actors whatever is within them, and in his practice, he is fanatical about precision and an enemy of anything coincidental, unclear and uncontrollable (1963: 12-3). The emphasis on the spectator implies a specific perspective on *Werktreue*: it does not mean, for example, staging Goethe's *Faust* without cuts, in a performance lasting for seven hours, but to make cuts so as to make the play more accessible to an audience that may not have the patience for the uncut work (1963: 23). Contemporary director Michael Thalheimer, too, emphasises that *Werktreue* does not necessarily mean, or at least imply, faithfulness to the (full, uncut) text of the original play (2008: 192).

In working on a production, for Gründgens any personal opinions take a background position, and he works solely to make the best of the context of work, time and actors. He endeavours to track down the play, to make its dramaturgy his own, and to find the style, mask and movement that are its own. Finally, he endeavours to give the actors security in performing without ambiguity all those aspects of the play, which he discovers together with them. (1963: 29). Thus, the work of the director is never an end in itself, but only ever a means towards an end, with the director as the mediator between play and audience. Gründgens was convinced that it is very easy indeed to direct a production in such a way that it becomes a scandal. To create something from nothing is an example of cheap art, while it is much more difficult to create something from something (1963: 141-2).

In a speech of 1948 to the German Stage Association, with the rebuilding of the German theatre landscape after the Second World War in mind, Gründgens emphasised the need for productions that follow the *Werktreue* approach. He defined it as the requirement to interpret the play as it was intended by the author. The director's creativity does not mean for the directors to put themselves on stage together with the play; rather, creativity begins where the director is able to exemplify in a production on stage the dramatist's vision and desire, and possibly to boost it. In this context, Gründgens argues that at that particular time in German theatre history, it is not important whether productions are good or bad, but whether they are right or wrong—whether it is possible to recognise, unambiguously, a specific play even if the production is only of moderate quality, or whether all that is recognisable are the director's vanity and ignorance. Even the most self-centred conductor is bound by the score, and the director should be bound by the play text. Gründgens pleads with directors to be rather less glowing but right, than fascinating but wrong (1963: 161-2).

With closer analysis, the concepts of *Werktreue* and *Regieoper* appear to be less of binary opposites than much discussion seems to imply. Both have at their heart the desire to bring the opera in question as close as possible to the spectator, to engage the spectators, to make them relate to the opera, be that by feeling uplifted by the beauty and sublime nature of the work (which is allegedly achieved better by a *Werktreue* approach), or by thinking critically about the opera and the contemporary relevance of its contents (which is allegedly achieved better by a *Regieoper* approach). In the next section of this chapter, I describe and discuss a 2012 production of Wagner's *Tristan und Isolde* to exemplify some of the debate surveyed so far.

Tristan und Isolde in Minden, Germany

There is a Richard Wagner Association in Minden, Germany, a town of 83,000 inhabitants on the river Weser in North-Rhine Westphalia. There is also a municipal theatre in the town, built in 1908 and refurbished in 2012. The theatre does not have its own company, it is a receiving house only. In 2002, Jutta Hering-Winckler, a solicitor in Minden and chair of the Richard Wagner Association, arranged a professional production of *Der Fliegende Holländer* to be produced in Minden and performed at the municipal theatre. In 2005, a production of *Tannhäuser* followed, in 2009 came *Lohengrin*, and *Tristan und Isolde* in 2012. The music on all four productions was provided by the *Nordwestdeutsche Philharmonie*, conducted by Frank Beermann. The production had been publicised, in the local newspaper, with special reference to Matthias von Stegmann as the director as a guarantor of the *Werktreue* approach. Von Stegmann had worked for many years as an assistant director at the Bayreuth Festival, including with Wolfgang Wagner on numerous productions. He had assisted Wagner also for the 1997 production of *Lohengrin* at the New National Theatre in Tokyo, where he returned to direct his own productions of *Der Fliegende Holländer* (2009) and *Lohengrin* (2012). Von Stegmann has been known, in Germany, as an actor in dubbing; he has written German dubbing scripts, and directed dubbing; in particular, he has been in charge of the German dubbing of *The Simpsons* (translation and direction) for a number of years now.

In one of the numerous articles in the local newspaper, *Mindener Tageblatt*, prior to the opening night on 8 September 2012, von Stegmann pointed out that he does not always consider the intellectualising of certain contents as healthy. For *Tristan und Isolde*, the spectator must take part in the life and the suffering (Koch 2012a). The set for the production supports this directorial approach, designed by Frank Phillip Schlößmann, who created the set design for production of Wagner's *Ring* cycle for the Bayreuth Festival, launched in 2006 and in the repertory until 2010, directed by Tankred Dorst. The orchestra pit in the Minden municipal theatre is too small to accommodate an 80 musician Wagner orchestra. Thus, the pit was covered, and the opera's action took place on top of it. In this constellation of the theatre space, the singers were literally within reach of spectators in the front row. Von Stegmann considered this proximity as a danger, but also an exciting challenge to develop the level of authenticity needed for spectators so close to the singers to believe their emotions fully and at every moment (Koch 2012a). Some of von Stegmann's explanations to the singers at the first rehearsal were documented in the *Mindener Tageblatt*: "I want pure emotion up there. That will be demanding. At every second you need to know what you are doing and why you are doing it". With regard to the proximity of stage and spectators, he pointed out that "large gesture of opera will not work" and advises the singers to "think in filmic terms: the end result should look like Chekhov or Strindberg". Von Stegmann emphasised again that he does not want to hide behind a concept that he superimposes on the opera from the outside. He told his singers that they would all get to their emotional limits in working with this opera but assured them that he was on their side (Koch 2012b).

The orchestra was further back on the stage and separated from the stage space allocated to the action by a gauze. The orchestra was thus in full view of the audience. The stage floor was built as a slope, rising towards the back of the stage. The front part, up unto the gauze, was made from wooden floor boards painted in a light lilac colour. At the very back of the stage, behind the orchestra, was a screen on to which different shades and colours of light were projected, in line with the music and the plot. Overall, the set created the image of a ship, with the screen shaped as the bow, and the auditorium as the stern, with the stage up to the gauze as the main back part of the ship and the conductor as the helmsman. Within this image of a stylised ship, the breath of the audience could be considered almost as the wind in the ship's sails.

When the audience entered the auditorium, the stage was open to view fully, lit by the lights in the auditorium. The orchestra musicians were at their desks behind the gauze, which was lit blue. When the house lights went down, the lights on stage came on, Isolde took her place in one of the boats, Brangäne sat near another boat, and Kurwenal was in the background. The conductor arrived, the overture started. Isolde was reading in a book, not quite able to concentrate, a number of books were piled on the floor next to the boat she was in, she flipped the pages, read here and there, nervous, agitated, possibly bored. Real life took place in front of our eyes: music, set, changing light, singers, singing, libretto, facial expressions, gestures, glances, all became one, illustrating in surprising detail what is likely the genuine meaning of *Gesamtkunstwerk*, total work of art.

Repeated viewing could possibly allow spectators to pick up on, and remember, all of the minute detail of what happened on stage. Most striking moments included the way Tristan and Isolde behaved when they had drunk the love potion instead of the death drink. Both became love-struck teenagers, in very different, but clearly masculine and feminine ways, respectively, very moving and only slightly comical, so as not to distract from the serious nature of the situation as highly problematic within the opera's overall plot. Neither could help the power of the potion, neither was able to "think straight" any more, all they knew was the attraction to each other, which is love in both a spiritual sense, as Eros, and a physical sense as sexuality. The production managed to make this holistic level of their experience clear, for example when Tristan and Isolde moved closer to each other as if to kiss, only for Isolde to break away from the kiss when their lips were almost touching, to place her face on Tristan's chest in a loving embrace.

Kurwenal was very surprised at what he observed, helpless, confused, and the realisation of what she had caused hit Brangäne quite visibly. Both had to use the maximum physical strength they had available to literally tear Tristan and Isolde apart so as to keep up appearances when King Marke arrived. When Marke discovered Tristan and Isolde at the end of Act II, the colour of Isolde's dress matched that of Marke's coat and suit. While Marke lamented Tristan's betrayal, sitting on the sea trunk, Isolde came over to him and sat next to him, sad at his suffering, sad that it was caused by her, but at the same time not showing any signs of feeling guilty: she was under the influence of the love potion, and was thus not responsible for Marke's misery, and neither was Tristan. There is no conflict here for her, or for Tristan.

At the beginning of Act III, we saw Tristan resting in a derelict boat; Kurwenal was busy washing out bloodied bandages from Tristan's wounds. There were many of them, and they were quite bloody, and Kurwenal tried his best with them, without achieving much. It is an image for the moving care that Kurwenal took of Tristan, but it showed also the helplessness of the rather rough man in carrying out this work that he probably never thought he would be doing: he was awkward with the movements, clumsy, quite inefficient, without any idea of hygiene, as one would expect from a man like him, but the fact that he still tried, and tried so obviously hard to do something almost against his very nature was genuinely moving.

Contrary to the ending of the opera as suggested in the libretto, according to which Isolde sinks, in Brangäne's arms, on top of Tristan's corpse, in the Minden production Isolde left the stage in very bright white light.

It is revealing to analyse the way critics wrote about this production. Some notice and convey a brief impression of the detail of the character's actions and motivations. Critics described some of the nuances of the production with regard to the singers, generally pointing to their intensity and authenticity (Helming 2012), and describing Andreas Schager's Tristan as a boisterous, passionate firebrand and dare-devil, whose ego does not have space for self-doubt (Helming 2012) and noting the tear that Dara Hobbs sheds as Isolde during her *Liebestod* at the end of the opera (Groenewold 2012). Other details noted by the critics included the splinter from Morold's sword that Isolde wore as a memento on a necklace, with Tristan entering with the rest of the sword (Brockmann 2012). In a detailed review in *Der Neue Merker*, Pfabigan comments very favourably on a phenomenal person direction that renders every breath, every glance, every step and every phrase into a spectator's very personal experience.

Critics also note the imaginative, detailed use of light throughout the production, such as velvety blue for the love scene in Act II, complete with starry sky that changes its light constellation in line with music and libretto. The skeleton of a boat that hung high from the ceiling over the orchestra in Act III, was lit red during Tristan's long monologue of suffering (Groenewold 2012). Groenewold refers to the production as a concentrated psychodrama, in which the effort to choreograph movements, gestures and glances as naturally and precisely as possible is evident, so as not to allow pathos to seep in. She attests a fine sense of stage dynamics, and awareness of the power of calmness to von Stegmann (2012). In her review in the national newspaper *Frankfurter Allgemeine Zeitung*, Eleonore Büning concludes that it has been a long time since audiences were able to see emotion on stage and not only in the music (2012). Brockmann combines observation of detail with more general writing, emphasising what the director did not do rather than what he did, or what the effect may have been of what he did: von Stegmann told the story *without* wrong additions, interpretations, or references to Wagner's biography (2012). Helming describes the production in general terms as "directorial chamber theatre" and adds that it "abstains from updating and re-interpretations characteristic of *Regietheater*" (2012). Similarly, Manuel Brug in the national newspaper *Die Welt* calls von Stegmann's production simple but moving, with nothing negative distracting from them music (2012).

Thus, the reviews of the Minden *Tristan und Isolde* praise the production; some describe some instances of detail, others combine general comments with indications that the high quality of the production was achieved because of various things the director could have done but did not do, fortunately. Altogether, however, it is fair to say that directors of the *Regieoper* category can expect to get many more words for their concept and its details, even if that does not entail praise. Such an imbalance of direct critical attention to the director's work raises the question to what extent sparse comments on a director's high level of praiseworthy, but (?!) uncontroversial achievement, in comparison to more detailed and precise comments on controversial *Regieoper* directors, do in fact tempt or seduce particularly younger directors to abandon any attempt at *Werktreue* in favour of *Regieoper*. Remember that according to Gründgens, not much effort is needed to direct a scandal, and if that brings more public attention, as measured by lines, or time, allocated to the production in the media, why bother with the eminently greater effort it takes to direct a genuinely moving, emotionally rich production? Both national reviews, by the way, misspell the name of the tenor (Schager becomes Schlager and Scharger, respectively).

Von Stegmann emphasised in interviews that several aspects of his production were based on gut feeling and intuition rather than intellectually conceived in terms of a concept. The violet colour of the wooden floor boards is an example, as is Isolde's exit at the end of the opera. In the latter he was inspired by the music, which does not suggest sadness any longer, but calm departure and closure: she is liberated, it is almost a kind of apotheosis, a dissolving. It may be that she dies, or that she moves into a different dimension.

Spirituality perspective

Some productions, according to some spectators, miss, in some instances by far, the spirit of the libretto and the music. However, even directors who admit to being, and wanting to be, provocative, insist that they are directing in line with the spirit of both libretto and music, with the overall aim of making the opera in question relevant to themselves, their team and the audience. I will not discuss further the conspiracy theory that "dark forces" take hold of some directors and twist their minds in such a way as to allow the least possible amount of bright, positive spiritual energy potentially contained in an opera through to the performance, so as to deprive both team and audiences of that potential positive spiritual energy, and to fill the production and reception experiences in turn with negative, dark energy conducive and nourishing to themselves. I also discard the possibility that those provocative directors are disingenuous when they claim to be inspired by the spirit of the opera (music and / or libretto) in their approach that is considered distant from that same spirit by some spectators and critics.

In some cases, critics at least seem to grow accustomed to an initially confusing directorial concept, or consider the confusing elements, or those they consider distracting or out of tune with the libretto and / or music, as secondary and pardonable in view of a very strong direction relating to the interactions of the characters. Neuenfels's production of *Lohengrin* for the Bayreuth Festival, launched in 2010, is a good example: in this production, the opera is set in a laboratory, with the chorus of Brabantian noblemen and women made up of rats. When Lohengrin, at the end of the opera, reveals Elsa's brother, Gottfried, as returned from the Grail, Gottfried emerges from an egg, complete with umbilical cord, as an adult-shaped baby, some disgusting alien creature from a horror movie. The production's overall concept and some of its details caused concern, confusion, and disagreement at first; however, Neuenfels's way of interpreting and conveying the interaction of characters, especially Lohengrin and Elsa in the bridal chamber scene at the beginning of Act III, was indeed very strong, for example Lohengrin's deep sadness when Elsa has asked the forbidden question. In addition, while the concept of this production was provocative and unexpected, Neuenfels was able to be consistent within it, while a good number of other provocative productions fail to achieve such consistency. Thus, one criterion of whether a

Regieoper production "works", in the sense that the intended provocation leads the spectator to think critically about the vision presented in the production, or to reject the production without further thought, might be whether the production is still able to tell a story consistently, stringently and convincingly.

An opera will be able to trigger a range of responses in different directors who consider directing it. Such responses will depend on the nature of the individual director in relation to the opera itself. The director's nature is particularly interesting with regard to the different percentages to which their masculine and their feminine sides have developed, and, related to that, to what extent their creative activities are influenced, possibly dominated, by the analytic, masculine, left or the synthetic, feminine, holistic right hemispheres of their brains. I have pointed out elsewhere (Meyer-Dinkgräfe 2011) that according to certain spiritual traditions, such as that of ascended master St Germain (2010), the purpose for souls to incarnate as humans on planet Earth is for them to learn to develop the feminine side of their nature and have argued that opera serves to develop the feminine side of humans, associated with the right hemisphere. *Werktreue* productions are better placed to achieve that aim. This argument is based on the assumption that music for opera has been composed, and the libretto written, intuitively, by the composer and librettist respectively, in unconscious service to this overarching aim. If we set this as the axiom, then the approaches to conducting and directing that seek to get as much as possible out of the score and libretto *on their own terms*, are likely to achieve development of the production team and audience's feminine sides to a larger extent than productions not governed by this aim. From the opposite angle, if a director adheres to a *Regieoper* approach, and seeks to put on stage ideas triggered by, or in relation to the opera (i.e., on the director's own terms, rather than that of the score and libretto), this approach will be dominated by masculine, left hemisphere influences and the potential for developing the feminine side inherent in the opera will not be fulfilled.

This argument implies that many people appear opposed to the *Regieoper* approach ultimately because that approach tends to shirk the purpose of opera to develop the human feminine side. The argument also explains why cogent and interesting character direction within an overall *Regieoper* approach serves to mitigate objection: such character direction picks up elements of the opera more inherent in the music and libretto, and thus more conducive to developing the feminine side of the spectators than other, non-inherent and superimposed *Regieoper* aspects conceived by the director's left brain and masculine side.

Kirsten Harms is an example for an opera director who sees a difference between her own approach to directing compared with that of her male colleagues: she draws conflicts in opera differently than her male colleagues. Many male colleagues, for example, see *Tannhäuser* as the conflict of a man to decide between the holy woman and the whore. While this level of interpretation may have been interesting for the 19th and 20th centuries, Harms believes that the piece says much more fundamental things about the nature of love. She was interested in the archetypical constellations in the relationship between man and woman that represent obstacles to happiness. Ultimately the characters break down in view of an image of woman that is too far from reality: a woman is expected to be both sexually attractive and a lone, chaste ideal. The discrepancy between these two cannot be bridged, and that ruins Tannhäuser and Wolfram just as much as Venus-Elisabeth. For this reason, it was natural for the same singer to portray both facets of this image of a woman (Königsdorf 2008).

Conclusion

The terms and related concepts of *Regieoper* and *Werktreue* do not serve much purpose any more for discussion and critical analysis of opera productions as long as they are used in their conventional connotations as binary opposites. Directors who explore an opera on its own terms, can achieve a very exciting, thought-provoking and moving event, as von Stegmann's *Tristan und Isolde* production in Minden demonstrates. Similarly, directors who are inspired by a given opera to explore it in different terms can achieve an equally engaging, interesting, thought-provoking and moving event. Examples for this are the widely praised *Parsifal* production by Stefan Herheim for the Bayreuth Festival, or his cogent presentation of *Tannhäuser* in Oslo, although it may not work every time for the same director (for example Herheim's *Lohengrin* in Berlin). The criterion of critical success for a production that seems to deviate from the original context of the opera is the extent to which the new interpretation, or revisioning of the opera, is consistent and cogent within the parameters it sets for itself in making sense of the contents as specified in the libretto and further developed in the music. Thus, the context is still determined by the opera itself: as soon as the director transgresses such a cogent and consistent operatic context, which may be obvious immediately or become obvious only with some further thought, in favour of private contexts that remain private, the production itself becomes arbitrary and unengaging for those (many) spectators who do not happen to know the private context at the origin of such a production.

From the perspective of spiritual development, finally, both exploration of the opera *per se*, and stringent narrative for a revisioning of the opera serve the purpose of allowing opera to fulfil its spiritual purpose, of developing the feminine aspect of members of the production team and of spectators.

CHAPTER FIVE

HOLISTIC EXPERIENCE OF OPERA AND THE *INTERNATIONAL OPERA THEATER* (IOT)

[First published in *Studies in Spirituality* 26 (2016), 373-392; reprinted here with permission from the publisher, Peeters]

Contextualisation

In the summer of 2012, I received an email from Karen Saillant, who introduced herself as a former opera singer, now artistic director of an innovative opera company, International Opera Theater, based in Philadelphia, USA. Every year, she stages a production in Italy, at the Municipal Theatre of Città della Pieve, of a new opera, with a libretto in the Italian language, and music composed as close to a contemporary lyrical Italian style as possible. Saillant felt that I might be interested in her work because of my interest in performance and consciousness—she had come across my name through various searches on the internet. Communication continued via email and skype, and I arranged to attend the opening night and one further performance of their 2013 opera, *Camille Claudel*, composed and conducted by IOT's music director at the time, Gianmaria Griglio, whom I had an opportunity to meet earlier in 2013 as a competitor in the OperaUpClose Flourish New Opera Writing Competition in London. A curiosity of peer review: an earlier version of this article was rejected for publication, in a different journal, following a peer reviewer's comment that it is in principle impossible for any human being to have, or have had, the experience that I describe and that is central to the article.

Introduction

This article is based on my experience during two performances of International Opera Theater's 2013 production of the new opera *Camille Claudel*. I describe the experience in as much detail as necessary to convey its essence to the reader. I define the experience as spiritual: spirituality is to be understood for the purposes of this article in a non-religious context, with the implication that "spirituality culminates in the full development of mind", and "any move in the direction of this fullness can be called spirituality" (Malekin and Yarrow 1997: 90). Subsequently I critically explore the experience in a range of relevant contexts of opera, theatre, performance and consciousness studies. My approach is part of the paradigm shift in consciousness studies from third person approaches to first person approaches, in so far as the experience I describe, and on which my argument is based, is at this point my own experience alone.

International Opera Theater (IOT)

Since its formation in 2003, by Karen Saillant, IOT, based in Philadelphia, USA has presented one new work per year, commissioned by IOT and created in conjunction with it. Seven of the operas were based on or inspired by Shakespeare's plays (*A Midsummer Night's Dream* [two different operas], *The Tempest, A Winter's Tale, Romeo and Juliet, Taming of the Shrew* and *Othello*). Other productions were based on the *Decameron* by Boccaccio, and *Buffalo Soldier,* based on the true story of the WWII segregated 92nd infantry division and the Italian Partisans who helped liberate Italy. The company also presented *Brundibar and the Children of Theresienstadt*, a production that tells the story of the children who gave 55 performances of the little opera *Brundibar* in the Theresienstadt concentration camp during WWII. In addition to the presentation of the short opera, *Brundibar and The Children of Theresienstadt* contains additional music that was performed in Theresienstadt; songs in German, French and Italian, by Ravel, Strauss, Dvořák and Mascagni. The piece uses spoken dialogue and is sung in four languages, English, French, German and Czech; Saillant wrote the libretto for this piece and compiled the music. In 2014, IOT presented *Azaio*, a combination of elements from Shakespeare's *A Winter's Tale* and Coleridge's poem *The Rime of the Ancient Mariner*. This opera featured a cast mainly of children, in addition to a bass-baritone for the mariner himself. The 2015 production was based on Shakespeare's *Comedy of Errors*. All productions were directed by Saillant.

Camille Claudel

The opera was composed by Gianmaria Griglio, with a libretto by Eleonora Gai and Griglio. It has two acts, Act One consists of a prologue and two scenes, Act Two consists of four scenes. The plot is framed by sculptor Camille Claudel (1864-1943) in old age (mezzo) remembering, in the prologue, her younger self (soprano) in a conversation with her brother, poet Paul Claudel (1868-1955) (tenor), before leaving for Paris, then being in Paris with Paul (Act One Scene One) and falling in love with sculptor Auguste Rodin (1840-1917) (baritone, Act One Scene Two). Act Two focuses on the nature of that relationship, the artistic and personal tensions brought about by their sharing of a studio, and Rodin's relationship with Rose Beuret (soprano). Scene One shows Rodin and Rose and Scene Two Rodin and young Camille. In Scene Three there is a fight between Rose and Camille, at the end of which Rodin takes a sheet off one of his sculptures to cover Rose, revealing to Camille that Rodin copied some of her own work into the creation of which she had poured all her life. Old Camille, who has been observing from a distance throughout, gets increasingly involved in the action in Scene Four, and in the end, Paul returns and old and young Camille merge into one. The stage presentation is directed in a non-realistic, symbolist manner, with a large amount of green gauze covering the stage and used imaginatively by the performers throughout. The works of art are represented by a structure resembling the model of a crystal, and a live dancer.

The experience

My experience of *Camille Claudel* was one of totality, where the libretto with its words and character, the music, the singing and the staging (concept, direction, acting, design) formed a genuinely holistic entity that went along with a mode of reception that involved more than the single focus of any one aspect or sense, or even of two aspects or senses, simultaneously. Single focus on just the score, or just the instrumentation, or just the singing, or just any isolated aspect of staging, or single focus on one of these after the other, even with the aim of thus arriving at a more complete picture, were quite well known to me from many years of attending opera performances. However, those insights were bound to remain fragmented, and such fragmentation in turn led to aspects of (intellectual) criticism that diminished or even disappeared in the holistic experience (which includes the intellect but is not limited to it). For example, fragmented analysis of the voices revealed strained delivery, uneven intonation, and problems with the vibrato, in the case of one of the singers. In my holistic experience, those deficiencies did not disappear, but at the same time the holistic dimension meant that the full potential of every aspect of the opera resonated at every moment; thus, while aware of any shortcoming on an intellectual, analytic level, I was at the same time also experiencing the ideal potential of all aspects of the production and performance, because my experience was not limited to the intellect but addressed all levels of consciousness. Afterwards I was reminded of Mozart's description of the holistic nature of opera in Shaffer's *Amadeus*.

> (…) That's why opera is important, Baron. Because it's realer than any play! A dramatic poet would have to put all those thoughts down one after another to represent this second of time. The composer can put them all down at once and still make us hear each one of them. Astonishing device: a vocal quartet! *(More and more excited)* ... I tell you I want to write a finale lasting half an hour! A quartet becoming a quintet becoming a sextet. On and on, wider and wider—all sounds multiplying and rising together—and the together making a sound entirely new! ... I bet you that's how God hears the world. Millions of sounds ascending at once and mixing in His ear to become an unending music, unimaginable to us. *(To Salieri)* That's our job! That's our job, we composers: combining the inner minds of him and him and him and her and her—the thoughts of chambermaids and Court Composers—and turn the audience into God. (1980: 60)

In the case of *Camille Claudel*, my experience was new not only because of the nature of the music, the sound, as in this credo of Mozart. Rather, in addition to the music there were the integral aspects of the production. In the holistic experience, music, libretto, characters, light, costume, movement, aspects of the set, in particular for *Camille Claudel*, the dancer representing Camille's creative spirit, the large amount of green gauze fabric on the floor, and the sculpture (in Act One) and the parts of the sculpture (in Act II) created in the shape of a crystal lattice or DNA, resonated together. For me, this holistic, and in that sense spiritual experience (in a non-religious sense) went beyond the experience that operas by Wagner, for example, can enable: in them, an emphasis on the emotions clearly dominates all aspects of libretto and score, and productions either intensify this approach by focusing equally on the emotions, or they go against this emphasis and dilute it, most likely without being able to add other dimensions because the weight of the emphasis on the emotions in libretto and score is so overwhelming.

My experience of *Camille Claudel* was holistic, and because of this, any fragmented approach at making sense of that experience is doomed to failure. In the same vein, a description of the individual components must remain fragmented and non-holistic. My experience of *Camille Claudel* went beyond such fragments and allowed all components to take their effect together in unison, in a state of simultaneity. The question for me is: how did this holistic experience arise? There is likely to have been some level of openness within myself to allow this experience to manifest.

Seeking to define that openness further is not part of this article. Here I want to explore whether it is possible to isolate causes in the production I saw that may have triggered or contributed to the experience.

Roesner argues that predominantly, theories of and approaches to music theatre (which includes opera) "investigate theatre as a synthetic vision, as a *Gesamtkunstwerk* (Hiß 2005) or as a 'musical multimedia' (Cook 1998)", but that "these ideas still talk, for the most part, about performances with clearly distinguishable components and how to read them historically and analytically" (Roesner 2013: 165). Those components are the "libretto/book, lyrics, music/score, set and lighting design, musical and scenic direction, interpretation by the performers" (Roesner 2013: 166) which come into existence in this sequence and must be excavated, in the process of interpretation/analysis/critique, in reverse order. In contrast, Roesner proposes considering the components of music theatre not as "additive but 'fusional' phenomena" (Roesner 2013: 166). Roesner finds the theoretical and methodological underpinning of this approach in the context of intermediality. I also argue against an approach to understand my holistic experience at the centre of this article against the conventional context of seeking to explore the individual components; however, the theoretical and methodological context for my approach is not that of intermediality, but that of consciousness studies, in particular the concept of holistic experience. I define holistic experience as an experience that comprises all the conventional components, but goes beyond them to form an experience that is more than the sum of its parts, in which the parts may be found and recognised, but in which they are not isolated or solitary, and where even the analysis of the parts does not do justice to the role those parts play in the creation of the holistic experience—even further, an analysis of the parts in which a holistic experience may lead to the uncovering of problems with the parts that do no longer exist in the holistic experience. I propose that such a holistic experience is at the same time a new experience of the concept of Gesamtkunstwerk.

In the following sections of this article I therefore discuss the extent to which selected frameworks can help to explain the nature of this holistic experience. Those frameworks are selective (there may well be more that I do not cover in this article), and they come from a range of contexts—in an attempt to provide as broad as possible an exploration. The frameworks are other reported extraordinary experiences in opera performance, Csikzentmihalyi's concept of *flow*, Maslow's concept of *peak experiences*, Gabrielsson's concept of *strong experiences with music (SEM)*, Peter Brook's concept of *total theatre*, and the model of consciousness developed in Indian Vedanta philosophy.

Conceptualising and contextualising the experience

My holistic experience of *Camille Claudel* sits within the context of desirable extraordinary experiences encompassing all singers on stage at the time of the experience, and the audience as well. As I discussed elsewhere in more detail (Meyer-Dinkgräfe 2011: 42; Meyer-Dinkgräfe 2013a: 143-159), Matheopoulos quotes from, and comments on an interview with Montserrat Caballé (b. 1933):

> "I know this may sound strange to many people, an example of what I mean are those extra-special moments that occur from time to time in every artist's career, moments when you no longer feel you are on a stage making music but in a different dimension, inside, at one with music, and no longer aware of the act of singing or conscious of yourself or your body. The body is a concrete thing made up of physical matter. But when you are in this state of fusion with music, you are totally unaware of it. You feel light, weightless, and afterwards (…) you feel so heavy again". Sometimes during performances Caballé is aware of colleagues or conductors experiencing the same sensation "this sort of trance when all of us feel we are not wholly here, and suddenly it's over in a flash, we look into each other's eyes and know we've just woken up and are no longer in another world but down here, on the stage, making theatre. I don't know why this happens, or how to explain it, but I know that it does and that audiences feel it, too. One of the worst things that can happen at such moments, when you are suspended in a dimension beyond, out of time and space, is applause. (1991: 61)

Anna Tomova Sintov (b. 1941) emphasises the need for opera singers to remember, while they are on stage, that "we are mere instruments in the realisation of a work and that our function is to merge with our colleagues until we are at one with them, the conductor, and through the latter's imagination with the composer" (Matheopoulos 1991: 221). Sherrill Milnes (b. 1935) provides this report of the most extraordinary, spiritual, of performances he participated in (a performance of Verdi's *Otello* at the Vienna State Opera):

> Right from the start we felt a sort of electricity in the air, the feeling that tonight the stars are in the right place—a Sternstunde as it's rightly called in German—and by the end of our Act II Otello-Iago duet the place exploded! It went berserk! At the end, we took our bows, the soli, the tutti, and half an hour of forty to fifty curtain calls after, we were still there. By then we were all getting tired of smiling, the way that you do at wedding receptions, and finally, an hour and a half and 101 curtain calls later, we got away! (Matheopoulos 2000: 178-9)

Barbara Bonney (b. 1956) describes the spiritual magic of a performance of *Der Rosenkavalier* by Richard Strauss during the Vienna State Opera's tour of Japan in 1994:

> (…) it took off in such a magical way that we all felt that this is it. Now we can all be run over by a truck because we have described their exceptional, most desirable experiences on stage often in terms of religion and spirituality. Thus, mine is not an isolated experience. This evening we made this work come alive in the way we feel Strauss wanted. Nothing can ever be like this performance. Even the remaining performances of the run under the same near-ideal conditions were a disappointment after what we had experienced on that fourth evening. (Matheopoulos 1998: 7)

Thus, mine is not an isolated experience; while the artists quoted above, however, underline that such an experience does not happen often or repeatedly, mine occurred over two consecutive performances of the same production—not before nor since in other performances of different productions.

Conceptual frameworks for making sense of such spiritual experiences have been developed in a range of contexts. In Transpersonal Psychology, Abraham Maslow developed the concept of peak experiences, which represent rare and transforming moments in peoples' lives. The experience of unity (Caballé, Tomova Sintov, Milnes, Bonney) is one of those peak experiences. Csikzentmihalyi's concept of *flow* was added to the characteristics of peak experiences. It is a "state of consciousness where people become totally immersed in an activity and enjoy it immensely" (Bakker 2005: 26). Bakker studied flow in the context of theories of emotional crossover or emotional contagion—how and why "positive and negative emotions can crossover from one person to another" (29)—and found that the peak experience of flow does indeed cross over from teachers to students. It is likely (a hypothesis, in empirical terms) that the occurrence of flow (or other peak experiences) in opera spectators crosses over to other spectators, and that similar crossovers take place among opera singers and between singers and spectators in both directions. Crossover can thus be related to the experience of unity as described by opera singers, as one possible way in which such unity can emerge.

Peak experiences in music, including opera, have been discussed in terms of *strong experiences with music* (SEM). This research has been pioneered by Alf Gabrielsson of Uppsala University. Subjects were asked to describe "the strongest, most intense experiences of music that you have ever had. Please describe your experiences and reactions in as much detail as possible" (2010: 551). Supplementary questions were whether this experience occurred only on the first time of listening to the music, or as well on subsequent occasions of listening; how the respondent felt "before and after the experience", "what the experience had meant in a long-term perspective" (551), the cause of the experience, and whether such experiences were encountered in situations that had nothing to do with music. In total, 953 people participated in the project, 250 of those provided more than one report, so that the analysis is based on 1354 reports (552). The analysis takes the shape of a descriptive system for SEM (SEM-DS), with seven basic categories, each with a different number of sub-categories. The basic categories are: general characteristics, physical reactions and behaviours, perception, cognition, feelings/emotion, existential and transcendental aspects and personal and social aspects. The experience of unity comes under the cognition category, within the sub-category "changed experience of situation, body-mind, time-space, part-whole" (557).

The unity of play, actors and spectators is at the centre of Peter Brook's concept of *total theatre*. In our problem ridden society, according to Brook, transcendence is difficult to achieve; however, he maintains that despite all movement, destruction, restlessness and fashion, there are "pillars of affirmation", rare moments when during a theatre performance actors, play, and spectators merge collectively in a "total experience, a total theatre" (1972: 151). Brook further characterises such experiences: "At these rare moments, the theatre of joy, of catharsis, of celebration, the theatre of exploration, the theatre of shared meaning, the living theatre are one" (1972: 151).

In the context of consciousness studies, the holistic experience makes sense within the framework of the model of consciousness proposed by Indian *Vedanta* philosophy in terms of higher states of consciousness. At the centre of the *Vedanta* model of consciousness are distinct states of consciousness, each with its own range of experiential and physiological characteristics. Humans share the experience of three conventional states of consciousness, waking, dreaming and sleeping. Several layers make up the levels of experience characteristic of the waking state of consciousness. They can be imagined as six concentric circles around a core. The six levels are senses, desire, mind, intellect, ego, and feeling (together with emotions and intuition). The core is pure consciousness. Pure consciousness is a fourth state of consciousness and serves as the basis for the six expressed levels of consciousness characteristic of the waking state of consciousness. Pure consciousness is also at the basis of the states of sleep and dream. It can be experienced either on its own, or together with waking, dream or sleep. Experienced on its own, it is a state of consciousness that is devoid of any contents otherwise associated with the senses, desire, mind, intellect, ego, or intuition, feeling or emotion. A person experiencing pure consciousness on its own is not aware of anything other than consciousness itself. The experience of pure consciousness together with waking or dreaming or sleep is characteristic of higher states of consciousness as defined in the *Vedanta* model of consciousness. In the highest of these, unity consciousness, the field of pure consciousness is directly perceived as located at every point in creation; the experiencer experiences himself and his entire environment in terms of his own nature, which he experiences to be pure consciousness (for further details, see Meyer-Dinkgräfe 2005: 24-29). As the frequency of the experience of higher states of consciousness increases, so does the clarity of the experience, and its depth. To a person initially unfamiliar with experiences of higher states of consciousness, they will come across as unique. Initially, at least, they are short-lived (as reported by the opera singers quoted above). The experience of unity is typical of higher states of consciousness within the *Vedanta* model, as the highest level of experience is characterised by the very unity of the experiencer with everything and everyone in the world (Meyer-Dinkgräfe 2005).

Triggers of the holistic experience

Now that I have described the holistic experience and contextualised it in a range of relevant explanatory frameworks (reported extraordinary experiences in opera performance, Csikzentmihalyi's concept of *flow*, Maslow's concept of *peak experiences*, Gabrielsson's concept of *strong experiences with music (SEM)*, Peter Brook's concept of *total theatre*, and the model of consciousness developed in Indian Vedanta philosophy), it is possible to discuss the characteristics of the production that may have contributed to this experience. I identify them in the key characteristics of the work of *IOT* to date, and the role in that work of the founding artistic director, Karen Saillant, and the hen music director, Gianmaria Griglio.

The lyrical style
For the scores for all of IOT's new operas, Saillant aimed for an Italian lyrical style, and the librettos were written and performed in Italian. These are the first two dimensions in which to search for potential components of the trigger of the holistic experience at the centre of this article. Although not a composer herself, a long career as a classically trained opera singer has given Saillant the ability to develop an ideal for the kind of music she would like to have for IOT's operas—an ideal that the composers working

with her on IOT's productions have been achieving to different degrees, perhaps depending on the extent to which they subscribe to the position that quality works in the Italian lyrical style can no longer be achieved, following the pinnacle of the style in the nineteenth- and early-twentieth century works of Italian greats Verdi and Puccini. The Italian lyrical style Saillant has in mind should come across to the listener as sounding lyrical and melodious in the same way that Verdi or Puccini's music sounds but should also retain a certain relevance for today's audiences and avoid direct imitation of its nineteenth-century precursors.

Defining the Italian lyrical style as such is a complex matter. Writing about Puccini's late style, Andrew Davis, following work of Leonard B. Meyer, defines distinct levels of musical style: style can be construed on the level of a single work, such as "the style of *Turandot*"; a group of works, such as "Puccini's mature style"; a single composer, such as "Puccini's style"; a group of composers, such as "the style of the *giovane scuola italiana*" (i.e., the "young Italian school" of the late nineteenth century), a genre, such as "the style of nineteenth-century Italian opera"; or a historical era, such as "the late Romantic style" (2010: 8-9). At any of the various levels, style can be defined further with reference to specific features of the melody and texture (in which melody is central at all times and, furthermore, in which the melody manifests a delicate balance between stepwise motion versus motion by leap), orchestration (often an emphasis on strings, especially to double the vocal melodies), harmony (a predominantly consonant harmonic language in which dissonance is present but tightly controlled), voice leading (an emphasis on smooth voice leading and on certain anti-historical features, such as the suppression of functional dominant harmonies), and rhythm and meter (including, most distinctively perhaps, the use of a written-out *rubato* that lends the music an improvised quality). Davis explores in detail these constitutive components of what he calls Puccini's Romantic style, as well as deviations from that style that mark his last four operas, *Il tabarro, Suor Angelica, Gianni Schicchi,* and *Turandot.* Within the contexts and definitions developed by Davis, it will be possible for musicologists to discuss and pinpoint the precise characteristics of the *Italian lyrical style* that Saillant aspires to for IOT's operas, specifically within the scores of the fourteen new operas premiered by IOT so far.

Italian librettos
The second characteristic if IOT's work, and that of *Camille Claudel* in particular, which can have contributed to triggering my holistic experience at the centre of this article, is that the scores of IOT's productions are in

Italian. According to Griglio, Italy and Italian classical music and lyrical opera have had considerable influence on the history of classical music and lyrical opera beyond Italy: for example, Vivaldi's non-operatic work was much admired by J.S. Bach. Griglio points out that Wagner completed *Parsifal* in Palermo and worked on *Tristan und Isolde* while in Venice, implying a possible influence of the environment on the composition (2013). Paolo Valenti (in conversation with Saillant), considers further that not only is Italian the language of the first operas ever written (in Florence at the turn of the seventeenth century), but the Italian culture is synthetic; dominated by foreign cultures throughout history, it has been able to absorb into its culture the finest aspects of its foreign dominators. In Venice we see Jerusalem. In Sicily we see Arabia, in Turin, France, in Naples, Spain and so on. In its ability to adapt, it has synthesized, opened and accepted the finest parts of other cultures. Italy has given us what many consider to be the most significant collection of diverse art on our planet.

The nature of the Italian language itself also may be one of the triggers for the holistic experience of this work; that is, the language itself has been seen historically as enabling or, indeed, as demanding a particular musical style. It would take further linguistic study to substantiate Valenti's idea of the Italian language as holistic in the sense that that country's architecture or culture might be considered holistic, but with regard specifically to libretto and music. Griglio, who also co-wrote the libretto for *Camille Claudel*, has commented in more detail on this point:

> On the subject of music and text, I can say that, at least for myself, the music mostly comes out of the text: I see the Italian language as generally curving, where English for instance has more angles. Therefore, generally speaking, an Italian text demands a rounder type of music, but at the same time the music follows almost automatically by reflecting the text. Specifically, it has to do of course with the abundance of vowels present in the Italian language, where not a single word ends with a consonant (unless it was borrowed from another language) and the vast majority of words have less than three consonants in a row (but even then, like in the word "applaudire", the three consonants are followed by a diphthong, the vowels making up for the use of the consonants and softening them). I think of it as modelled on the hills of Tuscany, with a natural flow that is not interrupted by rough angles. The music follows the same pattern, so, even in situations where you'd expect it to be more angular (like in a scene of rage), it's still soft around the edges. (2013)

The anecdotal evidence for the impact of the Italian language on the spectator is substantiated by research into the relationship between language and consciousness, Travis et al. have pointed out that in human languages, the relation between sound and meaning is not inherent in the sound itself (2001: 72). Even if the listeners do not understand the words uttered, they still perceive them, and the perceived sounds are bound to have some impact on them, depending on the language. Travis et al. were able to demonstrate that reading aloud a text written in Sanskrit even without knowing the meaning of the words read produces effects otherwise associated with meditation, such as reduced skin conductance and enhanced EEG alpha power and increased EEG coherence (2001). It should, therefore, be possible to develop studies specifically to establish the extent to which the Italian language has an impact on consciousness, especially the emotions, possibly comparing opera libretti with everyday texts, such as newspaper articles, and comparing Italian with other languages.

Commedia Dell'Arte

A further influence on the Italian direction of IOT's work is Saillant's long exposure to and interest in Commedia Dell'Arte.

> Commedia characters live their lives totally in the present, not thinking about the future or living in the past. They are also aware to live their lives on the stage and this is why there is no 4th wall. For this reason, there is a constant communication between them and the audience. For this reason, they are never alone. They are not necessarily talking to the audience, but there are many forms of communication, for example emotional communication between the character and the audience. In comedy, you know that you are communicating well when you receive laughter. There is also the communication of the internal thoughts. Nothing in commedia is psychological. Everything is out, exposed. You are essential, naked in front of the audience. You allow them to see everything, even those parts that are imperfect. You use that as a way to stimulate laughter and at the same time heal the audience, letting them know that if you can expose all of your flaws (and you can laugh about them) that they can do this too and feel better about themselves. It is a spiritual and at the same time a physical exchange that exists between stage and audience. You are healing them and yourself and the same time. (2013)

Cannot a new production of an existing opera be new and separate from the interpretation of others? Only in the rarest of cases, because many directors, conductors, musicians, singers and others involved in such a "new" production will by nature of their profession have experience with that existing opera, and spectators are highly likely to be influenced in some ways, even if unconsciously, with regard to an existing opera, in the form of expectations, for example. Saillant is adamant that the opera produced by IOT should be new, in order for the properties to be original and drawn from the imagination of the individuals creating the work, rather than being culled from interpretations of others who have performed the work in the past.

The intense rehearsal process

For IOT's productions, the production team comes together for a month in the summer of each year in Città della Pieve, Italy, for rehearsals. Those rehearsals serve as the framework for the exploration of intuitive communication modalities at the centre of Saillant's work. Saillant believes that IOT's singers need to self-organise themselves with the support of the directors so that they can bring their individual histories to the realisation and elevate the spirituality of the experience. Rather than informing the singers of the blocking in advance, Saillant allows blocking to develop organically while the singers are in movement. In the example below, Saillant elaborates on the opening scene of *Camilla Claudel*:

For example, *Camille Claudel* opens with the character of Old Camille sitting on the chair and two singers are underneath her cape, so that was a direction, that is how we began the opera. Then I said you are going to open your cape first to one, then to the other. I didn't say on measure 37 you are going to open your right arm, on measure 45 you are going to open your left. I just said you are going to open your arm and discover Camille Claudel in your past which this cape is representing and then her spirit of creativity even fills you more in your imagination as you are delving into your past. Then the music is explaining it too. (2013)

The vocal work is part of this process—further analysis of Saillant's specific approaches in that respect follow in the next section. IOT seeks to create experiences that foster self-discovery and acceptance, which Saillant believes are at the heart of empathy and therefore meaning-filled intercultural communication. Opera is the complete integration of all of the arts and is therefore IOT's main medium. A main objective of IOT is to bring artists of diverse backgrounds together to create pieces that break through boundaries of communication. In working with those intercultural communities in her productions, rather than having an idea in her mind and then make it happen, Saillant would rather not have an idea in her mind and leave everything as possibilities in working with the people who come to do the project, taking what they bring and allowing it to percolate into some kind of unexpected creation.

To the production process in Città della Pieve, Saillant brings her underlying understanding of her work as a woman. In principle, Saillant identifies her work as a battle with the masculine side: the feminine side has tended to come across as overly emotional, and this has made it very difficult even for herself as a director in what she perceives as a man's world of opera directing. She argues that as a culture we are very visual, we do not know how to listen, to each other, and to hear. This phenomenon has been explored in depth by Berendt (1987). Therefore, Saillant maintains, what the singer presents visually has an impression on the brain, with different areas of the brain responsible for processing sound and sight. For Saillant, related to this is the issue of singers trying to be entertainers, because the audiences are more easily able to identify them and relate to them. In comparison, real artistry is much subtler, lighter, and more delicate and nuanced.

> Men are women and women are men, we all have both aspects within us. Thus, women are not that different from men, especially from men that have a well-developed feminine side. The feminine side is very important in terms of creativity, but you need the masculine side to make it happen. The art form of dance has been dominated by women, but in the world of opera women have not had that level of opportunity. As an older woman I have particular problems that a younger woman might not have. Younger singers project their feelings towards their mother or grandmother on to me and may have problems accepting my authority as a director, especially when I ask them to work in a way they have never worked in before. (Saillant 2013)

Saillant also brings a clear understanding to the rehearsal process of how information flows in conventional and unconventional ways between and among the members of the production team. Biophotons, Saillant feels, are the essence that is transmitted by an artist—especially when the artist has a feeling of well-being. This feeling, however, has been mostly eliminated by the way artists are "taught" in our society and the way art is made. IOT's mission is to change this. Biophotons, argues geobiologist Hans Binder, are referred to as "quanta of light" in new physics and alternative medicine, or as "ultra-weak emission of photons of biological origin" (2012). Leading researcher into the biophoton phenomenon, Fritz-Albert Popp uses biophotons in processes to establish the quality of food, or to analyse tumour tissue (2006). Binder considers the "light in our cells, people's atmosphere, the spark of light in us, the core of our life-light, divine light in the cell of life, or the spark of life once sent out as the soul" (2012) as synonymous with biophotons. Saillant comments: "There is an Italian word for this: scintilla—the meaning of this word during the Renaissance was 'the light inside an individual which can never be extinguished'" (2013).

Design

In terms of design, for the last nine productions, Saillant has worked with cloth or net on stage. It started out as an exercise in rehearsals, when Saillant covered singers with chiffon fabric while they were lying on the floor doing exercises. Then she used net fabric in her productions, very small initially, but increasing in size, up to 80 yards in 2012.

> I just kept adding. Even with a small amount it was an unwilling collaborator because you can't predict it. It was so interesting between the acts to see the singers dealing with the fabric. I had a lot of fabric on the floor which makes it dangerous and they have to pay attention to the fabric so in the intermission they would come out and make a little pathway across the stage. Everybody is barefoot, and I believe the fabric grounds everyone, it is under their feet, so they have to be aware of it. Even the way you walk is different so there is a tension in the present moment. Even when people are auditioning I ask people to take their shoes off. I think it is impossible for people to be connected to their full vulnerability or potential with their shoes on. (2013)

She used the net fabric in rehearsal to help the singers stop thinking so much and to force them to be in the moment, because the net is very unpredictable, and it also has a certain sculptural quality. In auditions it was very interesting when she put the net into somebody's hands, saying: "Oh, this will interest you". She can see immediately by the way they manipulate the net whether they understand metaphor. What happens when she gives them the fabric is usually one of two things: either the singer starts using the fabric in a literal way, such as rolling it up, or folding it into equal bits, or measuring it, straightening it, doing something with it that makes sense. Or the singer uses the fabric in a metaphorical way, using it and continuing imaginative, creative movement with the fabric throughout their audition piece. The colour is different every year, reflecting the opera's essence in a spiritual sense: in 2012, for example, it was peach. On underwater images of the Caribbean, Saillant saw a fish that was extremely beautiful, the red lionfish, which had a particular colour of peach that she selected for the production. The beauty of the colour was in contrast to the villainous nature of the fish, but in line with the colour representing the major theme of the production, oppression. Usually, Saillant arrives at the colour choices for her productions intuitively, adding rationalisations later in some cases, but not all.

Voice work

In addition to the specific nature of the music and the libretto for IOT's operas, and the dimension of the production, with its components of directorial concept and design, Saillant places considerable emphasis on working with the singers to liberate the full potential of their voices. Here, Saillant can go back to her own training and professional practice as a singer. According to Saillant, many actors and opera singers are trained in an academic environment that supports a lot of thinking. From her experience of having worked with many opera singers over the years as colleagues during her own career as a singer, and within IOT in her role as director, many singers are not able to be present while they are performing. They are thinking about the technique they have been taught to follow. For example, Saillant noticed that singers think about their uvula or their tongue, or are excessive in opening their mouths, which leads to often visible tension on the jaws, and staring of the eyes. For Saillant, singing with fixated, wide open eyes, and wide-open mouth, is therefore a mistake. It is not necessary. Many photographs suggest that this has become a false impression that people have, because they do not understand how pronunciation occurs and what consonants we use our jaws for—there are only five and otherwise the jaws should be completely free. Especially in large opera houses, many singers engage in great tensions in their bodies and their faces. Saillant explains the cause of the problem with the wide-open mouth with reference to physiology: the optic nerve is closely related to the phrenic nerve, which monitors the blood gases and controls the respiratory system, especially relating to the diaphragm. An example may help to illustrate this specific aspect further: in summer 2012 Saillant was working with a soprano who was making that mistake, and she was able to convince her that it is not necessary. The singer was shocked at the freedom she had when she was not dislocating her jaw by over-opening her mouth.

There is much harshness in the delivery of singing, singers are often forcing their sound into their environment rather than allowing it to arrive. Saillant observed that many singers do not hear the first few notes they sing and are thus worried that their voices will not come out. That is one of the reasons they force sound out and try to hold on to it. Many changes and transformations through the *Luminous Voice* workshops (in Rome, November 2012) happened without Saillant having to point explicitly to the problems. For example, one tenor hardly ever had his left heel on the ground for his first audition. Saillant did not mention this to him directly, but the topics of being grounded, of being in character, breathing exercises, and exercises locating and subsequently working on areas of the body that were tense, were part of the workshop. At the final audition his foot was firmly on the ground. This approach ensures the singer never gets obsessed with what they perceive to be their own problems, although all issues are being addressed.

Another problem Saillant has observed in working with singers has to do with tension in the shoulders, as seen in elevated shoulders. There should only be one finger space between the edge of the bottom of the ribs and the top of the pelvis. Jutting the jaw forward is also problematic. The jaw goes back into the hinge in the skull and so when it is jutted forward it is actually dislocated and creates tension. The jaw should only be used for five consonants, so it is important that the jaw is free and relaxed. Fixated eyes are problematic because they indicate some kind of tension that occurs in the optic nerve that is then experienced in the phrenic nerve which is the nerve that controls the diaphragm. So, there is a holding of the breath. Listening to a very brief excerpt of soprano Dara Hobbs as Isolde from *Liebestod* on Saillant comments that Hobbs has a lovely voice, but she is not yet at the point where she has achieved the ability to be fully in the moment in the sense that she still thinks the words as she is singing them. Saillant explains that the way the voice works is that the phrase appears in the unconscious mind and then is sung, without thinking. However, some singers are thinking, and it affects their breathing: they hold their breaths, even if only a little. The reason for this, Saillant found, is probably that most singers do not know the text on its own. They know it as related to the music, but not separate from it. In order for the respiratory system to know how much breath to take for a phrase, there is a change for every vowel pitch and intensity in terms of the minute muscular changes that occur in the system and in the larynx, in every part of the vocal mechanism. Her work with singers led Saillant to conclude that if the singer does not know without a doubt, totally unconsciously, the complete text of what it is they are saying, they will hold their breath at some point or another. Holding the breath is the number one cause of a lot of problems such as emphysema, asthma, and vocal problems. Singers' bodies thus need to know what it is they are going to sing.

When the singer makes such mistakes, Saillant argues, it prevents the audience from experiencing a transcendent presentation. In contrast, Saillant has observed that when a singer is balanced, and in harmony, especially with his/her breath, with the way that the breath is flowing over the vocal folds, and the spontaneous reflexive synergy of breath, then the sounds are very natural and beautiful.

Overcoming Shortcomings

Finally, the holistic experience of *Camille Claudel* occurred despite the perception of undeniable shortcomings. In this context, writing about Hans

Werner Henze's *We come to the River*, with a libretto by dramatist Edward Bond, Robert S. Hatten argues that a number of issues with the composition "undermine the dramatic effectiveness of the music in the opera as a whole" (1990: 297), but concedes that apart from moments when the opera "degenerates (…) into a mere echo of life's multiplicities", the opera can overcome those flaws and can "generate irony, and even sustain a dialectic among ideologies" (1990: 308).

Spirituality of Karen Saillant's life

For all humans, their individual paths in terms of spiritual development, include the necessity to make decisions, major or minor, at many junctions and crossroads. There were at least two major crossroads for Karen Saillant. She had many aspirations for her life when she left her foster family at the age of eighteen, with whom she had been living ever since shortly after her birth. The director of Children's Aid told her that because of her childhood in foster care, and despite a full scholarship to Indiana University, she would not be able to survive in this world. This was a decisive moment in her life, and against the odds of the system she decided at that point: "You have to keep going and you must not let anything stop you, and then you can succeed" (Saillant 2015a).

Her brother, also in foster care, but with many families over the years, not with one as in Karen's case, was initially considered as retarded by the authorities, who hoped he would turn out suitable for a career as a farm hand. He, too, broke through this net of expectations, and ultimately graduated with a PhD in chemistry, was vice president with Ford Motors and developed into a major player in the field of sustainability. The second crossroads came with events that began on 8 February 1999. Her husband stopped a man from attacking her in front of their house in Philadelphia. He managed to hold the man down until the police arrived but collapsed with a massive heart attack while resting on the neighbour's steps. In a Facebook status update sixteen years later, Saillant wrote:

> The rescue squad arrived & they resuscitated Bernie. It took 27 minutes. They saw that Bernie was young & they hadn't wanted to give up. Bernard came back from college & eventually left school to help Christian & me care for Bernie. One time Bernard physically carried his dad in his arms into the emergency room when Bernie spiked a high fever & had to be rushed back to the hospital. We exercised Bernie & danced with him in bed. I sang to him & bought a small piano to fit in the space next to his bed so I could play for him. We read him stories & Christian played & replayed his favorite Honeymooner episodes over & over. We did everything we could to give him a beautiful experience. My cousin Mike & his wife Barb & their children came with picnic dinners (even the

silverware & tablecloth). We spread it out across his hospital bed, always including him in conversation. Healers & acupuncturists & chiropractor friends came to try to revive him. Strangers called saying they had heard about Bernie & wanted to come by to help, so we opened our doors to them. I strapped Bernie into his wheel chair & took him all over center city. One day it was to The PA. House of Representatives home care hearing as an advocate for in home health care. We all cried. I took him in his wheelchair on walks to The Reading Terminal & even to concerts at The Academy of Music. Christian & Bernard & I took him to see Toy Story 2. Bernie loved nothing more than to laugh & we believed that if anything would wake him up, it would be laughter. We danced & loved & exercised & carried him & sang to him & shared our lives for that year & a half. But Bernie never woke up. He died on June 15, 2000, with his sons & myself by his side.

It was shortly after his death that Saillant felt the absolute need to create the work she has been involved in ever since.

Conclusion

In this article I have described an experience I had in relation to two performances of a production of *Camille Claudel* by the *International Opera Theater*. I explored that experience in a range of explanatory contexts, and discussed potential factors characteristic of IOT's work that, on their own or together, can contribute to the creation of the holistic experience. I conclude with the conviction that empirical research can establish the frequency of experiences of unity (such as mine, serving as the basis for this article, or the ones referred to by Caballé, Tomova Sintov, Milnes, and Bonney, among others) across wider cohorts of opera singers and spectators, for example by using questionnaires. Empirical research can also explore in more depth the validity and strength of the explanatory contexts I introduced in this article, with regard to peak experiences, flow, SEM, Brook's concept of total theatre and the Vedanta model of consciousness. Finally, empirical research can establish the validity and importance of each of the special features of IOT productions on their own and together, both for the past productions and for forthcoming ones: the music in a holistic Italian lyrical style, the libretto in Italian, and the approaches to production, design and singing.

Comment 2018/1 - Opera in crisis?

Every now and then, art forms are considered as undergoing a crisis. Those who make that diagnosis are usually critics for the media or from an academic background. In 2015, Detlef Brandenburg, editor of the German *Die Deutsche Bühne*, published twelves statements about the current state of affairs of the art form of opera, with focus on the German scene, with its opera houses and opera sections at multi-section theatres.

Brandenburg argues that many new operas are being composed and staged; however, hardly any are taken up again at other opera houses after their premiere production. Thus, these operas do not become known to a wider opera audience, and the composers do not get a chance to develop their work further to gain experience for future compositions. Conventional, canonical opera has attracted its audience because of very specific characteristics. These include a very emotion-laden plot, and, most importantly, beautiful music and singing. Many tunes, melodies or arias from canonical operas have become well-known because of their beauty. For some reason, contemporary composers seem to be developing a different understanding of musical beauty, which has not yet caught on widely, or they go against the canonical concept of beauty, or they are not trained or capable of creating beautiful sounds. I have not yet found a convincing argument in this context, but I find hardly any of contemporary opera music or singing beautiful. I am therefore not surprised that opera houses do not often revive new operas, and I admire the courage of artistic managers to invite new work to be created in their houses if they can predict that the result will not sound beautiful.

Brandenburg refers to potentially problematic assumptions that audiences tend to be conservative, and actually happy with an apparently never-changing status quo of conservative productions of a conservative repertoire. Artistic managers therefore hesitate to introduce too much by way innovation, both in terms of innovative productions of the core repertoire and introduction of new work. As far as innovative productions are concerned, they can be refreshing and interesting, but they are very rare. The reason that many productions of the *Regietheater*, director's theatre, however, may be problematic is that they just do not make any sense in relation to the music and the libretto. Directorial concepts then come across, at best, as inconsequential and not much in the way of the music. I remember an interview with Peter Schneider where he talked about a production of Wagner's *Götterdämmerung*. In one of the scenes in which the three Norns weave the rope of destiny, the music is fairly dramatic. However, the scene had been directed with the Norns sitting down doing some knitting. Schneider showed some despair in his comment that it is simply impossible to conduct the dramatic music of this scene as "knitting music". At worst, unfortunate directorial choices or concepts are downright annoying, constituting obstacles to the enjoyment of the performance, and to the achievements of the musicians. As with theatre, there is no objection to innovation in principle. If it works well, it can be great, as with Thomas Ostermeier's 2005 production of *Hedda Gabler*, that I still consider as the best example of a very successful contemporary approach to a canonical play text. I have not yet encountered an opera production quite reaching the consistency of narrative of that Ostermeier production. I have commented extensively on that production (2013a, 85-92).

In the same special opera issue of *Die Deutsche Bühne*, Falentin considers the problems of a repertory system, where a season might consist of a few new productions and predominantly revivals of older productions. Those revivals may be problematic because lack of time does not allow the cast (many of whom will be new to the production) to learn more than basic blocking, which can lead to such revivals lacking life, coming across as under-rehearsed and lack-lustre all the way to embarrassing. The semi-stagione system may have benefits where it is possible to implement it, with only a few operas, three to five, per month, in series of four to eight performances.

Comment 2018/2: The craft, art and magic of conducting

The activity of conducting an orchestra for a concert or in opera, and the role of the conductor, have been discussed predominantly in poetic terms. Just as in any other form of art, or probably even in any field of life, there is the average performance of the activity of conducting, in which the conductor displays a certain achievement in the techniques associated with the activity, certain acquired, learnt and practiced skills that can be taught in person or through manuals—the kinds of movements that are needed, reading the score, and transmitting the score to the orchestra. Conductors need to have musicality and need to be able to communicate mainly through gesture, without words (at least in the performance, very often also the rehearsal). Conductors need to know how to handle people (after all, their orchestra consists of up to 100 or more instrumentalists), and need authority (but, some say, without alienating the orchestra players). Eye contact is important for this, as Bernard Haitink demonstrated in a master class (Masterclass Media Foundation 2015). Extraneous movement is not needed, also demonstrated vividly by Haitink in masterclasses—

suggesting to one trainee conductor to engage less in head movements (Masterclass Media Foundation 2015), and holding the left arm of another young conductor down when she was doing too much with it, unnecessarily (Karina Canellakis, winner of the 2016 Sir Ggeorg Solti Conducting Award; nmz Media, 2015: 5:00). Conductors need to listen in the head and then compare, to check whether the sound the orchestra produces matches what they hear inwardly. Perfection that a conductor may aspire to exists only in the conductor's head: as Yakov Kreizberg put it: "You can determine what your goal is, and you can strive to achieve that goal (…) but you're not likely to completely fulfil it" (Duffie 2002: 37-38).

In addition to interviews with conductors, or articles about conducting in newspapers or magazines, there are some scientific, empirical studies of this art. Biasutti, for example, concludes on the basis of a qualitative study involving 10 conductors and 10 performers:

> The conductor needs a good memory, listening skills, clear gestures, a suitable choice of repertoire; he or she must be able to project his or her musical interpretation, respect compositional ideas and understand the musical character and style of the piece. The conductor has a holistic approach which combines technical, expressive and interpretation issues with consideration of the music as a whole. High-level instrumental technique, listening and feedback are important aspects for orchestral players, but also social skills since players have to work collaboratively, following the conductor's instructions and sharing the assignments with other members of the orchestra. (2012: 68)

Khodyakov studied the relationship between guest conductors and the orchestras they work with, in terms of the concepts of power, authority and legitimacy. He concludes that "because of the temporary nature of guest conductor–musicians relationships, the success of this negotiation depends on the extent to which guest conductors can signal their readiness to build trustworthy and respectful relationships with musicians and invest in impression management" (2014: 64).

Koivunen and Wennes explored the role of the conductor in terms of leadership qualities, such as authority, physical and mental fitness, ambitions, intelligence, communication skills, and charisma (2011: 52). They refer to Ladkin's 2008 study of beautiful leadership, a "bodily embodied practice" which consists of "mastery, congruence and purpose" (2011: 56). They further point to research suggesting that many conductors are in fact not loved but hated by the musicians in their orchestra (2011: 58). They do not suggest correlations between love or hatred and beauty of the experience of the music created by orchestras where either one or the other dominates the conductor-orchestra relationship. I would expect that hatred is not conducive to great art.

There is a marked difference between average performance and great achievement, and it is here that technique remains as the necessary basis but is being surpassed in peak performance (evoking Maslow's concept of peak experience, 1968), or the concept of flow (Csikzentmihalyi 1993). The phrases then used to describe the experience of being in the presence of a great conductor, of music conducted by a great conductor, become poetic: magical or alchemical (Burton-Hill 2014), implying a "cosmic level of music-making" (conductor Mariss Jansons quoted in Burton-Hill 2014). Charisma comes into the discussion here as well: it is the only concept in this context that has been subjected to hesitant and mainly inconclusive empirical study, where the result does not go much beyond the insight that charisma is an important part of a conductor's ability, and some conductors have more charisma and other less (see for example, Running 2011). An exception is the study of collective virtuosity, collective peak performance in an orchestra, by Marotto, Roos and Victor (2007).

Conductor Tara Simoncic explains that "there is an electricity and energy that exists between the conductor and musicians. If you bring the right energy, they will know exactly what you want from the music through your physical movement, facial expressions and energy" (2013). The great conductor passes a current from one sphere to another, and what happens then between a great conductor and her or his orchestra is possibly a form of telepathy. Antonio Pappano commented: "You can feel it, strangely enough, when people say that there's a great atmosphere in the house. That has a lot to do not only with your performance and the performances coming from the stage, but how the audience is reacting to it at the moment (...) You feel the silence (...) That's why people come to the theatre, for that (...) frisson" (Duffie 2008: 34).

Werner Thärichen, timpani in the Berlin Philharmonic, reports that, trained also as a conductor and composer, he would have the score on his instrument during rehearsals. On one occasion, he noticed a beautiful, new sound developing. It did not come from the conductor running he rehearsal, but then he noticed Furtwängler standing in the entrance. He was carrying the sound within him so strongly that his mere presence drew it from the musicians (nuevamusicologia 2012, 55:19).

In conversation with Hans Binder, whose philosophy I have explored in detail in my book *Observing Theatre: Spirituality and Subjectivity in the Performing Arts* (2013b), the following further aspects of the "mystery" of conducting emerge: when the conductor and the orchestra come together, they form, and unite within, an energy field. This energy field is composed of the energy fields of all players and the conductor, and all aspects of the conductor's profile that I discussed above come into this. The energy field of orchestra and conductor together can be characterised by less or more harmony. The extent to which the players' and the conductor's consciousness has been developed feeds in to this energy field, as does their dedication to their art, and the extent to which they have developed their heart energies and allow those to enter the energy field of the orchestra-conductor encounter in rehearsals and performances. A warm heart and a high level of sincerity are essential qualities for a conductor— Dimitrij Kitajenko recalls that one of his foremost teachers, Yevgeny Svetlanov, "told the orchestra musicians everything with his magic hands and his heart" (2015).

According to Binder, all humans are on earth for a very individually specific purpose. If that purpose is to be a conductor, then different conductors will have different tasks in relation to their art and craft, in relation to the purposes and needs of the players and the spectators / listeners. Some will be more sensitive and cater for those players and audiences who need or appreciate that aspect of music, while others may well have the task to communicate more raw aspects of the music, which will be highly appreciated by others. This explains the differences in our perception of music but does so without the need to take recourse to value judgments. We can agree to disagree when we find that someone else does not like the conductor we admire, and vice versa, without attributing weakness or other negative characteristics to either the conductor or the fellow-listener.

PART THREE:

THEATRE AND CONSCIOUSNESS

Chapter Six

Liveness:
Phelan, Auslander, and After

[First published in *Journal of Dramatic Theory and Criticism* 29:2 (2015), 69-79; reprinted here with permission from the publisher]

Contextualisation

In 2014 I wrote and submitted an ultimately unsuccessful bid to the ERC (European Research Council) on the nature of human experience in the context of theatre. Professor Brian (Les) Lancaster, formerly of Liverpool John Moores University, where he held the first chair in Transpersonal Psychology in the UK, and Dr Jesscia Bockler, worked closely with me on the grant application. They now both engage in the successful activities of the Alef Trust which they founded in 2014. In this contextualisation, I present the conceptual framework of the 2014 application, which served as the basis for my revision and reassessment of the idea of "liveness" in the article that follows.

We encounter life in the form of our experiences. We all have various experiences in life. Love, hate, being pleased/displeased, being rewarded/punished, seeing a tiger, smelling the fragrance of a perfume, touching a table, happiness, sorrow, being afraid of, or threatened by somebody, reading, writing, being a child in school, being a father or mother, trying to understand a concept, theory or problem and succeeding or not succeeding in that attempt, being in the waking state, dreaming, half asleep, soundly asleep, in agony, anxious, comfortable or in difficulty, conducting/observing religious rituals, social customs, playing different games, and so on. Each of these may have different kinds of sub-categories of experience: for example, loving my parents is different from loving my friends, both are different from loving myself. Just as experiences are innumerable, understandings of experience can be innumerable as well. To complicate matters further, we are bombarded by claims of approaches to experience that are supposed to help us live our daily lives, from the marketing associated with various lifestyle and consumer choices (exercise, dietary protocols, "mindfulness") to the poorly defined yet allegedly virtuous concepts of academic fashion.

Initially, religions and philosophy sought to develop understanding of experience, later followed by the sciences. However, history has also shown that new understanding of human experience cannot have any impact unless our individual minds are radically affected to the point where habitual responses such as anger, greed, grasping and aversion are radically transformed. Understanding is one thing, but we would need to feel so inspired by this new understanding that we are compelled to act on it. Only when this becomes internalised can people benefit. Gautama Buddha and Jesus of Nazareth both came up with radical new understandings of human experience and there are Buddhists and Christians who are of benefit to others through this and some who are not. This shows that understanding without wisdom is futile.

Experience is central to human existence in so far as we all engage with experience at every moment of our lives. Experience is related to and influenced, shaped and determined by a vast range of factors within and beyond our control. This considerable complexity of experience would suggest that every effort should be made by representatives of academic disciplines to work together so as to establish holistic approaches and yield holistic insights, rather than exclusively delving even deeper into the increasingly isolated areas of interest characteristic of those disciplines. Strategic efforts by some funding bodies have realised this need by actively supporting such collaboration.

The quest to explore human experience lies at the core of all theatre, most other artistic endeavours, and all study of the mind. For most of the 20th century, conventional methods of enquiry across the natural and social sciences focused on the objective and uninvolved description, definition and prediction of the objects of their research. Quantitative methods were favoured over qualitative approaches which were "recommended only as interim strategies that might provide suggestions or hints for later quantitative and/or experimental determinations" (Braud and Anderson, 1998: 5). It was the general assumption that valid knowledge of the world could be obtained only through neutral observation of external phenomena. In this drive for objectivity humanity's unique capacity for inner experience, for self-awareness, introspection and intuition was almost entirely ignored. The fundamental binary opposite between the outer objective and the inner subjective led to the assumption that the domains of objective science and of subjective arts and humanities are mutually exclusive.

There have been recent attempts to achieve multi-disciplinarity and integration of disciplines. Such attempts tend to emphasise process over state and performance over text, participation, interconnection, appreciation and transformation over detached description, prediction and control (Braud and Anderson, 1998). These recent attempts do not exist in isolation, nor are they new. In fact, the results of such attempts approach long-held ideals such as direct experience of Plato's *idea*, and Schiller's principle of *universality* (1789). Those ideals are eclectic, interweaving, interactive, transcultural, transpersonal, and holistic, and the approaches seek to be rigorous, as well as respectful, in a methodological sense. The changing view of experience opened up by these recent developments places emphasis on the subjective, *first person* dimension (Varela and Shear 1999) in areas including the perception of time, the nature of emotions, embodied cognition, and access to tacit and intuitive means of gaining knowledge.

Over the past three decades, researchers in the human sciences have become increasingly aware of the limitations of so-called objective research practices and have begun to develop approaches which acknowledge subjective experience as a valid source of knowledge (Polkinghorne 1983). Braud and Anderson assert that a complementary, transpersonal research paradigm has begun to emerge which "can more adequately apprehend the complexity, breadth, and depth of our world and of humanity" (1998: 6) by offering a less constrained, less fragmented and more meaningful picture of human nature and potential. The new paradigm repositions human experience, allowing for a multiplicity of voices and relating the individual to the larger whole within which all experience is co-created. It moves away from purely instrumental and utilitarian values that emphasise the need to manipulate and control, and it champions participation and appreciation, placing greater value on complexity, ambiguity and complementarity. The benefits that this new paradigm generates can affect all domains of human society, reshaping social, cultural and economic norms and perspectives. In the field of health, for example, we are witnessing the emergence of a new, participatory recovery model which expands medical treatment options by enhancing partnership work and self-directed care, leading to greater choice, control and empowerment for people experiencing illness (McNiff 1998; Care Services Improvement Partnership 2007; Mental Health Foundation 2014).

A number of new research methods have evolved which emphasise the value of alternative, participatory modes of knowing, e.g., Intuitive Inquiry (Anderson 1998), Organic Research (Clements 2004) and Heuristic Inquiry (Moustakas 1990). Within these approaches "[R]eality is contacted through physical sense data, but also [...] through a deep intuitive inner knowing. Awareness includes (objective) sensation as well as (subjective) intuitive, aesthetic, spiritual, [and] noetic [...] aspects. Understanding comes [...] from identifying with the observed, becoming one with it" and the "entire spectra of states of consciousness are of interest [...]" (Moustakas 1990: 10-11)—a notion echoed by Tart (1972)—who advocated the development of *state-specific* sciences, suggesting that non-ordinary states of consciousness are likely to yield new insights which are not accessible by conventional methods.

Alongside alternative modes of knowing these new research methods embrace an extended range of tools for data collection and analysis, allowing the researcher to engage with the topic in a holistic, deeply embodied and immersive way. The researcher's immersion in the research topic may include active engagement with the practices of research participants (e.g., through workshops and seminars), contemplative and meditative practice, body work, dream analysis, and work with symbols and metaphors, highlighting the creative dimensions of the complementary research approaches.

The trend just discussed is growing, but as it grows it also meets with increased objection, which developed from ridicule of not taking the trend seriously to harsher criticism as it is being perceived as a threat to the status quo. It would be well worth exploring the extent to which the UK's Research Excellence Framework is in fact a suitable tool for bricking in the status quo. Many disciplines still do not "talk to each other", or at least not fully, openly, directly, intentionally, freely and effectively. The same applies to sub-areas within disciplines, old and new, because each area considers its position and other positions in the discipline as mutually exclusive rather than as positions that, while different, add to the overall understanding because they are approaching the same phenomenon from different angles.

Despite these efforts, therefore, we are still stuck, to a large extent, with a world view that is based on binary opposites. There is, in particular, still the gap between the sciences and the humanities identified by C.P.Snow (1905-1980) in his Rede lecture of 1959. I already pointed to neuroscientist Vilayanur S. Ramachandran's position that as a scientist he can "talk only in terms of what science can achieve at any point in time, but I am also trying to push the boundaries of science for science to be able to grasp a little bit more of what is still out there, and which I am aware of".

What we need is, to invoke Schiller, "philosophical minds" to identify synergies and links between areas that may come across as not related, rather than sticking to the status quo of fragments that provide a safe haven to "bread scholars" who have learnt a whole lot about the fragments, but who see any development that might challenge their knowledge about fragments as a threat to their own very essence, and who will thus fight genuine progress with all possible means. In this article I reassess liveness from a range of consciousness-studies-related angles.

Introduction

Live-cast and recorded theatre (LCRT) such as National Theatre Live has expanded rapidly into a major industry since its launch in 2009. In academic terms, this development has been discussed predominantly in the context of audience demographics. The development merits, however, a reassessment of the liveness debate launched with the seminal contributions by Peggy Phelan's 1993 book *Unmarked: The Politics of Performance,* and Philip Auslander's 1999 study *Liveness: Performance in a Mediatized Culture.* Auslander argues that before mediatisation in the forms of sound recording and film, all audiences encountered performance in a mode that we now call "live." However, that term was not yet relevant then, because it makes sense only in relation to an opposite, such as the "mediatized" (Auslander 2008, 56). In this sense, the live does not precede the mediatized and cannot claim superiority because it came first (Auslander 2008: 11). Once the live emerges as a category of experience, in opposition to the mediatized, those people who are representatives of the live in production or reception contexts develop an anxiety about the perceived threat that the live is allegedly exposed to from the mediatized (Auslander 2008: 7). They address that anxiety by attributing higher value to the live by arguing that it is real, whereas the mediatized is not real (Auslander 2008: 3). An alternative is the attempt to make the live as alike to the mediatized as possible (Auslander 2008: 6). In that case, those who favour the live over the mediatized seek to recreate a mediatized image in a live setting, thus invoking our nostalgia for "what we assumed was the immediate" (Auslander 2008: 43). For this response to anxiety, Auslander refers to the helicopter in *Miss Saigon* as a prominent example (Auslander 2008: 26). Another is the suggestion that a live recording is somehow better than a studio recording (Auslander 2008: 60).

Auslander rejects the arguments developed by those in favour of the live when they feel threatened by mediatisation. The live, he argues, is not first and therefore stronger. The claim that the live is real and that the mediatized is unreal, Auslander argues, does not work because the mediatized is just as much a human experience as the live. Auslander also rejects the implication of the higher value of the live recording over the studio recording in terms of the problematic semantics: "This expression is an oxymoron (how can something be both recorded and live?) but is another concept we now accept without question" (Auslander 2008: 60). In an article reflecting on the first edition of Auslander's book, Martin Barker had argued that audiences experience live performance "as if it had elements of uniqueness" (Barker 2003: 28). This argument was strongly developed by Phelan (1993). In the second edition of his book, Auslander responds to Barker, suggesting that the audience's hope that a live performance is unique is an illusion. Auslander refers to Barker's qualification that for a live performance of a theatre production to be successful, a performance needs to be such that the "actual variations are probably minimal and insignificant" (Auslander 2008: 64). In the same vein, Auslander denies that live performance functions to bring performers and spectators into an experience of community. Instead, he suggests that the nature of performance is founded on difference, separation, and fragmentation that exclude unity. Auslander refers to the failed attempts by Grotowski and Boal to achieve such desired unity (Auslander 2008: 65). He questions the need for a spectator to be present in the same space as the performance to enjoy the experience of watching a performance (Auslander 2008: 69), and ultimately concedes only that live performance may afford social prestige to the spectator who can boast to have been present at a live event which carries the value of being memorable by peers (Auslander 2008: 66). Live and mediatized, Auslander concludes, are not ontological opposites, but rather cultural and historical contingencies define their opposition (Auslander 2008: 11).

Despite the fact that Auslander, in his writing about liveness, brought what Barker called a "deep pessimism" to the debate about liveness (Barker 2013: 43), many critics continue the discussion of the nature of liveness. For example, Reason has addressed the concerns about documentation in relation to live performance (Reason 2006). In the context of her argument relating to utopian performatives, Jill Dolan writes that "live performance provides a place for people to come together, embodied and passionate, to share experiences of meaning making and imagination that can describe or capture fleeting intimations of a better world" (Dolan 2005: 2). Bundy et al., and Reason have considered liveness in the context of audience research with younger audiences. Bundy et al. have identified the following:

> Characteristics that young people identified as key components of their experience of liveness . . . : audience; the comfort and discomfort of presentness; performer vulnerability, risk and uncertainty; proximity to the

> live action; perceptions of realness; a sense of relationship with the actors; and the intensity of engagement. (Bundy et al. 2012: 18)

Writing about secondary school pupils in the United Kingdom attending a performance of *Othello*, Reason observed that these spectators experienced the cinema audience as an audience of peers, while they constructed the theatre audience as *other* people (Reason 2006: 223). With regard to the young spectators' responses to the liveness of the *Othello* performance, which includes their references to "directness, immediacy, responsibility, realness," Reason argues that it is necessary to include in the discussion "the wider social phenomenon and experience . . . , the public experience of the event" (Reason 2006: 239). He concludes:

> the experience of being in a theatre audience is always going to be largely about something very different from simply sitting down and watching a play ... the acuteness of this social experience was heightened by the live nature of the theatre performance – the real presence of the actors, the danger of something going wrong, the risk of missing something all provide an urgency to the situation, increasing levels of tension and potential discord within the audience. Like the complex realness of the live actors, so is the theatre audience a heightened, intense and peculiarly real environment. (Reason 2006: 240)

Paterson and Stevens discuss liveness in the simulcast phenomenon on the basis of *NT Live,* and propose a "new conceptual framework that can be termed 'Super Bowl Dramaturgy,' whereby the qualities of the 'live' performance are subsumed within a dramaturgical logic that parallels the branding, staging, and viewing experiences of a major mediatized sporting event like the American Super Bowl" (Paterson and Stevens 2013: 147). As part of that discussion, they argue that the advent of the simulcast implies that "live" is being redefined to include reference to "a live screening where the spectator can view the performance in the same temporal moment that it occurs, though they may be separated by vast spatial distances" (Paterson and Stevens 2013: 155). Under the influence of new technologies, the concept of liveness has developed to only refer to temporality (if the event in the theatre and in the cinema happen at the same time, the event in the cinema is also live), at the expense of the once indispensable feature of corporeality (Paterson and Stevens 2013: 155, referring to Dixon 2007: 127). That redefinition is characteristic of the marketing for the simulcast events—whether the audience really experience those events as live in the same sense as live theatre is a different matter altogether. Conventionally, Paterson and Stevens argue, liveness has been associated with "presence, immediacy, authenticity, community, ephemerality and unpredictability," and the marketing for *NT Live*, for example, exploits these in the "nostalgic and affective resonances" of its branding (Paterson and Stevens 2013: 156).

Paterson and Stevens point out that the live performance in the theatre that serves as the origin of the simulcast has been created for the purposes of that media transfer and is not the same performance as other live performances of the same production. Given that the filming on simulcast nights prioritizes the simulcast performances over the live experience of the audience, with cameras obstructing the live spectators' views and actors performing as much to camera as to the live spectators, the experience of the live audience is also different from a conventional experience in the theatre.

Auslander further developed his positions in the 1999 and 2008 editions, and in 2012, wrote: "[I]t may be that we are now at a point in history at which liveness can no longer be defined in terms of either the presence of living human beings before each other or physical and temporal relationships" (Auslander 2012: 6).

Reassessment 1:
Liveness as Physical and Temporal Copresence

Auslander's position and its later modifications are in need of reassessment given the developments that occurred across a range of relevant fields since they were published. The history of theatre should have demonstrated by now that no matter what the perceived threat to theatre may be in any one era, the oft-evoked crisis so far has not led to its ruin, demise, or disappearance. Throughout history, theatre has faced challenges in terms of its institutional contexts and artistic forms. There has always been an attempt to attract new audiences, and research suggests that through the recent development of live simulcasts of theatre performances into cinemas, new—or at least more—spectators have been attracted to local theatres (Bakhshi and Throsby 2014: 1-8). While the existence of media in relation to theatre does not threaten the very existence of theatre, it does mean that theatre makers must be aware of these developments and respond to them while maintaining the integrity of their art form. That might mean integrating aspects of the media into theatre productions and performances. These integrative approaches are taught at the university level in academic and vocational programs and discussed in a variety of academic contexts.

The integration of media into live performance, however, does not make such a performance less live. It is still the case that in such performances the spectator and the performers are in the same space at the same time—they are "co-present in space," to invoke a concept frequently mentioned in liveness debates (Barker 2013: 43). In the cases of cinema and television, the spectator is not in the same space and time as the performance, and in the case of the simulcast the spectator is not in the same space, but at least almost at the same time—any transmission over distance, analogue or digital, comes with a time delay, even if imperceptibly small. It would be futile to try to deny those differences; and moreover, it is unnecessary to remove the unhelpful dimensions of implicit or explicit threats of one medium or art form over another, and the correspondingly implied value judgments. There is sufficient space and a sufficiently large number of potential recipients to render hostile competition obsolete.

Reassessment 2: Subjectivity

Of particular importance here is the nature of the experience of liveness and how that experience has been expressed. Auslander refers to "the magic of live theatre," the "energy" that supposedly exists between performers and spectators in a live event, and the "community" that live performance is often said to create among performers and spectators (Auslander 2008: 2). Live experience in theatre tends to be expressed in terms that make intuitive sense: in addition and close relation to the ones mentioned by Auslander, Dolan, and Bundy, Reason and Barker, for example, identify "immediacy, intimacy, buzz, learning, and being (in) the audience" (Barker 2013: 65). These are very subjective experiences, and the concepts employed to capture them have been intuitive, metaphorical, and subjective. Watson's description of theatre artist Eugenio Barba's writings applies here as well:

Barba is essentially a creative artist, a poet both in the theatre and in his writings about it. This poetic quality calls for a careful reading of his ideas since he favours poetic metaphors over the more traditional intellectual approach of deductive logic to sustain his arguments (Watson 1993: 18).

Auslander is explicitly sceptical about such experiences, which he considers to be "traditional, unreflective assumptions" that invoke "clichés and mystifications" (Auslander 2008: 2).

The subjective nature of the experience of liveness in the theatre, and consequently, the way such experiences are reported, has led to concerns about that subjectivity. That concern is closely related to a predominantly positivist, materialistic, and scientific worldview, for which the subjective is suspicious by definition. The methods and concepts of science have been unable to capture the subjective and have therefore ruled it out in favour of objectivity. Nonetheless, in recent years science has begun to incorporate subjectivity in the form of first person approaches to consciousness, especially in the context of consciousness studies (Varela and Shear 1999). A number of new research methods have evolved to emphasize the value of alternative, participatory modes of knowing, e.g., Intuitive Inquiry, Organic Research, and Heuristic Inquiry (Anderson 1998, Clements 2004, Moustakas 2004). Within these approaches, "[R]eality is contacted through physical sense data, but also ... through a deep intuitive inner knowing. Awareness includes (objective) sensation as well as (subjective) intuitive, aesthetic, spiritual, [and] noetic ... aspects. Understanding comes . . . from identifying with the observed, becoming one with it," and the "entire spectra of states of consciousness are of interest ..." (Moustakas 2004: 10-11). This is a notion echoed by Tart, who advocated the development of *state-specific* sciences, suggesting that nonordinary states of consciousness are likely to yield new insights not accessible by conventional methods (Tart 1972).

Part of this turn toward first person approaches in consciousness studies, probably very closely related to the performative turn in the arts, as well as in the humanities and social sciences, is the consideration of traditional wisdom forming the heritage of different cultures as potentially fruitful in innovatively and rigorously addressing pressing issues. The model of consciousness proposed by Indian Vedanta philosophy is one such example. It has been used in different contexts to help explain phenomena of literature and theatre in more consistent ways than other models (Malekin and Yarrow 1997; Meyer-Dinkgräfe 2013). This model is applicable to the liveness debate, and it can therein develop a better understanding of the subjective experiences reported in relation to it. It does so without becoming redundant and without destroying any poetic aspect of current reports of that experience.

According to the model proposed by Vedanta philosophy, consciousness comprises three conventionally experienced states: waking, dreaming, and sleeping. At their basis is pure consciousness or *turiya*. Malekin and Yarrow describe it as follows:

> *Turiya* is an underlying unconditioned consciousness, which appears limited when reflected through the three contingent states of the individual mind. In itself it is a self-effulgent radiance akin to the intelligible sun of St Simeon and the irradiation from the One of Plotinus. It is, in the deepest sense, the reality of the mind and, according to Gaudapada and Shankara, Reality itself. (Malekin and Yarrow 1997: 38)

When waking, dreaming, or sleep coexist with pure consciousness, thus defined, a "higher" state of consciousness has been achieved—the ultimate aim of human spiritual development. "Higher" means "more comprehensive and more integrated." (Malekin and Yarrow 1997: 39)

In terms of the consciousness studies debate, the Vedanta model offers a solution to the *hard problem* invoked by Tom Stoppard's new play with the same title (Stoppard 2015). David Chalmers argued that the hard problem of consciousness is how to explain why and how certain physical processes give rise to a rich inner life (Chalmers 1996). If adopting the Vedanta model of consciousness, the causal relationship in need of explanation is the reverse. The Vedanta approach argues that physical processes are a concretization—or manifestation—of consciousness and provides information as to why and how consciousness proceeds to manifestation (Meyer-Dinkgräfe 2005). The hard problem is thus solved, first and foremost, on the level its formulation set out to discover in the first place: experience. The Vedanta model fulfils Chalmers' demands to take consciousness as a fundamental entity in nature; it even goes beyond Chalmers in proposing consciousness as the ultimate fundamental entity, the very basis of fundamental entities in physics, like space and time, for example. The latter are set as fundamentals because physicists cannot, at present, explain their existence any further. Such relative fundamentals are thus an intellectual construct. Consciousness as the basis of all creation as proposed by Vedanta is no such intellectual construct: instead, it is the linguistic/verbal rendering of the deepest experience possible to the human mind. Why was the hard problem taken to be so hard that some authors, such as McGinn, claim it can never be solved? McGinn is perfectly right to state: "it is quite predictable that our *intellects* should falter when trying to make sense of the place of consciousness in the natural order" (McGinn 1999: 105). The intellect on its own, isolated from the basis in pure consciousness, by definition, cannot grasp levels of reality that are originating from a subtler level. Intellect informed by pure consciousness, however, is able to fathom the very depths of consciousness, thereby enabling intellectual understanding of experiences encountered at subtle levels.

In the context of the liveness debate, the Vedanta model provides an enhanced understanding of the concepts that Auslander and others have considered with scepticism, the aspects that make liveness so attractive to audiences. Pure consciousness, (according to the Vedanta model), is omnipresent: it is the basis of everything in the universe, and humans can directly experience it in or through their own minds. The physiology of the brain is the complex tool that permits that experience. Through their creations at all levels, humans can also directly give expression to pure consciousness if a dramatist creates a play or an actor creates a character. This act of creation implies imbuing the created work with pure consciousness. That human creation, the play or the performance of the character, will partake in, consist of, or reflect pure consciousness to the extent that it has been put in by the dramatist or the actor, depends on the level of consciousness they have been able to achieve in their respective lives. The recipient, reader, and spectator can, in turn, experience pure consciousness to the extent that they have developed their own consciousness relative to viewing a performance. Development of consciousness is here to be understood as the extent to which those individuals have integrated pure consciousness with waking, or dreaming, or sleeping. The higher the level of consciousness, the more of pure consciousness people can bring to that which they experience, and consequently, the more they can perceive and access pure consciousness in the world around them. They will then refer to experiences of pure consciousness, which are within the range of every human being, culturally different in terms of the language and concepts at their disposal. In the Chinese context, those experiencing pure consciousness might refer to it in terms of the subtle energy form of *chi*, in contexts of Vedanta, *prana*. In Western cultural history, Paracelsus wrote about "archaeus," Newton about "cosmic aether," Mesmer about "universal fluid," and Sheldrake about "morphogenetic fields"—this list is by no means complete (Rosch 2009: 297. I propose that these phenomena are exchanged between performers and spectators during a performance: in Vedanta terms, pure consciousness. When we are in the waking state, we experience consciousness in terms of contents: we perceive through the senses, and we think, for example. Pure consciousness on its own is experienced as devoid of such contents. All that exists in that state of consciousness is pure bliss. When pure consciousness coexists with other states of consciousness, the experience of bliss remains. Consequently, the more of pure consciousness the actors are able to integrate into their acting, and the more the spectators can experience it, the more enjoyable the experience will be for both. The art form of theatre has particular potential for allowing those involved in it—actors and spectators—to reach intensive experiences of pure consciousness, more intensive than in other areas of life. What is in fact an experience of pure consciousness is conceptualized in lay terms as "energy" that spectators can "feel" to exist in the theatre.

If we thus understand better what happens in terms of energy in the theatre, such better understanding cannot diminish our experience of it. On this basis we can go even further in our attempt of understanding. In the context of meditation practices, empirical science has researched psychophysiological correlates of pure consciousness (Travis and Pearson 2000). It should therefore be possible to design further empirical research to explore the hypothesis that actors and audiences will express a stronger experience of energy, or the "magic of theatre," in direct correlation to the extent to which actors and audiences experience pure consciousness. These studies would likewise include refined breathing (suspension of breathing between 10-40 seconds during the experience of pure consciousness), related skin conductance responses at the onset of changes of the breathing pattern, and measurements of the brain activity through EEG readings. I have offered suggestions for an enhanced understanding of the reasons why live performance may be perceived as different from a performance that is not live, and why the experience of liveness is often associated in audience reports with references to intangible aspects such as energy. These suggestions offer opportunities for readers to bring their wide spectrum of interests and areas of expertise to the debate (all the contexts for subtle energy, consciousness studies, and qualitative and quantitative empirical approaches). These suggestions also open up opportunities for cross-disciplinary communication: the findings in different areas about the same phenomenon need not be (considered as) mutually exclusive! In the same vein, with repeated emphasis that the nature of the live experience of performance does not imply a value judgment, further research can investigate the specific characteristics of the experience of film and television that make it different from (not inferior than) live performance. If the physical presence of the performer allows the direct exchange of energy between performers and spectators, different mechanisms must be at work in creating the impact of film and television on the spectator. The impact of the creative process on film and TV actors is also likely to be different as they are not in the presence of their spectators. In physiological terms, for example, it should be possible to hypothesize, and subsequently put to the test, that live actors will provide the brain with 3D stereo cues that are not present in conventional 2D screen viewing. Further thought and subsequent empirical research could address the question of whether the same or different brain areas are active in response to true 3D, and screen 3D (given that the projection of 3D is onto a flat screen), or whether the same brain areas respond to these different cues in subtly different ways (Banks et al. 2012). Or are the differences between true 3D, screen 3D, and 2D more to do with subtle "liveness" perception or immersion than with the visual cues themselves? (Apostolopoulos et al. 2012).

Reassessment 3:
Simulcasts

Thus far I have established the difference between live and non-live and have suggested ways for explaining the attraction of the live in relation to experiences exclusive to it in terms of the direct exchange of pure consciousness between actors and spectators. The simulcast happens almost at the same time, but spectators and actors are not in the same physical space. There is anecdotal evidence, supported by a number of empirical studies, that people can influence other people independent of physical copresence. Here is an example in the context of theatre:

American director Peter Sellars made an experiment: actors in one of his productions were on stage and played a scene, as rehearsed, which contained by nature a number of specific emotions. Neither those on-stage actors, nor the audience knew that backstage, a further group of actors were doing a range of exercises intended to allow them to engage deeply with specific emotions. Sellars's idea was that these backstage actors would be radiating emotions. The emotions he instructed them to engage in were either exactly the same emotions portrayed by the actors onstage, or exactly the opposite ones. Both onstage actors and spectators noticed a difference in atmosphere. Actors commented on most successful performances with a special ease of portraying emotions when the backstage group had enforced their emotions, and of a tough and frustrating performance with difficulties of getting into their emotions when the backstage actors had engaged in emotions opposed to theirs (Meyer-Dinkgräfe 2006).

The findings of this experiment make sense when considered in relationship to the Vedanta model: consciousness is a field that is omnipresent. This position may well have unexpected impact on the liveness debate. If consciousness is indeed omnipresent, spectators in the cinema watching a live-cast should, through the very nature of the event, become part of the field of consciousness created in the theatre; the reverse functions similarly, given that experiencing the performance in the theatre and in the cinema for the duration of the performance and its simulcast is one subfield of consciousness in the overall field of consciousness. This does not apply to the reception process for film and television, because there is no live event—past or present—that could constitute a subfield of consciousness outside the cinema or the viewing experience of TV typically in the living room. The film or TV broadcast will have its subfield of consciousness specific to its history and processes of creation. Thus, the viewer's consciousness will be influenced by both the contents of what they watch on the screen, and by the subfield of consciousness that emerges from the history and processes of creation. The liveness of the actors and production team that created the subfield of consciousness is a minor part of the components that make up the subfield. The liveness of the actors on the stage from which the production is simulcast into the cinema is comparatively a much stronger contributor to the subfield of consciousness, and therefore, its impact on the viewer's experience must be assumed to be stronger.

Conclusion

There are clear and undeniable differences between live performance, simulcast, cinema screening, and TV broadcast in terms of creation and reception. These differences do not imply value judgments, and the different art forms or media do not represent threats to each other. Consciousness studies, especially the Vedanta model of consciousness, facilitates an enhanced understanding of experiences reported by spectators in relation to liveness, thereby enabling an appropriately refreshing context for understanding the new phenomenon of simulcast. This understanding of liveness for the theatre and simulcast opens up many opportunities for further cross-disciplinary dialogue and research.

Comment 2018 - Live-casting

Live broadcasts of opera, dance and theatre performances from leading arts venues such as the Metropolitan Opera House, New York, Royal Opera House Covent Garden, National Theatre, and Royal Shakespeare Company, to numerous cinemas world-wide, have become part of the arts scene since their launch by the MET opera in 2006. At the same time, live streaming to the internet has been developed (for example by the Vienna State Opera), and live broadcasts on television continue, predominantly for sports events. Initially, live casts to cinemas were advertised as the opportunity of seeing live theatre, only not in the theatre, but in the cinema. Over the years, producers and audiences have realised that the experience of a theatre or dance or opera production live-cast into a cinema is not the same as seeing the production in the theatre or opera house. Nor is it the same as watching a recording of such a live-cast, or the film of a stage production. Live theatre, opera or dance, live-casts to the cinema, screenings of recorded live-casts, filmed stage productions, live-streaming to the internet, and live broadcasts on TV are different from each other. Each form has its own technology, its own contexts of production, and its own aesthetics of reception. The cinema live-cast emphasises the communal aspect—hence the RSC's explicit decision, for example, to rely on the local cinemas' public sound systems rather than issuing headsets to each live-cast spectator in the cinemas.

In the theatre, the spectator can decide what to look at, the stage or other spectators, and what on stage to focus on, or not. In film and the in a live-cast or live streaming, the decision of focus is made for the spectator by the director. In live-casts you do get close-ups that are not available in the theatre. I saw the recent National Theatre production of *Hedda Gabler* both in the theatre (first) and as a live-cast (later). In the theatre, I was impressed by the dynamics of the vast space. That dynamics was nearly completely lost for me in the live-cast, but I was able to combine my memory of that dynamics with the interesting close-ups of the actor's faces that I had not had in the live performance. Thus, the impressions of live performance and live-cast combined into a new, richer experience that neither the live performance nor the live-cast would have been able to achieve. Research into this might consider the extent to which that combination of experiences is due to my extensive experience in the context of theatre.

A distinct disadvantage of the live-cast format can be for comedy when the live audience is heard laughing about something that is not in view at that moment. Technology itself, or the venue's equipment, or the venue staff's ability to use the available equipment appropriately, are still problematic for live-casts as well. I have attended a sizeable number of them, but there has not been one without a temporarily frozen screen. The actor's words tend echo around the cinema—they do not do that in the theatre—sometimes so much so that the cinema technicians decide to turn off all but the speakers at the front of the cinema. Where live-cast directors choose not to select specific aspects of the stage but show the entire stage from a certain distance necessary to capture the stage's width and depth, they sometimes still shift camera focus or angle slightly, very slowly, almost unnoticeably, and for me and several others I talked to, this kind of camera movement caused dizziness, headache and nausea. This medium has potential but needs to address current shortcomings.

CHAPTER SEVEN

PERFORMANCE AS PHILOSOPHY: THE UNIVERSAL LANGUAGE OF THE THEATRE REVISITED

DANIEL MEYER-DINKGRÄFE AND ANITA S. HAMMER

[First published in *Nordic Theatre Studies* 28:2 (2017), 97-118; reprinted here with permission from the publisher]

Contextualisation

I first met Anita S. Hammer at the 2006 world congress of the International Federation for Theatre Research in Helsinki, Finland, where Jade Rosina McCutcheon and I launched the IFTR working group on *Performance and Consciousness*. Hammer attended the 2007 and 2011 conferences on *Consciousness, Theatre, Literature and the Arts* which I organised in Aberystwyth and Lincoln, respectively. Her book on *Between Play and Prayer: The Variety of Theatricals in Spiritual Performance*, came out in the Rodopi series on *Consciousness, Literature and the Arts* as volume 27 (of currently 53 published titles) in 2010. 2008, 2011 and 2014 she contributed articles to the *Consciousness, Literature and the Arts* journal. In 2015 I had started thinking about revisiting the issue of universality in the context of theatre, as I had written about it some ten years ago, and those ten years had seen seminal work on "literary universals" by Patrick Colm Hogan. I then came across the call for papers for a special issue of *Nordic Theatre Studies* on "Theatre and Language". I submitted an abstract and received positive response from the then journal editor, Laura Gröndahl, who alerted me to the need to have a Nordic/Baltic focus that could be provided by the topic or by a Nordic/Baltic co-author. Hammer was interested in collaborating with me on this, I sent her a first draft of my own thoughts in February 2016, a few intensive weeks of writing and revising followed, we submitted at the end of February 2016. In June 2016 we received two positive and one negative peer reviews, revised in line with comments received, made further revisions in the journal's internal editing process, and submitted the final version, which appears below, on 23 September 2016.

Introduction: Dialogue

We have known each other as academic colleagues interested in similar aspects of our experiences in the theatre for a number of years, and over those years we have regularly shared the development of our thinking. When Nordic Theatre Studies published its call for submissions for its special issue on Theatre and Language, the time had come to take our ongoing dialogue a step further and seek to share our thoughts as dialogue with the readers of NTS. In all modesty, we are exploring for the 21st century the ancient Greek model of Plato's dialogues, adding the dimension that while, for Plato, the dialogue mode was the product of one author's (Plato's) thinking, who gave his words to both dialogue partners, in our case, there are two genuine partners and voices involved. In our dialogue, we also add the format of genuine exchange to the established convention of co-authored articles in the sciences where no individual section of the article is attributed explicitly to one of the co-authors. The experience of theatre comes into being through, and exists in, the dialogue of stage and spectators. Our dialogic performance on the page brings out insights that we would not have been able to create on our own. Perhaps our readers (as spectators) can share both the insights and the ways in which they came about and enter their own dialogue with ours.

Context: concrete experience versus abstract speculation

Meyer-Dinkgräfe
At its beginnings, across cultures, philosophy was a practical tool to enhance knowledge and, through that enhancement, increase well-being profoundly. Over time, philosophy has become restricted to the context of intellectual reasoning, analysis and argument, devoid of the experiential component that was originally considered as an integral part of its nature. Philosophy is no longer based on practice, but theory alone, speculation. This shift of emphasis has led to philosophy losing its essential role in life, on the levels of both the individual and of society. I view the history of Western philosophy as a series of attempts by philosophers not at reasoned speculations, but at sharing with their readers, in the form of reasoned

argument, the essence of their own experiences (Meyer-Dinkgräfe 2013b: 125-130), for example:

> "Husserl (1859-1938) wrote that I, the meditating I, reduce myself to my absolute transcendental ego through the phenomenological epoché (Cartesian Meditations). Phenomenology was to be the discipline to study this new domain of the experience of pure transcendental consciousness. Epoché was a method of suspension of judgment in the mode of the natural standpoint, such that everything came to be understood as a phenomenon within consciousness, accessible by going within to analyse consciousness. 'I experience my own conscious existence directly and truly as it itself' (Paris Lectures). We direct the glance of [--] theoretical enquiry to pure consciousness in its own absolute being" (Ideas). (Meyer-Dinkgräfe 2013b: 129)

Hammer
This may be a very generalised position, but let's start with it. It would perhaps be true to state that there has been a tendency in writings in the field of theatre studies, as well as generally in the fields of philosophy and the humanities, that the more abstracted from the experience itself, from its materiality and from its specifics, the higher the status and the publishing points of the writings.

Meyer-Dinkgräfe
But such abstractions can be a trap. The practice of writing itself may be a trap of language and a barrier of semantics rather than opening to a philosophy of performance that cannot grow through anything other than concrete, specific experience attained through the human senses. The recent revival of debate about the relationship between philosophy and performance was spearheaded initially within PSi, TaPRA, and IFTR and, while continuing in those umbrella organisations, is now located within its own dedicated organisation, Performance Philosophy. That debate has, at its core, the restoration of experience to philosophy by means of the practice of performance. This acknowledgement can take the shape of employing performance to express philosophy — in more immediately experienced ways than verbal language is ever able to convey.

Hammer
It is this focus on the function of performance as philosophy — central, as you said, to Performance Philosophy — that is also central to our discussion. We want to tease out some further aspects of how performance can be more than "mere performance" and how performance can be philosophy. We should give some indication where we come from?

Meyer-Dinkgräfe

My research is anchored in consciousness studies, defined as the "the study of how we think, feel and act, why we think, feel and act as we do, and what it feels like to think, feel and act as we do" (Meyer-Dinkgräfe 2013a: 11). From within consciousness studies, I focus further on positions of spirituality to provide explanatory contexts for phenomena of theatre and performance. I understand spirituality in a non-religious way, with the implication that "spirituality culminates in the full development of mind," and "any move in the direction of this fullness can be called spirituality" (Malekin and Yarrow 1997).

Hammer

I find it interesting that you approach spirituality in an explanatory way. For myself, I am aware that my use of the concept of spirituality has been more of an approach in searching to find a way of describing aspects of experience of great importance that would otherwise have been left out. Now, you are also raising the question if spirituality may have something to do with religion? Yes, there may be spirituality in religious worship, but often that is spirituality gone wrong. Spirituality is about empowering the self, on the deepest levels. Religion is, so often, about structure and power. This is another big discussion, of course, and too far-reaching and important to be explored in the present context. But let me just say that I believe there is an urgent need for humans to take back their own spiritual individual power, as from their own experience, not letting themselves be reduced to non-spiritual beings, neither to let religious creeds steal their spirituality by imposing explanatory concepts that may in fact be distorting. Deploying spirituality itself as an explanatory context, as you suggest above, seems to be a good way of getting out of an old mess.

So, back to our argument — how can performance be philosophy — philosophy in action? There is a close connection between making general statements and those of a high level of abstraction. And in research, even in the humanities, and as can be seen also in the field of theatre studies, there is still a need to distance oneself from one's own experience, as if such experience is suspected of not being valid according to an unspoken norm of "objectivity", which has long since been consciously overridden during the history of research methods in the humanities, but which, nevertheless, still seems to be working ghost like in the shadows, depriving specific, personal and true experience of its validity. The steady need for abstraction, distance and general statements, with less importance given to the specific that is experienced through the senses, is continuing in the humanities, and in theatre studies specifically, due to a lack of will for research of the self, and how emotions, thinking, feeling and living are intertwined, also in the writings of philosophy (Hammer 2010).

Meyer-Dinkgräfe
The writings of William James still hold ground in this context of continuing scepticism towards the subjective component of experience when he refers to science as being shallow, as long as the totality of experience is not considered: "The reason is that, so long as we deal with the cosmic and the general, we deal with only the symbol of reality, but as soon as we deal with private and personal phenomena, we deal with realities in the complete sense of the term" (James 2002).

Hammer
Another of the forefathers in the philosophy of the arts, John Dewey, has commented on the established cosmologies and theologies, which have held power over human imagination "through a direct appeal to the sense and sensuous imagination" (Dewey 1934: 30). Dewey strongly argues against isolating arts by "placing them in a realm of their own, disconnected from other modes of experiencing" (Dewey 1934: 45). The private and the personal, revealed through sensuous imagery shared as emerging experiences of meaning, now exist as a possibility in performative practices; opening up to viewing performance practices as a concrete act of philosophy.

Performance and /as embodied philosophy

Hammer
A more recent attempt at rendering philosophy more useful than it promises to be if taken as a set of speculations is the emergence of the concept of embodied philosophy. This can develop only through sensuous experience. What would be a better way of making philosophical ideas tangible than the creation of performative events that, in themselves, can embody what abstraction loses in its own process?

Meyer-Dinkgräfe
We will have to justify why older frameworks are still relevant while more recent ones need further contextualising because they are new and, if we are not careful, they are discounted outright as "esoteric".

Hammer

Indeed, the point of justification needs to be addressed. In several fields in the humanities there have been arguments for the human mind and subjective experience to be considered in research, particularly influenced by the writings of Merleau-Ponty.

Meyer-Dinkgräfe

And there is transpersonal research methodology (Anderson-Braud 2011). But often Merleau-Ponty emphasis on "bodily experience" is understood as merely bodily — or it is considered but overridden by other methods and approaches that are more evidential, and therefore considered to have a higher status.

Hammer

As is very well known in our field of research, the twentieth century experiments of physical theatre (Artaud, Grotowski, Schechner) gained their inspiration from the practices of various eastern traditions of theatre and ritual. However, sometimes these practices got so embodied that they became closures rather than openings to the very ideas that they embodied. The post-Grotowskian field of performance experiments is rich and varied, from the poorer than poor simplicity of Marina Abramovic to independent groups here in Scandinavia, established groups as different as Verdensteatret, Baktruppen, and SIGNA, but also more recent appearances, such as a dance production by Dreamscreen productions/Kristina Gjems (http://www. dansenshus.com/forestillinger/this-is-a-world-of-dew/). Several of their works may in fact be seen as ways of transgressing sensuous boundaries exactly for this good reason, namely to penetrate the human experience in such a way that it awakens our senses to embodied ideas and ideals.

Examples of Scandinavian performance practice and their theoretical contextualisation

Meyer-Dinkgräfe

Can you elaborate on examples from Scandinavian performance practice?

Hammer

In other contexts (Hammer 2008 and Hammer 2007) I have respectively described my reflections on the experiences of two such performative events — that of SIGNA's Seven Tales of Misery and of Verdensteatret's *A Concert for Greenland*. These two events differ, almost to the extreme, in their aesthetics, but nevertheless to me functioned as a trigger of awareness on several levels of consciousness. I have described my experience of Seven Tales of Misery as creating fluctuating states of awareness between individual and collective realms, allowing a confrontation with the fluctuation of my own consciousness, between individual independence, insecurity, and drive towards ritual surrender when focusing on personal experience as embodied philosophical experience (Hammer 2007).

Meyer-Dinkgräfe
What kinds of theoretical contexts for this practice have you explored?

Hammer
When experiencing Verdensteatret's performance of A Concert for Greenland, I turned to the French philosopher Gaston Bachelard in order to find concepts by which to try to turn an intimate bodily and imaginative experience into writing. Bachelard, in his works, proposes the existence of a material imagination, a concept I consider helpful for the understanding of performance as philosophy. He points out the existence of images of matter, that is to say, imagery that is created directly from matter without which there is no possibility of gaining an understanding of how human imagination works (Bachelard 1983: 2). Bachelard opposes the existentialist's critical approach to imagination and replaces this with an approach to human imagination that celebrates it and proposes human fantasy as a function of a vision into the future. To Bachelard, the experience of reality as materiality is the ground for all imagination; thus matter, emerging from bodily experience, is decisive to the quality of all imagination and sensation of matter present in human imagination. This has far-reaching epistemological consequences. Imagination is described as irreducible. This is because imagination emerges and is inseparable from bodily sensuous experience. When applied to the context of performance as philosophy, this means that the sensuous expression of the performer and all the other elements of performance, as well as the experience of the same by every member of the audience, are regarded as non-reducible subjective experience, and simultaneously as a shared experience of scenic imagined imagination. Their irreducibility makes them philosophical statements. "When forms, mere perishable forms and vain images — perpetual change of surfaces — are put aside, the images of matter are dreamt substantially and intimately. They have weight, they constitute a heart" (Bachelard 1983: 1).

Meyer-Dinkgräfe
Thus, Bachelard's positions work best for you to make more sense of your experience of the performance?

Hammer
In my experience of A Concert for Greenland, I propose, with reference to Bachelard that the performance itself states a "Dreaming Consciousness" and the dialectics between inside and outside that Bachelard refers to as, "The two kinds of space. Intimate space and exterior space," here, "keep encouraging each other, as it were, in their growth" (Bachelard 1994: 201). In viewing performance as philosophy, all material elements may be considered as philosophy enacted by means of spatial imagination of matter. The quality of the materiality unfolding in the performance may be considered as constituting images of philosophy, irreducible and true to human experience.

Meyer-Dinkgräfe
In general, one may say that contemporary performance has, at its core, the levelling out of the hierarchy, which has canonised the semantics of language. Bodily expression, sound, light, movement and kinaesthetic, not giving itself over to reference to already accepted or presumed previous sensuous experience, is often at its core.

Hammer
To take this further, some performances are, by the very sensuous experience that they reveal, actualizing experiences of what may be named "other realities". Such performances reveal dimensions of reality in which inner and outer dichotomies are on the verge of, or are being, dissolved. In some instances, these performances go to the core of the questioning of human sensuous experience and our idea of its limitation and possibilities. (See for instance Kim Skjoldager-Nielsen's description of the Islandic artist Olafur Eliasson's installation Your Blind Passenger) (Skjoldager-Nielsen 2016).

Performance philosophy as practice (1): energy

Meyer-Dinkgräfe
How can we let philosophical ideas penetrate our consciousness through the experience of performance?

Hammer
It is simple, really, but hard to do. Human consciousness, on the immediate level, is contradictory. Therefore, we tend to leave out elements of reality that do not fit into previously accumulated ideas of it and focus instead on those with which we are familiar, or by which our pre-understandings are not challenged. This is what in some contexts is referred to as "blocking" experience. If I go on doing this, my experience will be only partial, and I will not be able to put to use all those capacities that human consciousness has as its potential. Bodily presence of imagery that emerges from imagination rooted in matter, speaks directly to the whole of the human being in ways in which matter and mind cannot be separated. Neither can facts and non-facts, nor can inner or outer worlds. Performance that plays with imagery by means of the bodily and the sensuous, on a variety of levels or fields of experience, has the capacity for uprooting blockages of pre-conditioning. Performance, seen in this way, functions as philosophy of ideas that, were it not for their embodiment, would not be visible.

Meyer-Dinkgräfe
How can ideas be expressed and created concretely and without abstraction?

Hammer
Let me explain this by way of alignment to another subject field, namely, a comparison between western and eastern medical traditions. Western medicine has been built on the principle of cause and effect by understanding the bodily functions of a human being through using methods of research based on scientific evidence. Great achievements to human health have come from this. Eastern medicine, represented by ancient Chinese traditions as well as Indian traditions, represents a holistic approach. Chinese medicine proposes, for instance, that the meridians that run through our bodies are streams of life forces that not only can be found in the physical body, but also in additional "bodies" that are extended from these meridians both inwards, to the organs, as well as outwards, towards levels of energy in and around our bodies. Using both western and eastern approaches to medicine, a Norwegian doctor, Audun Myskja, proposes what he names an "energy paradigm" (Myskja 2014-2016). At the core of this paradigm is the understanding that the field of energy of a human being is not limited to the body, even if this energy field is situated in the body while we are alive. The energy paradigm, therefore, transgresses the body/mind boundary because all human emotion, thought, imagination, and experience, past and present, exist in these many-layered fields of

energy in and around a human being, and express themselves in subtle or more articulate ways, according to their qualities.

Meyer-Dinkgräfe

This concept of the energy paradigm is very close to the concept of energy fields that I have discussed in terms of German geo-biologist Hans Binder's practical philosophy. As this is a new development in philosophy, I will spend some time to explain it. Across the universe, every manifestation can be considered as an energy field and each experience that we engage in is formed of a confluence of energy fields from past and present in the current moment in the current location in space (Meyer-Dinkgräfe 2013b: 105). In her performances, Aurelia Baumgartner, who is a dancer with an MA in Philosophy and considers herself as a dancer/philosopher, seeks to lead the audience to an experience of philosophical contents. She calls it body-thinking. She exposes herself to a range of energy fields (in the form of concrete objects, contexts, ideas and associations) and then, guided by intuition, expresses the energy field that emerges from that confluence through her performance — performance in action. I will elaborate on her work further below.

Hammer

Baumgartner's body-thinking seems to be a way of exploring various levels of individual, interactional and collective experiences. Imagery, as well as bodily sensation are integrated parts of such experiences in which they complete and enhance each other, even if considered contradictory to the logical mind. Therefore, knowledge of ourselves is available to us on many levels and in many shapes and forms, and in several dimensions, to the extent that we are willing to open our consciousness up to them. Saying this, I am aware that during the last decades, there have been many schematic representations of such philosophy delivered from ancient eastern sources and over to the west. But this has not really been working for western human beings. Why is this? This is because the western human being has the need to experience for herself the bodily energy fields, both her own and other fellow human beings' — only then can this become a reality to her. It is, therefore, imperative to state that the energy paradigm is not an abstract model, but a way of opening up to experiences that are at the core of philosophical performance. Live on stage, philosophical performance, as such, will necessarily transgress all model thinking by appealing to trust in personal experience, considering it trustworthy and superior to speculation and abstraction.

Taking this into account when considering performance as philosophy, it is clear that engaging sensation by including the body, and extending bodily imagination by sound, rhythm, light and colour, and the space of the stage, can be no less than the ideal way of staging a philosophy that has human experience through the senses at its core, and that may pave the way for experiencing contradiction and conflict, oneness and diversity in oneself and in the other. This is because such performance is "experience" in the Deweyan sense.

Meyer-Dinkgräfe
Here the concept of embodiment helps considerably to make sense of concepts such as energy, which can come across as abstract as well, even if we are seeking to reduce abstraction in favour of something more concrete. It is through our bodies that we experience energy.

Performance philosophy as practice (2): imagination and archetypes

Hammer
Imagination is at the core of embodied philosophy — imagination is created bodily — and goes through the mind again into the body for renewal in an everlasting spiral of life forces. Abstract philosophy does not have the advantage of taking us through such a process. But may not all appearance in the sensuous world serve this purpose, if humans are willing, not only performance? The answer is yes, but in the process of performance embodying philosophy we have, literally, a stage through (or "on") which we may take the opportunity to consciously be aware of our own consciousness and the way it works because we are made into consciously aware participants by the qualities embodied in the performance itself.

It may be timely here to remind ourselves of Victor Turner's etymological analysis of the word "performance" — from parfornuir (thoroughly furnish, making full [completion of]) (Turner 1982: 13-14) and combine this with a quote from Bachelard: "If we cannot imagine we cannot foresee" (Bachelard 1994: xxxiv). Philosophical performance is about making philosophy fully human, as experience, in order to foresee who we really are.

Meyer-Dinkgräfe
The question has been raised, however, if such performative experiences may be considered as philosophical if they cannot reveal any general statements about the world that may be shared by many.

Hammer
This is where the concept of archetypes comes in, another "old concept", perhaps, but one that still fulfils the purpose of adding to our understanding. The question arises whether all mythologies (regarded as the ancient language of philosophy) share the same archetypes. When Jung spoke of archetypes, he did not speak of specific contents, but of structures/patterns existing in the human psyche in what he referred to as the "collective unconscious". He called these patterns archetypes because he identified these as having a tendency to shape typical, perhaps similar, or nearly identical contents in the collective artistic (philosophical) works of different cultures. The observation that content is different on surface levels is therefore no argument against the notion of archetypal patterns by itself.

Bachelard's descriptions of material imagination could not have been developed without reference to C.G. Jung (Bachelard 1994: xxxii). Jung was in no doubt that the various imagery-manifestations needed to be considered as precise and irreducible as possible. This means that images produced by the human mind can be seen for what they are rather than being taken as a "cover up" of hidden dangerous impulses of desire, as would be the case according to the psychoanalytical tradition. One may suggest that the reduction of images to fantasy (and thus untrue), and fantasy to nonsense, is due to the manifestations of human imagination not being taken seriously. In contrast, we argue that such images refer to extremely precise psychic realities and, if taken seriously, there is hardly any interpretation needed for understanding them. When I (with Bachelard), categorically state that no interpretation is needed, this is in order to underline the limits of the use of deduction or induction as well as hermeneutics of meanings as methods of interpreting imagery. Only if the mind can clear itself of the assumption that deductive or inductive interpretative processes are assumed when approaching imagery, can one get close to experiencing the image-forms. Jung puts it the following way: "The form, in fact, does not need any interpretation; it portrays its own meaning" (Jung 1969: 90, Hammer's translation).

From working with imagery in dreams, ethnographic material, and fantasy, Jung argued for the existence of "collectively existing, unconscious conditions." He thus proposes the method of "active imagination", whose purpose is not to trace imagery back to any prior figure, but to create a synthesis of passively existing contents of consciousness and unconscious influences.

Jung described active imagination as a form of spontaneous amplification of archetypes (Jung 1969: 90, Hammer's translation). In his last work, published posthumously, Jung strongly emphasised the need for precision in the interpretation of "dreams and symbols" (Jung 1964a: 92). He warns us against turning these interpretations into a "mechanical system" and then cramming them into "unimaginative brains (Jung 1964a: 92). He concludes: "One can explain and know only if one has reduced intuition to an exact knowledge of facts and their logical connections" (Jung 1964a: 92). Images reveal their contours as form. Amplification of these forms does not disturb or alter the form itself but helps us see these contours more clearly.

Meyer-Dinkgräfe
To come to an understanding of the concept of archetypes and how to make it useful for the understanding of consciousness, the spectator must be rooted in experience, not in theory.

Hammer
Archetypes are, according to Jung, irreducible images that do not appear as expressions of the personal psyche, but which rather express the collective cultural realm by spontaneously manifesting themselves in the cultural field. The most common approach to archetypes is to consider these images in terms of their contents. There is, however, a twofold difficulty in this approach. The first difficulty is the tradition of Jungian interpretations. Various specific content has somewhat "automatically" been ascribed to certain archetypes, solely based on content only, sometimes making us blind to the fact that these are emerging as form. This creates a difficulty in approaching the manifestations of archetypes altogether, since the term is so loaded with historically related manifestations of content. Archetypes are mythological images and mythologies can be archetypes. Regarding mythological contents, it is of importance, then, to consult with how Jung describes the notion of archetype. "It is necessary to point out once more that archetypes are not determined as regards their content, but only as regards their form, and then only to a very limited degree" (Jung 1964b: 79). Jung bases this explanation on the position that these primordial images can only be determined when they get into the conscious realm of the psyche. Therefore, they can only be defined by the material that is conscious to the

psyche, and that is by contents. This does not mean, however, that the "archetype" is identical to the "content". "Its form, however, [--] might perhaps be compared to the axial system of a crystal, which, as it were, performs the crystalline structure in the mother liquid, although it has no material existence of its own" (Jung 1964b: 79).

Meyer-Dinkgräfe
I wonder, here, whether the Jungian approach to archetypes includes reference to the experience of the source of those archetypes on the level of the unconscious — in parallel, for example, to the position that the basis of all manifest content of consciousness, pure consciousness, is open to direct experience. This is the position held by Advaita Vedanta. Vedanta is one of the six orthodox schools of Indian philosophy, and within Vedanta, Advaita Vedanta is associated with the concept of non-dualism — the subjective monism that consciousness is all that exists.

Hammer
The thought of such a possibility is inspiring. It also leads me to think of Rudolf Otto's notion of the numinous (Otto 1959) as the experience of spontaneous revelation as well as William James who, in his important work, refers to "religious experience", experiences that are "ineffable", and have "noetic qualities" (James 2002: 295). I would rather refer to such experience, in this context, as "spiritual" — but again, as James points out, often set off by sensuous experience — and this could relate directly to experience of performance. Concerning Jungian archetypes, however, the discussion above leads me to the second difficulty, namely that trying to reveal the immaterial structure of archetypes would seem to be an impossible project, since these manifestations may only be available to consciousness through manifestation of contents. Jung proposes archetypes to be transgressive, meaning that they manifest across time/space in both psychic and physical spheres (http://www.terra psych.com/jungdefs.html). Spontaneous amplification is a technique used in order to illuminate, or amplify archetypes appearing in personal as well as in cultural contexts. Returning to the energy-paradigm sketched above, the field of energy of a human being may be manifest through the structure of the energy field as well as through the imagination. Contents and form are then no longer separated. Contents may appear as form and form as contents, completing each other and describing manifestations on many levels of consciousness, pointing towards the archetypal in our lives. It may be argued, then, that such amplification is precisely what takes place

in performances engaging body and mind in the way that, for instance, Aurelia Baumgartner's work exemplifies.

Performance philosophy as practice (3): case study Aurelia Baumgartner

Meyer-Dinkgräfe

What you just described adds to our understanding of works of art, such as Baumgartner's. That is particularly the case when, in her intuitive way of working, Baumgartner finds herself inspired by myths and related archetypes, as for example in her work influenced by the Eurydice myth (see further below) and her work with horses, which also appear in mythology and have archetypal dimensions. For a 2012 performance, she presented a history of human horse interaction in several episodes, culminating in her pas-de-deux with her Arab Grey Pegasus. At the centre of her 2016 *Dancing Horses — Different Others* was the interaction of Pegasus with an autistic adolescent, an encounter between two individuals, one horse, one human, whose major mode of existence is fear. It was very striking to see how well those two interacted, overcoming fear.

Hammer

Performance cannot perform archetypes by choice of contents, but by immersing the theatre makers and the spectators into a process that engages the participants and the recipients in such a many-layered way and on such a variety of levels that the archetypal structures open themselves to new contents and changing contents. This is, perhaps, at the core of how performance may be understood as philosophy.

Meyer-Dinkgräfe

The many-layered nature of Baumgartner's performance as philosophy is interesting in that context and the number of layers increases with each performance she creates. It is no longer merely dance, or merely choreography. This approach defies linearity and her performances go way beyond their contents and require the spectator to open up to this ultimately new mode of creating.

Myths and archetypes have been considered as universal. Fischer-Lichte has considered the search for a universal language as one of the three components of intercultural theatre (Fischer-Lichte 1989: 115). Peter Brook and Suzuki Tadashi, for example, Fischer-Lichte argues, base their work on such a universal language of the theatre on archetypal and biological grounds. However, such a reasoning is problematic. Recent research into myths, she argues, deny the archetypal aspect of myths. Research also suggests that although humans all over the world share the same basic needs, and behaviours, such as eating, sleeping, walking and standing, the ways in which those activities are carried out are culturally determined (Fischer-Lichte 1989: 118). Fischer-Lichte suggests several levels of theoretical discourse. The first implies the question as to what could be communicated in such a universal language of the theatre. The second level deals with the specific conditions that would enable a universal language of the theatre. The third level is the function of such a universal language of the theatre.

In this context I have argued that as long as we remain on the verbal level, because that is culture-specific, we are unable to reach the genuinely universal level — that of the language of nature (as Artaud put it) (Meyer-Dinkgräfe 2005: 153). Just as much as philosophy can be understood not as a series of speculations, but as philosophers communicating and sharing their experience, performance can communicate from the universal level that is beyond verbal language; we can experience such performance first and think about it later.

Hammer
Can you elaborate more on Baumgartner as philosopher?

Meyer-Dinkgräfe
Aurelia Baumgartner's father, Hans Michael Baumgartner (1 933— 1 999), was a highly respected professor of philosophy in Germany, and Baumgartner is a philosopher. Her work is philosophy, both what she has to say and what she does in her practice. In what she has to say, she has referenced the philosophers that she thinks about, thinks in terms of, and that have guided her thoughts. All that thinking is interwoven with her practice. For her, practice is thinking, and takes the shape of her performances. It is philosophy in practice, just as much as it is possible to understand the history of philosophy as practice — as the writings about personal experience. Philosophers encountered their own revelatory experiences and wrote about those experiences to make sense of them for themselves, and to share them with others to enable others to make sense of their own respective experiences, and to enable others to have the same, or a similar, experience. For many, the first encounter with such experiences was new, unexpected and life-changing.

Hammer
So, Baumgartner's performances seek to bring philosophy back to the realm of experience, reclaiming them from the context of mere speculation?

Meyer-Dinkgräfe
I would say so. Perhaps she has found the key in performance that fine artists and musicians appear, or claim, to have found in their understanding of Practice as Research, which has left the restrictions of verbal language behind.

Baumgartner's performance of Catch me if you can: *Euridice 2012 Reloaded* was presented on 11 June 2015 at the 6th International Conference on Consciousness, Theatre, Literature and the Arts at St Francis College, Brooklyn Heights, New York, and was developed into a performance installation for the 2015 annual conference of the Theatre and Performance Research Association (TaPRA); it is the first of her performances I want to discuss in the context of this article (Baumgartner 2016: 1-16).

The components of Eurydice interweave and interact, mediated from prepared audio and video material, and immediate components, unmediated through the live body on stage, and the arrangement of the live space. Module art adds to this diversity, which, despite, or, actually, because of the disparate nature of its components, coalesces into a whole that constitutes a new dimension. The performance moulds this new dimension and explores its facets, nuances and external textures. The formation of this new dimension is given to the recipient's experience — I am using this term because the term "spectator" is restricted to the visual and the term "audience" to the auditory senses. These terms do not do justice to the more comprehensive experience aimed at, enabled and taught by Eurydice. Either gradually, or in a sudden phase transition, the new dimension opens up to experience. While we know the sudden transition from the sudden shift that allows us, with Rubin's vase, for example, to see either a vase or two faces in profile, but never both at the same time, in Eurydice, in the new dimension, we are able to experience all aspects simultaneously. We can think and talk about this experience in academic terms, but that is not the same as the experience itself that we try to capture in this way. The performance has become embodied thinking, bodythinking, which is a more holistic way of experiencing the world — a performative idea of utopia.

Hammer

If only we could encounter the real world, whatever that is, in such a way. In that sense the performance, which we cannot grasp fully through words, has a didactic nature because the performance is not limited to the verbal "dimension". The nature of Baumgartner's performances, as you describe them, is such that they enable a philosophical experience in the recipient, and the performances are created in such a way that they intentionally and explicitly aim for that experience in their recipients. Any performance that does not have that intention and is "just a performance" may still trigger philosophical experiences but would not count as "performance as philosophy" because it does not have the explicit intention of causing philosophical experience. There has to be an intention, and this intention is consciousness of consciousness, which can be experienced as a certain kind of "awareness", sometimes, and with regards to philosophy — awareness of ideas revealed.

Meyer-Dinkgräfe

Baumgartner's art is a good example of an art in which dance plays an important role, but which goes far beyond the traditional forms and structures of dance without denying, or ignoring them, and without reducing their current or past values. Through initial training and continued engagement with new material, intuition and openness for the world, interest and curiosity, together with hard work, Baumgartner has at her disposal a large pool of material to create from — it goes beyond dance forms across the world to include video art, module art and scenography as equal partners in the creative process. All these forms and aspects of art are enveloped and permeated by philosophical thinking. The variety goes against the linear, the telling of stories that can be retold and then, and thereby, ticked off. You will find less and less linearity in Baumgartner's work. Complexity increases instead, as does the multi-layered nature of her productions. The spaces are both physical by the way of mise-en-scène and by the way of a spiritual horizon. The very multi-layered approach brings forth a new, higher, larger, and denser unity. The spectators can experience this unity if they are prepared to enter the adventure of these productions in an unprejudiced way and if they do not attempt to use their reason to find something linear, or to be able to understand something. It is a principle that is central to many spiritual traditions worldwide: the principle of "letting go".

Dancing Horses — Different Others was the performative video installation that Baumgartner presented on 29 January 2016 as part of the symposium BodyThinking in the context of the topic of Art and Inclusion.

It is a project that seeks to bridge the boundaries of verbal language and linearity. We see video projections that constitute art, not mere documentation, through the camera, editing and sound. There are scenes of Baumgartner's pas-de-deux with her Arab Grey, Pegasus, and mare Mabrouka. A male flamenco dancer appears in a video and dances live on the stage, in front of the video screen, or in front of the empty screen. Three young female dancers dance together live; Baumgartner also dances live. In the video, we see an autistic adolescent, Christos Tsaoussidis, interact with Pegasus. Later, he comes onto the stage live joining in a scene with the three female dancers. He cues sounds and the dancers move in line with those sounds — they have learnt a sequence of movements for each sound and Tsaoussidis choreographs their movement through the cues he selects. There are further details that could be enumerated, relating to the stage, the dance, and the video. The details, how they may relate to each other, and whether we can make them fit through our intellectual analysis, are specifically not essential for the experience of this performance. The details merge into a holistic experience without any input from thinking, pondering, or rationalising — an experience that does not require the boundaries and limits of verbal language.

Conclusion: Modes of Performance

Hammer and *Meyer-Dinkgräfe*
We have created a wide net in our conversation about the possibility of performance as philosophy, about the possibility that philosophy need not remain distant from human life as speculation. The main overarching focus was on embodiment, taking up a current trend that seems to want to reassure people that philosophy is comprehensible in a very concrete and tangible way for everyone, not only for a cerebral elite. We provided an analysis of concrete examples of performed philosophy / philosophical performance with reference to Scandinavian companies and productions, and with reference to the dance work of Aurelia Baumgartner, and discussed underlying principles and patterns at work in all of these examples with reference to the concepts of energy and image and archetypes. The sequence in which we presented this material led from the abstract (philosophy understood as speculation) to the concrete (philosophy understood as experience that can be enabled or achieved in or through performance) and, via further substantiation of the concrete (Scandinavian performance examples), to more abstract considerations (energy, image and archetype) and ended with the concrete (Baumgartner's work). In this way, not only

the contents of our dialogue, but also its alternation of abstract and concrete represent written aspects of a performance of philosophy.

CHAPTER EIGHT

IN TRANSIT:
WAJDI MOUAWAD'S *SCORCHED* IN BREMEN,
GERMANY AS THEATRE OF ANTICIPATION

YANA MEERZON
AND DANIEL MEYER-DINKGRÄFE

[First published in *Critical Stages* 14: December 2016; reprinted here with permission from the publisher]

Contextualisation

At the 1998 conference of the International Society for the Study of European Ideas, ISSEI, I offered a workshop to which Yana Meerzon contributed what turned out to be her first conference presentation. We have kept in contact since then, meeting at a number of theatre studies conferences. In 2012/13, Meerzon and UK-based colleague Benjamin Poore, worked together on a long chapter on Nostalgia for my 2013 book *Observing Theatre: Spirituality and Subjectivity in the Performing Arts.* Given Meerzon's interest in exile theatre, we had considered a joint project about Zoo Indigo's *No Woman's Land* (see below, in chapter 12), but were unable to obtain funding for this. In October 2015, Meerzon received the information about the Call for Papers for a special issue of *Critical Stages* on statelessness. Rather than proposing our work on *No Woman's Land*, I suggested focusing instead on the production of Wajdi Mouawad's *Incendies* (*Scorched / Verbrennungen*) at the municipal theatre in Bremen, Germany, a production that was one part of a whole range of productions and other, related activities at the theatre. Mouawad's work is central to Meerzon's research. In November 2015, I went to see the production and interviewed the production's assistant director, Friederike Schubert, and Simone Sterr, who had been in charge of the refugee theme at the theatre as its lead dramaturg for a few months by then, having taken over from Regula Schröter, who had been in that role when the refugee theme was launched and when *Scorched* was first presented. In April 2016, Meerzon and I submitted a first draft of the joint article to the editors, Stephen Willmer and Azadeh Sharifi. Following a range of revisions, the article was published in December 2016.

Introduction

Any person coming to Germany who is persecuted politically or in another way in their home country (as in Syria by the terror militia of the so-called "Islamic State") has the right to be considered for refugee status and to apply for asylum. While the person is awaiting the result of the check, and if refugee status and asylum are granted, it is then the responsibility of the state to assure dignified treatment of the applicant or refugee. In Germany, since 1953, 4.6 million applications for political asylum were received, of which 0.9 million were received between 1953 and 1990, and 3.7 million since 1990. In the last few years, the figures are 127,023 for 2013, 202,834 for 2014, 476,649 for 2015 and 181,405 for January to March 2016. While the federal government of Germany is keen to see refugees integrate into the state, bureaucracy is sometimes blamed for inappropriate delays of dealing with applications, and there are concerns about the appropriateness of the very concept of *integration* and the related marginalisation of migrants across generations. The names and the looks of these immediate refugees, as well as German-born second and third generation immigrants who came to Germany decades earlier make these people to be perceived as non-German and alien (Sharifi 2014, 35). The question remains: what have the state and its cultural institutions done to change these stereotypes? Sharifi points out that at its annual 2011 meeting the German Dramaturgische Gesellschaft noted that Germany's cultural diversity was not yet represented appropriately in the core programme of German municipal theatres (as opposed to special events). Hence it urged cultural institutions to develop more activities of this nature and provide alternatives to out-dated concepts such as integration. In this, Sharifi concludes that theatre can and should support the acceptance of migrants as a positive feature within German society (2014: 43).

Following this suggestion, in the 2014/15 season, the municipal theatre in Bremen put on a total of fifty-two events relating to migration, under the heading of *In Transit,* to start developing alternatives through arts to such out-dated concepts as integration. The activities of the *In Transit* initiative ranged from full productions of classical and contemporary plays to discussions with the audience, and events staged for specific refugee groups. The majority of these events came ahead of the massive wave of migration in the summer of 2015. For the 2015/16 season, the theatre wanted to go further and focus on telling a story of the vehemence, weight and impact of an ancient Greek play with its selection of Wajdi Mouawad's *Incendies/ Scorched*, directed by Mirko Borscht. In the following, we discuss how Borscht's staging addressed the issues of migration in general, and specifically in the context of Bremen theatre's outreach activities.

Meyer-Dinkgräfe
The theatre in Bremen is a typical German city theatre, programming drama, dance, musical, operetta, opera and theatre for children and youths. It has three stages, with a total seating capacity of 1426. Overall, the theatre has sold between 150,000 and 290,000 seats per season since 2000. The theatre launched its innovative *In Transit* under the leadership of its artistic director, Michael Börgerding, and dramaturg, Regula Schröter, who wanted to find out more about the people who were moving into Germany. They were also interested to learn how migration affects the German people themselves. With hindsight, assistant director Friederike Schubert and the newly appointed leading dramaturg Simone Sterr commented that this season marked Bremen theatre's artistic team as proactive and not merely reactive: "We predicted what might happen and now it is daily life" (2015). They chose to put on *Scorched* to provide no longer only a thematic context, as in the *In Transit* season, but to ground the insights gained through this initiative within historical discourse. I travelled to Bremen to see the production in November 2015, inspired by reading about *In Transit*, and keen to see the extent to which this theatre might have regained at least some of its position at the forefront of developments in the German theatre scene that it had held in the 1960s when it made the national headlines with ground-breaking productions by a young Peter Stein, among others. The production certainly developed its own aesthetic, much in line with other municipal theatres' attempts to better represent diversity on stage (Sharifi 2014). Now I am keen to explore how this staging relates to Mouawad**Error! Bookmark not defined.**'s own artistic project.

Meerzon
The poetics of *performative testimony* defines the dramatic and performative structures of Mouawad's theatre. His plays "bear witness to the national tragedy of Lebanon, work through the trauma it caused, and offer hope to the survivors. Instead of inspiring dread, fear, horror, and pity leading to

catharsis, these plays re-enact violence, memorialize the victims, and perform mourning work in order to renew our shattered faith in humanity" (Moss 2001: 174). The play *Scorched* is the second instalment of his cycle, *Le Sang des promesses/The Blood of Promises* (1997 – 2009). It tells the story of a twin brother and sister on the quest to uncover the mystery of their mother's silence during the previous five years. A contemporary re-telling of the Oedipus myth, it examines what kind of cultural, collective and individual memories inform the journeys of exilic children. The text employs the elements of testimony and autobiography; and it engages with the simultaneity of dramatic space and time.

Introducing *Scorched* to his Avignon audience (2009), Mouawad stated that every artist tells the one and only story of his life; and if this story reaches beyond this artist's personal preoccupations, it can achieve a dramatic and existential universality. In his plays, Mouawad tells the tale of unkept promises, abandoned children and sacrificed hopes. The parable of the Binding of Isaac, in which God asks Abraham to sacrifice his son, finds a special echoing in Mouawad's theatre. He renders the story of Isaac's sacrifice as Abraham's ignorance of his sin. Hence, Mouawad's plays question the responsibility of parents for their children. In *Scorched,* the abandoned infant of the young Nawal, the fruit of her first true love, turns into his mother's torturer, the father to his own brother and sister. The Lebanese civil war serves as the background to Nawal's fight for love, her resistance, torture, and testimonial silence.

Mouawad's personal experience of the Lebanese civil war is marked by what Susan Suleiman calls the *1.5 generation effect*, the traumatic survival experience of children, who during the time of the atrocities were "too young to have had an adult understanding of what was happening to them, but old enough to have *been there*" (2002: 277). They experienced the trauma prematurely, "before the formation of stable identity that we associate with adulthood, and in some cases before any conscious sense of self" (2002: 277).

Born in 1968 in the Lebanese village of Deir el Kamal, Mouawad was already a bystander, no longer innocent, by 1975, when the war started. He had witnessed the street-fights and listened to the bombs falling. In 1978 his family moved to France and in 1983 to Quebec, so his childhood was forever to remain "the knife stuck in one's throat" (Mouawad 2009: 5). By the year 1990, the official date of the end of the civil war, it was estimated that up to 250,000 civilians had been killed, up to one million of the population had been wounded, about 350,000 people had been displaced, and countless others had gone into exile.

The war's shocking episodes made their way into Mouawad's plays and productions; so, the unresolved childhood trauma dictates the testimonial nature of his theatre.

Meyer-Dinkgräfe
It is interesting to see how closely related the play is to the author's personal experience, and how he seeks to abstract from that personal dimension, making the experiences of the characters transcend the boundaries of the specific context of Lebanon to a universal context that reflects the experience of migrants, of exile, in general. The audience can follow the plot and understand the contexts and implications of war without the detailed knowledge of the Lebanon conflict. In the Bremen production, the notion of "anywhere and nowhere" was transmitted through a bleak set dominated by a trench filled with water, three industrial fans, and a predominance of grey in its colour; so, the stage turned from the representational site into that of memory and troubled imagination.

Meerzon
This tendency to go from something concrete to something abstract marks Mouawad's dramaturgy in general: *Scorched* bears a visible tension between the real historical events that took place during the civil war and its fictional representation. For instance, the scene in notary Alphonse Lebel's backyard unfolds simultaneously in several temporal and spatial settings but is placed within a single locale on stage. The notary invites the twins to sign Nawal's testimony. Here, he mentions Nawal's "bus phobia" and begins telling the story of Nawal's witnessing the attacked and burned bus. The scene in Lebel's backyard overlaps with the other one, in the earlier time-frame, when Nawal tells her friend Sawda the truth: she was a passenger on that bus (Mouawad 2005: 43). This horrifying episode, which appears in the play as Nawal's recollection and on stage as her personal experience, "is not a figment of Mouawad's imagination. The attack occurred on April 13, 1975 and is widely seen as marking the beginning of Lebanon's civil war" (Arsenault 2007). The incident involved a group of gunmen who killed four members of the Lebanese Christian party and militia (Phalangists). So, for Mouawad, Lebanon remains the country of a "childhood lost in pieces"; the place that theatre is called to restore by bringing peace to the artist's memory. In his work, Lebanon appears, as Salman Rushdie would have it, as "two countries, real and fictional, occupying the same space, or almost the same space" (1997: 22). Here, the war is experienced as the child's memory – removed in time

and distorted in imagination. In its original staging *Scorched* allowed Mouawad to escalate the story of his personal suffering to the universals of abandoned childhood, to reach in its language the realms of poetic expression, and to make memory a separate, almost tangible entity on stage. I wonder how Mirko Borscht approached this issue in his staging in Bremen?

Meyer-Dinkgräfe

Hendrik Werner, Bremen's theatre critic, characterises Borscht's style as an aesthetics of violence. According to Werner, Borscht's "Berserkerfantasien / berserk imagination" (2015) does not have its strengths in psychological subtlety, which is evident in his production of *Scorched*. He chose the small auditorium of Theatre Bremen to compress the action of Mouawad's play into a small, dark, and claustrophobic set, and brought it close to the audience. Spectators sat on raked rows in front of the stage. The first impression of the set was striking because of its lack of colours—the stage comes across as a crowded space in shades of grey, not very brightly lit with cold light. There were large industrial extractor fans, one left, one right, and one in the back, arranged asymmetrically. Towards the front of the stage was a large rectangular trench filled with water, within it an area that looked like an island. This distorted visual perspective served as a counter-balance to the language, which Schubert described as "flowery", so as to avoid any sense of *kitsch* (2015). As a result, the production resorted to sensational moments where linear performance, based on the strength of the actors' speaking, would have been better. While there was more of that in the stronger second half, by that time the audience was no longer interested in catharsis (Werner 2015). In her review for Radio Bremen, Christine Gorny, too, showed disappointment at the directorial concept. At times, the action went "over the top", there was too much shouting, wriggling and splashing at the expense of making the production's impact even more stirring than it already was (2015).

Meerzon

Genre-wise, *Scorched* balances somewhere between tragedy and melodrama, which might affect its language as well. Mouawad often relies on the poetic traditions of the French neo-classical theatre. His texts often carry the shadow of an Alexandrine, but also bear the input of Mouawad's actors/collaborators who actively participate in making the story. Although he wrote the first four of his plays alone, working on the cycle, Mouawad realized that to make a show together, as a group, inspires him more than writing the text first and then directing it. Roughly, the process could be described as the following: Mouawad comes up with an idea for a play and gathers a group of collaborators who eventually "dream" and "invent" the future performance together. Using the rehearsal period as a trigger for the participants' emotional breakthrough constitutes the basic principle of Mouawad's theatre writing. I think that this collaborative process might have informed what Schubert described as the distorting perspective of the text. People who were forced to flee their countries often see their past and present through these distorted lenses. Such a perspective, I believe, often instigates an avant-garde form of writing/performing, marked by the devices of fragmentation, distancing, hyperbole, grotesque, and syncopation.

Meyer-Dinkgräfe
As Schubert explained, the set was inspired by the film *Interstellar*: "In the film there is a scene in which the main character exists in a gap, which does not have time or space. This is represented in the film by a stripy effect" (Schubert 2015). In the production, this stripy effect was recreated through rectangles with grey stripes hanging above the stage.

Meerzon
This is very interesting; it tells me that *Scorched* has achieved the status of a "canonical" text. It can be translatable and transferable into a new context, and even a new temporal setting. I don't think Mouawad really thought about the sci-fi potential of this script; whereas here you have another director who re-imagines this story through new lenses. He turns its central conflict into a compelling visual image.

Meyer-Dinkgräfe
In her notes on the production, the dramaturg, Regula Schröter, describes the play as being "about the search for truth and the entanglement with a past characterised by civil war and senseless violence". She acknowledges Mouawad's position in the context of exile but emphasises that the author does not write his own specific history but focuses instead "on a family story and approaches it via individual fates which represent the collective collapse of war" (Schröter 2015). She points out that "Civil wars of the last years do not only show similarities in their complex mesh of causes but also the expressions of violence and counter violence, the development of militias and intentional expulsion of people are the same". Similar thinking informed Borscht's take on this issue:

Our society produces victims as well as perpetrators at the same time. The truly crazy thing with such so-called civil wars appears to me to be that in most cases they are not being carried out by those who caused them and are only ended when they don't have any purpose anymore, when the economical and ideological resources of this war have been exhausted. War is a branch of economy. War regulates relationships of power, new markets and strengthens the economy. You have to bear that there are no simple truths in this play. Should one fight with weapons or with words? How is killing legitimised? Does the history of the twins begin with love or with a crime? Is it correct to confront one's own children with their true identities or does it make you guilty not to do it? (qtd. in Schröter 2015)

I think, Borscht tried to implement this through the casting choices. First, he changed the solicitor into the female character called Madame Lebel. Then he changed the character of Nawal's mother into Nawal's father.

Meerzon
In general, I would not object to cross-gender casting if such a choice serves an artistic or political purpose, but it seems to me that turning Nawal's mother into her father is fundamentally wrong for the play's premise. Such a choice, I'm afraid, shifts the story of *Scorched* into a more or less clichéd discourse of gender struggle and the power of patriarchy. By no means do I want to suggest that the society of Nawal's youth, as it is depicted in *Scorched,* imagines equal rights for men and women, it definitely does not. However, what is more important is that as her personal coming of age Nawal takes on a very important task: she is there to break the chain of wrongdoings which rests in her family with poverty, anger, and lack of education, specifically lack of power and voice for women. As Nazira, Nawal's grandmother, says: "poverty is to blame for all of this, Nawal. There's no beauty in our lives. No beauty. Just the anger of a hard and hurtful life". (Mouawad 2005: 19)

The story of Nawal begins in 1951, when a fourteen-year old girl falls in love with a young Palestinian man, named Wahab, from the Deressa refugee camp. In her Christian village, such love is forbidden; and hence Nawal faces a choice of either rejecting her love and giving away her child or leaving her own family in shame. Uneducated, scared, and weak in her will, Nawal follows the tradition, as it is spelled out by her mother: "This child has nothing to do with you, Nawal [...] Nothing to do with your family. Nothing to do with your mother, nothing to do with your life" (Mouawad 2005: 18). In the previous scene we hear Nawal telling Wahab that "something has been set in motion and nothing can stop it"; and now as we – the new family – are coming together, "everything feels better" (Mouawad 2005: 17). Here, Mouawad puts forward one of the major issues of this play: it is the question of destiny – "something has been put in motion"; and it is the question of personal responsibility. The moment

Nawal gets pregnant she becomes responsible for the new life: the mother assumes responsibility for her child. But what can a young woman do to fight history and tradition? Nawal's family will not accept Wahab as one of their own (he would be killed soon) and they won't keep his child, so a new cycle of hate, shame, and betrayal is set in motion. When Nawal realizes the mistake she made by obeying her mother's rules and giving into the tradition, she decides to set things right. In this, she is prompted by her grandmother's plea, who on her deathbed explains to Nawal the history of her country and her family's hatred: "[…] the women in our family… are caught in the web of anger. We have been for ages: I was angry at my mother, and your mother is angry at me, just as you are angry at your mother. And your legacy to your daughter will be anger too. We have to break the thread. So learn to read, learn to write, learn to count, learn to speak. Learn. Then leave. […] Learn to think, Nawal. Learn" (Mouawad 2005: 22). Nawal keeps her promise: she learns how to read and write, leaves the village to find her son, joins the resistance to avenge all the abused women of this country, and fights further for their freedom. Nawal's journey – as Mouawad depicts it – becomes as heroic as tragic and mythological. An echoing of the *Oresteia* cycle is found in this part of the text. It is only after Nawal's death that her children, Jeanne and Simon, will be able to break the thread.

Meyer-Dinkgräfe
All this, of course, suggests that Mouawad was truly inspired by the genre of tragedy. Schröter quotes him directly when she says, "Nawal understands that truth and lies are only two slopes of the same mountain, and that from now on she has no other chance than to understand and to try to balance on the ridge and to maintain her balance. This balance is expressed in her silence". (2015)

Meerzon
I imagine then that this play was chosen for its artistic value: it only indirectly provides new light on the emotional and historical baggage that refugees carry when seeking asylum in Europe, when settling on the streets next to those audience members who come to see this show in Bremen. Symbolically speaking, this play tells the story not only of the sacrificed child; it tells the chronicle of a sacrificed nation, the Lebanese civilians left alone to face the destiny of their unjustifiable suffering.

Meyer-Dinkgräfe

You referred to Moss earlier in terms of the play working through trauma and offering hope to the survivors. For the theatre audience in a place as remote from the source of trauma as Bremen, *Scorched* can bring the distant events closer because they can relate to the personal tragedy of the characters. The Bremen spectators see on stage situations they can understand, because the situations are presented to them by people they can relate to. They can then transfer that experience to the current refugee crisis. I still wonder, though, whether the Bremen production actually misses a dimension of the play that Mouawad certainly brought out in his own work. The Bremen production is grey, is messy because of the water, and there is no counter-weight to the bleakness—it is in fact difficult to see the hope that the play offers by solving the riddle of Nawal's silence and by offering the possibility of closure to the children. What this production lacks is the distance between the spectators and the characters. In Mouawad's own work, that distance was created through the poetic language. The Bremen production shied away from it. The translation into German itself comes across as rather sober, expressed in a contemporary idiom, and any poetic language left in it was carefully evened out. The scenography of Mouawad's own staging was non-realistic; it used strong colours, which, together with his poetic language, created distance from the characters and events. This stylistic elevation of the horror to the level of contemporary tragedy invited the possibility of catharsis, something that was hardly the intention of Bremen's production. Here, Borscht was more interested in the ambivalence of the relationships between victim and perpetrator. (Schubert 2015)

Meerzon

This is a very important point, specifically in terms of a historical gap between the time when this play was written and its staging in Bremen. As we know, every new mise-en-scène concretizes the chosen text for its new audiences. Focusing on the moral and historical ambiguity inherited in this play provided Borscht with an opportunity to bring this story closer to his audiences in Bremen. Perhaps it forced them to think deeper about the fate of the migrants, those who reached Germany a long time ago and those who are seeking asylum today.

Conclusion

The 2014/15 season in Theatre Bremen, with its 52 events under the *In Transit* heading, the subsequent production of *Scorched*, and the resulting personal involvement of Theater Bremen team members in working with current refugees, created, as Schubert and Sterr point out, a very strong network among their theatre colleagues across the country, as well as internal bonds between cast and crew. The company has now progressed from discussion to action, making the facilities of the theatre available to the refugees and aspiring to present the issue of migration in a historical context: "All these people who come over to Germany have their histories, they have their stories and we want to know what that means" (Schubert and Sterr 2015).

While it was possible to ignore refugees in the past (with the exception of their peak in 1992 and 1993, with 438,191 and 322,599 applications for political asylum, respectively, as part of the Yugoslavia civil war) because their numbers were smaller; the current influx of asylum seekers and media attention makes it more and more difficult for German authorities and the municipal theatre scene to ignore the situation. Theater Bremen's concern with the situation reflects the daily presence of migrants in Bremen—a reality that has become the daily life for their German hosts as well. Following the staging of *Scorched* from September 2015, Theater Bremen is currently putting together sessions in which the audience is informed about the countries from which the migrants have come to Germany and working directly with different communities of migrants. It is not surprising that women remain the most vulnerable subjects within these communities. As Schubert and Sterr explained,

We find that women of the migrant community are much less empowered than the men. In conversation we then found, for example, one particular group felt especially sad that they didn't have the opportunity of dancing together but also, even more than that, cooking together, which they are used to from home. We realised that no matter how important little gestures are, gestures are not enough, and so more substantial action is needed. [...] For example, when we were planning a meal together with a group of 200 refugees including their children, we made a point of not having plastic crockery and cutlery and cheap soup and whatever else might make it look like a kitchen for the poor, but we made sure that it was all presented very well, very nicely with proper table cloths, with proper cutlery and crockery and high-quality food (Schubert and Sterr 2015).

This reflection may lack theoretical and conceptual underpinning and may therefore come across as naïve but represents an example of artistic initiative beyond that developed under the auspices of the state. Altogether, *In Transit* was not only anticipatory, it was visionary. It reminded European society how urgent it is today for each European country and every one of their citizens to finally begin, and take seriously and carry through, the process of self-education and exchange, since only dialogue can break the act of silence and horror, as Mouawad's play *Scorched* tells us.

CHAPTER NINE

CONSCIOUSNESS STUDIES AND EVOLUTIONARY BIOLOGY IN STOPPARD'S *THE HARD PROBLEM*

DANIEL MEYER-DINKGRÄFE AND GREGORY F. TAGUE

[First published in *Etum* 2:2 (2015), 47-58]

Contextualisation

Gregory F. Tague was one of the first contributors to the *Consciousness, Literature and the Arts* journal and later joined the editorial boards of that journal and of the book series of the same name with Rodopi (now Brill | Rodopi). I contributed an introduction to his 2008 book *Ethos and Behavior: The English Novel from Jane Austen to Henry James*. In 2009, we co-edited *Origins of English Dramatic Modernism 1870-1914*. In 2011, Tague was keynote speaker at the 4th International Conference on Consciousness, Theatre, Literature and the Arts in Lincoln, and in 2015 he co-hosted the 6th (and so far, final) of these biannual conferences with me at his home institution, St Francis College, in New York. When, after a hiatus of several years, a new play by Tom Stoppard was announced, excitement was intense. When it emerged that in *The Hard Problem*, Stoppard addresses evolutionary biology and consciousness studies, the foci of Tague's and my research, respectively, in relation to literature and theatre, we agreed to write an article together. It was published, after full peer review, in the online journal *Etum*. Sadly, the journal has since disappeared. It is therefore particularly useful to include the article here.

Introduction

At the Royal National Theatre Platform (RNT) Performance with Tom Stoppard on 6 February 2015, host Nicholas Hytner, then still director of the RNT, started the conversation by quoting from a letter Stoppard had sent Hytner in 2013 (Hytner 2015). In the letter, Stoppard indicates that he wanted to combine writing about the banking crisis and the possibility of a person's altruistic goodness in the context of evolutionary biology (Stoppard 2015). The resulting play, *The Hard Problem* (Stoppard 2015) directed by Hytner at the Dorfman Theatre (World Premiere on 28 January 2015), was at the centre of that platform discussion, and is at the centre of this article. It was Stoppard's first stage play since 2006, and the first play for the National Theatre since 2002. The new play by one of the leading playwrights in the UK and the world thus came with high expectations, and

The critical reception showed some disappointment. Susannah Clapp, for example, writes in *The Observer*:

> The joy of the play, his first for nine years, is that it brings this problem to the stage and poses it crisply. The difficulty is that Stoppard then glides away from examining it. Often taxed with being too intellectual as a playwright, he is here not intellectually stringent enough. The great adventurer looks strangely conventional. (Clapp 2015)

In the article we provide an analysis of the play's use of references to evolutionary biology and consciousness studies, and how these references relate to the characters, the plot, and the RNT production. Stoppard has been well-known for using complicated intellectual concepts and frameworks in his plays. He plays with existentialism in *Rosencrantz and Guildenstern Are Dead* (1966), in *Arcadia* (1993) there are chaos theory and thermodynamics, as well as various distinct philosophical positions, which are also at the centre of *Jumpers*. Quantum mechanics is central to *Hapgood* (1988). In each of these cases, Stoppard works with a relatively well established framework. Those frameworks are complex, and within those frameworks there may be different opinions on detail, but the frameworks represent known and accepted paradigms, philosophical schools or approaches. The plays take up those frameworks, and the plays' wit and intellectual brilliance are caused by the characters challenging common sense opinions of life against the backgrounds of the frameworks. Stoppard's approach is successful because he can assume a certain level of familiarity of the audience with the frameworks. On that basis of familiarity Stoppard adds further factual information and crafts the challenges. The same is true for Stoppard's focus on evolutionary biology in *The Hard Problem*. Evolutionary biology may be controversial, in so far that some people agree with its tenets and others do not, but in itself it consists of a range of related insights about life on this planet, including human life. It is these tenets that Stoppard teases out in *The Hard Problem*, and in that respect this play is no different from the others. The next few paragraphs therefore discuss the play from the context of evolutionary biology.

The Hard Problem and Evolutionary Biology

To start with, evolutionary biology works with averages, with typical events, the norm, and, as any kind of science, does not like "outliers", data that do not meet this criterion of average. In line with this tenet, the play's characters cannot be extraordinary, and they are not. At the beginning of the play, the main character, Hilary Matthews, is a 3rd year student of Psychology at Loughborough University. We learn later that she had a baby at the age of fifteen and dropped out of school as a result, giving the baby, a girl she named Catherine, up for adoption. Because of these circumstances it is likely that Hilary is a mature student, a little older than the typical age of 20-21 for a 3rd year student. Readers and audiences have to work this out for themselves—a device characteristic of the entire play: to get to its depths, the depths from which the writing originated, we have to work. In the play's first scene, Hilary is in her bedsit with her tutor, slightly older Spike, who has agreed to give her a lift to her home to offer a private tutorial, and to see whether he cannot only get into "her good graces", as he puts it, that way, but also into her bed — he can. Hilary seems hesitant about "the biology", as Spike puts it (Stoppard 2015: 6), at first: "I'd rather not complicate..." (Stoppard 2015: 6), but Spike's response makes her laugh: "Hey, I'm your tutor, it would be an abuse of trust without precedent in higher education" (Stoppard 2015: 6). This line also created the loudest laugh from the audience at the matinee performance on 2 May 2015. It was an open, genuine kind of laughter, in response to a line in the opening minutes of the play, when the context was being established. Hilary has been applying for research posts to start after her graduation and has been successful in obtaining an interview at the Krohl Institute for Brain Science, where she had had least hopes, and had applied only "for sheer cheek" (Stoppard 2015: 12). She is aware that she needs a miracle for her interview to be successful (Stoppard 2015: 16), also given that she will graduate with a II.1, which, in the UK higher education system, is not the highest category. While her university, Loughborough, has a good reputation, it is not in the first-rate category of

Oxford and Cambridge in the UK, or CalTech (California Institute of Technology) in the USA. Amal Admati, Hilary's competitor for the Krohl job, has completed his undergraduate degree in mathematics at Cambridge and is currently studying for his MA in biophysics at Cambridge; in terms of educational background, therefore, he is much more promising than Hilary. Later on in the play, when Hilary has been with the Krohl Institute for a number of years, a new recruit, Bo, "a young Chinese-American woman" (Stoppard 2015: 34), has degrees from Shanghai, CalTech and Cambridge.

So, Hilary is an average third year student, and the way she debates with Spike the issues that she is interested in, is very characteristic, in the context of psychology (consciousness studies and evolutionary biology), of an average student expressing and formulating her ideas. What she has to say will be pleasing to hear for her university teachers, because they can see that she has begun to think about the issues on her own, rather than merely regurgitating taught and learnt material. However, what she has to say is not in any way brilliant, nor is the way she says it other than average. In Hytner's production, Olivia Vinall captures this profile very well indeed: she comes across as an attractive young woman with a level of interest and competence in her field that is average and a bit dull. It is a difficult profile to achieve for an actor, and it is not very rewarding even if done, as in this case, very well, because it is an impossible task to maintain audience interest in and attention for, a slightly dull character. Moreover, such a character is not an ideal vehicle for getting complex contents (evolutionary biology and consciousness studies) across to an audience, even if in conversation with characters who are presented as supposedly less dull, more charismatic — less average and more extraordinary. As Jerry Krohl suggests in the final scene, there is a spectrum of possibility in reality, represented in Cathy for him; for the audience, Hilary represents an outlier on what Jerry calls the 'distribution curve'. She has yet to stabilise her beliefs and find her place.

Spike is a high flyer in academic terms, progressing from a junior post at Loughborough University to a professorship in one of the high prestige UK universities, University College London, and then to a high-profile post at the Krohl Institute, within a relatively short period of time. This suggests that he is above average in his academic abilities. He has found his field, is certain about its boundaries, its potential, and has no doubts about those parameters at all. This allows him to focus well within the established context, and that is the basis for his success. His focus, however, also comes across as rigid, and that makes it ultimately as uninteresting as Hilary's ideas. Within his own context, Spike is dull as well.

At the beginning of the play, Hilary, the average student who will be lucky in due course with getting the Krohl job, and Spike, the high-flying but still average academic/scientist, are seen discussing the so-called prisoner's dilemma. This scenario is well known in the psychology of game theory. The prisoner's dilemma, in its simplest form, goes as follows. Two criminals are captured and separately interrogated. If one confesses while the other remains silent he gets a plea deal. Both could confess or remain silent. The dilemma is in not knowing what the other criminal will do, and this raises questions of individual self-interest or group cooperation. Spike tells Hilary that in a prisoner's dilemma all that matters are the innate and ancient "survival strategies" (Stoppard 2015: 5), not the individuals. He is quite pessimistic and says that altruism is "an outlier" (Stoppard 2015: 5). While he is correct to say that cooperation is a strategy, over the long process of evolution organisms learned that cooperation is the best strategy. So, altruism is not quite an outlier but an extension of cooperation. Many believe that cooperation evolved from the mother-child bond, extended to male parenting, to alloparenting, to kin (William D. Hamilton's inclusive fitness theory, 1964), and so on. However, Spike is correct to suggest that an evolutionary biologist would be reluctant to use the word *good*. What matters are motives to survive and especially to reproduce successfully. Nevertheless, a biologist who favours group selection might insist that behaviours can evolve for the good of a group. Many species have evolved tit-for-tat strategies (Robert Trivers' reciprocal altruism, 1971). There might be cases of pure altruism, but in the human world people want or expect reward or recognition, even unconsciously. Nevertheless, Jane Goodall (1986) and Frans de Waal (2013), to name two, offer accounts of apes that literally sacrificed their own safety, and in some cases lives, to help a conspecific or even a human being.

In reference to Hilary, Spike uses the expression "nature-nurture". This is a popular misnomer. There is no simple dichotomy, and any evolutionary biologist would hesitate to over-emphasize one more than another. It is somewhat closer to a fifty-fifty split, though in the case of social species, instincts can be shaped and moulded by learning, which is cultural. Hilary wants to get entry into the famed Krohl Institute with a model entitled Nature-Nurture Convergence in Egoistic and Altruistic Parent-Offspring Behaviour. The title reflects more on Hilary's situation, as we are to learn. Most evolutionary psychologists believe the mother to be of primary importance in care giving. We see this even in certain chemicals produced by the mother, such as oxytocin. In *Braintrust*, neuro-philosopher Patricia Churchland says that the ancient brain chemical oxytocin is an important operator in our moral systems. Originally implicated in reproduction, oxytocin is prevalent among vertebrates. However, only in mammals is oxytocin involved in infant care, and the theory is that eventually pro-social emotions so evolved. This is because oxytocin activates when the mother experiences stress against her offspring. Parental care by the father probably came much later in terms of pair-bonding with a female of the species and in terms of parental investment. Spike is correct to say that, however, there is competition between the mother and child. David Haig (1995) has done work in this area, and it is a simple fact that while in the womb the child is ever hungry for resources. But in line with Richard Dawkins' ([1976] 2006) misnamed notion of the selfish gene, the mother is able and willing on both an instinctual and conscious level to make this investment, since the infant not only holds her genes but is the machine that will produce offspring that will carry such genes into the future. Technically, fitness is reproductive success. Making healthy offspring ensures a line of descent. Hilary, however, tends to be anthropocentric, trying to find or apply *good* to such a natural process. Hilary wants to believe there are virtues in nature. Nature is neither good nor bad; it just is.

Hilary is upset that Spike is a strict materialist. We see this in their conversations about consciousness where he stresses matter. She seems to believe in a special ingredient, what Bergson called the *élan vital*, whereas Spike finds only neurons and synaptic connections. In Scene Five Hilary suggests that she wants to believe in "soul", her word, and cannot accept that she is connected to the animal world in a long line of evolution. She's guilty of what Frans de Waal (1999) has labelled anthropodenial. Much of this makes sense later when we find out about Hilary's teenage pregnancy. Clearly her decision of adoption has haunted her. Over the years, she has wondered and worried about her child, looking for meaning in the world that has made her into what she and others could consider a bad mother.

In the third scene there is talk of the Turing test — whether or not a computer can think. Hilary has applied for a number of jobs, including one which she is sure she does not have a chance to get, at the Krohl Institute for Brain Science owned by a rich financier, Krohl. Her competitor for the Krohl job, self-interested and unsympathetic Amal, likens the brain to a computer. This is an outdated analogy. He favours the computer over the brain. But the brain is organic and the product of selective forces. Amal's talk seems merely a foil to Hilary who vocally states that a computer is incapable of emotions. As a psychologist Hilary is less concerned with *how* the brain works and more concerned with how it seems to create a mind, an identity. She posits a dualism that marks her as a Cartesian in sharp contrast to Spike and the others. Introduced in this scene is the notion of luck, which is later tied to coincidence (and betting in Scene Four). In terms of natural selection, technically there is no randomness. In the first edition of *On the Origin of Species* (1859), one cannot even be sure Darwin uses the word random, favouring, instead, the concept of variation. Phenotypes emerge adaptations that evolve. Randomness would come by other means of evolution, such as mutations or genetic drift. Many mutations do not survive, and some are harmful. In terms of altruism, Trivers' (2006) model has been tested and proved: if we give, we expect something in return, so it is not a blind force of chance. Rather, it is an evolved trait.

In Scene Four, Hilary has been working at the Krohl Institute since the time depicted in Scene Three. The Institute is run by a billionaire capitalist, Jerry Krohl, hence the importance of the metaphors of luck and gaming. In this scene Krohl's eleven-year-old daughter Cathy asks her father if she were an orphan. She is concerned about creation and origins, which fits into the evolutionary theme of the play. We learn from this that she was adopted and that she knows this. We are also wondering about the likelihood of the coincidence of Krohl's adopted daughter Cathy being the same as Hilary's daughter Catherine. Darwin did recognize how chance factors into variation and circumstances and such chance can be beneficial to an organism and thus passed on. Stoppard's fabrication stands out here — what are the odds that Krohl would hire the birth mother of his adopted daughter? Does the answer to that question play into Hilary's ideas of God or into evolutionary biology?

In Scene Five, Hilary meets Cathy, who happens to walk into her office. At this point the audience wonders about the power of coincidence. Hilary does not yet know this is her child. Stage direction: "She doesn't know Cathy" (Stoppard 2015: 35). Oddly, there is no recognition of the child, which surely because of genetic inheritance must bear some facial resemblance to her; Hilary only pauses when she learns the child's name is Cathy. This is an important scene in that Hilary, who has not yet become sceptical of human nature, insists that "accountability, duty, freewill..." (Stoppard 2015: 37) do not appear in a brain scan. She is one hundred percent correct. The scan can show which areas light up when stimulated, but that does not account for or predict outcomes. The ultimate question seems to hover around how biology and genes can account for behaviour, such as altruism, or for consciousness. A few lines later, Hilary tells her research assistant that their work is not trying to measure empathy

(Stoppard 2015: 39). Could that include her empathy, one wonders. The research involves testing young children of varying ages in terms of egoist/altruist values. Personal information on the questionnaires, then, is discarded, since if read could lead to "special cases" (Stoppard 2015: 41).

In Scene Seven, Hilary and Spike meet up again at a conference. Here, too, Hilary complains about Spike's hard-core materialism that leaves no room for the "sublime" (Stoppard 2015: 48). Spike is somewhat critical of her inability to do mathematical analysis, which apparently is the strength of Hilary's research assistant. This is telling since it was not until the mathematical models of the early and then mid twentieth century that much of Darwin's theory about gradual, natural selection was confirmed. Cathy by now is ready to turn thirteen, and Spike learns of Hilary's daughter for the first time. As at the opening of the play, in a scene with Spike, Hilary prays. The difference now is that, exasperated by his scepticism, she practically begs him to pray. In this scene she offers a rather puzzling line, perhaps deliberately ambiguous reflecting her own self-doubts and doubts about science: "somewhere between ape-men and the beginning of religion, we became aware of an enormous fact we didn't understand" (Stoppard 2015: 51). She has been living in shame, either for getting pregnant so young or making an adoption plan. In terms of evolutionary biology, she seems to be unaware of what evolutionary psychologists Jerome Barkow, Leda Cosmides, and John Tooby have dubbed as the adapted mind — as indicated by those comments about the apeman. Popular culture depicts human evolution as linear, but it is not. Closer to Darwin's conception, evolution is a slow branching process with fits and starts. Hilary's use of the non-scientific term ape-man demonstrates her lack of evolutionary knowledge. There were many hominin and hominid species alive at the same time, and depending how far back one goes, some of our ancestors did have more ape-like behaviours, such as preference for an arboreal habitat. But we did not technically descend from chimpanzees or gorillas, our great ape cousins. Rather, we descended from an ancestor we held in common with the chimpanzee. On a related note, in the long process of hominid-hominin evolution, the brain evolved and expanded to selection pressures. An organism does not need a large brain and higher cortical functions to survive. Monkeys, lesser apes, great apes, human beings, and even other social mammals like dolphins have encephalized brains because of their complex social structures. As the brain evolved, put simply and to borrow from Howard Gardner and then Steven Mithen, separate intelligences related to awareness (such as those dealing with communication, sound, space, movement, and body) began to interact. Different areas of the brain became more fluid and flexible. Over time, the human mind itself adapted to the environment of other human beings, which gave rise to tool use and manufacture, complex hunting, mating preferences and practices, and advanced social structures. Given that we are evolved creatures, consciousness is an evolved mechanism.

When Hilary refers to the ape-man, she just blurts that out and Stoppard must have been aware that it does not make much sense. She might know but does not want to confront her own ultimate origins, the truth (which might make sense considering the secret she has been carrying). She is either an A student who pretends not to know, or she is a B- student who is out of her league. Her getting the job at the Krohl Institute seems too coincidental, but believable in the context of the interview. Hilary is an attractive European woman, dressed nicely. Amal is an Indian man and wears, according to the stage direction, a cheap suit. Amal is interviewed in the bathroom. Dr Leo Reinhart, the interviewer, we are told, likes the hard problem in spite of his penchant for the material side of brains (Stoppard 2015: 22). Hilary at this point does not even know the terminology "Hard Problem". Amal is too focused on the mechanistic, computational analogy to the brain, whereas Leo understands that brains think and that there is something we call mind (Stoppard 2015: 22). Amal suggests that a computer can do more than what a brain can do (Stoppard 2015: 23), which seems to miff Leo. This conversation / interview has moved out of the bathroom and into the reception area where Hilary is waiting her turn. She overhears and interrupts, saying that while a computer has speed, it has no depth, no thoughtfulness. When Leo asks Hilary what is her idea of deep, she responds brilliantly with "A computer that minds losing". If we were to take Hilary to be, overall, a character of average rather than exceptional intelligence, this unambiguous instance of brilliance is a (welcome and much needed) "outlier". The stage direction here is important: "Leo takes a moment to reconsider her" (Stoppard 2015: 23). That is where she has clinched the job. Amal is the better candidate, but Leo has a feeling about Hilary. She might not know what the hard problem is, and she might not know about biology or evolution, but she knows that a human being possesses an emotional mind, which a computer (so far) does not. And the whole point of the Krohl Institute is to study this, not to examine, as does Amal, mathematical computations. Amal already has (he believes) the answers — he says so: "There is overwhelming evidence that the brain causes consciousness" (Stoppard 2015: 23). Hilary counters and so demonstrates that she can work on the hard problem, since she sees mind, matter, and consciousness as problems (Stoppard 2015: 23).

But Hilary is a bit of a cheater. When pressed by Leo concerning the emergence of consciousness she begs ignorance and says: "I thought that's why we're here. To crack the Hard Problem" (Stoppard 2015: 24). In the same scene, two pages earlier, she was not even aware of the so-called hard problem. The question here arises whether Hilary is an operator. She is plagued by the adoption plan, and now she has managed to get this dream job. Has she compounded her feelings of guilt by snatching away from Amal this opportunity so that she tries to make amends later in accepting blame for the botched research? If she were not selfish, she would have raised her birth daughter and would not have, essentially, lied to Leo about knowing the hard problem.

The research Hilary had done concerning young children of various ages and egoist/altruist values is published in a journal. As published, the research demonstrates that children become more egoistic as they get older. The problem is that the research assistant who is expert in equations fudged the numbers. The published paper is all wrong. Magnanimously, later, Hilary tries to take all of the blame herself. Is she therefore altruistic? Why would she have trusted the greenhorn research assistant so much? Because she was good with numbers or because she suspected she could manipulate the numbers. In fact, the research assistant claims that she faked the equations to help Hilary. It's almost as if Hilary wanted to sabotage her career in science as an excuse to do something else. The question of self-interest plagues this play. However, there is a big difference between self-interest and selfishness. Is Hilary selfish? This is ironic in that forms of deception and cheating have and will always be around, but ultimately cheaters do not win. (Note, again, how Hilary's paper is entitled "Ultimate Goods".) Hilary tried to prove that there is good in nature. Is she good for taking a fall? Besides, she should know we don't grow less caring and less helping as we age. We would not have survived if we were all cheaters. Spike thinks she's saying human nature is separate from animal. According to extensive research by Jessica Flack and Frans de Waal (2002), who chart ape (chimpanzee and bonobo) continuities with human beings, there is at bottom a common denominator of empathy. If she is separating human/animal nature she is wrong, since there is no strict separation, just a long continuum with differences.

Although Charles Darwin and Alfred Russel Wallace were the first naturalists to introduce the idea of evolution by means of natural selection, there had been a long line of evolutionary theories before them, but none explained precisely the mechanism of evolution. Natural selection is a long process of weeding out what does not work by refitting it with a working alternative. Operating through an individual organism, natural selection elicits adaptive traits that increase survival and reproductive potential, and these traits are eventually passed on. While Darwin knew there is a struggle for existence, other thinkers, such as Peter Kropotkin in 1902, wrote about mutual aid.

Clearly the notions of self-struggle and reciprocal helping are critical to Stoppard's play. For Darwin, there is no teleological design in nature, only adaptations, and we see Hilary grappling with this thesis and essentially rejecting it. Nevertheless, even Darwin's theory had gaps with his ignorance of gene theory, and this was not fully explained until the early twentieth century by J.B.S. Haldane (1932), Ronald Fisher (1930), and Sewall Wright (1931) who introduced complex mathematical equations about population genetics to prove Darwin's ideas sound. All of this is central to the play, since the subjects of consciousness, altruism, and parenting are products of natural selection. However, the playwright is careful to demonstrate how evolutionary information is shaped by the values and beliefs of individual characters. There might indeed be a problem, but how willing is any individual to accept a hypothetical answer?

Not surprisingly, by the end of the play Hilary is to leave England and go to New York to study philosophy. She learns that her daughter had been adopted by her wealthy ex-employer, but she is okay with that. Odd, considering how anti-materialist she is, happy her daughter will not want for anything. Perhaps she can, finally, justify her adoption decision by saying that her daughter has been and will be well cared for. The really hard problem seems less about any theory of consciousness and more about Hilary's decision, age fifteen, to make an adoption plan and now, with her professional career in ruins to leave England and so leave Cathy.

The Hard Problem and Consciousness Studies

The way in which Stoppard discusses, as we have shown above, evolutionary biology within *The Hard Problem*, is similar to the way he deals with other concepts and theories of philosophy his play and science: he plays with a set of given parameters and sheds interesting light on the lives of characters in *The Hard Problem*, and our lives, in the process. A separate study can develop those parallels in detail. In, Stoppard does not only deal with evolutionary biology, however, but also with consciousness studies, referenced in the very title of the play. Consciousness studies as an interdisciplinary field of study emerged in 1994 with the first biannual conference *Towards a Science of Consciousness*, held by the then recently founded *Center for Consciousness Studies* at the University of Arizona in

Tucson, USA. The conference was attended by around 1,500 delegates. The launch of consciousness studies in the context of this conference represents a concerted multidisciplinary and transdisciplinary effort to address questions about human life. Questions of the nature of the mind and its relation to the body have been central to Western and Eastern philosophy (including Plato, Aristotle, Plotinus, Descartes, Hegel and others) and mysticism (Meister Eckhart, Jakob Boehme) since the onset of history. I have argued elsewhere, based on Shear's lectures for Maharishi International University in the 1970s, that the entire history of philosophy could be rewritten as the history of writings about human experience of consciousness (Meyer-Dinkgräfe 2013b: 125-9). In line with Stoppard's contribution to the programme notes for the National Theatre Production, the characters in the play discuss two positions on consciousness opposed to each other: dualism and materialistic monism. Dualism suggests that mind and body are separate entities. Monism suggests that only one substance exists primarily, either matter (body) or consciousness (mind, soul). Either matter is primary and gives rise to consciousness (materialism), or consciousness is primary and gives rise to matter (subjective monism). Independent of the conceptual backgrounds from which people discuss consciousness, it tends to be central to their argument that consciousness holds an elevated position, usually the highest in a hierarchy. From the materialist perspective, which materialists refer to as "bottom up", consciousness arises from matter; it can be reduced to matter but is still somehow more than matter. The "hard problem" of consciousness studies, for materialists, is the question of how that matter gives rise to consciousness (Chalmers 1996). The perspective of subjective monism, on the other hand, considers consciousness as the primary substance, again at the highest position of a hierarchy, from which matter emerges.

> The arts and humanities disciplines contribute to this understanding to some extent, but to a larger extent the arts and humanities benefit from the insights of other disciplines under the umbrella of consciousness studies in developing the understanding and knowledge specific to their own disciplines. (Meyer-Dinkgräfe 2013a: 13)

Stoppard does not consider subjective monism, in line with the position of current science, which subscribes to materialism. Stoppard's choice is also in line with evolutionary biology, which, as a science, is equally materialistic. This is the context for the materialistic take on consciousness in *The Hard Problem*. That materialistic approach, in reducing consciousness to matter, can leave many people, including Hilary, disappointed because they tend to feel that there must be more to consciousness. In the play, Hilary realises the need for breaking down boundaries of materialism and exploring new ideas; as a result, she asks interesting questions, but she does not find the answers to those questions within the frameworks and contexts of the disciplines she works in. Her questions relate to consciousness studies, more so than to evolutionary biology. Many academics claim that it is impossible, or very difficult to define what consciousness is in the first place, and Hilary and Spike struggle with that aspect of consciousness as well. Asked by Hilary to "explain consciousness", Spike impatiently, as he is not really interested in this question, "*takes her finger and holds it to the flame of the candle for a moment before she snatches it away with a little gasp*". Then he says: "Flame – finger – brain; brain – finger – ouch" (Stoppard 2015: 11). Spike is able, Hilary concludes, to explain is made of mechanisms, but nothing beyond, such as sorrow. The reason for this, for Hilary, is that "the body is made of *things*, and things don't have thoughts" (Stoppard 2015: 12). Such reasoning, expecting there to be more than materialism allows for, leads her to find the "God idea" (Stoppard 2015: 12) more attractive. Stoppard develops Spike as Hilary's main antagonist, but in foregrounding Spike's evasiveness when it comes to talking about his materialistic world-view, Stoppard offers the audience the opportunity of considering Spike as a rather reluctant materialist. He is a scientist, and as a scientist he has learnt to follow certain rules of the discipline. His thinking is limited by the boundaries of what science can comprehend and explain, although he may well have intuitions that do not square with his scientific mind-set. Anything that does not fit that mind-set represents a threat to the mind-set; when challenged to discuss consciousness, Spike is reluctant to engage, because such engagement might open up the threat to his established mind-set. He is aware of that threat and seeks to avoid it if possible.

When Hilary has been working at the Krohl Institute for five years and prepares for a conference paper, she runs a number of possible ideas in the context of consciousness studies past Ursula, who also works there. Those questions encompass subjective monism — could the cosmos be teleological (No). What about panpsychism (No. Nature isn't conscious. Trees are not conscious). And materialism: Functionalism (No. A thermostat is not even a tiny bit conscious). What about quantum-level brain processes to explain consciousness? ("Will you show me how Gödel's Proof means a brain can't be modelled on a computer?") (Stoppard 2015: 45-46).

New recruit Bo offers a take on one of Hilary's own research projects in ways that open up a new dimension hitherto not detected by Hilary. In addition, Bo develops a research project of her own, and comes up with results that go some way of addressing, and answering the essence of Hilary's own research questions about human goodness. However, it turns out that Bo, in order to please Hilary, whom she loves, manipulated the data in ways unacceptable in scientific methodology. This is the ultimate professional misconduct in the social sciences and science, comparable, perhaps, to an art historian intentionally certifying a forgery as genuine. Triggered by this event, at the end of the play, Hilary, faced with the choice of either seeing Bo lose her current job and any good further prospects, or taking the blame for the publication that needs to be retracted, decides to take the blame. She will leave her post at the Krohl Institute and study philosophy at New York University, because there someone is teaching philosophy "whose ideas are [...] undemonstrable" (Stoppard 2015: 75). The philosopher is probably Thomas Nagel. He is famous for the question, "What is it like to be a bat?" Amenable to Hilary, he pretty much seems against any reductionist (his word) explanations of consciousness. She hopes to be able to find answers to her questions there, unable to find them in science. The play thus does not answer her questions, and leaves them for Hilary's encounter with philosophy — perhaps Stoppard will provide the answers in his next play?

The play seems to say there is a hard problem, but does not really define it fully, just as consciousness studies has not defined it fully, for in doing so, some argue, it would have answered it or abandoned it as a problem that does not really exist. Stoppard leaves the hard problem thus appropriately open. Stoppard hints at possible links between the hard problem of consciousness studies and evolutionary biology, but just as consciousness studies is still struggling to agree on a working definition of consciousness, those links are not explicit and definitive in the play. Stoppard asks: if consciousness is biologically evolved, and if like great apes we are social creatures, does that logically mean altruistic behaviour is mostly evolved and only in part learned? Stoppard takes these problems of science and gives them flesh and blood in characters like Hilary and Spike. The issues are implicit to the story of Hilary's life. The hard problem in consciousness studies, the question of *how* the body produces consciousness, has not been solved by science (Spike and colleagues at the Krohl Institute), and Hilary will look for it in the philosophy of New York University.

That Stoppard leaves open the definition of consciousness, permits inconclusive dialogue between Hilary and Spike, and sends Hilary off on a philosophical quest simply validates the existence of the hard problem. Especially through Hilary the play shows that both helpful and harmful behaviours are dependent on consciousness. Stoppard links the hard problem with Hilary to demonstrate how consciousness is less a scientific puzzle to be resolved but more so a real-life dilemma concerning altruism. In fact, the play implies that the brain might be incapable of solving its own hard problem. Consider the image of the box at the end of the play, which Hilary fills and then empties. The playwright symbolises materialism (consciousness from matter – the filled box) and subjective monism (matter from consciousness – the emptied box). There is a continuum of choices seen in Hilary's active shuffling of the contents. Good art is silent, so Stoppard does not supply any professorial definition to the hard problem but directs the audience to consider alternatives so as to posit its own hypotheses. Are answers about consciousness and altruism inside the box (proximate science and the how) or on the outside (ultimate philosophy and the why)? When does brain function or form (box) become conscious content (goods)? Stoppard leaves these as open questions but suggests that with further training Hilary will continue the conversation between evolutionary biology and philosophy. In *The Hard Problem*, Stoppard raises issues that are central to science and to life. He raises some of those issues directly, some implicitly and indirectly, through characters that are average (like the majority of people in the world, and thus the majority of readers or spectators), and ultimately it might be up to readers or spectators, Stoppard seems to suggest, to answer the difficult questions that the play raises. Consciousness studies is not like evolutionary biology in *The Hard Problem*, and the other concepts, approaches, theories and paradigms that Stoppard works with in many of his other plays. While those concepts are relatively well defined and understood as frameworks, consciousness remains elusive; different positions in the field are fiercely claiming to be exclusive and mutually incompatible with others, vigorously resisting attempts at building bridges.

The hard problem faced by some materialists simply does not exist for other materialists and does not arise for subjective monists. In *The Hard Problem* Stoppard thus enters what is for him, in the context of his other plays, new territory, in working not within a given, and thus relatively safe, framework. The openness of the play reflects this new territory.

CHAPTER TEN

SCIENCE IN LUCY PREBBLE'S *THE EFFECT*

Contextualisation

Dr Bernhard Kupke, a brilliant biology teacher at my school, Theodor Schwann Gymnasium in Neuss, Germany, inspired my interest in biology, and sciences in general. I embarked on studying Biology and English at university (Düsseldorf), but the way the science was taught there was too different from what I had been used to at school. The professors considered their teaching duties as having to waste their time on "all of you pick-a-daisy and stroke-a-dog pseudo-biologists", and in each area, I found that many narrow positions about what constituted scientific fact competed with each other. I changed subjects from Biology to Philosophy after two years. However, my interest in science continued and has influenced my work over the years, culminating in two funded research projects in collaboration with Elizabeth Valentine, then Professor of Psychology at Royal Holloway, University of London. I was, therefore, also interested in the development in contemporary drama of playwrights making forays into science, placing scientists and science topics on stage. Working in the same School as Andy Jordan, who was involved with the creation (as dramaturg) of all of eminent scientist Carl Djerassi's science plays, and produced all of them and directed most, allowed me to gain very close access to this field. I was keen to understand, with regard to Prebble's *The Effect*, how the science referred to in that play was seen by real-life scientists (Prebble is not a scientist, but a dramatist). I thus asked three scientists to read the play and discussed the use of science in the play with them.

Introduction

The Effect opened at the Royal National Theatre, London, in a co-production with Headlong Theatre Company, directed by Rupert Goold, on 12 November 2012. It was written by Lucy Prebble, who had scored a major critical success with *Enron* in 2009. The cast were Anastasia Hille as Doctor Lorna James and Tom Goodman-Hill as Dr Toby Sealey, Billie Piper as Connie Hall and Jonjo O'Neill as Tristan Frey. *The Effect* is set in a drugs testing facility. Triallists Connie and Tristan have volunteered to stay in the facility (a hospital) for a four or five-week trial period to undergo testing of a new antidepressant. The drugs are administered by Dr Lorna James, and the trial is overseen by Dr Toby Sealey. The play itself is set up like a drugs trial, reflected in the text (such as references to the age, weight and height of the characters in the list of characters, and the stage direction at the start of the play "experiment begins") and the performance, with Connie's heart rate, for example apparently visible or audible for the audience to see / hear at appropriate moments in the play).

With its medical context, *The Effect* is placed on the spectrum of plays that deal with science in one way or another. Kirsten Shepherd-Barr points out that plays that deal with science have been around for several centuries, but that since the mid-1990s, there has been an unprecedented wave of such plays, which has not abated since (2006: 1). The science plays come from Britain, the USA, France, Germany, Switzerland, Greece and other European countries, and encompass "neurology, physics, biology, evolution, genetics, reproductive technology, epidemiology, biochemistry, mathematics, and astronomy" (2006: 1). Shepherd-Barr identifies a number of recurrent features in science plays: they cast the scientist as hero or villain (or indeed both), they engage with "real" scientific ideas, they portray complex ethical discussion, and they demonstrate an "interdependence of form and content that often relies on performance to convey the science" (2006: 2). As far as the form of science plays is concerned, Shepherd-Barr notes the diversity, ranging from realism to documentary theatre, from Brechtian theatre to non-realistic approaches, often combining "textual richness with scenic restraint" (2006: 2). A leading exponent of science in theatre plays, Carl Djerassi, is keen to ensure that at least in his plays, the science is as accurately presented as possible. In that sense his plays are also didactic.

At the core of this article is an exploration of the extent to which the science in *The Effect* is accurate, of the instances where the play deviates from knowledge, approaches, protocol and scenarios in science as practiced today, and of possible reasons and impact of such accuracy or deviation. The article analyses the play in terms of the institutional context it presents, the relationship of the scientists and the volunteers, common assumptions about psychology, and the specific procedures of the trial presented in the play. This exploration is based on discussing the play with Dr Paul Grassby (Head of the School of Pharmacology, University of Lincoln), Dr Graham Lappin (then Reader, School of Pharmacology,

University of Lincoln) on 13 October 2013 in person, and Dr. Wayne Macfadden (then Senior Medical Director, Hoffman-La Roche Neuroscience) on 17 October 2013 via skype.

The institutional context

The Effect identifies Connie and Tristan as healthy volunteers who are to stay in the trial institution, a part of a hospital, for four weeks for the doctors running the trial to establish the impact of a new antidepressant. The volunteers undergo a series of pre-trial tests, then the drugs are administered in increasing doses, and further measures are taken to establish the impact of the drugs on the volunteers. Paul Grassby agrees that clinical trials at their beginning stage are expected to work with people who are healthy. Wayne Macfadden expands on this by pointing out that "after a drug is shown to be not dangerous in animals, it progresses to healthy volunteers to determine what the maximum tolerated dose is". According to both Grassby and Macfadden, this is a relatively short procedure, and would not take a month, as the trial in the play. In addition to establishing the doses that are safe for humans to take, the first phase in current trial practice tests for pharmacokinetics, "what the body does to the drug", which is "the movement of the drug into, through, and out of the body". Once safety and pharmacokinetics have been established in healthy volunteers, pharmaceutical companies will start testing the new drug on volunteers who have actually had the disease, not another group of healthy volunteers. Macfadden goes on to point out that the purpose of the anti-depressant medication that is being developed in the context of Prebble's play is to improve symptoms in people who are suffering from a Major Depressive Disorder, as described in DSM-5: "therefore one wouldn't give it to a healthy person as it wouldn't really tell you anything, as you wouldn't of course expect to improve their mood as they are not clinically depressed". Macfadden's observation in this context relates to Grassby's position that what is presented in the play is not really a clinical trial but more of a research project. "It is the first experimental attempt to put the active ingredient into a human and it is not a rigorous randomized, double blind clinical trial".

Thus, in terms of the scenario that provides the frame for *The Effect,* the play collapses several stages of a real-life trial, ranging from pre-trial experiment via test for safety and pharmacokinetics with healthy volunteers, to the long-term trial with volunteers who are suffering from the symptoms the drug is supposed to address. When the doctors talk amongst each other, Toby says "an antidepressant effect in healthy volunteers. Pretty extraordinary." (2012: 23) This is a further instance to suggest that the scenario in *The Effect* is a research project and not a clinical trial because as Macfadden says, "presumably this drug is being tested for a Health Authority approval- so one wouldn't primarily be studying its psychoactive effects in healthy people". In drug trial testing at the clinical trial stage researchers would be looking at ill people. "They would not be doing psychiatric depression rating scales in normal healthy individuals so again this points to the fact that what they should actually be doing is not a clinical trial but only testing the drug for its safety and tolerability". The length of the trial period in *The Effect* is also contested by the experts: what happens in the play suggests a pre-trial research project or testing for safety and pharmacokinetics, which would not take four weeks.

The play suggests that there are more male volunteers than female ones. Grassby points out that the rule of thumb is that the first participants in a trial or experiment are always male. Pharmaceutical companies do not use females at all, because for new drugs, studies of how an unborn foetus may be affected by the drug cannot have been carried out yet. There may be exceptions, depending on the general target for the drug. "If you had a small number of females in there, I don't think you will be breaking some big rules, but they are mostly males at the first stage". Macfadden agrees that there are usually more men, and in the case of female volunteers, the testing institutions have to ensure as best as they can that the female volunteers are not pregnant and will not get pregnant for the duration of the trial.

Further within this context of the institutional conditions surrounding drugs trials, Connie and Tristan discuss that for some projects English has to be the first language and subjects have to be articulate. This assumption probably implies that these subjects will be able to express the kinds of experiences that they have in relation to the drugs—by further implication, for other kinds of drugs they might the companies might select volunteers who do not fit that description. Lappin points out that in clinical trials there is a need for informed consent. "That means that subjects usually have to read quite a lot of material before they start and then understand it before they sign off". Thus, all trials require a certain level of literacy from their subjects. It should be noted, however, that, as Grassby comments, much of this work of clinical trials is sub-contracted by pharmaceutical companies and many clinical trial units that they set up tend to be in the poorer areas "so they tend to capture people who do this for money".

So far, the following picture about the use of science in *The Effect* emerges: the scenario that Prebble sets up for *The Effect* is somewhere between first experiment and first trial phase with healthy subjects to test for security. The four-week duration of the trial is not compatible with either experiment or first trial phase. The socio-political context is similarly ambiguous regarding the information about level of literacy required, and with the presence of a female subject more of an exception in real life situations.

Towards the end of the play, when an overdose of the drug has had devastating effects on Tristan, Dr Sealey discusses events with Dr James and concludes that "nothing will be published obviously" (2012: 97). Macfadden wonders whether this is an indication that the researchers would not be publishing all the results: in a real- life context that would not be acceptable. The question then arises as to the personal interest of the doctors involved in this case with the outcome of the project and here Macfadden comments that physicians like Dr James should not have any financial interest in whether the trial succeeds or not because she is presumably paid only for her time, so it shouldn't matter to her whether the drug works out or not. For Dr Sealey the matter is likely to be different: "he is probably a stockholder in the company and he would want the tests to work and that is why in the real life scenario he should not have anything to do with the actual patient care and he would certainly not know which patient was receiving placebo and which was not". Macfadden emphasises that companies (sponsors of research) are very keen on monitoring their procedures very strictly:

In general, clinical trials are closely monitored by the sponsors, as information may need to be provided to health authorities. To start with, the placebos are supposed to look exactly like and taste like the real drug. The unblinding codes are strictly maintained, so nobody in the company knows who is on active drug and who is receiving an active drug, unless there is an urgent safety issue. Then a patient may be "unblinded", and the treating physician is informed about what they are receiving. There are also specific contractual arrangements with the investigators; they must not be overpaid, nor given extra financial incentives. They must be paid only for their work on the project. For example, it is forbidden to give investigators extra money if they recruit more patients than other investigators. Finally, there is an obligation to publish all the data within 12 months of the end of the study.

The scientist – volunteer relationship

In the early stages of the trial, independent of whether it is an experiment or whether it is a clinical trial, the question is whether the scientists running the experiment would be on the ground with the subjects at the stage of their admission to the trial facility, doing the blood pressure tests, swabs, giving medicines and discussing their questions, or would this be done by their assistants only? The very first encounter in the play between clinician and volunteer, Dr James and Connie, gives rise already to the question as to what kind of scenario the play is taking as its focus: where, in a real pharmaceutical company testing its new drugs on humans, would we find the contexts described in the play? The play begins with Dr James asking Connie: "have you ever suffered from depression?" (2012: 5). The play then continues with the discussion between Dr James and Connie of what it means to be depressed and whether Connie herself is depressed. Dr James proceeds to ask Connie about pregnancy, contraception, smoking, drinking, drugs, medicines, irritable bowel syndrome, cancer (specifically of throat, lungs and skin), arthritis and diabetes. What the play seems to be covering here is anything that could possibly have an effect or be related to the drug in question, or even further, where they do not expect anything, but they are testing for those influences anyway. According to Grassby and Macfadden, this range of questions, and the fact that the questions are asked by the doctor involved in the trial, rather than an assistant of some kind, makes sense in comparison to their experience in drugs trials. Lappin adds that there would be a very close relationship with patients and medical staff at this first stage.

However, Grassby, Lappin and Macfadden also agree that the play shows too much of familiarity between the doctor and the patients, which according to Macfadden,

> most people in the profession would probably view as inappropriate doctor/patient contact, for example Dr James telling Connie about her previous affairs and her love life [2012: 61-62]. Even in a psychotherapy situation most people would view such behaviour as not within the boundaries of normal practice. In a clinical trial it is even more important to remain neutral to the subject and ask open ended questions- so their responses are not influenced by their personal feelings towards the investigator.

Especially the scene in which Dr James suggests that the male volunteer, Tristan, could give the urine sample while she is present is certainly not part of what would happen in real medical circumstances, as Lappin points out "those samples are not normally supervised, there are rooms that you go into and you produce the samples and they collect it, and they wouldn't mix male and female".

A further example of this over-familiarity is the long joke that Dr James tells Connie

> There is this medic at a conference and he has fallen for a girl there who hasn't looked twice at him. He knows dopamine is the initial trigger for falling in love but also that dopamine is stimulated a new, exciting experiences. To try and get the girl he arranges for them to go bungee jumping together to set up his own chemical reaction. The instructor ties them together and they stand over this incredible valley and he has got his arms around her and they fall long into this incredible, adrenalin/filled rush – and their dopamine levels go higher. Eventually they get lifted back onto the bridge, they get their breath back and he looks into her eyes and says, 'wasn't that amazing!' and breathless she answers, 'yes and isn't the instructor handsome!' (2012: 22)

Macfadden observes that it is not so much the question of whether this is an in-joke amongst psychiatrists but that this is an instance where more intimate conversation takes place and "a breaching of the objectivity that one would expect from a physician interacting with a subject when testing a psychiatric medicine".

All three specialists confirm that scientists involved in drugs trials, no matter at what stage, would never know which patient received the real drug and which received a placebo. It is thus not realistic that Dr James knows that Tristan is receiving a placebo and not the drug. In consequence, it is equally not realistic that her own reporting is tested as well for bias (i.e., Tristan in fact gets the drug, not the placebo). Macfadden explains that this would not happen in real life scenarios,

> as you can't test investigators that way and especially because those involved as researchers in such a procedure would never be trusted with the knowledge of who is getting the real drug and who is getting the placebo—not until the end of the experiment—as that would introduce too much bias, especially in psychiatry where many patients respond to a placebo pill only, and thus one needs to be as neutral as possible.

Knowledge of and assumptions about psychology

Across the play, the volunteers, Connie and Tristan, as well as the scientists, Dr James and Dr Sealey, talk about the testing of drug-related aspects of psychology and psychiatry in general, and with regard to depression in particular. Given the play's emphasis on the volunteers, I will consider them first in this context. Connie is a psychology student and asks Dr James directly whether her knowledge of the Stroop test may or may not interfere with the results. Dr James explains: "In most cases being aware of your own bias doesn't actually mean you can affect that bias" (2012: 19). Macfadden confirms this. Grassby, however, is of the opinion that if the subject knows the test, knowledge can be a problem. In some cases, Macfadden adds "if you repeat a psychological test there is a learning effect the second time around". He argues that knowing about the contents of tests in general may not matter as long as the subject did not undergo the test too recently.

The play demonstrates in dramatically interesting detail how the two volunteers break every rule in the book. They go out of the prescribed area, they smoke, they use their phones, and they have sex. Should they not be eliminated from the data set? Lappin explains, first of all, that the rule not to use mobile phones is not something he recognises from the drugs trials he was involved in. In terms of the problematic behaviour, he points out that volunteers get compensated financially for doing a trial. In case of minor infringements of their contracts, they get fined and the money they receive in the end goes down. In case of major infringements, they are excluded from the trial and do not receive any money. The infringements presented in the play would certainly count as major. Macfadden confirms that on the safety trials it might be appropriate to have volunteers in overnight and if one where to lose a certain person for hours at a time, one may need to eliminate them, but it is a judgement call of the investigator. "If, however, they are missing for 12 hours one would certainly eliminate them and then they might be removed from the project as unreliable". Macfadden adds that in describing the experiment, the assumption is that there might be "protocol violators" and the scientists may need to exclude those person's data and start fresh with another person until they have the requisite number of subjects necessary. Therefore, in those properly protocoled experiments it would not ruin an experiment if one or two subjects had to be removed from the project.

The play references general attitudes towards mental illness with the assumption that mentally ill patients rock to and fro (2012: 31). Grassby comments that such a pattern of movement is normally due to the side effects of the drugs they are given, anti-psychotics, and not part of the mental illness itself. Lappin adds that there is a whole range of repetitive behaviour, with rocking or walking up and down among them. According to Grassby, patients know that they are doing it and could try to stop doing it for a short period of time. Macfadden explains that people with severe mental illness like schizophrenia may rock back and forth, but medication can make this worse.

The constellations in the play are interactions between the volunteers, Connie and Tristan, or between Dr James and one or both of the volunteers, and interactions between Dr James and her line manager, Dr Toby Sealey. They discuss the rationale behind the development of new drugs, with Toby arguing: "It's why we are developing new generations of ADs in the first place" (2012: 24). Macfadden comments that pharmaceutical companies attempt to develop improved, differentiated products. Toby wants to be associated with something that is eventually improved. In the same context Dr James continues with "Because the old ones have been discredited", to which Toby responds: "No they haven't been discredited, the studies that discredited our original trials have themselves been discredited now" (2012: 24). Macfadden comments that there is inaccuracy here, because nothing has really been discredited per-se regarding antidepressant clinical trials, although there have been different interpretations of the data through the years.

The play also references the image of psychiatry as a discipline within medicine. In a long speech "at an industry event" (2012: 28), Dr Sealey introduces himself like this: "I am Toby, I 'm a psychiatrist, I'm afraid" (2012: 28). Then he talks about the serious representatives of medicine, the heart surgeons, in comparison to the Cinderella of medicine, psychiatry. Psychiatrist Macfadden confirms that psychiatry is indeed commonly disparaged by other specialities in medicine because it is not always an evidence-based science and there are a lot of variations in clinical practice amongst psychiatrists. For this speech, Toby brings a real brain in a bucket with him. Macfadden find this unusual, arguing that it is also possibly unethical & maybe illegal: "you just can't harvest body parts for the purpose of a talk".

The actual drugs trial

When Dr James administers the first dose, 25 milligrams of the agent RLU37, she gives Tristan a pill "that has been emptied into a plastic cup and then a plastic cup of water to wash it down with" (2012: 12). Dr James says "5, 4, 3, 2, 1", he then swallows it, his mouth is checked, Connie is next, Dr James indicates she should wait, she does. Dr James repeats her "5, 4, 3, 2, 1". "Connie takes hers, her mouth is checked, it continues theoretically with other volunteers" (2012: 86). Macfadden comments on this description of the process in the play as accurate if it were a drug trial, but possibly a little too elaborate for the testing for security that he considers the scenario in the play to represent. Lappin also notes in the context of the medical tests and their application that what normally would happen is that one person is dosed and then a team would wait for several hours to give the same dose and medication to the next person. "That is a rule that they have to stagger because if they give everybody the dose and then there is a problem then they will all have the problem. If you stagger them, only one gets the problem".

In the play the dosage increases from 20-50 milligram and so on upwards and later goes on to 50-100-150 milligrams. Macfadden comments that this is what would indeed happen, it is called a single ascending dose and a multiple ascending dose, which is the format in which one would use to test the safety intolerability and try to find out the maximum tolerated dose when people start to get side effects.

The play suggests that nicotine inflates dopamine levels. Macfadden comments that nicotine stimulates dopamine but not correct to say that it elevates dopamine for "hours". Connie and Tristan talk about the telemetry devices which they themselves detach and reattach. According to Macfadden this is possible, but the investigator would know when exactly at what time it came off and exactly at time it was put on again just as doctors would definitely not know who is on the placebo and who is not on the real drug and so there is no opportunity for them to tell the subjects whether they are on placebo or not. Macfadden adds here that in the US it is considered unethical of the doctors to give placebos in the first place so Dr James's comments in this regard would not be applicable to the US but might apply in the UK. The side effects that the play mentions are irritability, paranoia, aggression, extra blinking response. They are the type of thing one would want to see early in a healthy volunteer, maybe in a single day but again not in a month long locked procedure.

Towards the end of the play, when Connie and Tristan have developed a love relationship and are not sure whether their feelings are real or the result of the drugs, we have the situation where Connie gets her tablets, another increase of the dose. The doctor fails to check her mouth, Connie rushes to Tristan and kisses him full on the mouth. She has kept her pill in her mouth and in the kiss transfers it to him. She assumes that he is given the placebo and wants him to have the real drug. However, he has been getting the drug all along, so on this occasion in effect he gets a major increase of the dose that he had been given before. He should have been going from 200 to 250 but does go from 200 to 500. Within seconds, Tristan "makes a strange sound, he staggers, loses consciousness, falls to the fall, stiffens. His limbs jerk and twitch, his mouth gurns, he is fitting. He bleeds from his mouth and wets himself, it is horrific" (89-90). In this context the experts comment that it is not likely that a patient will be bolting away and transferring a pill to another patient like this because it is more likely that they are receiving their pills independent of each other: "typically it is a relatively private encounter between the study staff and subject when you give the person the medicine" (Macfadden). One reason for this is that one would not want to see what the other person is getting. Lappin confirms that to go from fairly mild symptoms to symptoms described in the play by more than doubling the dose is extremely unlikely. Grassby adds that the kind of side effects or the amount of side effects could happen, but they would not happen that fast.

Tristan then suffers from "transient global amnesia" and he also has got "tardive dyskinesia". Macfadden comments that with tardive dyskinesia people can rock back and forth but that is the condition that people can get when they take anti-psychotic medications usually at a high dose for a very long time. This effect would not likely happen after a single dose in such an individual even if it is a very high dose. This is medically incorrect for a number of reasons: the effect would be coming from a different kind of medication and people need to take higher doses over a long period of time. The amnesia is described as transient. Transient means, according to Macfadden, that it fades away so it should decrease but it does not seem to decrease in Tristan: so, there is an inconsistency there. The description of Tristan's symptoms rather suggests that he suffered a "cerebral vascular incident, i.e., lack of blood flow to the brain". The other inconsistency is that the play suggests that Tristan has undergone a blood transfusion. That is strictly speaking not accurate "as in the case of an overdose like this one would not get a blood transfusion but a dialysis".

The play reveals that Tristan had a history of seizures in childhood, which was undisclosed (2012: 96) and Dr Sealey blames the strong effect of the overdose on that. Macfadden comments this is an example of somebody who may be hiding symptoms for the purpose of being eligible for a clinical trial. It was not discussed whether the trial team would rely on self-disclosure or whether they would ask for medical records of the volunteers.

The end of the play suggests in the stage directions that Tristan has recovered sufficiently to be discharged from hospital, but he remains vulnerable, his physicality is of a different man without some of the former bounce. It is left unclear whether it is something that he would be like forever, whether he is forever damaged in some form, or whether this is something that he is like now and there might be a chance of further improvement. Macfadden points out that this is unlikely to be the result of a single dose, but it is not impossible because the overdose might have caused a minor stroke, which would in turn leave more permanent damage.

Conclusion

To conclude, Macfadden thinks that the idea of confusing a placebo response with developing real feelings is an intriguing notion. He also thinks that some of the things that he referred to and I asked him about would not be picked up easily by someone who is not a specialist. Therefore, for the conventional spectator who does not have this specialist knowledge, it will not be received as preposterous or fictional, as a figment of the imagination. People might recognise that the doctor should not really be that close to people and talking about their love life but other than that it was fun.

CHAPTER ELEVEN

"AN OPPORTUNITY OF A LIFETIME"? ETHICAL CONSIDERATIONS OF CASTING CHILDREN IN PLAYS WITH "ADULT THEMES"

Contextualisation

In 2013 I began working with Swiss-born, New Zealand-based psychologist Amanda Maria Young-Hauser on a book (to be published with Cambridge Scholars Publishing in August 2018) on *Paedophilia and Child Sexual Abuse in Drama and Theatre.* In our research and discussions, we came across the ethical implications of casting child actors in roles of children who are subjected to sexual abuse. We decided not to include a detailed discussion of this aspect of our topic in our book. In the text below, not previously published, I provide my position on this debate from a consciousness studies angle.

Introduction

A good number of plays, past and present, or television drama or films, for that matter, have characters who are not adults. The term *adult* is defined, in this context, as a person who has reached the legal age of majority, which for many countries across the world is eighteen onwards. The question that arises for the team of any production of such a play is whether to cast the characters of children and adolescents/teenagers with actors of an age similar to that of the characters, or with (young-looking) adults. For the 1974 National Theatre production of *Spring Awakening* by Frank Wedekind, for example, the adolescents were played by young adults (with Michael Kitchen aged 26, Jenny Agutter aged 22, and Peter Firth aged 21). Ethical issues arise with child actors in terms of the potentially damaging implications of stardom. In this article, however, I focus on the issues arising from the impact that the subject matter may have on the child actor. I summarise the important work Ott has done on this topic in her MA thesis in 2009 at the University of Oregon, USA, expand this with more recent examples, and develop an additional perspective from the context of consciousness studies to broaden the base for further discussion and research, for parents to make informed decisions about the lives of their children, and to inform policies of good practice in the entertainment industry.

Case studies: Ott and beyond

Ott considers four case studies of "plays with adult themes": *The Pain and the Itch* by Bruce Norris, in which the character of four-year-old Kayla is present when her parents have "intense, obscenity-laced screaming matches", and on one occasion she enters with one hand inside her pull-ups, which the audience interprets correctly as indicating that her genitals are inflamed and itchy from a sexually transmitted disease, presumably from her uncle (Ott 2009: 1, 28). With regard to a production of *The Trojan Women* by Euripides, Ott discusses social violence, loss and grief as potentially problematic contents, moving to physical abuse and torture in Martin McDonagh's *The Pillowman,* and ends with the topic of child suicide in Pirandello's *Six Characters in Search of an Author* in the version by Headlong / Rupert Goold and Ben Power (2008). The age range of the child actors in those productions was five to fourteen. Only the young girl in *Six Characters* was played by a young-looking adult actor, probably because of the dangers involved for a younger person in carrying off the drowning in a fish tank special effect for her suicide scene.

Ott discusses a range of positions and options. Rating systems, similar to those for cinema and TV audiences, might help, but it is also problematic to justify setting a specific age limit before a child actor can safely engage with specific adult material, because children develop at different rates within a spectrum of development. Parents have the legal and ethical role of protecting and guiding their children, and "Involving a child in a positive way rather than using them for their naïve services is the ethical option" (Ott 2009: 18). In terms of artistic merits, involving child actors on stage in the context of adult themes may have a shock effect on the audience and thus allow an audience to become engaged in a new way. However, Ott also warns: "On the other hand, some productions use the child on stage as a token shock element: manipulating the audience into an unearned, strong emotional response. This decision deserves pause" (2009: 22).

In the context of her case studies, Ott identifies in official statements on websites and in letters to the editor supported by her own interviews, the ways in which company representatives and parents deal with the challenges of casting children in plays with adult material. In one company, the children were under constant supervision during rehearsals and performances. One parent noted that her child did not understand the meaning of some of the words used on stage and was happy with that as sufficient to ensure the child would not be harmed by such language, even if exposed to it on a daily basis over the rehearsal period and the production's run in the theatre. When pornography was playing on the on-stage TV set, cast and director ensured the children's backs were turned. The mother of one of the girls performing in *The Pain and the Itch*, said: "I would call her a casualty if we had said no and deprived her of the opportunity of a lifetime because we were more interested in insulating our world from what others might think than putting her interests first" (Ott 2009: 34).

Where the company does not provide reassurance of some kind to audiences that they did take care of the child actors, problems can arise. For example, Ott left the theatre after the performance of the Goold / Power production of *Six Characters* "with many questions and concerns wishing that there had been a talk-back with the cast and crew to attend. More communication with the audience would have benefited this production that I experienced" (2009: 61). Another problem is that in some instances, according to Ott, the casting of a child actor for a child character without thorough prior reassurances of the audience is actually not helping the cause of the play. She quotes the critic of the *Chicago Tribune* in the review of *The Pain and the Itch* that "instead of drawing the audience in, the child actor in Steppenwolf's production of "pulled audiences out of the world of the play because of the concerns her presence raised" (Ott 2009: 33, quoting Istel 2005: 115). She also points out that some authors do not provide instructions as to the age of the actors playing the child characters (such as McDonagh for *The Pillowman* (2009: 49). In contrast, Jennifer Healey adds an author's note to her play *The Nether* (2014):

> It is important to cast Iris with an actress who will appear on stage as a prepubescent girl. The child actor takes the audience *out* of the play (Bert States, *Great Reckonings in Little Rooms: On the Phenomenology of Theatre*, Oakland: University of California Press, 1987), which is desirable considering the contents of her scenes. The audience is assured nothing awful will be enacted upon the child, whereas they have no such confidence with an adult posing as a child. A young actress also adds warmth, which is critical to the chemistry of the play. (2014)

To provide the context for this, The *Nether* of the title is the former Internet, which has taken over much of the world, to the extent that some people choose to cross over and continue living there permanently. Morris is a young female detective working to maintain law and order in the Nether; she is investigating business man Sims, who has developed an area of the Nether in which "in-world" people can take on alternative identities and engage in activities considered immoral and criminal in conventional current and future ethical and legal contexts. Sims brings his customers, in their alternative identities, together with Iris, herself an avatar creature of the Nether, a child, with whom the customers then can have sex, and then they can kill her with an axe. Iris appears on stage, as does Sims in his avatar identity Papa, and one of Papa/Sims's customers, Woodnut, who turns out to be an agent working for Morris and her force. Iris turns out to be the avatar of Doyle, a middle-aged male science teacher, whom Morris also interrogates. In his review for the *Telegraph*, Spencer insists that "you never worry that the young girl playing the beautiful Iris in the nether world will be traumatised by the play she is appearing in."

Spencer did voice concern about the well-being of the 13-year old actor playing the "original party piece" in Philip Ridley's *Mercury Fur* (2005). The play is set in London in a dystopian future characterised by violence and a breakdown of law and order to the extent that the government decides to have the army systematically eliminate the population of entire areas. The play focuses on two male teenagers, Darren and Elliott (17 and 15 respectively), who work for a slightly older man, helping him organise parties in derelict houses with a "party piece" as central attraction for the client, the party guest. In this case the party piece is a 10-year old Asian boy who will help the guest fulfil his Vietnam-war inspired fantasies, which Darren and Elliott will film for him on a camcorder—thus creating a real-life snuff movie. The party-piece is sickly and frail and dies before the guest can begin the torture—he is replaced by the older boy who found shelter in the derelict house and has joined Darren and Elliott in preparing for the party. The sexual dimension of the torture and murder of the original party piece and its eventual replacement is evident in the text. All violence happens off-stage, the audience hears screams, but does not see any violent act being carried out, only the result when the stand-in party piece returns to stage from the torture in its first stages.

It may not be as much of an ethical issue, some of Ott's arguments seem to imply, if the characters and actors are older, closer to the age of majority, as, for example, in *Scarborough* by Fiona Evans (Royal Court, London, 2008). In the first half of this play, we see 15-year-old Daz with his 29-year-old teacher Lauren in a Scarborough bed and breakfast, while in the second part of the play, the characters in the same room, and with virtually the same lines, are 15-year-old Beth and her 29-year-old teacher Aiden. Lauren and Aiden reveal to Daz and Beth, respectively, that they want to end their relationship, which they had engaged in only to have some fun, and because they are in a long-term relationship, with Chris. Chris, now 47, was Lauren's male swimming coach who seduced her when she was thirteen. Chris, now 47, was Aiden's female swimming coach who seduced him when he was thirteen years old. Aiden is about to marry Chris, and Lauren is about to marry Chris. Thus, the play invokes the victim-abuser cycle characteristic of paedophilia, the suggestion that often a person abused as a child becomes an abuser later in life. *Scarborough* also suggests that the adults have more power (in this case to break off the relationship), and the child is always the one to suffer most (Billington 2008).

To address the issues she raises, Ott proposes a set of guidelines covering parental involvement, company and cast involvement, supervision, aspects of the rehearsal process, communicating with the community, prospective and actual audiences, as exit interview and evaluation. All these guidelines work on the basis of what the child actor perceives through their senses of the potentially problematic contents of the play, the extent they understand the contents correctly, and how they are supported in dealing with the contents if they do understand it. This perceptual framework does not, however, take into account possible less tangible, but nevertheless equally important, aspects.

Spirituality and chakras: a new perspective

In my 2013 book *Observing Theatre: Spirituality and Subjectivity in the Performing Arts*, I introduced the philosophy of German geobiologist Hans Binder as the basis for discussions of aspects of theatre as varied as *nostalgia* in theatre, intuitive collaboration, praise of acting in theatre criticism, practice as research, digital performance, theatre and philosophy, the canon, applied theatre and aspects of acting including helping actors cope with stage fright. For the remainder of this article, I will apply his thinking to the ethical implications of having children perform in contexts of adult themes in theatre, film and television.

Binder explains his background and the development of his abilities in the following way. Even as a child, he had a special relationship with nature because, when he was one with nature, he was able to perceive the aura of many trees and plants as well as being allowed to hear the fundamental oscillation of the universe, the OM sound of nature. This should, however, gain greater significance only in the second half of his life. He learned the crafts of reinforced concrete construction and horticulture and was very successful in these areas for decades. In horticulture, he had a major business, which he gave up when his skills to investigate fault zones in houses, and to provide analyses of persons were in such demand that he was able to dedicate himself to them alone. In earlier times he used to dig deep into the gardens of the people, today he can do that in their subconscious minds to help them with the design of their lives. Until all was ready, he was able to learn a lot through training and studies. To this day, he continues researching and experimenting on his own in the field of consciousness studies. He has supplemented his natural talents with the study of the Veda, of Vastu, dowsing, and geomancy, and has acquired knowledge of all the materials and radiations, as well as the anatomy of all human body parts, organs and all their features. This bundled set of skills and all the knowledge he acquired are invested into all the holistic analyses and in development and manufacture of products.

The entire universe, according to Binder, can be understood as an energy field that integrates smaller units also as energy fields and interacts with the parent field, and other fields, since they are in turn connected to each other via the "everything that is" principle. Each planet has therefore its own energy field and is connected via the "unified field of natural law" again with the great whole. On Earth, there are then earth energy fields at each level of manifestation, for all plants and each plant, and for all animals and for each animal, and for all people and every individual (2013: 105). Everything that people have ever created and create, have manufactured and manufacture, in what form and with what material whatsoever, and what people have ever thought and think at this very moment, also represents energy fields, brought into being by the respective activities of manufacturing, creating and thinking. All levels of complex energy fields interact with each other and react to each other, in the sense that like attracts like in turn (2013: 106).

Each theatre production has its own energy field, which is an amalgam of the energy fields of the contents, the writer, the production team, and the performers. When the production is shown on stage, the energy field of the production further merges with the energy fields of the spectators at each performance. The same applies for the creation and screening and broadcasting of radio, film and television contents. The energy field of a theatre, film or television production affects all people involved in the production, whether they know it or not. It stands to reason that the production of a play "with adult themes", such as the ones discussed above, will develop an energy field that is informed by those themes, and the ways in which the cast and crew think about the play, its themes, and themselves in relation to the themes. From an objective angle, the cast and crew's thoughts may all be morally sound and ethically acceptable, but this still means that while working on the production, a lot of thinking about the contents is going on for both cast and crew, and the energy field of the production reflects that thinking about that subject. No matter how carefully a child actor's parents and chaperones and wranglers and directors and fellow-actors try to prevent any harm coming to the child actor because of the adult material, and even if all the criteria developed by Ott are adhered to, the energy field is still in existence. Potentially, this energy field will have a stronger impact on the child actor than on the adults involved in the production. This has to do with the way energy is conceptualised in this context, and the ways in which it is absorbed, stored and used.

In Sanskrit, the term *prana* is translated as *absolute energy*, and the Chinese call it *chi*. The human energy system consists of:

the subtle energy body
the *chakras*
the *nadis*, also known as energy channels

The *nadis* have the task of supplying the energy bodies with life energy that was previously created in the *chakras*. In the human body there are a few thousand energy channels. The most important ones are called *Ida*, *Pingala* and *Sushumna*—we know them also from acupuncture, where they are known to us as meridians.

Within the human energy system, the *chakras* serve as the receiving stations, transformers and distributors of the various frequencies of *prana*. The *chakras* draw certain energies from the subtle bodies as well as from the environment and especially from the universe, transform those energies and, in turn, pass them on via the *nadis* back to the subtle bodies. Body, soul and spirit need these energies for their preservation and development. There are ancient writings that describe a number of over 80 000 *chakras* in the human body, with the result that there is hardly a point in the human body that is not suitable and intended for the reception, conversion and transmission of energies. However, most of these *chakras* are very small and play only a minor role in the energy system of the person. There are about forty minor *chakras*, which are of greater importance. The most important of these are located in the spleen area, in the neck, the palms and the soles. The seven major *chakras* that lie along a vertical axis at the front centre of the body are critical to the function of the most basic and most essential areas of the human body, mind and soul.

The *chakras* also take up vibrations directly from the environment, vibrations that match their respective frequencies. In this way they connect us through their various functions with the events in our environment, in nature and in the universe, by serving as aerials for the whole range of energy vibrations and information that go beyond the physical realm. They are the openings that connect us with the unlimited world of subtler energies. Similarly, the *chakras* radiate energy directly into the environment, thus changing the atmosphere around us. Through the *chakras* we can send out healing vibrations and conscious or unconscious messages and thus influence people, situations and even matter in a positive and negative sense (2013: 142-4).

The seven main chakras relate closely to major bodily and mental human functions. The root *chakra, muladhara – chakra* is located between anus and genitals, connected to the tailbone, and opens downwards. It is associated with the fiery-red colour, the element of earth, and the sense of smell. It is symbolised by the four-petalled lotus, its fundamental principle is physical will (as opposed to spiritual will of the seventh chakra). In the body, it is associated with the spine, bones, teeth, and nails, with anus, rectum, colon, prostate, blood and cell structure, as well as the adrenal gland. In astrological terms, the root chakra is associated with Mars / Aries, Taurus, Scorpio / Pluto, and Capricorn / Saturn. The root chakra links us to the physical world and channels universal energy to the level of physical energy. If it functions in harmony, it allows us to be well-grounded, full of energy, stability, contentment, and inner strength. If the root *chakra* is out of balance, it can function in a disharmonious manner or in terms of sub-function. In the case of dysfunction, thinking and action focus predominantly on material possession and security, on sensual stimuli and indulgence. People thus afflicted will have difficulties to give and receive openly and honestly. Their inability to let go and their desire to hang on to things often lead to constipation and obesity. In case of sub-function, people tend to be weak, with a lack of mental and physical resilience. They have increased feelings of insecurity, of having no proper grounding below their feet, and they perceive life as a burden.

The second chakra is the sacral chakra (*svadhisthana*). It is located above the genitals, linked to the sacral bone, and opens to the front. Its colour is orange, it is associated with the element of water, the sense of taste, and with the symbol of the six-petalled lotus. Its fundamental principle is the creative procreation of being. The physical associations are the area of the pelvis, organs of procreation, kidneys, bladder, and liquid substances of the body. Associated glands are ovaries, prostate and testicles. The sacral chakra is the centre of original, unmediated emotions, sexual energies and creative forces, and also the centre of the feminine principle. Through the sacral chakra we are part of the fertilising and receiving energies that permeate all of nature. If their sacral chakra is in balance and harmony, people will feel they are flowing naturally with life, and with their feelings. Disharmony of this chakra results in all kinds of problems with sexuality, sub-function takes the form a lack of feeling of self-worth, as well as emotional, mental and sexual callousness, depression, aggression and blaming others.

The third chakra is the solar plexus chakra (*manipura*), which is located by the width of two fingers above the navel. It opens to the front. Its colour is yellow to golden yellow, associated with the element of fire, and is symbolised by the ten-petalled lotus. The solar plexus chakra is associated with the lower back, the nervous system, the psyche, stomach, digestive system, liver, gall and spleen. The related gland is the pancreas. In the context of astrology, the solar plexus chakra is associated with Leo / Sun, Sagittarius / Jupiter, Virgo / Mercury and Mars. Through the solar plexus chakra, we absorb the energy of the sun and of the universe; we engage actively through this chakra with other people and the world, and this chakra governs our interpersonal relationships, preferences and antipathies. It is the seat of personality. The solar plexus chakra purifies the energies generated in the root and sacral chakras, channels and makes use of their creative energies consciously, and manifests the energies generated by the fourth to seventh chakras in the material world. On a physical level, the liver, governed by the solar plexus chakra, has the task, in conjunction with the digestive system, to analyse food, to separate useful and useless components, and to transform the former and pass them on to appropriate places in the body. When this chakra functions in harmony and balance, we feel inner harmony and peace with ourselves, with life and our position within it. We can accept ourselves, our feelings, desires and experiences in life fully and can respect the feelings and idiosyncrasies of other people. Because this chakra is associated with the element of fire, harmonious functioning of this chakra allows us to be full of inner light and full of strength, enveloping our bodies with light, which protects us from adverse influences and has a good influence on the environment.

Disharmonious functioning of the solar plexus chakra leads to the need for people to want to influence everything according to their own wishes, and to control our inner and outer world, to exercise power and to conquer.

This is driven by inner restlessness and dissatisfaction. They seek in the outside world the kind of confirmation and satisfaction that they lack inwardly. They develop an incredible level of activity, with which they seek to cover up the nagging feeling of incompetence. They lack serenity and they find it difficult to let go and relax. Certain that they can achieve everything, they tend to control and suppress undesired feelings and emotions. These accumulate and are released in due course in the form of irritability and uncontrollable explosions of anger. Sub-functioning of the solar plexus chakra leads to people feeling despondent and disheartened. They see walls and obstacles everywhere.

The fourth chakra is the heart chakra (*anahata*). It is located in the middle of the chest at the level of the heart and opens to the front. Its colour is green, pink and golden; it is associated with the element of air, and the sense of touch. It is symbolised by the twelve-petalled lotus. In terms of body, it is associated with the heart, the upper back with ribcage and thoracic cavity, the lower part of the lungs, blood and the blood circulation system, and the skin. In terms of gland, the heart chakra is associated with the thymus gland. Its astrological associations are Leo / Sun, Libra / Venus, and Saturn. In the heart chakra, the three lower and the three higher chakras are linked. The chakra provides us with the ability to empathise and to feel with others. We perceive the beauty of nature, of the harmony of music, of the performing arts and poetry. Here, images, words and sounds are translated into feelings. If in harmony, the heart chakra is the centre of unconditional love, which exists only for its own sake, and which you cannot own or lose. We radiate natural warmth, geniality and happiness, which opens the hearts of other people, generates trust and gives joy. Compassion and readiness to help are further characteristics resulting from a balanced heart chakra. Our feelings are free of turmoil and conflicts, free of doubt and uncertainty.

If the heart chakra's function is disharmonious, people might still want to give as much as possible, but that attitude is not unconditional, but related to expectations, and when those are not fulfilled, they people get frustrated and unhappy. Sub-function makes people easily vulnerable, and dependent on the love and affection of others. If such a person is then rejected, they feel deeply hurt, especially if they were courageous enough for once to open up. They the retreat even more into their shell, afraid of further hurt. If a person's heart chakra is completely closed up, this will show in their coldness, apathy and heartlessness. Those people need particularly strong stimuli to feel anything at all.

The fifth chakra is the throat chakra (*vishuddha*). It is located between the pit of the neck and the larynx. It arises from the cervical spine and opens to the front. Its colour is light blue, also silvery and green-blue; it is associated with the element of ether, and the sense of hearing. Its symbol is the sixteen-petalled lotus. In terms of the body, it relates to the areas or throat, neck and jaws, ears, voice, vocal cords, trachea, bronchia, upper areas of the lungs, oesophagus, and arms. The related gland is the thyroid, the astrological associations are Gemini / Mercury, Mars, Taurus / Venus, Aquarius / Jupiter. The throat chakra is the centre of human expressiveness, communication and inspiration. It serves as the bridge between thinking and feeling, between our impulses and reactions to them, and we express everything that is within us through the throat chakra. When this chakra is in harmony, we are able to express without fear our feelings, thoughts and inner insights. We can reveal our weaknesses just as well as we are able to show our strengths. While we can express ourselves fully, we can also remain silent and listen to others with our hearts and with inner understanding. Our language is full of imagination but also very clear, full, and melodious. When faced with difficulties and obstacles, we remain true to ourselves, which includes the ability to say "no". We are not influenced or engrossed by the opinions of others, but we maintain our independence, freedom and self-determination.

If the throat chakra lacks harmony, the communication between mind and body is disturbed. As a result, either people find it difficult to reflect about their feelings; feelings are pent up and released through rash action. Or people cocoon themselves within rational thinking, denying the existence and the wisdom of their feelings. Their way of speaking is either unpolished and rough, or rather matter-of-fact and cool, often accompanied by stuttering. The voice tends to be relatively loud, but without deeper content. These people will not allow themselves to come across as weak but try to present themselves as strong at all costs, exposing themselves to much pressure in this way. They use their language to manipulate others or try to attract attention by their ceaseless stream of talking. Sub-function of the throat chakra leads to a similar difficulty to express oneself, but people thus affected are rather withdrawn and shy, or they tend to talk only about inconsequential things of outward life. When pressed to say something about what they think deep down, they tend to feel as if they have a lump in their throat, and their voice sounds pressured. They tend to orient their thinking and behaviour according to what they think other people will appreciate, and do not know all that much about what they want themselves.

The sixth chakra is also called the third eye (*ajna*). It is located a finger's width above the root of the nose in the middle of the forehead. It opens to the front. Its colour is indigo blue, also yellow and violet. It relates to all the senses, also in the form of extrasensory perception. It is symbolised by a 96-petalled lotus. In terms of the body, it is associated with the face, eyes, ears, nose, sinuses, cerebellum, and central nervous system. The related gland is the pituitary gland. Astrological associations are Mercury, Sagittarius / Jupiter, Aquarius / Uranus, and Pisces / Neptune. The forehead-chakra, or third eye, is the seat of the highest mental powers, of the ability of differentiation, of memory, and will, and on the physical level it is the command centre of the central nervous system. It is also the link between soul and mind. If this chakra functions in harmony, we have an alert mind that allows us insights of deep philosophical truths. We realise increasingly that the outward appearance of things represents symbols in which a mental principle manifests on the material level. The more the third eye is developed, the more our thinking is based on a direct, inner realisation of reality. Abilities such a clairvoyance and insights into and visions of other dimensions emerge in dream or in meditation. In disharmony, people rely too much, sometimes exclusively, on their intellect and reason. As a result, people accept as truth only what they can grasp on that intellectual level. If people do have access to deeper levels, they are not able to understand the true meaning of the images perceived at those deeper levels. The images mix with one's own ideas and phantasies, becoming so dominant in the process that one can lose all relation to reality. In case of a sub-function of the third eye, people will be open only to the outward, visible world, and their lives will be determined by material desires, physical needs and unreflected emotions. They will reject spiritual truths because they consider them as based on mere illusion and representing only nonsensical dreams without relation to reality. Their thinking is geared predominantly towards prevailing opinions. In demanding situations, such people will get forgetful. They also often have problems with their eyesight.

The seventh chakra, crown chakra (*shasrara*) is located at the highest point in the middle of the head and opens upwards. Its colour is violet, also white and golden. Its physical association is the cerebrum, the related gland is the pineal gland; the astrological associations are Capricorn / Saturn and Pisces / Neptune. It is symbolised by the 1000-petalled lotus. The crown chakra is the seat of the highest perfection humans can reach. It is the source and point of origin for all the other manifestations of the other chakra energies.

Conclusion

This very brief survey of the chakras demonstrates that their dysfunction or sub-function affects all areas of human life. If chakras absorb energies that are not conducive to their intended and balanced functioning, then the inappropriate energy blocks the chakras, prevents them from absorbing and radiating the energy they are meant to deal with, and this leads to dysfunction or subfunction. Adults can develop the ability to close their chakras against absorption of inappropriate energy. However, by definition, unlike adults, children cannot close off their chakras to prevent them from absorbing inappropriate energy. I established earlier in this article that the energy fields that form in the production process of a play for theatre, film or television with adult material are shaped and moulded by that contents. The resulting energy fields will be defined by and saturated with the energies relating to a combination of physical, emotional, and sexual violence, personal suffering and misery, and all other kinds of contents of events in life and resulting moods that we would rather like to avoid in daily life—indeed, members of many professions work hard in attempts at prevention and treatment. It stands to reason that subjecting children below the age of eighteen, who cannot close off their chakras for the purpose of self-protection, to such energy fields is highly problematic, because the energy of those fields must be assumed to be such that they will block all chakras, thus leading to a vast range of adverse effects, some of which I mentioned in the brief survey of chakras, their functions, and the symptoms of dysfunction and sub-function. This is why it is very important that parents listen to their inborn tendency to protect their children and act accordingly.

CHAPTER TWELVE

TOWARDS A THEATRE OF THE HEART

[First published in *Annals of the University of Bucharest: Philosophy Series*, LXVI: 1 (2017), 199–221, reprinted here with permission from the publisher]

Contextualisation

Across the last decade, I repeatedly, and increasingly encountered a kind of theatre practice that appealed strongly to me. Looking back at those encounters in the summer of 2016, I decided to develop a new concept to capture those experiences, *theatre of the heart*. I presented a shortened version of the article below as a public lecture at the invitation of the Faculty of Foreign Languages and Literatures at the University of Bucharest, Romania, in November 2016. The full text was later published in a journal published by the University of Bucharest.

Introduction: the heart

The conventional paradigm of science, with its predominantly positivist and materialistic contexts, seeks to exclude the subjective by definition. As a result, the methods and concepts of science have been unable to capture the subjective and have therefore ruled it out in favour of objectivity. Nonetheless, in recent years, science has begun to incorporate subjectivity in the form of first person approaches, especially in the context of consciousness studies (Varela and Shear 1999). A number of new research methods have evolved to emphasize the value of alternative, participatory modes of knowing, *e.g.*, Intuitive Inquiry, Organic Research, and Heuristic Inquiry (Anderson 1998, Clements 2004, Moustakas 1990). Tart advocated the development of *state-specific* sciences, suggesting that non-ordinary states of consciousness are likely to yield new insights not accessible by conventional methods (1972). This development owes much to the emphasis on subjectivity in non-Western traditions, and on the basis of research into that dimension, the recognition that subjectivity has existed in the Western context as well, making the alleged and assumed West/non-West binary opposite obsolete.

In my book *Observing Theatre: Spirituality and Subjectivity in the Performing Arts* (2013b), I introduced the philosophy of German geo-biologist Hans Binder as the basis for discussions of aspects of theatre as varied as *nostalgia* in theatre, intuitive collaboration, praise of acting in theatre criticism, practice as research, digital performance, theatre and philosophy, the canon, applied theatre and aspects of acting including helping actors cope with stage fright. In this article I want to continue this discussion with some thoughts on the nature of the heart in the context of theatre practice.

The relatively recent cognitive turn in theatre and performance studies (McConachie and Hart 2006) highlights an existing emphasis on ratio, on reason, on the biochemical and electro-physiological processes in the brain of theatre and performance makers and their audiences. Emotions, hitherto the major domain of the theatre, have been subsumed under the cognitive regime, and, in line with the materialistic paradigm characteristic of the scientific approach of cognitive science, have been reduced to brain activities.

Apparently in contrast to this emphasis on the brain is the endeavour to foreground the heart as much more than merely an organic pump, and to understand it in terms of the seat of the soul, and a core centre for human spiritual contexts (where spirituality is understood as relating to human nature in both religious and non-religious terms). In this article I want to explore the heart in relation to spirituality in general terms, and then consider the relevance of the insights of that exploration for theatre and performance practice. The purpose of this consideration is to re-assess the nature of the experiences of creating theatre and of watching a performance in a way that does not seek to reduce it to brain activities but allows a wider perspective that in turn can be shown not to rule out the dimension of brain activity as mutually exclusive. For the science-minded, the argument I present in this article can be operationalised, and turned into a set of hypotheses, which can be tested empirically.

The heart chakra

In the context of knowledge from a range of knowledge traditions, subtle energy is circulating in and around our physical body. Chinese medicine is aware of these energies in terms of the meridians of acupuncture, while in Indian philosophy there are the concepts of *prana* and of the *chakras* – centres in the body that serve as hubs for subtle energies flowing in up and down the spine. The heart serves as one such *chakra*. In Sanskrit it is called *anahata chakra*, its colours are green, pink and gold, it is associated with the element of air, and with the sense of touch. It is also referred to as twelve-leaved lotus. It is further associated with the heart, the upper back with ribcage and chest cavity, the lower area of the lungs, blood and blood circulation, and the skin. The associated gland is the thymus, which regulates growth and the lymphatic system, and stimulates and strengthens the immune system. In terms of astrology, the heart chakra is associated with leo/the sun, for warmth of feelings, geniality and generosity, with libra/Venus for contact, love and striving for harmony, and with Saturn relating to overcoming the individual ego as the basis for making selfless love possible in the first place.

As the fourth of seven chakras, the heart chakra forms the centre of the chakra system, connecting the lower three emotional-physical chakras (root, sacral, solar plexus) with the higher, mental-spiritual chakras (throat, forehead, crown). The symbol of the heart-chakra, the hexagon, demonstrates vividly how the energies of the three lower and upper chakras intertwine in the heart chakra. The heart chakra's relation to the element of air is what gives the heart flexibility. The heart is what gives us the ability to empathise and be attuned to one another, to resonate with each other, and to experience beauty of nature, in the harmony of music, in the performing arts and in poetry. In the heart chakra, images, words and sounds are transformed into feelings. The main task of the heart chakra in human life is unification through love. Any yearning for unity, harmony and love is expressed through the heart chakra. In its purified and fully opened form, the heart chakra is the centre of pure, unconditional love, which exists only for its own sake and which you cannot own or loose. The path of the heart leads from the loving and understanding "yes" to ourselves as the condition to the "yes" to the other and to life. This kind of "yes" creates a vibration that does not allow negative feelings to take hold – they dissolve. Loving ourselves, in the sense of lovingly accepting our very essence from the depths of our hearts can thus fundamentally transform and heal us – thus creating the basis for a fulfilling love for others, for compassion, understanding and deep enjoyment of life.

When the heart chakra is developed and open, people will radiate natural warmth, geniality and cheerfulness, which opens the hearts of those they interact with, creates trust and gives joy. Compassion and readiness to help others are, of course, matters. The feelings of such people are free from inner tumults and conflicts, of doubt and insecurity. They love for the sake of love, from the joy they feel when they give, without expecting anything in return. They feel secure and at home in all of creation. They do not know fear and engage in all they do with their whole hearts.

People whose heart chakras do not function in harmony might want to be there for others and want to give, but without being in tune with the source of love, they still, even unconsciously, expect to receive something in return (recognition or appreciation) and find themselves disappointed if those do not come. Sub-function of the heart chakra renders people easily vulnerable and dependent on the love and affection of others. If such a person is being rejected, they feel deeply hurt, especially if such rejection comes after they had had the courage, for once, to open up. This then leads to sadness and fear of further hurt. If the heart chakra is closed completely, people will come across as cold, unresponsive and heartless. Opening the heart does not mean to approach everyone carelessly with open arms and to hug everyone – it means employing the tools of intuition and wisdom to separate the wheat from the chaff.

The heart and non-linear theatre

According to St. Germain, one of the Ascended Masters in theosophy and other esoteric traditions, the balance of feminine and masculine values is the purpose of spiritual development across a long sequence of a living being's incarnations. Beings, whose masculine side is over-developed, are incarnated as humans on earth, since earth is considered, in this context, as an essentially feminine planet. Thus, the purpose for souls to be incarnated as humans on the planet earth is for them to be able to develop the feminine side of their nature, irrespective of whether they are born as man or woman (2004). For this development, the heart has a crucial role, as does a proper balance between heart and mind. The heart works through love, and vice versa. In the course of human development, the feminine, the heart and love will become more and more evident and foregrounded in all areas of life, including the arts and theatre. This means that art and theatre will deal more and more with these subjects and the contents will become more and more genuine (as opposed to the superficial nature of many romantic films, for example). New forms of expression of theatre will come into existence. The nature of theatre of the heart, for example, will be non-linear and multi-dimensional in presentation and reception.

Precursors
According to the psychology of the senses, although we may develop an ability to process sensory impressions as if they were simultaneous, and develop, therefore, considerable skills of multi-tasking, in fact our sensory perception is ultimately linear, we can process only one input at a time. "Multi-tasking" is therefore a misnomer. The theatre has sought to develop

modes of perception that allow true multi-dimensionality. Peter Brook's rehearsal exercise, which he demonstrated at a National Theatre platform performance (5 November 1993), is an example. From the stage, he asked the 1200 members of the seated audience in the semi-circular auditorium of the Olivier theatre to stand up. After a lot of shuffling, when everybody had stood up, Brook instructed the audience to sit down. Then he alerted them to the need to be prepared for standing up, for this activity to become more efficient and faster. The next time around he asked the audience to get up, speed and efficiency indeed improved. Then he alerted the audience that they had in fact at least 180-degree vision and instructed them not to look only at him at the centre of the stage, but to become aware of the full range of vision, of the other spectators. With that visual awareness, the impulse for getting up, and subsequently sitting down again, was to come from among the audience, not from him. This worked, a little hesitantly at first, and more and more in synchrony as Brook repeated the exercise four or five times. He concluded this part of the Platform session with the information that he did this exercise with his performers at his Théâtre des Bouffes du Nord in Paris for 45 minutes to an hour at the start of each rehearsal, so as to create synchronicity among the performers.

Different modes of perception were also central to the work of David Freeman with Opera Factory Zurich, where he staged a production of Mozart's opera *The Marriage of Figaro* in such a way that in addition to the main (and usually only) focus on stage, on the singers currently singing, the audience could also see other characters going about their business: for example, while Susanna and Figaro measure their new bedroom, Basilio is composing, the maids are baking bread, Marcellina has a cold and is helped by Bartolo by administering a hot foot bath, Antonio is tending to his garden, the Countess is having her breakfast, the Count is chasing after the maids, as is Cherubino. Freeman's London two-part production of *Morte d'Artur* started off in the Lyric Hammersmith theatre. During the interval of the first part, the audience walked across to the church in Hammersmith, where the first part ended, and the second part started. For the second half of the second part, the audience returned to the theatre. In the church, the pews had been removed, and the action of the play continued simultaneously on at least five pageant wagons arranged across the space of the church. I have discussed this in more depth elsewhere (Meyer-Dinkgräfe 2006a).

Aurelia Baumgartner's *Catch Me if You Can: Euridice 2012 Reloaded*
This kind of experimental performance can, I would like to suggest, trigger an experience that is different from that of conventional sensory experience. The implication is that it might in fact be the experience of genuine simultaneity that these performances enable, which should yield different results in psycho-physiological terms. In the remainder of this section, I discuss two more recent examples of such performance, which achieve a similar impact in quite different ways. The first is dancer/philosopher Aurelia Baumgartner's performance of *Catch me if you can: Euridice 2012 Reloaded*, presented on 11 June 2015 at the 6th International Conference on Consciousness, Theatre, Literature and the Arts at St Francis College, Brooklyn Heights, New York, and developed into a performance installation for the 2015 annual conference of the Theatre and Performance Research Association (TaPRA). The second is the four-part production of the *Iliad*, by Mike Pearson and Mike Brookes, presented at the Ffwrnes Theatre, Llanelli, Wales, from 21 September to 3 October 2015.

At the beginning of Baumgartner's *Catch me if you can: Euridice 2012 Reloaded*, the auditorium lights go off, there is darkness. A projection on to the large screen at the back of the stage shows buildings behind trees, accompanied by a sound reminds me of cicadas, but may also be high-pitched radio or electrical interference – it lacks the pulse of the cicadas' voices. The camera short shifts from the row of houses to a large building, with trees in front, with the camera driving past, handheld, a little shaky. The camera shifts to capture different city images, including car traffic, less trees. A female voice-over on the video, speaking in English with a German accent, speaks individual words or phrases – fragments which may or may not relate to the images. The word "predestination" appears on the screen, top right, while the scene captured by the camera shifts to interiors, with words "café", "Kasse Kaufkarten / ticket office" providing some orientation. The soundscape reflects the noise of many people speaking at the same time. The female voice-over meshes with recording referencing train announcements over a tannoy at a railway station. Meaningless sequences of small and capital letters now fill the screen, their ordered appearance from top to bottom jarring with the impossibility of making sense of the letters in terms of words. This description covers only about a minute of the 69-minute performance. The first human appears on stage after around four minutes – Flamenco Puro dancer Jairo Amaya appears in silhouette in a round beam behind a screen, launching into a flamenco number – the rest of the screen remains in darkness, the screen is dark as well, no more projections for the moment.

Aurelia Baumgartner's father was a highly respected professor of philosophy in Germany, and Baumgartner is a philosopher. Her work is philosophy, both what she has to say and what she does in her practice. In what she has to say, she has referenced the philosophers that she thinks about, thinks in terms of, and that have guided her thoughts. All that thinking is interwoven with her practice. For her, practice is thinking, and takes the shape of her performances. It is philosophy in practice, just as much as it is possible to understand the history of philosophy as practice – as the writings about personal experience. Philosophers encountered their own revelatory experiences and wrote about those experiences to make sense of them for themselves, and to share them with others to enable others to make sense of their respective experiences, and to enable others to have the same, or a similar, experience. For many, the first encounter with such experiences was new, unexpected and life-changing. Sadly, this experiential aspect of philosophy was marginalised in the writing of the history of philosophy, leaving philosophy to be considered speculation (Meyer-Dinkgräfe 2013b, 125-9).

Baumgartner's performances seek to bring philosophy back to the realm of experience, reclaiming it from the context of mere speculation. Perhaps she has found the key in performance that fine artists and musicians appear, or claim, to have found in their understanding of Practice as Research, which has left the restrictions of verbal language behind.

The components of *Eurydice* interweave and interact, mediated from prepared audio and video material, and immediate components, unmediated through the live body on stage, and the arrangement of the live space. Module art adds to this diversity, which, despite, or, actually, because of the disparate nature of its components, coalesces into a whole that constitutes a new dimension. The performance moulds this new dimension and explores its facets, nuances and external textures. The formation of this new dimension is given to the recipient's experience – I am using this term because the term "spectator" is restricted to the visual, and the term "audience" to the auditory senses. These terms do not do justice to the more comprehensive experience aimed at, enabled and taught by *Eurydice*.

Either gradually, or in a sudden phase transition, the new dimension opens up to experience. While we know the sudden transition from the sudden shift that allows us, with Rubin's vase, for example, to see either a vase or two faces in profile, but never both at the same time, in *Eurydice*, in the new dimension we are able to experience all aspects simultaneously.

We can think and talk about this experience, as I and you are doing now, in academic terms, but that is not the same as the experience itself that we try to capture in this way. The performance has become embodied thinking, body-thinking, which is a more holistic way of experiencing the world – a performative idea of utopia. If only we could encounter the real world, whatever that is, in such a way. In that sense the performance, which we cannot grasp fully through words, has a didactic nature because, the performance is not limited to the verbal "dimension".

The *Iliad* by Mike Pearson and Mike Brookes

Iliad was the third production for National Theatre Wales by Mike Pearson and Mike Brookes, following on from their 2010 production of *The Persians* by Aeschylus in the Brecon Beacons and their 2012 production of *Coriolanus* by Shakespeare near Cardiff. For *Iliad*, Pearson and Brookes used the poem *War Music* by Christopher Logue (1926-2011). Inspired by Homer's *Iliad*, Logue's poem at the centre of the Pearson/Brookes *Iliad* begins at the moment when Achilles refuses to continue fighting, until the point when he does resume. The production was presented in four parts, each lasting between 90 to 120 minutes. The four parts were presented on consecutive nights, and over two marathon performances of all four parts across 12 hours, one daytime (10.30am to 9.30pm) on 26 September, and one night-time (6pm to 6am) on 3 October.

The main hall in the arts centre in Llanelli was stripped of seating, the floor covered in beige-coloured tiles of flooring, not carpet, but softer, and hence more comfortable to the feel than laminate. There were stacks of plastic garden chairs, which spectators were invited to use and place wherever they chose if they wanted to sit. Many used car tyres were located in different areas of the space, and what appeared to be stage hands, but turned out to be fully trained actors, shifted those tyres, piled them up and placed large plywood sheets on to them, thus creating make-shift performance platforms. Sometimes, spectators were instructed to move away from certain areas, which were then used for and by the actors. Sometimes, the plastic chairs were used as part of the performance, to shape the space, to represent a mountain range, or to allow for the cast to express emotions such as anger by throwing the chairs, on one occasion throwing chair after chair, what must have hundreds of them, high into one corner of the venue, to reach almost to the ceiling. Microphones hung down on their cables from the ceiling, and the actors used them to recite their lines. Monitors around three sides of the space projected the text in autocue format. At other times, the characters of the Greek gods appeared on the monitors – they were pre-recorded, played by adolescents from the area. The gods, this dramaturgical device suggested, were teenagers, with all the stereotypical assumptions about adolescent emotional inconsistencies and vulnerability – leading to arbitrary support or punishment of the humans at their mercy.

I am still impressed by the clarity of the vocal presentation by the actors, the decision to have trained actors as the "stage hands", who in the end did so much more than just shift people, tyres, chairs and so on, to contribute to the overall atmosphere of the production. The multi-layered nature of the event, with actors, stage hands, the auto-cue monitors, the gods on monitors, the landscape film in the background with its very slowly shifting image, the audience on the move, the text in itself, the rendering of the text by the actors, the Welsh accent, and the layer of distance between the audience and the performers despite relative physical proximity – too many layers to even try to make sense of them intellectually, and always approximating, and sometimes gaining, the nature of new dimensions of experience. All of this suffused with, permeated, informed, carried and sustained by something as yet not really theorised, but more and more frequently the essence of great theatre: a very deep quality of the heart, an unconditional love for the art and its expression in the performance space, which includes the audience.

The heart and atmosphere in the theatre

In the introduction to her 2012 anthology on *atmospheres*, editor Christiane Heibach points out that atmospheres are omnipresent, and their existence can, therefore, not be doubted. Nevertheless, they evade analytic, scientific consideration predominantly because of their diffuse nature and because they resist categorisation. Etymologically, Heibach explains, the word originates from Greek *atmós*, steam, mist, and *sphairos*, globe, and this situates the word within the discipline of physics. This kind of atmosphere is central to climate research. The enveloping, invisible and nevertheless perceptible nature of atmosphere as subject of physics is then transferred to human life, where it is currently not measurable (Heibach 2012: 9). Heibach differentiates first-, second- and third-order atmospheres. First order atmospheres are occurring naturally, they are those described by physics. Second-order atmospheres are anthropocentric: atmospheres that come into being in and through interaction of people with other people, and with spaces, things, and environments. Third-order atmospheres are intended atmospheres as parts of societal and cultural reality: planning of buildings and cities, environments of consumption and wellness, mono- or multi-medial forms of art, and theatre and performance (Heibach 2012:

11-12). Totalitarian regimes are cut off to the outside and manipulate people internally in their spaces of living and thinking to create toxic atmospheres (Sloterdijk 2004: 189).

I propose to understand atmosphere as the result, and experience of, interactions of subtle energy. I have explained what I mean by subtle energy as follows.

The entire universe, according to Binder, can be understood as an energy field that integrates smaller units also as energy fields and interacts with the parent field, and other fields, since they are in turn connected to each other. Each planet has therefore its own energy field and is connected via the "unified field of natural law" again with the great whole. On Earth, there are then earth energy fields at each level of manifestation, for all plants and each plant, and for all animals and for each animal, and for all people and every individual. The deepest and most important energy field of each person is that of their very own life plan.

> Since this plan of life for every human being is different and individual, according to their own primordial tasks of learning and *karma* from previous incarnations, each individual has the opportunity to change the past by living in the present and by addressing the tasks resulting from her life plan in daily life. (...) Everything that people have ever created and create, have manufactured and manufacture, in what form and with what material whatsoever, and what people have ever thought and think at this very moment, also represents energy fields within the unified field of natural law, brought into being by the respective activities of manufacturing, creating and thinking. All levels of complex energy fields now interact with each other and react to each other, in the sense that like attracts like in turn. (2013b: 105-6)

I have also proposed that physics has developed a model allowing to explain and understand these subtle energy interactions (2006b). These subtle energies come together in the experience of atmosphere. For example, if people are happy, they build up energy fields of happiness which resonate with all existing happiness in the universe, tapping into that universal field of happiness energy, and receiving nourishment from that universal field, as well as in turn further nourishing that universal field of happiness with the energy of their own happiness. This energy field is first and foremost experienced, and then describable and communicable, as atmosphere. This is why "atmosphere" can relate to the experience of one person, or more people who are together. If a person's heart is well developed, he/she will have an organic, natural atmosphere of that quality, and that quality, that atmosphere, will also characterise his/her work, whatever it may be. The principle of resonance is important in this context. I described it, from Binder's perspective, as follows:

Our emotionally substantiated and stored beliefs generate a tremendous resonance field and everything that oscillates within this resonance field is taken up by this resonance field and cannot help but resonate, just as all the strings on a guitar resonate when a string is plucked. The law of resonance teaches us how everything in the universe communicates with one another via resonance. All things and beings in the universe have a natural oscillation and communicate with each other, as well as all the cells and organs of our body and of matter vibrate with each other, usually in different frequencies. Other people, beings, things or events cannot escape the resonance field that we generate, when they resonate with our generated frequency, for like always attracts like. (2013b: 110)

Based on this principle of resonance, a person whose heart is open will attract other people who have similarly open hearts, or are ready, in their spiritual development, for impulses that allow their hearts to grow.

Peter Brook's theatre

I propose considering Peter Brook's theatre, his productions and the Théâtre des Buffes du Nord, the actual theatre space that was his from 1974 to 2010, and which remains the venue that continues in his spirit and where he still presents his productions, as representative of the theatre of the heart. The heart is certainly at the centre of Brook's most recent production, *Battlefield*, which is a 70 minute "continuation" of his 1985 epic 9-hour *Mahabharata*. The programme for the performances at the Young Vic in London provides a poignant quote from the play: Yudishtira, who becomes King after the end of the war that is central to the *Mahabharata*, is shown in conversation with Krishna, the god:

Krishna	*You won't have a choice between peace and war.*
Yudishtira	*What will be my choice?*
Krishna	*Between a war and another war.*
Yudishtira	*The other war, where will it take place?*
	In the battlefield or in my heart?
Krishna	*I don't see a difference*

(Brook and Estienne 2015)

The theatre space that has been Brook's for nearly four decades carries his atmosphere, which is characterised by a deep, heartfelt love, awe towards, and veneration, reverence and respect for the art (form) of the theatre. This atmosphere originates from Brook's work and permeates, saturates, and pervades it. In a more neutral performance space that has not developed this particularly unique atmosphere, Brook's productions lose some of their impact. In such venues, they have to create the atmosphere of the theatre of the heart afresh with each performance, which takes more effort, and the intensity of the atmosphere will be less. In comparison, performances at the Théâtre des Buffes du Nord, in which the atmosphere of the theatre of the heart has been established very strongly over the years, the performances are carried by that atmosphere and increase it further. Atmosphere transforms a mere, and neutral, space, into a place that is characterised by its atmosphere.

The heart and love

According to Binder, there are three levels of love, related to the heart and the heart chakra: interpersonal love, partnership love and universal love of the heart. Ultimately, Binder argues, the first two categories of love have not much to do with universal love – they are predominantly bonds that serve specific purposes, such as an increase of economic/financial and social security, to live one's ego, to get mutual recognition, and not to have to live alone. On that basis it is possible to consider interpersonal and partnership love as "needy love", which is based on a deficit, and can lead to people manipulating each other for their own gain. Two people in a "needy love" relationship can easily, when the needs are not met as expected, ruin each other's freedom and respect, leading to hatred and jealousy.

Universal love of the heart, on the other hand, never tries to change the other in line with our expectations, accepting him or her as he or she is. It is self-sufficient and allows those who live universal love of the heart to be able to forgive. Universal love of the heart structures an aura, a complete energy field, for each person that can radiate inside or outside, as needed depending on the situation we are in.

Under the Covers and *Blueprint* by Zoo Indigo
Zoo Indigo was founded in 2002 and is based in Nottingham. The company describes itself as an "Anglo-German contemporary performance company". Its founding members are Rosie Garton and Ildiko Rippel.

Garton is a lecturer in drama and performance arts at De Montfort University, and in creative writing at the University of Nottingham. Rippel, originally from Germany, is senior lecturer in drama and performance at the University of Worcester. Thus, both combine their performance practice with careers as academics. In 2008/9 they premiered *Under the Covers*, in which they had a live skype link to infra-red cameras in their homes filming their infants in their cots. That footage was shown live during the entire duration of the performance. The framing device was for Garton and Rippel to tell the audience that as young mothers they had failed to find babysitters for the night, but not to worry, as the audience was now taking on the collective role of the babysitter – the audience would now have to watch the children on screen while at the same time also watching Garton and Rippel perform, and would have to become active when they noticed the children waking up, or crying, by singing a lullaby to them, or embarking on any other activity suitable to calm the child/children in question. I would like to argue that the performance of *Under the Covers* represents theatre of the heart in so far as the material comes immediately and without mediation from the heart – the performers both open up and frame what comes out (pure love of the mother for the child) in the artistic context of the performance. There is utter fullness there, and the performers as mothers can give as much of that as they like without feeling any depletion. The fullness comes from their shared love for their children: as the video clip of excerpts demonstrates. In *Zoo Indigo's* 2012 *Blueprint*, the mother child relationship is expanded: Garton and Rippel, and, in one version of the production two other performers on stage, are linked by skype with their respective mothers, with whom they playfully interact. The performers introduce their mothers, ask them to show us their environments at their homes, ask questions about their mothers and about themselves as children, and they play themselves as children, and they play biographical monologues as their mothers about the mothers and their own younger selves.

The heart and age / wisdom in the theatre

In current Western society, in general (with some minor regional differences), the norm is defined by people aged 25 to 45, give or take a few years. Any person below that age or above it runs the risk of being considered, by those that define the norm, as not within the norm. Anyone who does not fit within the norm is not fully understood and therefore considered at best with surprise or suspicion. The position outside the norm, which those below 25 or over 45 have not chosen for themselves, makes them vulnerable. Society has realised this to the extent that it provides funding for, or at least tolerates the existence, on the basis of charitable donations, of organisations that protect the young and the old from the norm (National Society for the Prevention of Cruelty to Children,

NSPCC, and Age Concern in the UK). The young are considered predominantly in terms of what they need to do to achieve well when they have reached the norm, without much attention to their here and now during those years. The old are considered predominantly in terms of what they have or could have achieved while they were the norm. Hope, the frequent attitude towards the young, is replaced by sadness that not much may have been achieved, or sadness that in comparison with all that has been achieved, the status quo of the aged person assumed to be so much less than that achievement. From the perspective of the norm, youth is considered in terms of growth towards a goal, while older age is considered in terms of deterioration. Goal and deterioration are not within the grasp of those defined by it. The here-and-now of the young and the old does not count on its own terms, as the terms of comparison and judgment are that of the norm, and youth and age both deviate from the norm.

There are some alternative approaches to youth, for example that developed by Maria Montessori, and while there are many laudable attempts to bring such innovative approaches to bear on public opinion, they have not become mainstream in the sense that they determine policy that schools have to follow. There is some recognition that an increasingly ageing population will bring challenges with it, buzzwords have been created and are circulating, and research funding bodies have latched on to this development and have made funds available for research to study well-being and dignified ageing, for example.

In attempts at shifting perceptions about ageing and the aged, frequently the idea is referenced that old people are wise and younger people should acknowledge and respect that wisdom. The concept of *wisdom* goes back to Greek times in the Western context, and to comparably early times in other cultures. With this strong history of wisdom in our lives and culture, we all seem to know the word, and have an idea of what it means. However, writing in 1997, leading wisdom researcher Monika Ardelt pointed out that wisdom research has been a relatively recent addition to sociology and psychology, and that after well over a decade of research, there is no uniform definition. The range of wisdom definitions reaches from wisdom as "an expert knowledge system (expertise)" (Baltes & Smith 1990, 87) and "a form of advanced cognitive functioning" (Dittmann-Kohli & Baltes 1990, 54) over wisdom as the art of questioning (Arlin 1990) and the awareness of ignorance (Meacham 1990) to an elaborate description of wisdom as a two dimensional model with intrapersonal, interpersonal, and transpersonal aspects on one dimension and the domains of personality, cognition, and conation on the other (Orwoll & Achenbaum 1993, 1997,

15). Ardelt emphasises that wisdom is not merely a different form of descriptive knowledge or the accumulation of facts: "Wise people do not necessarily know more facts than other individuals, but they comprehend the deeper meaning of the generally known facts for themselves and others" (1997: P16).

More recently, Ardelt defined wisdom as "as an integration of cognitive, reflective, and compassionate personality characteristics" (Kallio 2015: 34). The *cognitive* wisdom dimension relates to the search for the true and deep meaning of phenomena and events. To do this, wise persons are able *to look at events from a multitude of perspectives*; they are not merely stuck on their subjective preferences, and they are able to ponder the questions deeply (the *reflective* dimension of wisdom). Finally, deeper understanding and less self-centeredness are supposed to lead to compassion for others (the *compassionate* wisdom dimension) (Ardelt *et al.* 2013). Lee et al. address the debated issue of whether wisdom is a universal or culturally-specific construct, by comparing USA and Korea (2015).

Conventionally, growth of wisdom is associated with increase of age – the older the person, the more wisdom they have gained and exhibit. Psychological research sometimes confirms this, sometimes not. A 2013 study by Thomas and Kunzmann, for example, "suggests that any phase of life offers opportunities for the attainment of wisdom-related strengths as long as an individual is willing and able to actively engage in life's ongoing challenges" (2013). Other studies suggest that middle-age correlates more highly with wisdom than young and older age (Webster, Westerhof and Bohlmeijer 2012). Studies of wisdom also consider aspects of gender. Ardelt found that women "tended to score higher on the affective dimension of wisdom than men. By contrast, men tended to outperform women on the cognitive wisdom dimension only among the older cohort" (2009: 9). Vladimir Soloviev used to equate holy wisdom with beauty and the principle of feminine divinity (McCannon 2004, 458). In this construction, it is the woman who – as if pregnant – bears wisdom and nurtures it. It is left to man to make wisdom manifest and active. This effectively parallels not just Jung's pairing of *anima* and *animus*, but any of the female/male dualities whose unions are considered to reflect cosmic revitalization and spiritual perfection. Sophia and Logos. Shakti and Shiva. The Church with Christ as her bridegroom (McCannon 2004: 475-6). For more on Soloviev and the female divinity, see Galtsin 2015.

The aim of development is integration of masculine and feminine, which is then the peak of wisdom. In line with this, Ardelt concludes that the "results might reflect gender-specific socialization practices and changes in those practices for the younger cohort. As predicted, no significant differences between men and women were found in the three dimensions of wisdom among the top 25% of wisdom scorers, suggesting that relatively wise persons have integrated the cognitive and affective dimensions of wisdom" (2009: 9).

Zacher, McKenna and Rooney found that "the effects of composite wisdom on life satisfaction and positive affect were fully explained by composite emotional intelligence" (2013: 1711). Zacher *et al.* describe several dimensions of emotional intelligence.

The first emotional intelligence dimension is appraisal and expression of emotion in oneself (*self-emotions appraisal*), that is, "an individual's ability to understand his or her deep emotions and to be able to express emotions naturally" (Law *et al.* 2004: 484). The second dimension is appraisal and recognition of emotion in others (*others-emotions appraisal*), defined as "an individual's ability to perceive and understand the emotions of the people around them" (Law *et al.* 2004: 484). The third dimension is use of emotion to facilitate performance (*use of emotion*), defined as "the ability of a person to make use of his or her emotions by directing them toward constructive activities and personal performance" (Law *et al.* 2004: 484). Finally, the fourth dimension is regulation of emotion in oneself (*regulation of emotion*), that is, "the ability of a person to regulate his or her emotions, enabling a more rapid recovery from psychological distress" (Law *et al.* 2004: 484; See also Law et al. 2013: 1698-9).

If we understand these dimensions as dimensions of the heart, we can argue the link between wisdom, the feminine, and the heart.

Public opinion lags far behind, however, and is still dominated by the norm in terms of growth and deterioration, associated with, ultimately, hope regarding the assumed potential of the norm, and fear of the decline associated with age. Drama and theatre, in this context, most certainly have held the mirror up to nature. Do they recognise, acknowledge and take seriously their potential of bringing real change in the minds of the spectators? The 2013 production of *Much Ado About Nothing* directed by Mark Rylance, put that question to the test in a major way by casting Vanessa Redgrave (b. 1937) as Beatrice and James Earl Jones (b. 1931) as Benedick. The production ran from 6 September to 30 November 2013 at the Old Vic theatre in London. The majority of critics panned the production, in some cases in worryingly ageist terms.

David Benedict considers the casting choice an "interesting notion that collapses in execution", qualifying that this is "the least of the show's problems". He does come back to the age of the two leading actors later in the review, however, arguing that "casting actors this old renders numerous lines and situations preposterous". He provides as an example the impression that "Redgrave's Beatrice is old enough to be Hero's grandmother. Why do they share a bed?" Benedict is even more dismissive of Jones, referring to his "rambling, shambling Benedick", who "looks wholly detached from all his scenes, using his bassoon-like voice more as narrator of his thoughts than as a man engaging with those around him" (2013). Brown (*London Theatre Guide*, 2013), Coveney (*The Stage*, 2013), Norrington (London Evening Standard, 2013),

Billington (*The Guardian*, 2013), Spencer (*The Telegraph*, 2013), Hemming (*Financial Times*, 2013), and Letts (*Daily Mail*, 2013) have similar concerns in relation to the ages of the lead actors. To expect, as those comments seem to imply, for Redgrave and Jones to appear on stage as they would have at, say, the ages of thirty-eight or forty-one respectively, is strange. They were not trying to play a younger age, or to hide their age, but they both performed in full awareness of their capacities. It is those capacities that reviewers should have focused on, rather than resorting to irrelevant belittling and insults. It may have been the very subtlety of their acting that was beyond the critics' vocabulary to describe, assess, or perhaps even to perceive in the first place.

Redgrave's and Jones's tremendous achievements as actors across a long and distinguished career are not in doubt, and critics of *Much Ado* acknowledge their appreciation of those actors' work elsewhere and up to now. To do justice to the critics, some of them have some words of praise to say about Redgrave and Jones in this production as well. Coveney finds that Redgrave: "delights sporadically". She is "buoyant and that familiar, penetrating voice casts its spell" (Norrington). She has "odd moments of unpredictable magic" (Billington) and a "still-potent charisma" (Coghlan). She is "great on her character's fierce independence and eccentricity (…) and can be poignant" (Hemming). She "carries great dignity on stage. Her voice is these days almost Shirley Williams" (Letts). She is the "expected reliable class act, energetic and sprightly" (Lee Tomlinson). "Jones brings twinkly charm and a lovely tenderness to Benedick" (Norrington). He is good "when he puts on a silly voice or gurns" (*Express*) and brings "tender warmth to the part" (Hemming). Only Sadler in the Huffington Post has only praise: "The playfulness and mischief they bring adds so much to the comedy in the production. And both of them have such wonderful tones to their voices as well as acting talent that you really could just listen to both of them spouting Shakespeare all day" (2013).

Conclusion

In this article I have written about a set of experiences with theatre productions over the last few years that have appealed strongly, in different ways, to my heart. To contextualise the phenomenon, I have coined the phrase *theatre of the heart*, and have provided an analysis of its manifestations with reference to non-linear theatre, atmosphere, love, and wisdom and age. I have provided examples for each of those contexts from recent theatre practice. I am sharing this experience and my interpretation of it, I hope to enable other spectators to make sense of experiences they have encountered but may not be able to place, or to open them up to such experience in the first instance. My considerations may also support theatre artists to be courageous and develop the theatre of the heart further.

Commentary 2018 (1):
Zoo Indigo's *No Woman's Land* -- a journey

In 1945, many people were evicted from their homes in East Germany and had to flee their homes, with whatever belongings they could pack up at very short notice. Many fled on foot, with hand-pulled carts, some more fortunate ones in their cars. Those fleeing on foot were vulnerable because of the weather, and always in danger of attack from soldiers. Many suffered from hunger, many died.

One of those who had to walk for many, many miles was Lucia Rippel, grandmother of Ildiko Rippel, who is a Senior Lecturer in Drama and Performance in the Institute of Humanities and Creative Arts at the University of Worcester. She and Rosie Garton form the Nottingham-based Anglo-German performance company Zoo Indigo. In summer 2015, Ildiko Rippel retraced her grandmother's journey of refuge, accompanied by Garton for much of the way, and other friends and members of her family for shorter periods of time. In May 2016, Zoo Indigo presented a performance of work in progress, followed by a discussion with the audience, at the Attenborough Arts Centre in Leicester. The first full-length performances took place in November 2016. The work is still being developed further and has had several tour dates for 2017, including the Drill Hall in Lincoln on 9 February, with more forthcoming.

It was interesting to observe the development of the performance over the three stages from work-in-progress (May 2016) to full performance (November 2016) to further performance (February 2017). It was a journey in itself. The framing concept of presenting the performance as a Berlin cabaret was there from the beginning and has remained. Rippel and

Garton are dressed in 1920s suits and explained the context of their performance when the lights went down. They told their audiences about their 2015 journey, and about the journey of Rippel's grandmother. They explained why there were two treadmills on the stage, and that someone would be on the treadmills throughout the performance, Rippel and Garton, but also members of the audience, who were asked to volunteer, allocated a number, and asked to come forward and step onto the treadmills when invited to do so during the performance. Rippel and Garton also checked which male audience members have a beard. Then they chose one and applied make-up to each other's faces to represent beards. This was part of the cheerful nature of the performance, as was the introduction proper of the cabaret, with Rippel speaking in German and Garton in English. The seriousness of the context, however, was brought home quickly and suddenly when they revealed that many of the refugee women dressed up as men to avoid being raped by Russian soldiers or pretended to be mad because allegedly the soldiers would avoid women they feared were mad. Rippel then revealed that her grandmother was not able to escape that fate of being raped. "Not again" and "not again in front of the children" were the chilling lines, in all three versions I.

The first full performance, in November 2016, was around 80 minutes long, compared with the 45-minute "work in progress" I had seen in May. Rippel and Garton had developed the material considerably, not only adding to the May work. In May, they had not yet developed the necessary distance from the summer 2015 walk and the emotional involvement in it – the frame of their performance, to create distance through a 1920s Berlin cabaret context and style, was then a device to create distance, and had now become a frame to express distance.

The two performers were now at home with the material, relaxed and confident. There was a good balance of fast-paced funny material and slower, more thought-provoking sections – often sudden one-line revelations that caught the audience off-guard and led to gasps and sudden silence. Extensive use of footage from the film *The Great Escape* had been reduced considerably. Footage from the German film *Die Trapp-Familie*, was shown as an example of the kinds of romantic film that the grandmother of a German friend of Rippel and Garton loved watching – she also had had to flee her home in the wake of the end of WW2. While in the work-in-progress performance that footage was merely shown without comment, with some spectators able to identify it and others not, in this performance they explained the context and contents. As in the work-in-progress performance, volunteers from the audience were invited to walk on the two treadmills – over the 80 minute-performance, together they walked around two miles – which was then compared to the 200+ miles that Lucia Rippel had walked in 1945, and that Ildiko Rippel and Rosie Garton had walked in 2015. The two performers also played with their language(s) – the fact that Rippel is a native speaker of German and spoke many of her lines in German, while Garton does not speak German at all – in some cases Garton's very dry, very brief renderings of Rippel's longer German sentences was very funny indeed, esp. for those who understood both languages, but also for those who did not.

The third performance I saw, in February 2017, showed that Rippel and Garton had further developed the performance—further reducing extraneous material and making it even more their own, slowly and at times still tentatively, cautiously abandoning the distance they initially needed to be able to cope with the magnitude of the original walk in 1945, and that of their re-tracing it in 2015

After the work-on-progress performance it had occurred to me, in relation to what I had seen of Zoo Indigo's work before, online video and an excerpt of their *Blueprint* as part of a conference at De Montfort University in Leicester, or indeed read about their work: the previous work came much more immediately and without mediation from the heart—Rippel and Garton both opened up and frame what comes out (pure love!) in the artistic context of the performance. There is utter fullness there, and both performers can give as much of that as they like without feeling any depletion. The fullness came from their shared love for their children in *Under the Covers*, and that for their parents in *Blueprint*. In the work-in-progress of *No Woman's Land,* they had not yet achieved that. This which may be why the audience kept on "wanting more" in the post-show discussion.

It seems that Rippel and Garton found a way to that fullness for *No Woman's Land* as well, building on the love they have for Lucia Rippel and her daughters. Of course, that love cannot be quite the same for Ildiko Rippel as a blood relative and Rosie Garton, who comes to this performance from a naturally bigger distance (also due to not having been able to join in the whole trip in summer 2015). However, neither proximity nor distance remained relevant in achieving a common ground of limitless love to serve as the basis for giving to the audience.

Commentary 2018 (2):
the (opera) masterclass and the heart

Many conservatoires across the world offer masterclasses as part of the education of their students, and many of those are open to the public, at low ticket cost, or free of charge. The master class teachers are artists in the field who have established their high level of ability beyond reasonable doubt; in many cases, they may be beyond the peak of their own performance career, allowing them time to expand into teaching. In this post I focus on opera master classes, as I have attended a number of these as a member of the audience. I expect that some of my observations can be transferred to masterclasses for instrumentalists.

In terms of arrangement, a master might visit a conservatoire to work with a selected number of students. Often, six students in a three-hour session get up to 30 minutes to work with the master, on one or two pieces (song or aria) they will have chosen and practiced with the piano accompanist beforehand. In many cases, the accompanist is a fellow-student. There is probably a very tough selection process for many students interested in being involved in a master class, and students are on record emphasising the honour it is for them to be selected, and how much they practice for the event. There are exceptions here, of course: at one masterclass I attended, the master concluded the session with one singer by asking bluntly (more saddened than annoyed) whether he was prepared to admit that he had not put in many hours of rehearsal with his accompanist, and the student did admit this. In other scenarios, young singers would attend a residence of several days with a master, again following a selection process. Those masterclasses are predominantly private, with a public showcase of masterclass and concert recital at the end of a week or two.

There is a certain etiquette around masterclasses: the student presents the rehearsed song or aria uninterrupted, while the master listens and observes closely. The master and audience applaud, then the master addresses aspects of technique and interpretation, often together. At the end, the student sings (part of) the song or aria again, and in all cases I have observed live or on video, the singer's performance is much better after having taken on board the master's advice.

Research into the masterclass has covered aspects of expertise, apprenticeship, etiquette, embodied pedagogy, the master's experience and personal authority, the impact of the students' experience, gender and level of study on their evaluation of a masterclass, and general views of students about their experience.

In a recent publication, I explored the heart in relation to spirituality in general terms, and then considered the relevance of the insights of that exploration for theatre and performance practice. I coined the phrase *theatre of the heart* and provided an analysis of its manifestations with reference to non-linear performance (Baumgartner's *Catch me if you can: Euridice 2012 Reloaded* and Mike Pearson/Mike Brookes *Iliad*), atmosphere (Peter Brook), love (Zoo Indigo), and wisdom and age (*Much Ado About Nothing*, with Vanessa Redgrave and James Earl Jones, 2013).

The purpose of this consideration was to re-assess the nature of the experiences of creating theatre and of watching a performance in a way that does not seek to reduce it to brain activities but allows a wider perspective that in turn can be shown not to rule out the dimension of brain activity as mutually exclusive.

From my experience of live masterclasses, they work best when the master teaches with an open heart.

CHAPTER THIRTEEN

INTERCULTURAL DIFFERENCES AND UNIVERSALITY OF CREATING AND PERCEIVING BEAUTY THROUGH / IN PERFORMANCE

DANIEL MEYER-DINKGRÄFE AND TANATCHAPORN KITTIKONG

Contextualisation

One of the participants in the working group *Performance and Consciousness* at the IFTR world congress in Warwick in 2014 was Dr Tanatchaporn Kittikong. She presented a paper on "Moving with a Free-Mind: Layers of self-consciousness in performing with Buddhist Vipassana meditation". That encounter resulted in a formal exchange between Khon Kaen University (KKU) and the University of Lincoln, signed in October 2015 on the occasion of a visit by a team from KKU, led by KKU's President, and a visiting professorship for myself at KKU in May 2016. The article below is the outcome of our collaboration during that visit, followed by email and skype communication.

Beauty: many perspectives and questions

In Western discourses of the arts, the concept of beauty is slowly gaining respectability again after many years on the fringes, where mentioning beauty in academic discussions was not considered appropriate. Creating beauty across the arts is actually quite challenging and difficult, it is much easier to create a scandal! Beauty has been considered as very subjective, as it is only "in the eyes of the beholder", and neuroscientific exploration of beauty has been criticised as being reductionist. Plato, however, considered the creation and experience of beauty as a major, and very powerful, tool for human beings to develop their consciousness. Meditative experience is beautiful, and often a meditating person is perceived by others as looking beautiful with (because of?!) their radiating inner silence.

In English and German, there are several words in the context of beauty. Humans can be described as nice, pretty, cute, hot, beautiful. This range of words encompasses the sexual, the erotic, and what transcends those. These words refer predominantly to members of the female gender—possibly with the exception of "hot", which may be a word used by teenage girls to refer to a sexually attractive male. The other words are not usually associated with men—a man would be handsome, or good-looking, but not beautiful. Denotation of outward appearance may be different in the male homosexual community. In the German language, the word equivalent to English "beautiful" is "schön". "Beauty" is "Schönheit", men would be described as "gutaussehend"; "scharf" could be the equivalent of "hot"—it is interesting here that the reference to "heat" in English changes to that of "spicy" in German. "Pretty" has is equivalent in "hübsch" and could be used for females but perhaps also to describe a good-looking gay man. The German "niedlich" could be related to English "cute", with both connoting a younger age, in the direction of childhood, and applicable to the description of members of both genders.

Research suggests that people who are considered beautiful are also more successful in life. This may be related to charisma—perhaps charismatic people are also considered more beautiful—or beauty is a characteristic of charisma, or beauty makes you charismatic? This link is not without ambiguity: beauty has been associated with virtue, with goodness. However, some charismatic people are the opposite of good—they are evil and dangerous, and no longer beautiful. Equally ambiguous is the relation between beautiful and attractive. A femme fatale, for example, is certainly attractive, but not necessarily beautiful. The femme fatale exploits her power of attractiveness (which she may consider as beauty, and which resembles beauty on the surface) to get what she wants, but this does not make her genuinely happy (and thus genuinely beautiful).

In terms of outward appearance, the ideal of beauty changes across time within and across cultures. In the English Restoration, for example, inspired by the French court, white-powdered faces with a beauty spot counted as beautiful. At other times, sun-tanned skin was considered more attractive and beautiful than pale skin deprived of sunlight. Tanning parlours with sun-beds or treatment with tanning creams are still popular (if controversial) today. In India, in long-gone times and today, lighter skin is considered more beautiful than darker skin. In Cameroon, men found women with very curvaceous shapes, especially in waist to hip ratio, more attractive than slim women, but preferred slightly darker-skinned women to those with lighter skin (Dixson et al. 2007). A further aspect of the embodiment of beauty is its relation to the senses: beauty is predominantly related to the visual sense. Sounds may be experienced as beautiful. Classical music is likely to be described and experienced as beautiful, and the same is true for at least some pop music.

There may be a status aspect to this as well—lower-class people, peasants, are more exposed to sunshine as they work outdoors, and that leads to their skin becoming darker. Another aspect of outward appearance in relation to beauty is to do with colour not of the skin, but of the hair, and the association, in Western (popular?) culture of blonde hair in women with assumed lower intelligence. This association is sometimes meant and received as offensive, sometimes as funny, or even both. The films and musical *Legally Blonde* are based on that association, as is a phrase like "having a blonde moment". There is also an often-repeated assumption that intelligent blonde women have to work harder to be taken seriously.

In principle, we respond to beauty by feeling enchanted. It is a pleasant feeling, desirable. In popular perception, someone who is considered beautiful is expected to be happy by nature *because* they are beautiful, so people are surprised if beautiful stars come out as suffering from depression. A person's self-image might also be related to this, even going as far as body dysmorphia. Might there be an additional dimension of cultural conditioning involved in self-image in relation to beauty? Maybe we are not supposed to think well of ourselves, or not too well, or not in terms of beauty because of ideas about modesty? There is also a difference between feeling beautiful in private and talking about it to others (which may then well be judged as inappropriately bragging behaviour).

Beauty is related closely to other concepts. One of those is knowledge. There is a difference in the way beauty is perceived, depending on the level of knowledge the perceiver has acquired about the object of beauty, and the extent of that knowledge the perceiver can actively bring to the perception process. The concept of the connoisseur (in the Indian context, the concept of *sahrdaya*) captures this aspect. It is important to note that by bringing in knowledge, beauty does not become restricted to the level of the intellect—knowledge here encompasses, and is built on, experience that transcends the intellect. However, the question remains whether an appreciation of an object of beauty is rendered more valuable or valid when it comes from a more knowledgeable person?

The Max Planck Institute for Empirical Aesthetics in Frankfurt studies beauty from an empirical perspective. Such approaches are affected by the training emphasis of the researchers involved: they are either scientists with an interest in the arts, or artists fascinated by science. Usually, the perspective is a scientific one. This again has an impact on the outcome. Artists work in very broad terms, often contextualising their art in terms of universality, or large arcs of space and time. For scientists, such dimensions are problematic. In comparison with arts and humanities researchers, scientists can well publish hundreds of papers—because those typically address very specific, and narrow (in the best sense of the term) issues. When science addresses issues of the arts, in many cases the findings are not new: arts researchers knew the outcome all along—what is new is that now science has developed the tools to confirm what was known all along by the artists and arts researchers.

From a different perspective, there has been the concern among artists and arts researchers that science, with its preferred materialist and thus reductionist methodology, diminishes the art object or process under investigation. Ramachandran confirmed that there are many experiences, also those in relation to the arts, that current science cannot yet understand. Aware of these limitations, he seeks to expand the boundaries of science to enhance its explanatory value. Funding and priority of focus are important factors. More money will be available for projects seeking to find ways of helping accident victims overcome a coma, than to explore the difference in brain structures for scenographers in comparison to non-scenographers, following the studies of larger brain areas in charge of spatial awareness in taxi drivers.

A few years ago, I attended a Bharata Natyam performance in Aberystwyth accompanied by Mohiniattam performer, Kalamandalam Radhika, who was visiting me from India. In the interval of the performance, which had a Bharata Natyam teacher performing with her students, Kalamandalam Radhika mentioned that she considered the Bharata Natyam teacher a good teacher, and, in response to my question, elaborated that her students' execution of some movements was better than her own (and would thus be considered more beautiful at least by a knowledgeable spectator), where her age did not allow her the perfect execution of the movement any more.

Very briefly, beauty is likely to be an important aspect of marketing. While beauty is commonly associated, for people, with youth, there have been discussions of the beauty of age. In the context of science, it is likely that beauty will play a role in human evolution. We love beauty and see beauty where something has been done with love. Animals are unlikely to have an intellectual understanding of beauty. Animals perceive frequency oscillations, not beauty as such. However, beauty has a positive frequency oscillation, and therefore, animals like beauty.

Thai language on beauty

> To be a beautiful (Ngām) person is at heart not face.
> To be a beautiful (Sūay) person is to have manners not beautiful eyes.
> To be an old person is to have knowledge not just living long.
> To be a rich person is giving ability not just owning a huge home.
> (translation from Thai poet with unknown author by Kittikong, T.)

In Thai language, there are two words relating to beauty, the first one is Sūay [สวย] and the second one is Ngām [งาม]. Sūay is often used to describe a pretty, gorgeous, charming girl or woman, but is not usually for a man. If Sūay is used to describe a man, the implication is that he looks very feminine. Sūay is also used to describe gesture, movement, and action, such as dancing, walking and smiling. The Thai dictionary (Royal Institute of Thailand, 2011) defines the word Sūay as something that has a satisfactory quality and is often used together with the word Ngām. The word Ngām is defined as an adjective that indicates the characteristic of satisfaction, for example Maan-ra-yart-Ngām (beautiful manners) or Rup-Ngām (beautiful form). This characteristic also suggests a perfected, completed and rich quality, for example, Ton-Mai-Ngām (beautiful tree), Fon-Ngām (beautiful rain – meaning enough rain). Ngām is also a synonym of good and plenty in the way of fulfilling the need, for example, Kam-rai Ngām (good profits). Thai people use these two words together as Sūay-Ngām, describing beauty as something that has satisfactory quality. Moreover, Sūay and Ngām are used predominantly for the visual sense. In the Thai language, other terms would be used for different senses such as Pai-ror (beautiful for sound), a specific term related to taste, A-roi (delicious, beautiful taste). In English, German or Thai, "beautiful" is not used for the senses of touch and smell.

These two Thai words related to beauty are not different in terms of meaning but have a different impact on feeling. The concept of Ngām can denote a higher level of beauty, and is used in the context of the arts and in an aesthetic context. The level of beauty represented by Ngām is higher than that captured by Sūay because Ngām goes along with ethically good behaviour—this will be interesting to compare with Schiller's ideas about moral education. Ngām implies a holistic experience rather than a limited perception. "Holistic" implies context and aura—as with the beauty of the King's or a monk's walk, greetings etc. The implication is also one of hierarchy. Highly-placed people such as the King or a monk are beautiful by the nature of their high position. Whereas Ngām is neutral as far as gender is concerned and more official, Sūay is more associated with the feminine and is used on a daily basis.

There were discussions in my aesthetics classroom on how the students use the words Sūay and Ngām differently or similarly. The discussion found that Sūay is the quality that is perceptible through the eyes, the sense of seeing, and Ngām is something to be perceived with the heart. Here are some examples provided by the students trying to categorize how they use the words Sūay and Ngām to describe different things. Certainly, all the abstract ideas (non-physical entities) can hardly be described as Sūay. Some students suggested that the two words have the same meaning, as in the North-eastern Thai dialect, only the word Ngām is used to describe something good and beautiful. Some students suggested that the two words belong to different generations: they rarely hear Ngām, or mostly hear it from grandparents rather than peers. It is quite interesting to assume that this current generation seems to recognize Sūay rather than Ngām. Perhaps in the current young generation, beauty is gradually losing the association with 'heart'.

Thai perception of beauty

The question of what constitutes beauty in the cultural context of Thailand, or, "what is Thai beauty", is really an aggregate of two closely related questions—what is "Thai" as (collective) identity, and what is the perception of beauty within, or according to that identity? The key to these questions is a third question: where and how is Thai beauty expressed?

The notions of nation, religion and monarchy, or the three pillars, play an influential role for Thai understanding of identity and cultural practice. Thai as national identity is a 'concept' that is deeply engrained in the cultural politics of Thainess, just like the Thainess that is presented in the marketing images of the country. This belief, in turn, shaped our idea of how we perceive and embody beauty.

The public image of Thailand is represented, staged and performed in terms of beauty. Clicking on the Thailand Tourism Authority website reveals some wonderful and beautiful images of Thai cultural practices. For me as a Thai person, these images bring to the fore the distinction between Thai beauty and Thai identity, "Thainess". Noting that Thailand has been creating its public image associating beauty with the exotic is very interesting. This marketing image might only have a function of luring the foreign tourist with something exotic, where exotic is identical with beautiful. Nevertheless, the Thai ideal of beautiful women is inconsistent. Different beauty pageants such as Miss Thailand World and Miss Thailand Universe have started to welcome the exotic-beauty as representatives of Thai women. While in the Thai market, whitening lotion and cream are popular, woman with darker skin were chosen as representative of Thai beauty. Ms. Nonthawan Thongleng, Miss Thailand World 2014, has caused controversy to the perception of beautiful Thai woman due to her darker skin tone. Later, the so-called darker skin as 'exotic look' gradually permeated other pageants like Miss Thailand Universe: Ms. Aniporn Chalermburanawong (2015) and Ms. Chalita Suansane (2016), where women with lighter skin tone are still dominating in the Thai society. Perhaps, Thai perception of beauty complexly intermingles with not only cultural practices but economy driven as Thai identity.

Thai embodiment of beauty

Thai etiquette elevates beauty as embodiment and displays of respect by means of 'showing' or 'paying' respect to adults, monarchy and icons of Buddhism. Farrelly noted that Thai etiquette becomes part of the Thai pride and Thai's relationship with the monarchy influences beliefs about status, hierarchy, obedience, and loyalty (Farrelly 2016). In addition, Howard noted that in the Thai student's text book introduces the Thai manner 'Wai' (an action of raising the hands and palms together) to pay respect, where the subtitle of the textbook reads 'Thai manners are more beautiful than any other country's' (Howard 2009). Howard argues, based on his experience of observing a Thai kindergarten student in the classroom in a village near Chiangmai, that Thai national identity is signified by 'ceremonial deferential pledges' that construct how students should behave in their inferior role and pay respect to their teacher (Howard 2009: 269).

An assumption of Thais being submissive to politicians or to the monarchy is rather superficial in this context, ignoring much more complex roots of Thai culture and beliefs. The observations by both Farrelly and Howard are prejudice to only show that Thai etiquette falls behind the political drive. I would argue that Thai perception of beauty is closely related to 'respectful qualities'. Respect relates closely to the notion of non-self, and they are deeply engrained in Thai culture and its main religion, Buddhism. Buddhism does not focus on obedience. Buddhism teaches its believers to be mindful and respectful. According to Maneephan Sakteera (2010), the concept of beauty that has been mentioned in Buddhist scriptures in two ways, which are external beauty and internal beauty. Sakteera's study concluded that Buddhism's perspective on external beauty is caused by internal beauty. In Thai Buddhist dhamma, the pivotal drive in nurturing beauty to the internal and external matter is mindfulness. Being mindful thus also raises the notion of respectful, consistent patience, and joy altogether towards wisdom. Therefore, the aim of the practice of meditation is to create beauty in both mind and body. From this Buddhist perspective, internal beauty is certainly not far from the context of spirituality and consciousness studies.

Central to Thai etiquette, respect is to perform body movement and gesture that are driven by the notion of lessening-self. Respectful gesture is Øn-Nøm [อ่อนน้อม] in Thai language, directly translated as soft and bend. The word is usually used together with Tøm-Tøn [ถ่อมตน] which means being modest or humble, directly translated as lower self. Thus, being soft and humble is the Thai respectful gesture in which Thai beauty is embodied.

The Thai greeting 'Wai' may serve as an example. The gesture employed in Thai culture for people to greet each other is known as 'Wai' [ไหว้]. Its movement is to put both hands together close to the chest, elbow beside the body. Then pointing both hands slightly towards the front, at the same time lowering the head and back to both hands until both thumbs are touching the forehead, keeping the elbows on the side of the body. This gesture is for greeting someone older than the one performing Wai. Depending on the status of the person one is greeting, there are different appropriate levels of respect where both thumbs touch upon nose or forehead.

Another example from what I have observed relates to how Thai people behave when they enter the temple. Their body movement and gesture are often noticeably changed towards the qualities of calm, self-restrained, composed, and controlled. These respectful gestures are performative as well as meditative. This respectful demeanour is performed in Thai culture not only in the temple but in all official and ceremonial events.

The art of moving the body with respectfulness and care could also be applied to read the Thai performing arts such as Thai classical dance. In Thai classical dance, the movement is slow, constrained, careful and delicate. It could be that respectful body movement is embedded as the deep root of Thai perception of beauty.

Beautiful mourning for the late Thai King Bhumibol Adulyadej (1927-2016)

Death and mourning are not usually associated with beauty. However, the mourning of all Thais for their late King Bhumibol Adulyadej can be considered as the most beautiful grieving of all time. The images of all the Thais from all over the country, dressing in black, queuing up to pay their last respects to the late King, waiting in lines for approximately 6-8 hours, can be seen as most touching, and it is undeniable that this was a beautiful event. Many artistic and volunteering activities for the passing father of the land have sprung up in all parts of the country. The willingness to pay respect to the monarch is vivid, and this respectful manner has initiated many strong performances to the King's remembrance.

From my point of view, Ngām - Thai beauty is expressed and performed within the embodiment of respect. Beauty reflects cultural embodiment represented in Thai etiquette and manner. This is not only how Thai people move and speak, it is also how Thais think and perceive. The notion of respect is not only in the movement or arts but in any performance of people. It could be difficult for Thais to consider any action that is Ngām without the qualities of being humble and respectful.

Beauty in the disciplinary context of consciousness studies

Consciousness studies has been defined as "the study of how we think, feel and act, why we think, feel and act as we do, and what it feels like to think, feel and act as we do" (Meyer-Dinkgräfe 2013b: 11). From the wide range of approaches to consciousness studies, from cognitive psychology to physics, we have selected the one that focuses on spirituality. That term needs definition.

From the earliest history, the arts have been associated with a beneficial impact on those exposed to it as makers or receivers. In the West, Aristotle in his *Poetics* wrote about the cathartic impact of theatre, while in the East, the *Nāṭyaśāstra*, the ancient Indian text about drama and theatre, which also includes music and dance, relates how dance/drama were created by Brahma, the creator, in response to the request of the Gods for him to create an art form accessible to all human beings and with the explicit purpose of restoring the golden age to humankind (Ghosh 1950). The use of the arts in therapy (drama therapy, dance therapy, and so on) confirms the validity of such early claims of the beneficial impact of the arts on humans in terms of increased well-being, as does research into that impact.

This role of the arts in improving our lives has been contextualized further in the fields of religion, philosophy and consciousness studies. The high currency of contextualizing the arts in these fields is reflected in academia in the emergence and continuing success of the 'Theatre, Performance and Philosophy' working group within the Theatre and Performance Research Association (TaPRA), the working groups 'Performance and Consciousness' and 'Religion and Performance' within the International Federation for Theatre Research (IFTR), the 'Performance Philosophy' working group within Performance Studies International (PSI), the network 'Performance Philosophy', and the recently founded journal *Dance, Movement and Spiritualities*, as well as, in the context of consciousness studies, *Consciousness, Literature and the Arts* (refereed online journal, book series with Intellect and Brill | Rodopi, and biannual conferences 2005-2015).

For most of these contexts, spirituality, explicitly or implicitly, is central, and in many, the term and concept of *spirituality* has been understood in a non-religious way. It is this understanding that forms the basis of our article, with the implication that "spirituality culminates in the full development of mind", and "any move in the direction of this fullness can be called spirituality" (Malekin and Yarrow 1997: 90).

In *Observing Theatre: Spirituality and Subjectivity in the Performing Arts* (Meyer-Dinkgräfe 2013b), I introduced the philosophy of German geobiologist Hans Binder as the basis for discussions of aspects of theatre as varied as *nostalgia* in theatre, intuitive collaboration, praise of acting in theatre criticism, practice as research, digital performance, theatre and philosophy, the canon, applied theatre and aspects of acting including helping actors cope with stage fright. In this article, we want to continue this discussion with some thoughts on the nature of beauty in the context of its description as an aspect of the feminine principle, associated with the Goddess.

The feminine principle is the receiving principle, in the form of accepting and absorbing. It is directed to the inside, and associated with spirit, feeling, creativity, gentleness, patience, humility, intuition as well as changeability, emotionality and feelings of guilt. The feminine principle is quiet and works from concealment. The feminine principle is associated with the element of water, in nature with everything soft, hilly, lissom. The associated planets are Moon and Venus. The Moon in turn is associated with the direction of north-west. It represents mind, feelings, motion, change, radiant brilliance in times of the full moon, the element of water, and the flowing of all kinds of energies. If dysfunctional in relation to humans, the Moon is related to difficulties with breathing, headache, migraine, issues with the nervous system, and weak vitality. The Moon regulates water on Earth in terms of high and low tides. Venus represents beauty directly, as well as fertility and material possession. Its element is also water, its direction is south-east. In a positive sense, Venus represents love, aesthetics, richness of feelings, enjoyment, beauty, plants, receptivity, and artistic sensitivity. In the negative sense, Venus relates to allergies, problems with the liver, asthma, problems in a partnership, envy, jealousy. Finally, Venus represents tests in our lives regarding temptations and ensnarement.

The feminine principle is associated with the second of the seven main chakras. They form part of the energy system of humans, according to Indian philosophy, together with subtle matter energy bodies and nadis, channels of energy. The nadis have the task to provide life energy to the energy bodies that had been created in the chakras. In the human body there are said to be several thousand energy channels. The most important of those are called Ida, Pingala and Sushumna. We know them as well from the science of acupuncture, where they are known to us as meridians. The chakras serve the human energy system as receiving station, distributor, and transformer of the different frequencies of prana—life energy. They draw certain energies from the subtle-matter bodies, as well as from the environment and the universe, transform them, and pass them via the nadis to the subtle-matter bodies. Mind, body and soul need these energies for maintenance and development.

There are old scriptures that describe more than 80,000 chakras in the human body. The result is that here are hardly any points in the human body that are not suited and intended to receive, transform and pass on energies. Most of these chakras are, however, very small and play a minor part in the energy system of human beings. There are some forty ancillary chakras that have more importance. The most important of those are in the areas of the spleen, in the neck and in the palms of the hands and the soles of the feet. The seven main chakras, which are situated along a vertical axis in the middle of the body facing the front, are most important for the functioning of the most fundamental and essential areas of body, mind and soul. Of these, the second chakra is most important in turn in the context of beauty.

The second chakra, Svadhistana-chakra in Sanskrit, is also called sacral chakra, and serves as the seat, in the human body, of the feminine principle. It is located above the genitals. It is linked with the sacral bone and opens to the front. Its colour is orange, it is associated with the element of water. In terms of senses, it is associated with the sense of taste. It is also referred to as six-leaved lotus. Its fundamental principle is the creative procreation of being. The physical associations are the pelvis area, the organs of procreation, kidneys, bladder, everything liquid such as blood, lymph, digestive fluids and sperm. The associated glands are gonads—ovaries, prostate and testicles. The function of the gonads is the development of male and female gender characteristics as well as the control of the female period. Its astrological associations are Cancer / Moon: richness of feelings, receptivity, fertility;

Libra / Venus: relationship in a partnership, sensuality, artistic sensibility, turning towards the other; Scorpio / Pluto: sensual desire, transformation of the personality through relinquishing the ego in the act of sexual union. In terms of tasks and function of the second chakra, it is the centre of original, unfiltered emotions and sexual energies and creative forces. It is associated with the element of water and this with the feminine principle, from which all biological life has originated. Through the sacral chakra we participate in the fertilising and receiving energies that permeate all of nature. We experience ourselves as a part of an ever-ongoing process of creation, which expresses itself in and through us in the form of feelings and creative action. The sacral chakra is often considered as the true seat of the feminine aspect of God in the form of creative force. Its sphere of action includes for men the organs of procreation, which carry within then the impulse for creating new life. In women, we find here those areas in which she receives the creative impulse and allows new life to arise from it. This is also the area where the growing being is protected, nourished and supplied with all it needs to thrive.

The water element purifies and purges. It dissolves and rinses away all that has congealed and stands against vital flow. In the body, this is represented through the detoxifying and eliminating activities of the kidneys and bladder. On the mental level, we experience it through letting go and allowing feelings to flow, which make us ready to experience life again and again as original and new. Our interpersonal relations, in particular those with the opposite sex, are shaped decisively by the functioning of the second chakra. The manifold variations of eroticism belong to its range of impact as much as abandoning the limited, small ego and the experience of a larger unity through sexual union.

The harmonious functioning of an opened sacral chakra shows itself in a natural flow with life and feelings. You are open and natural towards other people and the other sex. You feel that the flow of life in creation flows also through body, soul and mind. In this way you can participate better in the deep joy of creation and of life. The feelings are original and actions are creative. They fertilise your own life and the lives of others.

The malfunction of the sacral chakra often has its origin during puberty. The awakened sexual forces cause uncertainty, because parents and teachers are rarely able to convey how to handle these energies properly. In addition, often there has been a lack of tenderness and physical closeness from early childhood onwards. That is how it can now come to a denial and rejection of sexuality. As a result, the unselfconscious expression of its creative potential is lost and the energies focus in a malformed way against oneself or others. If sexuality does happen, it degenerates and uncontrollable behaviour can result. In both cases there are insecurity towards, and tensions with, the other sex.

Insufficient functioning of the sacral chakra comes into existence in most cases already during childhood. Often, parents have suppressed their own sensuality and sexuality and the parents themselves are lacking in sensual stimulation, touching and tenderness. The result of this is that the parents themselves have closed off all aerials. Mental abuse and violation come in as well. During puberty, the sexual energies that are welling up are blocked off completely. Their "successful" blocking causes a lack of feeling of self-worth, a congealment of emotions as well as emotional and mental coldness of feelings. Damage of soul and mind in the form of split-off parts of the soul is a logical consequence. When balanced-natural sexuality is disturbed, these forces are transformed into depression, aggression and attributions of guilt. You go into the victim position, manipulate, and all of the physiology is messed up.

Beauty: creation and perception in performance

Having considered beauty in general, in the Thai context and in the context of consciousness studies, we now proceed to consider beauty in the realm of performance. Critics sometimes refer to "beautifully acted", where "beautiful" relates to the art, not the appearance of the actor. In the Thai context, dance and movement are referred to as explicitly as beautiful, whereas praise of acting would be expressed as "well-acted" or "smartly acted". This does not imply that in Thailand, acting is not perceived as beautiful, but the language uses different expressions. This is different when referring to a performance of theatre, which can be classified as "beautiful" in the sense of being very impressive.

The environmental context of performance is often considered beautiful, such as the surviving Greek arenas, or richly decorated foyers and auditoria of theatres and possibly particularly opera houses in the Western context. In the context of Thailand, a proper theatre space is not that common. However, festivals that include performance often take place in a temple, a space that is richly decorated and special in term of spiritual practice, and in that sense beautiful.

The choices of the designer / scenographer are important as well with regard to set, costume and lighting. From an intercultural perspective, it would be fascinating to explore further whether designs that conform with rules of architecture proposed by Feng Shui or Sthapatya Veda, which are said to have a balancing, harmonising, beneficial impact on those encountering them, would be perceived as more beautiful? These questions go hand in hand with the issue of directorial decisions. Western director's theatre, for example, tends to be explicitly and intentionally not beautiful. It is, of course, arguably much easier to create an ugly image on stage than a genuinely beautiful one—eminent German theatre actor, director and artistic manager Gustaf Gründgens argued that it is very easy to direct a production in such a way as to create a scandal (1963)!

Sometimes, anecdotally, audiences are surprised to see in daily life an actor they considered beautiful in character on stage. Costume and lighting can contribute to an actor's stage beauty, but cannot take sole responsibility. Does performance make beautiful? Beauty has been related to radiance in various cultural contexts, and radiance is part of what constitutes an actor's presence on stage. The more present we perceive an actor to be, the more likely we are to perceive that actor also as beautiful. Presence as such, or its absence, is either agreed, or disputed. Body awareness enhances beauty, among performers and in daily life (Power 2008, Hofmann and Zorić 2017).

Beauty is important for many plays—such as the beauty of characters as perceived by other character (or not). In *Amadeus* by Peter Shaffer, composer Salieri grasps the full extent of Mozart's genius in terms of beauty: "I was staring through the cage of those meticulous ink strokes at an absolute beauty" (Shaffer 1980: 48-49). In the same play, Mozart's extolling of the role of music, specifically opera, can be regarded to be in terms of beauty, even though he does not use the term explicitly:

> ... That's why opera is important, Baron. Because it's realer than any play! A dramatic poet would have to put all those thoughts down one after another to represent this second of time. The composer can put them all down at once and still make us hear each one of them. Astonishing device: a vocal quartet! (*More and more excited*)... I tell you I want to write a finale lasting half an hour! A quartet becoming a quintet becoming a sextet. On and on, wider and wider—all sounds multiplying and rising together—and the together making a sound entirely new! ... I bet you that's how God hears the world. Millions of sounds ascending at once and mixing in His ear to become an unending music, unimaginable to us. (*To Salieri*) That's our job! That's our job, we composers: combining the inner

minds of him and him and him and her and her—the thoughts of chambermaids and Court Composers—and turn the audience into God. (Shaffer 1980: 60)

In Athol Fugard's *A Road to Mecca*, Miss Helen shares with the other characters and thus with the audience her memory of a vision that was central to her life. Miss Helen is a widow, seventy years of age, who lives in a small village in South Africa. After her husband's death Miss Helen started to create strange sculptures in her garden. The inside of her house changed as well: she placed numerous lamps and candles and painted the walls blue and golden. She is visited by Elsa, a young, energetic, politically active teacher from Cape Town. It turns out that the evening that is dramatized in the play gains special importance for Miss Helen: she also expects the visit of Marius, the village priest, who will ask her for a decision as to whether she wants to move into an old people's home or not. Elsa and Marius indirectly help Miss Helen to find herself and make her decision.

Miss Helen had a vision on the night of her late husband's funeral, which inspired her creative outburst: she actually tries to recreate her vision at home. She calls her vision "Mecca": "If my Mecca is finished, Elsa, then so is my life" (Fugard 1985: 47). Miss Helen's Mecca was her way out of her fear of death and darkness after her husband's death. At the end of the play Miss Helen tells Marius and Elsa about that vision: returned home from her husband's funeral, she had sat down in front of a candle, staring into the flame. It did not burn out, but became increasingly brighter and led Miss Helen to a distant place. At this point Miss Helen interrupts her story and asks Elsa to light the candles in the room:

[*She looks around the room and speaks with authority*]
Light the candles, Elsa. That one first.
[*She indicates a candelabra that has been set up very prominently on a little table. ELSA lights it.*]
And you know why, Marius? That is the East. Go out there into the yard and you'll see that all my Wise Men and their camels are travelling in that direction. Follow the candle on and one day you'll come to Mecca. Oh yes, Marius, it's true! I've done it. That is where I went that night and it was the candle you lit that led me there.
[*She is radiantly alive with her vision*]
A city, Marius! A city of light and colour more splendid than anything I had ever imagined. There were palaces and beautiful buildings everywhere, with dazzling white walls and glittering minarets. Strange statues filled the courtyards. The streets were crowded with camels and turbaned men speaking a language I didn't understand, but that didn't

matter because I knew, it was Mecca. And I was on my way to the grand temple. In the centre of Mecca there is a temple, and in the centre of the temple is a vast room with hundreds of mirrors on the walls and hanging lamps. And that is where the Wise Men of the East study the celestial geometry of light and colour. I became an apprentice that night. Light them all, Elsa, so that I can show Marius what I've learned.
[*ELSA moves around the room lighting all the candles, and as she does so its full magic and splendour is revealed. MISS HELEN laughs ecstatically*]
(Fugard 1985: 71-2)

Finally, it should be possible to interpret some of the last words of Emily in Wilder's *Our Town* in terms of beauty. Emily has died and joined the other dead on the cemetery. She requests from the Stage Manager to be able to return to Earth to relive a day of her choice. Granted her wish, she is unable to spend the whole day, because she finds that while alive, humans do not live in the present, in the moment. She leaves with these words:

Good-by, Good-by, world. Good-by, Grover's Corners...Mama and Papa. Good-by to clocks ticking...and Mama's sunflowers. And food and coffee. And new-ironed dresses and hot baths...and sleeping and waking up. Oh, earth, you're too wonderful for anybody to realize you. (Wilder 1938:100)

Emily's "wonderful" here at least implies beauty.

Summary

Beauty is a phenomenon that has been relevant to humans across times and cultures. The contexts are multiple and complex, ranging from individual to social, and political dimensions. In Thailand, beauty in performance (artistic and daily) appeals to the eyes and the heart. The notion of beauty as Ngām in performance relates to the heart through social values such as kindness, gratefulness, loyalty, and respect, as well as the charisma and presence of the performer/actor. The beauty as Sūay in performance relates to the qualities that please the eyes, such as right proportions, composition and sometimes extravagance. Many Thai performances are still made as 'mode of representation' to perceive beauty (pleasant to the eyes). The notion of beauty in the story itself is the social value (pleasant to the understanding of common value), but the discussion of beauty as a topic separate from the representational mode or value of society is not yet vivid in the Thai context.

PART FOUR:

PRACTICE AS RESEARCH

CHAPTER FOURTEEN

THEATRE WITHOUT CONFLICT:
PRACTICE AS RESEARCH

[This chapter will be published in *Time, Consciousness and Writing: Peter Malekin Illuminating the Divine Darkness*, edited by Theo Malekin and Robert Eddy, to be published by Brill | Rodopi, due out November 2018, printed here with permission from the publisher]

Contextualisation

For some time now, attempts have been made across disciplines in literatures and the arts of enhancing the dialogue between academics and practitioners; the latest phase in this development is the merging of the two in one and the same person: the academic who is an active artist, and the artists who reflect academically on their own artistic creation. The academic element in this merger is usually related to theory, while the artist's aspect is practice. Theory is predominantly on the level of discourse, of speaking and / or writing, and practice is doing. Prior to the attempts at merging theory and practice in this way, artists were free (?) to create independent of any theoretical restrictions. If academics wanted to read theory into their works of art, so be it. Academics were equally free (?) to approach any work of art of their choice and subject it to the theory of their choice. The merger of theorist/academic and practitioner/artist changes this picture. Academic ideas might now serve as 'inspiration' for artistic activity, and artists (are expected to) reflect their creation in academic discourse. The question arises whether either theory or art will be the same as before. Theory is likely to thrive, because with artists becoming fellow-producers of theory, more theory is certainly in the process of being written even now. There is thus a statistical chance that with more theory, more useful theory might result. It will be interesting to check, with hindsight, whether this statistical potential is met. Equally, hindsight will establish whether the kind of art created by reflexive artists, artists who not only continue producing works of art, but who (have to) write theoretically about them, is different from the art possibly still produced by artists who either never had the idea of turning reflexive, or who make a clear and conscious decision not to join the reflexive artist bandwagon. If there are differences, what could those differences be? I propose that reflexive art is likely to be different: I expect that it involves more of the artist's intellect, and less of other levels of the mind, such as emotions, intuition, feeling, ego, etc., and that, in consequence, it will appeal more to the recipient's intellect. The intellectuals among recipients are likely to be able to write about the works of art created by reflexive artists more readily, and further reams of theory will ensue. Less intellectually inclined recipients are likely to get less from those reflexive works of art. Reflexive art, on this argument, is potentially less inclusive than non-reflexive art, and its impact on recipients potentially less comprehensive than non-reflexive art. Clearly, such potential loss in inclusiveness and comprehensiveness has implications for any discussion of the value, worth, merit, or quality of the work(s) of art in question, no matter how despised such concepts may be in the present climate of political correctness.

Practice as Research (PaR), as defined and described by Robin Nelson

> involves a research project in which practice is a key method of inquiry and where, in respect of the arts, a practice (creative writing, dance, musical score/performance, theatre/performance, visual exhibition, film or other cultural practice) is submitted as substantial evidence of a research enquiry. (2013: 8-9)

While practice may be what the artist involved in PaR is most comfortable with, in a PaR project, theory should be imbricated within practice from the start of a project, rather than starting with practice and adding theory on (2013: 32). The relation between practice and writing about practice is important: PaR, according to Nelson, does not imply "a verbal account of the practice", and "certainly not" the requirement of a "transposition of the practice into words" (2013: 11).

Much of what happens in any arts practice is, to some extent, possibly to a very large extent, intuitive, works in terms of hunches, ideas, and relates to the concept of tacit knowledge. While Nelson acknowledges this with reference to relevant literature, he argues "against artists' claim to a special private knowledge which, based on intuition, is incommunicable other than in the artform" (58). He places "considerable emphasis" on the "processes to articulate the tacit", acknowledging that it may not "ultimately be possible to make the tacit thoroughly explicit (that is, expressed as propositional knowledge in writing), but, if practitioner-researchers wish their embodied cognitions to be better recognized, means of identifying and disseminating them must be sought" (39).

Thus for Nelson, neither theory nor practice comes, or at least should, come first, with the respective other coming second. Nelson would like to see the two as imbricated, and that means working hand in hand, closely linked, related to each other, informing each other, at all times, as a new mode of gaining knowledge, neither only theoretical nor only practical, neither starting with practice and applying theory to it, nor starting with theory and exploring it in practice. This is an ideal state of affairs, the aim and goal all PaR should strive for and be measured against.

Anecdotal evidence, which can serve as the basis for more detailed empirical study, provides an insight into how this imbricated mode of PaR works for different artists involved in PaR. Thus, German dancer/philosopher Aurelia Baumgartner is confident that in her artistic work, theory and practice do indeed go hand in hand. With regard to her 2012 performance *Dancing Horses: Reflections in Space*, in which she worked with horses, she comments:

> Naturally I always have theories at the back of my head. I work with structures, but I make sure or I try to ensure that these structures remain open. In some cases, I really go beyond established structures, for example with the question regarding animals, whether animals actually do have their own free creativity. This is quite an opposition to conventional approaches to animals which we consider as things. In my view animals need to be considered and respected as individual, auto-poetic and creative. Such a consideration of course brings with it quite a number of additional considerations of an ethical nature, for example: are we allowed to eat animals and where is the boundary between this and what could be called then cannibalism, where is the boundary? Further to this, how do we deal with nature, how we treat nature—all these are issues that I cannot answer in my work, but I can raise the questions through it. I can do this through my work by embodying these questions on the stage, and by thus inviting the audience to engage in the dialogue with the performance, with the questions. In that sense, I am a researcher who raises more questions than I answer. (2013)

Specifically about the need, in the university PaR context, of writing about, or in relation to practice, Baumgartner expands:

> I have to ask myself whether it is not the case that my performance work can say and express more than anything I could possibly write about it. I could link myself to some explanation of my work to some context but on the other hand I don't want to write an instruction manual. I would think together with Agamben that art becomes an example, a paradigm which enables or allows research to begin at a different level without ruining the artistic process. This might be achieved by somebody else doing the

research in relation to an artist's work rather than the artist him or herself so that the artist asks him or herself questions, has a lot of material to offer and probably also thinks him or herself about their own work. My first thoughts are integrated into the artistic expression and the researcher can then enter a dialogue with the artist about this expression. In this way it is not all focused on one individual. While the artist also has to become a researcher, a network is established, and it is the network that does the job. Such an approach would leave the artist and the scientist researcher their individual freedoms within their individual fields. (2013)

Kate Sicchio, US dancer and choreographer, considers herself as an artist/researcher. She remembers that even from a very young age on, she questioned her practice, and there is not much differentiation for her between her art practice and research, they are "totally integrated. I can't think of any research that I have done specifically that doesn't have a practical dimension to it but that is also who I am, I am a maker, I need to do stuff to understand it" (2014). When she decided on a career in academia, while the research dimension as such was not new or challenging, the dimension of intentional writing about her practice, over and above documentation, became a new aspect, which she found challenging to start with. She noted the difference between more relaxed expectations of writing in her native USA, and the more academic and rigorous demands on her writing in the UK, which to her goes in the direction of pseudo-social science frameworks. With the exception of one collaborative piece, which involved writing before and during the practical work (an approach she found particularly at odds with her way of working, which follows the principle of "I have to do it first, then I get it"), Sicchio has been able to write after the practice—which does not mean that practice and its reflection are disjointed, because writing is not the same as reflection.

While Sicchio thus does not have a problem with the core of PaR, she addresses an issue in need of further discussion. It relates to the perceived demand for the art work to constitute a research outcome or the answer to the research question. In the context of PaR, Sicchio asks whether it is enough for the creation of the work of art to serve as the process for, or tool of answering a research question.

Michael Pinchbeck considers himself, his practice and his relation to PaR as a product of the university environment. It was at university that he started a theatre company, and after graduation he took the company's productions to the university circuit, where the productions were "reflected upon in an academic context by students and staff" (2014). Pinchbeck's MA in Performance and Live Art at Nottingham Trent University shifted his focus to the visual arts, because that was the focus of the programme, "but I was still looking at the work through a research environment" (2014). While at Nottingham Trent, Pinchbeck added the writing dimension to the practice that occurred in a research context, accumulating a blog of around 40,000 words over a year. Writing this blog about his practice led to research questions about the role of the dramaturg, which developed into the central focus of his PhD research. Thus, practice developed in an academic context, presented to and reflected on by an academic audience, and reflectively written about by the practitioner, led to the research question at the centre of a PhD project. Recent practice then in turn emerged out of the research for the PhD. However, Pinchbeck's practice is not limited by research contexts. If he is commissioned to write a play, the trigger is not research, but nevertheless he will try to "create something that was not alien to the style of theatre I make as part of the PhD" (2014). Thus, for Pinchbeck, context is essential: "If you are writing for a mainstream theatre you might have to think about your audiences, if you are touring through a university theatre you might have to think about how your work sits within an academic context" (2014). He maintains a balance of the demands of contexts of research, articulating his practice and inspiration: "I try and articulate my research enquiry but there are times when also the work itself is unsure of where it is coming from; so, there are moments of not knowing that seem very important to a creative process that I also try and acknowledge" (2014). While he is not bound in principle by potential limitations of the research impetus, Pinchbeck does acknowledge that there may be occasions where an inability to articulate a hunch can be troubling. For those instances, he has developed a playful approach of openly acknowledging the problem in performance: "If there is a moment in the show which isn't working then you say to the audience 'I am not sure this is working', and after that you find a moment that may work. I am more or less trying to make visible the gaps or make the problems a narrative" (2014).

Sicchio is expressly an artist/researcher, and Pinchbeck asks directly: "When is practice not research?" (2014). Both have developed their careers in academia with practice and research as concomitant factors. The same applies for Andrew Westerside, although he is clear that he is an artist first in so far as he often thinks about the work first. The second question follows: "Is there a research question in here as I have to try and make what I do as a practitioner productive for both jobs" (2014). Adding the research dimension adds

a level of rigour to the questions I am asking about making a performance. Because we make new work and it is experimental work, there is always a sense of trying to move towards new territory or towards the unknown, which means that regardless of being a scholar or not, you want to stay at the cutting edge of whatever new practice is about, so having that research angle is really helpful. (2014)

In the context of Nelson's demand for, and justification of reflection of practice, as central component of PaR, Nelson seems to be dismissing those artist-researchers who appear to resist the demand for practice imbricated with theory when he writes: "for some arts practitioners, the requirement to do a little more to articulate their research inquiry is an unwarranted imposition from beyond their culture" (4). This apparent dismissal implies the assumption that the artists concerned have a choice. I want to suggest that they may not have a choice, and now I want to explore possible reasons of why not.

What are the concerns that some artists bring up in relation to PaR? The positions of Sicchio, Pinchbeck and Westerside suggest, as a working hypothesis for further empirical research, that individuals who have developed in an environment in which practice and research were both present, have been able to become secure in their awareness of the nature of their art practice to the extent that they do not encounter the research dimension as constituting a threat to their arts practice. Westerside confirms this position:

> What kind of an artist are you? If you are an artist with a fifteen-year career and then decide to do a PhD and become a university lecturer, then you have got a different game on your hands as you are going to have to think about your practice in a radically new way. (2014)

Central to that new way of thinking is to understand the questions many artists have in relation to their practice as research questions in an academic way. The questions may be the same in the end, but possibly the artist's perspective on the questions, and the terminology to express them in, may be different. Susan Melrose argues, in the context of the peer assessment of research in the UK under the framework of the Research Excellence Framework (REF), that

> perhaps we could acknowledge that practitioner-researchers in the case of PaR projects need to be able to argue for the status of their work as a mode of advanced enquiry driven by a creative as well as a research imperative, and to signal where and how these two meet, and to what effect. Does that mean that practitioner-researchers in HE need to be trained/mentored, to exploit research meta-narratives effectively in order to make that argument? Absolutely. The rest of us have been. (2013)

We must believe artists more literally when they report that they experience the process of the creation of their art as emanating from hunches, from intuition, and that they experience further that their artistic practice is influenced by the processes of theoretical reflection. They experience the influence as inevitable. The influence of theory on practice can be perceived by the artist as good in the sense that it supports their practice, leads to new insights, and new aspects of the practice that would not have come about without academic reflection on it. In contrast, the influence of theory on practice can be perceived by the artist as bad in the sense that it impedes, obstructs, blocks, or changes their art in ways they do not like. In these respects, the artists who report the experience of a detrimental impact of theory on their practice really do have that experience; they do not resist this aspect of PaR for the sake of resistance, or because of political or any other reasons except for their experiences.

If they thus come short of the ideal as developed by Nelson, we must not blame them as a result, and they must not feel guilty. No pressure should be exercised or felt in an attempt to achieve compliance, and supervision or mentoring must ensure to be sensitive: if the hunch, intuition comes first for an artist, this is part of the normal spectrum, and the role of the supervisor or mentor in such a scenario can only be to guide the artist to academic reflection on their own terms, with full understanding and empathy towards unfamiliar territory of that academic kind of reflection.

Westerside points out a challenge of PaR in the fact that much may be said, rightly so, about what constitutes research, but nobody can tell the artist what artistic practice is. "It is only when you know what your practice is that you can figure out how notions of research might apply to it" (2014).

Research into *verbal overshadowing* suggests one possible reason why some, not all, artists are not comfortable with the reflective aspect of PaR, and why they are not exaggerating their reluctance about the reflexive component of PaR because such verbal reflexion does have an undeniable, and perhaps even empirically measurable detrimental impact on their creative practice. In the phenomenon of verbal overshadowing, "describing memory for nonverbal stimuli (e.g. faces, tastes, or music) interferes with subsequent recognition performance". Further, findings of a 1998 study suggest "that individuals may be especially vulnerable to verbal overshadowing when their general perceptual abilities exceed their verbal abilities" (Ryan and Schooler 1998: S105). More recent studies have broadly confirmed the findings of the initial research and offered a range of possible explanations for the phenomenon. In some cases, studies have not been able to confirm predicted results, however, without being able to identify the reason(s).

Further potential reasons for the adverse impact of theory on practice for some artists could have to do with the concepts of sensitizer/rationaliser, or with field independence. Could it be that a structured approach to PaR is important, in which immersive creative phases, undisturbed by critical thinking, alternate with critical and reflective phases, with problems arising when such structure is not developed in the first place, or not adhered to? Other aspects of personality such as confidence, maturity, self-assurance, being comfortable with self-exposure and vulnerability, etc., could play their roles, too. It is likely to be a complex combination.

For those who do not perceive the critical dimension as a problem, reflection allows them to make sense of the practical, immersive experience, to consider their practice in a new light, and this in turn in many cases enriches subsequent practice. With hindsight, some argue that the critically reflective phase of their PaR was less a process of rationalising but one of integrating of consciousness and unconscious contents. They consider thought to follow naturally, organically from doing and moving, as suggested by Maxine Sheets-Johnstone: the boundary between verbal thought and thinking in movement might be more artificial than assumed (2009).

A further dimension is PaR in the disciplines of music and fine art: here, the need for verbal contextualisation is not necessary. Artists and musicians consider the creation of a work of art or a composition as research and can assess its merit as research without the need to put any of it into words. Researchers in the performing arts are unable to grasp this, just as researchers in music and art are unable to grasp the need for words. Imagine someone becoming an expert about all aspects of a strawberry without ever even considering the possibility of eating one him/herself.

Against this background, I engaged in what started off as a private PaR project in summer 2015, to explore the possibility of theatre without conflict. Later I wrote this up and proposed it for its inclusion in the book inspired by the late Peter Malekin. I first met Peter Malekin in 1988. I had heard about him within the German Transcendental Meditation movement and, while at Maharishi International University in the USA in the summer of 1987 on a four-week stint as researcher in residence, had seen a video recording of his conversation about poetry with Maharishi Mahesh Yogi. During my undergraduate studies of English at the University of Düsseldorf, I had developed what I considered a new interpretation of Eliot's *The Waste Land* on the basis of consciousness studies, which had, however, left my professors confused. I had visited London on a regular

basis since the late 1970s and wrote to Peter whether he could see me
during my next visit. We arranged to meet, I told him about my ideas, and
he simply said: yes, of course that is a very appropriate interpretation of
the poem, but not one that many literary critics today will accept, so no
wonder your professors did not understand what on earth you were writing
about. I then came to stay and live at Peter's house in Streatham from
1991 to 1994 while I did my PhD in drama at what was then Royal
Holloway and Bedford New College. I am grateful for many, many
conversations with Peter over those years.

Theatre and conflict

Over the years, in my own research, what I have been doing is to
interrogate and explore phenomena of theatre in the context of
consciousness studies, to seek explanations for experiences described by
theatre artists across the world in terms of consciousness studies. My
approach has been eclectic in so far as I have gone with the aspects of
consciousness studies that had, for me, the highest explanatory value,
independent of where any specific aspect might have come from. I have
found much value in Vedanta philosophy, much of that in the form of
Vedic Science as developed on the basis of Vedanta philosophy by the late
Maharishi Mahesh Yogi. In my 2013 book *Observing Theatre: Spirituality
and Subjectivity in the Performing Arts*, I introduced the philosophy of
German geobiologist Hans Binder as the basis for discussions of aspects of
theatre as varied as *nostalgia* in theatre, intuitive collaboration, praise of
acting in theatre criticism, practice as research, digital performance,
theatre and philosophy, the canon, applied theatre and aspects of acting
including helping actors cope with stage fright. In this chapter I want to
continue this discussion with some thoughts, and an account of practical
exploration, about what must be considered one of the most solid
principles of theatre theory and practice: that theatre thrives on, and can
possibly cannot exist without, conflict.

According to Binder, belief patters and dogmata and doctrines have
become so engrained in our lives that we take them for granted without
even a thought of checking their validity. They are, in fact, patterns of
belief, not of truth, even in the way we refer to them. We all tend to create
our own world in the realm of our thoughts. If that world corresponds to
laws of nature that rule the universe independent of what we are thinking,
then we are lucky. If the world we create in our thoughts does not
correspond to that set of natural laws, we have created, and are engaging
in, wrong belief patterns. These wrong belief patterns cannot be beneficial

for us. The longer we believe in those wrong patterns, the more they harden, and we come to believe that they are in fact laws of nature, which they are not. Some examples for individual wrong belief patterns are: Others always want to pull a fast one on me; others want to harm me; I must not attract attention; money makes you arrogant; men cannot be faithful; women cannot remain matter-of-fact; I mustn't contradict my partner; I am not likeable; I am only average; what would others say; that's how we have been doing this always. The examples show that the wrong belief patterns are often generalisations, which set in stone things that need not be accurate in this way for each individual.

Belief patterns form our innermost convictions, and these influence our thinking and action in a major way. We begin getting used to belief patterns in early childhood: our upbringing unconsciously makes girls believe that they have to be well-behaved and must not stand out. As adults, such women will be extremely adaptable, but also prone to put their own interests last. Boys have to be brave and must not have, or at least show, fear, otherwise they will be seen as milksops and expelled from their circle of friends. Other belief patterns accumulate through life experiences—if the colleague gets the dream-job more than once, this leads to the belief pattern "I am just not good enough". In some cases, wrong belief patterns may well have helped us. Patterns such as "I must not make any mistakes", or "I must be perfect in everything I do" may have brought us to the track of success we are on now, but suddenly such belief patterns turn from "right" to "wrong", or their nature reveals itself as having been wrong all along, and they turn from guarantor of success to dead weight.

Belief patterns give us a feeling of security, especially if they are well engrained in mass consciousness. We become part of an enormous energy field and feel supported by that field. However, in fact an energy field whose energy is no longer in line with natural law does no longer sustain its own energy, it needs energy from outside, from those engaging with the energy field, and thus we are drained of our own energy to support the energy field of the wrong belief pattern. We make our own lives miserable by adhering to such wrong belief patterns, because we close ourselves up to engaging in different, more rewarding experiences. Especially if we believe very strongly in a wrong belief pattern, we feed that pattern with a lot of our own energy, and if many people on earth have the same pattern, it gets very big and very strong, and forms a massive energy field. It takes a lot of effort and courage not only to find out that belief patterns are wrong, but even more so to free oneself from such energy fields.

I base what follows on the axiom that one of the most persistent false belief patterns is that "life is a struggle". The controversy, anger, frustration, disbelief, concern or merriment that such a claim might well stir is indicative of the extent to which this belief pattern has hardened. The strength of a belief pattern can be judged in relation to the extent to which we believe in something as a truth, the number of examples, or references which we can list to support the belief, the extent of attention we dedicate to the belief, the source of the belief, and the extent to which we yoke how many others for our beliefs. The overall principle, "life is a struggle", has a multitude of expressions that can serve as examples. In academic discourse, more is thought and written about struggle than its opposite. A search in the *Bibliography of British and Irish History* reveals 149 hits for *consensus* compared with 1735 hits for *conflict*, and 1617 hits for *peace* compared with 17,323 hits for *war*. In the context of the arts, the suggestion that the creation of great works of art must go along with a suffering artist is one example, supported in prose fiction, poetry and plays about artists, with even more hard-nosed "evidence" from psychology and the social sciences. If we were to look more closely, we will probably see a correlation between suffering and creative activity, where the correlation does not constitute causality; in addition, we know about the suffering of the artists because we are interested in the person because of the art. We are not interested in other people to that extent, and thus we simply do not know about their suffering: it is likely that many people we are not interested in and about whose private lives we do not know anything do suffer as well, only they do not create art. Thus, the causal link between suffering and artistic creativity is problematic at best. That it is problematic suggests that its basis, the assumption that life is a struggle, is problematic as well, in the sense of a false belief pattern as described and discussed above. Karen Saillant of International Opera Theater has voiced her concern about singers being prevented from achieving their best level of singing by following the false belief pattern that you have to open your mouth very, very wide to achieve full sound (2015). No matter how beautiful we consider a ballet performance, there is no denying that a dancer's body is worn out at a relatively young age. In classical Japanese Noh performance, the performer's elegant, and very slow movement is in stark contrast to the high rate of their body's metabolism, although the contents of the plays, when gods or goddesses are portrayed, may suggest a lack of conflict (Shepherd 2015).

When I talk about conflict, I am referring to the whole range of possibilities, such as plots and actions and dialogues that focus on, or are informed by, war, fighting, opposition, difference. Conflict, however, can exist also on the level of energies itself, as in the harnessing of dark energies in the heart chakra (energy centre) in Japanese Butoh. In some cases, audience well-being is achieved by the characters overcoming conflict, tense, difficult situations, but that is still drama/theatre with an emphasis on conflict. Theatre history across cultures confirms the position that theatre without conflict is problematic because conflict makes it interesting and lack of conflict enhances the risk of such plays and productions coming across as not interesting and boring. Rancière defines theatre as "bodies in action before and assembled audience", and with that definition, some form of conflict is implied as bodies in action will inevitably meet resistance (Julien 2015). Theatre presents human beings on stage, and the need to make decisions, ethical considerations, and various situations known to humankind often involve internal and external struggles (Newton 2015). Such theatre makes the characters in plays who undergo these struggles so attractive to their audiences. Furthermore, narrative thrives on change, and change thrives on opposition (Mangan 2015). Conflict may not necessarily have to be "in" the play, but can occur in the speeches, or "outside" the play. They are reported. But then they often have arguments between different positions, and that might be considered a form of conflict as well (Zorn 2015). Even drama/theatre that is experimental and seems to have no major conflict in the plot then establishes conflict between itself and audience expectations (Boyko-Head 2015). Stephen MacDonald's play *Not about Heroes* (1982) focuses on the friendship between Siegfried Sassoon and Wilfred Owen. In his review of the production, Guardian critic Michael Billington commented on the problems inherent in writing about a friendship, because a friendship does not provide room for tensions and conflict (1983). Finally, conflict need not be overt, as for example in film where a large percentage would probably self-define as romance or adventure: here the structuring around conflict resolution is masked (Punt 2015).

Alternatives to theatre based, directly or indirectly, overtly or covertly, knowingly or unknowingly, on conflict, might be found in the context of Dolan's utopian performatives (2005), even if many of these celebrate the overcoming of conflict. Theatre can include discoveries and surprising encounters that must be integrated into a new understanding (Brask 2015). A smaller or larger extent of conflict will also result depending on whether we understand theatre practice as collaborative, negotiatory, challenging, stimulating, life-enhancing, or provocative (Yarrow 2015).

In terms of energy fields, the energy field of the obsolete belief pattern of the need for conflict in theatre, dance and opera is part of the wider energy field that life is a struggle. Energy created from conflict is likely to be different from the one created from any context that lacks conflict, such as beauty. The strength of such energy is related to where society in general places more emphasis. In our time, most energy / attention is placed on conflict in the media, and in most people's thoughts. Therefore, artists and audiences are likely to respond more easily and strongly to energy in theatre relating to conflict. Similarly, it may be easier for dramatists to write conflict, for directors to direct conflict and for actors to act conflict. In this context, eminent German actor and director Gustaf Gründgens (1899–1963) argued that it is incredibly easy to direct a scandal but to create real beauty onstage is so much more difficult (1963). On each occasion that dramatists, directors and actors engage in conflict they tap into a massive field of that energy of conflict present in mass consciousness. By giving their attention to this field, they strengthen it further. In return, they feel strengthened. It is thus perhaps a "better" energy that does without conflict, but also one that will not be as attractive as conflict-generated energy to an audience used to the conflict-generated/related energy. It may be difficult for the performer to generate that conflict-less energy in the first place because the need for conflict in performance is so strongly engrained in mass-consciousness as a belief pattern.

What does all this mean for the practice of dance, opera and theatre? It means that there is vast potential for us, today, here and now, to develop really, genuinely, and truly "new", theatre practice. It is also a challenge, because anything really new cannot be predicted in its form, nature, characteristics, components, or aspects, at the stage where its possibility becomes evident, but it has not yet emerged, or its emergence has not yet been noticed as such. The nature of this challenge suggests that it is probably unlikely that new, conflict-free forms and contents of dance, opera and theatre will result from the activity at one level of the mind alone. They will need to work together on this one, mind, intellect, emotions, feelings, and intuition.

Practice as research

I wanted to put this theory to the test and explore it further in practice. For this I worked together with my two daughters, Lilwen (aged 14) and Myfanwy (aged 19), initially over a one-week period in August 2015, which forms the basis of the remainder article. They have engaged in improvisations around dramatic scenarios on a regular basis for many years, have created their own plays, and films, written numerous short stories and other pieces of fiction, and have also read many plays (esp. Myfanwy as part of her university studies of drama since summer 2014).

In discussing the potential of theatre without conflict, we began by thinking about the nature of conflict. It seems to be easier to begin with that and develop the lack of conflict on that basis. War was mentioned first, death second, although we also noted that death is a natural occurrence and our perception of it as something undesirable is probably a further example of a hardened and wrong belief pattern. We consider death as problematic because of lack of proper knowledge and understanding; medicine considers itself as a struggle ultimately against death, and that is where conflict comes in. Certain emotions are more associated with conflict than others, first and foremost anger. When we develop expectations of any kind, conflict immediately arises when those expectations are not met or fulfilled.

We shifted quickly from talking about conflict itself to discussing its opposite, lack of conflict. In peace there is no conflict. When we love unconditionally, without expecting, requiring, wanting something (love) back, there is no conflict. Positive emotions lack conflict, as does beauty. In Platonic philosophy, humans develop from appreciation of the beauty of objects to the beauty of individual persons to the beauty of all life to the experience of the form of beauty, a higher state of consciousness. Sustained innocence is also without conflict—here it is important to distinguish innocence from lack of education and ignorance. Conflict ultimately is personal, it exists, or arises, only in the person who creates it. Playfulness can be free of conflict. The plan of life, according to Binder's thinking, is important. Any situation a person faces according to a person's life plan, and their role within the divine plan, will allow a person to grow and develop. Conflict arises if people evade the situation, or make the "wrong" decision.

How to create theatre, on the basis of these insights, that is free of conflict? And: is it possible, even necessary, to define this kind of theatre not in the negative (lack of), but somehow in the positive? On the level of design, a neutral, empty space and generic costume might help. On the level of characters, idiosyncrasies become important. Opposites attract, and similarities create unity.

We decided to start the process by working on our own, creating a short monologue that we felt was without conflict. Writing the monologues was spontaneous for Lilwen. Myfanwy knew she wanted to tell a story. She also tried a poem, so as to be able to have special emphasis on the rhythm, but it did not work as well as with the story. In the story it proved easier to avoid conflict. Lilwen was always aware that the task was to avoid conflict. Myfanwy had to be aware that to avoid conflict, she had to get around the usual arc of storytelling which can, and usually does, include conflict. The task thus made her more aware of the structural aspects of storytelling. I closed my eyes with the intention of being able to focus deeply on the task; the question "Who are you" came up first, and the rest developed organically from that. I wrote, revised in the process, changed the position of sentences or parts of sentences in relation to each other, and noted that one phrase came across as rather aggressive, and thus characteristic of conflict, which I then cut. Lilwen wondered whether the use of "intend" in "I am me and I intend to remain this way" came across as aggressive (it did not).

Writing monologues tends to be in the first person (not always, as Myfanwy's monologue demonstrates), and if that is the case, there can be a tendency for the writing to be or become a reflection of ego. We have responded to a stimulus in our own individual ways. The writing at this stage was very personal, and with that came a certain level of vulnerability.

How to proceed from here? In the group, or individually, immediately, or after letting the material settle down and allow the tacit level to engage with it? We read out the monologues to each other, in the sequence of Lilwen, Daniel and Myfanwy. Further discussion led us to the sequence Lilwen-Myfanwy-Daniel. Additional work might be needed on the segues. Instead of words, the links could be created through passing a large dice (inflatable, to add playfulness) to the next speaker. Once the entire text has been created, we can add, at the beginning of the piece, a section of physical theatre inspired by / reflecting the text that follows. We discussed the costumes in terms of red hats, white, long-sleeved shirts, and being barefoot. The three of us would be in an isolated spotlight while speaking our monologue, while the others would remain as much as possible in darkness. At the end of my monologue, general cover light would come on and the three characters would see and then explore each other. Myfanwy suggested we take ideas from Bausch about the exploration, but we discarded that idea to allow us to be, and remain, original. We developed the ideas, which we later incorporated into the developing script, for each character to have an object. Myfanwy would have a book, Lilwen a dice, and I a picture frame. We also considered a signature sound, tune and movement for each character, and may come back to those ideas at a later stage. We considered these items as building blocks for multi-dimensionality. Spending about an hour of concentrated work in the morning after breakfast on the planning and writing of the material over six days, we took our material, as work in progress, to a two-hour rehearsal in the dance studio of the Lincoln Performing Arts Centre. The text below has been revised on the basis of that rehearsal and represents the current state of affairs in mid-August 2015.

Text

Spot 1 on Lilwen
Lilwen   *Holding inflatable dice*
         Let's play a game. Innocence is the theme. Nothing else. Just innocence. Because it should be sustained if it is the right kind. And if you are meant to be innocent, then that's that. Accept it. Cherish it. Sustain it. Because innocence counts. And so does individuality. Be you. That's why I enjoy my idiosyncrasy; my androgyny. I am not everyone out there. I am only me and that is a fact I hold close to my heart. I am innocent. I am an individual. I am me and I intend to remain this way. That's the game. I challenge you, positively, to be individual and remain innocent. The right kind of innocent. That is the game.

Throws dice into darkness

Spot 1 off to darkness

Spot 2 on Myfanwy who holds the dice

Myfanwy   Let me tell you a story. A story of a little girl who loved to read. She went each week to the same bookshop, took out and read thousands of books. As she grew up she still went. The one thing constant was the bookshop. She had moved from fairy tales to classics, from classics to gardening and cookery books. She knew the classics by heart, and fairy tales she told. "Haven't you read every book in the place?" they asked her. So she went around one last time. A golden book caught her eye. The cover was blank, there was no blurb. As she leafed through the pages, writing appeared. She sat and read, all was quiet. "It seems to me someone has penned my life in these pages. Some events are amiss, and some are there, yet I have not done them". "We never saw this book, know nothing of it", they said. "And how come I have not seen it before?" Maybe she wasn't meant to. We all have one, a life

penned, metaphorically. Whether fulfilled, that is our part
to play on the stage of life.

Throws dice into darkness
Spot 2 off to darkness

Spot 3 on Daniel who holds the dice

Daniel   Who are you? Who am I? Who I am… Do we have to put
           this into words? Do we have to define it, and why? If so, is
           it only for me, so that I know who I am, or is it for you that
           I can answer your question? I am pleased, perhaps
           flattered, perhaps excited, that you are interested. Thank
           you. Which areas should I cover? We can quite easily
           agree on more objective, measurable aspects such as
           weight, height, and category of body shape, hair colour,
           skin colour, and other outwardly visible aspects of what I
           am. Is that all that I am? Why don't you find out yourself
           who I am? I just am, and you perceive me through your
           senses, and tacitly as well, and you may or may not be
           open to that tacit level to the extent that you become aware
           of what it brings to you in finding out about me. Then you
           can answer the question for yourself, if you like, he is…
           And what if I am different afterwards, after you think you
           have found out what I am—who I am? Do you have to
           start all over again? Is that fun? It is probably a scientific
           approach: you observe me, note down your observations,
           and draw conclusion from the observations and notes.
           Then you observe me further, and adjust and modify your
           conclusions. Are your conclusions judgments? You could
           of course also abandon using observation to come to
           conclusions, possibly as judgments, and simply observe,
           innocently. Why don't you give that a try and see what
           happens?

Throws dice into darkness - front

Spot off to darkness – just before darkness, general cover light on

Lilwen, Myfanwy and Daniel see each other. Mime of exploration,
accompanied by music. Slapstick, funny.

Daniel   I wonder if they can talk…

Lilwen   Yes.

Myfanwy   *Yes.*

Daniel   Wow!

Lilwen, Myfanwy, Daniel. All at the same time. Precise lines to follow.

Stop. Pause. Look at each other.

They laugh

Daniel   We can laugh

Myfanwy   *pointing to the audience* Sometimes they laugh!

Lilwen   They're having a good time.

Daniel   Good time is good.

Lilwen   *To Myfanwy and Daniel* Are you here because you want to play my game?

Myfanwy   Yes.

Daniel   Yes.

Myfanwy   *To Lilwen and Daniel* Are you here because you would like to hear to a story?

Daniel   Yes.

Lilwen   Yes.

Daniel   *To Lilwen and Myfanwy, and the audience* Are you here because you want t to find out who you are?

Myfanwy   Yes.

Lilwen	Yes.
Myfanwy	*To Lilwen* What is your game? *To Daniel* What is her game?
Daniel	*To Myfanwy* What is her game? *To Lilwen* What is your game?
Lilwen	*To Myfanwy* What is her game? *To Lilwen* What is your game?
Myfanwy	*To Lilwen* What is your game? *To Daniel* What is her game?
Daniel	*To Myfanwy* What is her game? *To Lilwen* What is your game?
Lilwen	To be an innocent individual.
Daniel	Do we use the dice?
Myfanwy	It's a beautiful dice!
Lilwen	No counters, no dice, no winners, no losers. Just <u>you</u>
Myfanwy	*deflates dice / throw dice off stage* Good bye…
Lilwen	Pick your object from the washing line.

Lilwen, Myfanwy and Daniel pick an object, explore, and end up with "theirs"

Myfanwy	About the book (tbc)
Daniel	About the picture frame (tbc)
Lilwen	It's fluffy.
Myfanwy	Let's make a story of these things. Once upon a time…
Daniel	in a picture frame…

| Lilwen | a fluffy dice rolled on a one. Because I am one individual. It rolled on a three, because there are three of us. |

| Myfanwy | The three stages of a relationship… In a picture frame, a fluffy dice met and fell in love with another fluffy dice. Their love was true, they said it was meant to be, that they would be together till eternity. Besides fulfilling a basic need, besides completing a task, they learned through each other. They learned to love, learned to respect and appreciate, learned themselves, each other, and the world. There followed a love, a happiness, a life so rich, so beautiful yet natural. They had completed a task, learned love in life and were rewarded with…bliss. |

| Lilwen | I threw the dice one last time; a six – what did it symbolise? The factor of innocence, the rate of individuality, the probability of a story being told, the amount of times you look in the mirror every day and say, who am I? Not really. It just reflects the peace felt in this room as we attempt to create something never attempted or created before. It reflects the hope of how close we are to achieving our goals, reaching beyond our targets, until we can reach no further; we are at the top. We have reached what we intended to reach, and by doing this, we have bettered ourselves. So, what does the six on this fluffy dice represent? Our journey, and how it made us incredible people. |

| Daniel | People, once upon a time, were not either male or female. They were both in one, or none. Later these people split into two and became either man or woman. They have been searching for their dual souls ever since, so as to become one again. |

| Myfanwy | That would be the reason for all your longing and yearning? |

| Lilwen | We certainly always want something! I want food! |

| Myfanwy | I want money! |

Lilwen	I want a fountain pen!
Myfanwy	I want jewellery!
Daniel	And what if you get food? *Lilwen gets it from washing line*
Lilwen	Then I eat it. *Movement*
Daniel	And what if you get money? *Myfanwy gets it from audience*
Myfanwy	I spend it. *Movement*
Daniel	And what if you get a fountain pen? *Lilwen gets it from audience*
Lilwen	I use it. *Movement*
Daniel	And what if you get jewellery? *Myfanwy gets it from audience*
Myfanwy	I'll wear it. *Movement*
Daniel	And if you cannot get food, a fountain pen, money and jewellery?
Lilwen	We get frustrated.
Myfanwy	Angry, annoyed.
Lilwen	Yearning and longing cannot be the same as wanting!
Myfanwy	The aim of yearning and longing is much higher, and we do not know what it is we are longing and yearning for.
Daniel	I think so, too.
Myfanwy	So, what do we have to do to have a chance of achieving what we are yearning and longing for?

Lilwen	We have to be innocent.
Myfanwy	We have to stick to our life plan.
Daniel	We have to be aware of our identity.
Myfanwy	That is easy to say. How do we achieve all these, though?
Daniel	They are fields of energy. You can participate in that energy field, and consciously avoid its opposite.
Lilwen	Is that the same as with food? You know, with your favourite meal? You think about it, you prepare for the cooking, you do the cooking, and then you relish the eating. You feel very good afterwards. And the next time, you feel even better, because the energy field grows.
Myfanwy	Yes. But sometimes what you like to eat changes.
Daniel	It changes with time. There is a right time for everything. When the time is right, things have a high energy level. *Inflate balloon* When the time for something is over, the energy drops. *Deflate balloon.* You are fresh in the morning *Inflate balloon* and after a day's work you feel tired, with less energy *Deflate balloon.* You need sleep to build up energy again.
Lilwen	So, if you do lots of things that support and energy field, because what you do is right at this time, you help that energy field grow, and you get energy back from it. *Inflate balloon* You can do this for every one of the things we mentioned earlier, innocence,
Myfanwy	Life plan *Physical*
Lilwen	Identity *Physical*
Daniel	Meditation may have been the right thing to do 20years ago, *Inflate balloon* and might not be the right thing to do now.

Myfanwy   20 years ago, it would have given you energy, now it takes energy away from you. *Deflate balloon* You have to be careful and very alert to your intuition.

Lilwen   Right. You cannot find out any other way.

Myfanwy   Different activities have to do with different energy fields, don't they?

Lilwen   Yes, such as games

Myfanwy   And stories.

Daniel   And music, or paintings, or films.

Myfanwy   Across the history of all those, different movements or epochs and developments were in line with the times they arose in. *Inflate balloon*

Daniel   And then they lost that timeliness, and lost in energy and allowed new forms and developments to take hold. *Deflate balloon*

Lilwen   With time moving faster and faster, it seems. *Inflate and deflate. Audience?*

Myfanwy   Yes, movements are much more short-lived

Lilwen   This is the end of the game: we picked objects from a washing line, explored them, created a story that included then, before becoming rather philosophical. With balloons.

Myfanwy   None of us lost. We all won.

Daniel   *To Lilwen* We have played your game. *To Myfanwy* Now we come to your story?

Myfanwy   The game integrated a story and identity. My story will include identity.

Commentary 2018

In April 2018, I sent the following request to the e-lists of SCUDD (standing conference of university drama departments), and CLA-journal, made up of former contributors to the e-journal *Consciousness, Literature and the Arts*, contributors to the *CLA* book series with Intellect and Brill | Rodopi, and delegates of the six biannual international conferences on Comnsciousnessm, Theatre, Literature and the Arts.

> In each area of life, including academic disciplines, we tend to base many thoughts on tenets, axioms, principles and assumptions that we take for granted to the extent that we would probably even react with surprise if anyone doubted their validity. I would be keen to hear from you what you consider such strong tenets, axioms, principles and assumptions to be in your discipline.

Below I provide an anonymised, edited version of the responses received.

1. One of the core assumptions of Vedic knowledge is that there is an underlying infinite field of creative intelligence at the basis of all life and human creative potential. This can be experienced and expressed or articulated in artistic output.

2. Autonomy of the work of art: once the artist has created a work of art, he/she passes that work of art into the public domain and the work of art becomes autonomous, independent of the artist.

3. To what extent, if at all, is it possible to differentiate the work of art from the artist's political activities / convictions?

4. Theatre is an act of communication.

5. Theatre students develop self-confidence, resilience and teamworking skills.

6. People interested in theatre and performance are more open-minded and liberal than most people.

7. Theatre work is underpaid compared with film work.

8. It's important for theatre students to read widely and gain knowledge in areas outside their discipline. Study of history, literature, art and philosophy enhances the study of theatre.

9. Women and BAME people are under-represented in professional theatre especially in the higher positions such as artistic directors and producers.

10. Acting is behaving truthfully imaginary circumstances.

11. Theatre can transform lives.

12. Theatre is wonderful but creating a quality product is inevitably very hard work.

13. Aspiring actors do not have a realistic understanding of the field they hope to enter.

14. Some of them are, obviously, the ideas that date back to Aristotle's Rhetoric and Poetics, like the gradation of literary genres, or the notions of catharsis and mimesis. I can also think of the stable elements of plot structure as they were defined by Russian formalists.

15. Arts (specifically performance arts) students will never earn enough to pay off their student loans (so they shouldn't worry about them).

16. There is no place for logic or logical thinking in the (performing) arts, and organised thinking is for other less creative beings.

17. People in a drama department can't do maths (I think they are supposed to be 'above such earthly thoughts or something').

18. People who dress well, look good or obviously take care over their dress are less intelligent and are taken less seriously.

19. Being an actor is a tormentuous and ultimately psychologically unhealthy life.

20. Accidental, spontaneous discovery is the best kind of creativity.

21. People with autism have no empathy (this is unproven and, in my experience, completely false) and therefore cannot act or create productively and adventurously (actually recent research suggests that women with autism in particular choose acting as teenagers and are very good at it because they know what to do as someone else - better than they do in their 'real life' where expected behaviours are opaque).

22. The old trope that artistic process is by nature torturous and painful.

23. My governing tenet/axiom, the one that keeps popping up and reminding me what I should be doing not only within my "discipline" as writing instructor/editor/mentor, but also as a focusing guide for leading my life, has long been a simple observation by Ram Dass: *We're all just walking each other home.* Being periodically reminded of this seems to keep me going in the right direction.

24. As a journalist-documentarian, who, for a long time worked with the public-sector broadcasters, my colleagues tend to think they are better trained to discern 'the truth' (more so than private sector journalism). It's a WEIRD (Western Educated Industrial Rich Democratic) point-of-view littered with 'blind spots' and conceits how-things-ought-to-be.

25. I think one core belief in our discipline is the idea that theatre can transform our experience of the world. This seems to be a thread running through a number of discourses, for example phenomenological approaches to theatre, studies on affect, performativity and politics, as well as (in a different way) practices of applied theatre. In a sense, it would be surprising perhaps to find academics in the discipline who did not take this idea (in some sense), as axiomatic.

26. Another is perhaps the idea that theatre and the performing arts is confidence-building for students who study the subject. I think there is a widespread assumption that performance skills are highly "transferrable" and that the discipline develops students' interpersonal skills and so on. It's probably a core belief - I don't know if it is supported by concrete evidence?

27. Work of art aesthetics AS aesthetics.

28. Student centred learning - the virtues thereof.

29. Being research-active improves and enriches one's teaching.

30. We are all overburdened with administration today in the modern university.

31. The REF (and its equivalents) have significantly progressed the commodification of knowledge.

32. Students suffer from more mental health problems than they did in the past.

33. I came to University of [large city in USA/Canada] for a PhD and I realized that one of the axioms of making theatre in that city was getting state funds. There is a whole industry about how to apply to state funds, how it is distributed, and which key words need to be used in applications and so on. It took time for me to realize that my first-world colleagues were permanently damaged in their imagination by the state hegemony and they were made to believe that there is no possibility to make theatre beyond state funds and state approval. I really feel sad that this is an axiom that can never be questioned. This axiom is also very colonial because it creates a closed reasoning cycle: 1- Theatre can't be made without state funds. 2- Therefore in states that cannot afford to fund theatre, there is no theatre. 3- Therefore we have nothing to learn from people who are coming from countries where the state can't or won't fund theatre because there is no theatre there. 4- If people claiming to be theatre practitioners or researchers ever come to our country (in which we can afford to fund theatre) from the countries where the state doesn't fund theatre, we will never make space for them unless they learn our civilized ways of making theatre - aka our professionalism.

34. I have found over thirty years or more that 'theatre history' is understood to mean British theatre history, and for the most part nineteenth-century (and possibly eighteenth--occasionally) theatre history. It is resolutely and unapologetically monocultural,

and sees itself undoubtedly as the core, defining discipline of 'this' subject.

35. The second is the idea of performance and the primacy of the actor, promulgated by those infatuated with training. Performance has gained a ludicrous currency as a kind of essence, simply because it avoids close definition (as in 'what kind of performance?'). But there is not enough space here to track all of its abuses as a term, and the ideology that has been built on it across the discipline, which nearly always leads to the reification of a thing called 'contemporary performance', not to the study of performance as a cultural and historical diversity.

36. For the (opera) singer, there are (or there are explicitly not) diverse resonators or spaces of resonance in the body.

Chapter Fifteen

The View Across the Bay

A Novel

Contextualisation

The text of the beginning of the play in the previous chapter constituted the Practice as Research component of developing theatre without conflict (and which, incidentally, can serve as a further aspect of *theatre of the heart*). The novel below, published here for the first time, takes both the ideas that theatre is possible without conflict, and that there is a theatre of the heart, further and shifts these ideas to the medium of prose fiction. The heart was central in my writing process and is central to the way the characters understand and live their lives. While there is certainly conflict in the characters' lives, the novel emphasises how the characters successfully overcome that conflict to enable happiness and well-being.

Chapter 1

'You look different!' she said, with an intriguing mixture of so many facets of expression of eyes, face and voice: each minute, almost imperceptible, but so rich on their own and together that any actor would be envious. There was surprise at seeing him in the first place, although she could not remember, consciously, ever having seen him before. There was also surprise at seeing him in this place, where she would not have expected him to be. She was surprised that he was so different from what she remembered him to have been, although she knew she had not seen him before. This lack of logic surprised her, too, as soon as she noticed it. He was different from the other men she had encountered in the course of her entire life; although he looked young, he was a survivor. In the instant she saw him she knew, beyond doubt, deep within, that he had lived through difficult times and had made a conscious decision, early on in that phase of what was nothing but a severe test on the path of spiritual self-development, to endure rather than to give up, to observe rather than to get involved and entangled, and thus to live rather than to die. Seeing him proved to her that he had been successful, and the maturity he had gained in the process was at the core of what made him different from other men, other people she knew.

This insight added a further dimension, in addition to surprise, to the range of her expression that accompanied the words, 'You look different.' It was an almost objective, neutral, calm recognition of the depth and value of his achievement, combined with emotional admiration, strong feelings of being moved but without being overwhelmed by them at the same time. There were also happiness and joy that he had now achieved what she knew he had failed to achieve before, even though the circumstances eluded her—this did not give rise to concern as it was not relevant at this moment. In this moment, there was also an element of sheer excitement about meeting him so unexpectedly, about the mystery, the unanswered questions, the questions that did not need answers at this point, and the range of possibilities of where this meeting might lead.

Her words, 'You look different!' had come almost immediately when they had set eyes on each other, and their spontaneity, her spontaneity, had been obvious to him. Within the same set of what can have been only fractions of seconds came his immediate reaction.

Different. I am different, always, and eternally, different. That is what defines me, 'different,' nothing else. Nothing specific, particular, special: only 'different.' Everyone's immediate response to me: he is 'different.' I have accepted that I am being perceived as different, I know the reasons why others see me, immediately, as different. But it surprises me every time, again and again, when this happens, because I do not feel different, I feel as myself. I have a strong feeling of self-identity, and that is why I do not feel threatened, or attacked, or sad when others confront me with my difference, only surprised.

On this occasion, he noticed as well, the difference she talked about did not come in the statement of fact, as in 'You *are* different,' but was mediated, for the first time in his memory, through the sense of sight, vision: 'you *look* different. She had been *looking* at him, for quite a while, lost in herself, before she spoke, probably not aware of it. She had seen him and taken him in as fully as possible in that quiet, absorbing manner, and then reacted to what she had seen and kept seeing, with reference to the sense of sight, but suffused with all the other nuances of layers of surprise, knowledge, insight, being moved, admiration, joy, happiness and excitement.

In addition to these thoughts, insights, flashes in his mind, he knew that he knew her, had known her for a long time, for an eternity, but not here, not in this shape and form, neither his not hers. He took note of her physical appearance, quickly found it pleasing, intriguing and attractive, but did not dwell on it beyond.

All the events since he first saw her and since she first saw him, only a few seconds ago, had been within their respective minds, where they felt secure. He knew that he needed to respond because she had talked to him. She expected a response, because she had talked to him. Her utterance had been spontaneous in reaction to the sudden, and unexpected, encounter. She had opened herself up, almost involuntarily, and realised that she had left the security of her inside. She experienced the concomitant vulnerability. Her invitation to him to open up as well, through the response that had to follow, now, made him feel vulnerable in return. Anything he was going to do now was going to be a response, and she would experience it as such, even if he turned around and ran away. The time he would allow himself to pass between hearing her 'You look different' and his visible, audible or nonverbal response was already part of that response as well. He was aware of this, but it did not constitute an element of pressure or strain for him; he was used to maintaining his sense of self while exposing himself to vulnerability.

It had been a unique moment that they would never forget. They happened to have parked their cars next to each other to shop at the supermarket and had both returned to their cars with their trolleys full of shopping. They had casually looked at each other, and time stood still.

'I probably do, yes.'

She blushed. 'I am sorry, I don't know what I am saying, I don't even know you…'

'I think you do. I know you, I am sure. I recognised you as soon as I saw you.' He paused, hesitated briefly, then, seeing her not shutting off: 'Although I am equally sure that I have not seen you before. I still know you. I am Caleb, by the way. Caleb White.'

Kaya thought for a moment, without hesitating. 'Caleb,' she said, as if tasting the name's flavour, exploring its resonance within her. It sent shivers down his spine to hear her say his name aloud. His face showed curiosity. 'Oh, my name is Kaya, Kaya Jarvis.'

They were both still holding shopping bags in their hands, ready to put them into the boots of their cars.

Caleb smiled: 'Lovely name. Should we finish with the shopping and then go somewhere,' he paused, and looked at his watch, '12.30—for lunch? To talk some more?'

Kaya's response came quickly: 'Love that! You know the nice Italian around the corner? We can leave the cars here.'

'I only moved here recently, so I don't know that place yet, but Italian sounds good,' Caleb responded.

They put away their shopping, locked their cars, and walked across to the restaurant together, quietly, each deep in their own thoughts. As they walked, it happened quite naturally that they held hands. They looked at each other at the moment their hands met, surprised, curious and then acknowledging the fact by briefly firming up the grip on the other's hand.

***

They sat down in the restaurant, having chosen a table by the window that allowed a beautiful view over the promenade. They studied the menu and ordered.

They looked at each other, then spoke both at the same time: 'So, tell me all about…'

They stopped, laughed, and continued together 'you?!'

Kaya added quickly: 'You first, please, Caleb.'

'Yes,' he agreed. 'I just joined the university here. I teach drama.'

He paused, and Kaya took this as an invitation to respond. 'So, you are a lecturer?'

'Professor, actually,' he said modestly.

Kaya smiled: 'And you are so modest about it because…?'

'People in the UK are sometimes a bit sceptical about academics, the more so the higher up in the hierarchy.'

'I see.' Kaya sounded thoughtful. 'What is that hierarchy then, actually?'

Caleb was in his element: 'It starts at the level of lecturer, both in the old universities and former polytechnics that became universities in 1992, the new universities. In the old ones, you apply for promotion to senior lecturer, in the new ones you progress to that level automatically. Then comes the level of reader (again in both old and new universities), while in the new universities there is the role of principal lecturer. That is for people more into teaching and admin, while the reader-role is more for the research-oriented colleagues. From senior lecturer or principal lecturer or reader you can be promoted to a professorship, or chair. It's a personal chair if you get there through internal promotion, or an established chair if you have applied for, and are appointed to a professorship that was publicly advertised. Higher up the ladder are more managerial posts, such as Head of Department, Dean of Faculty, Pro Vice Chancellor, Deputy

Vice Chancellor and Vice Chancellor. The higher up in the hierarchy, the higher the salary. The teaching load also gets less the higher you get in the hierarchy.'

'Very comprehensive information,' Kaya commented, satisfied. 'Do you enjoy teaching?'

Caleb's response took a while. 'I do, yes, but over the years there have been ups and downs. You want me to elaborate?'

'Yes, please!'

'I have always enjoyed teaching. I think I came back from my first day of primary school telling my mother I wanted to be a teacher, and for that I needed a big car with a big boot to fit in all the students' notebooks I had to take home for marking!'

Both laughed, and Caleb rejoiced in the sound of Kaya's laughter, which cascaded and flowed like beads from a pearl necklace.

'I trained as a teacher at school level, especially for A-level English, where I was able to choose an emphasis on drama. But after that I taught only at university level. My approach to teaching is student-centred: I seek to enable student experience of the contents of the seminar or workshop first, followed by contextualisation within relevant history and theory. For a module on American Drama for UK students, I started with the insight that most students have never been to America, or if, then to Disneyland. I integrated student presentations and staff presentations on a wide range of topics, including food, political parties, family, healthcare, the military, sports, climate, American landscapes, religion in the USA, American cityscapes, economy and sales, US journalism, population, education, the relationship between the USA and Canada, crime and law enforcement, transport, actor training in the USA, culture beyond theatre, and American film and TV. This gave them at least an idea of what America is really all about and provided a context for the plays that take all this for granted. For courses at MA level, I have explored the approach of asking students to read a relevant chapter from a book, or a journal article, either set by myself or of their choice in relation to the session topic and develop at least ten precisely worded questions in relation to the chapter or article contents. This approach has led to student ownership of the contents, and the questions have sparked lively debate, adding to student engagement and achievement of learning outcomes.'

Another cascade of laughter from Kaya interrupted Caleb's fast flow of words. He was a bit startled: 'What?'

'Sorry,' Kaya comforted him, 'Only, you sounded almost like a letter of application just then, you know, for an American post where you need a teaching philosophy statement.'

Caleb laughed as well: 'You are right, I did sound very formal there!'

'Do go on, please,' Kaya pleaded.

'But then in the last two years I suddenly noticed a difference, students did not like my teaching any more, and I began to find teaching boring. It was quite a crisis, because I could not have continued working in such an environment.'

'I wonder whether your teaching had become merely functional?' Kaya ventured.

'How do you mean?' Caleb's question was genuine and revealed that he did have some inkling of what Kaya had in mind.

'Well,' she explained, gaining momentum, 'I guess with time, some kind of routine can creep in: you do the same thing year in, year out, it works, you don't have to prepare any more, and it gets boring. Less and less of your heart is involved, enthusiasm, energy; teaching becomes reduced to the contents you must get across and that is tested in exams. That's when teaching becomes functional, and that restricts the way the student can receive the functionality of what you teach them. They feel judged, and they close off.'

Caleb continued this train of thought: 'Yes, exactly. Thinking about it, there was also an increasing level of restrictions from the education system which added to the frustration. Student feedback is becoming increasingly important in staff appraisals, and therefore you are tempted to teach in a way that students praise your work, which they do first and foremost when you give them good marks.'

'But you cannot do that if the achievement just does not merit a good mark.' Kaya interjected.

'Quite,' Caleb confirmed. 'I also noticed that I was teaching at the same level I had been teaching for the past 20 years or so, and I then realised that that level was far too high for today's students. In their first year, they are at a level now that corresponds to year ten or so at secondary school twenty years ago. I discussed this with some colleagues in the education department, and they agreed. I took this on board and gradually the students came back to me, as it were, and I enjoy teaching again.'

Kaya considered this for a moment. 'You probably have to learn not to judge the students for being at a different level now than they were twenty years ago?'

'Yes,' Caleb agreed, 'it's not their fault that they know less, or different things, and that their entire ways of functioning, thinking, operating are different.'

'And being,' Kaya added.

'Yes, indeed, it goes as far as that, great.' Caleb nodded.

Their food had arrived, and they started eating, enjoying the pizzas they had ordered, his Margherita with additional sliced tomato, and hers Calzone without the usual red meat component.

'And how did you get into this kind of job in the first place--or should I say: how did you get to fulfil your calling?'

'Calling, definitely,' Caleb beamed. 'It was all quite straightforward: from school I went to university, did an undergraduate degree in drama at Royal Holloway, then an MA at Exeter, then my PhD at Warwick, and then straight into a lectureship at Middlesex, on to a senior lectureship at Brunel, and then the professorship here, which I started a few weeks ago. I seem to have been in the right place at the right time on several occasions.'

'And you *are* modest, this is quite an impressive career, even if some luck is involved,' Kaya admired. Caleb was pleased, smiling with shy pride at Kaya's words.

Kaya saw this and added: 'I think we should never hide our light under a bushel. Doing that is of course an English characteristic, but I think it's an old, wrong belief pattern.'

Caleb looked puzzled: 'I am not familiar with that concept, "old, wrong belief pattern". Can you explain, please?'

'Of course!' Kaya sounded happy and keen to be asked. 'Belief patterns and dogmata and doctrines have become so engrained in our lives that we take them for granted without even a thought of checking their validity. They are, in fact, patterns of belief, not of truth, even in the way we refer to them. We all tend to create our own world in the realm of our thoughts. If that world corresponds to laws of nature that rule the universe independent of what we are thinking, then we are lucky. If the world we create in our thoughts does not correspond to that set of natural laws, we have created, and are engaging in, wrong belief patterns.'

Caleb had been listening intently. 'But these wrong belief patterns,' he spoke those words slowly, still getting used to them, 'cannot be good for us.'

'No, not at all,' Kaya confirmed. 'The longer we believe in those wrong patterns, the more they harden, and we come to believe that they are in fact laws of nature, which they are not.'

'Can you give me some simple examples, perhaps, just to make sure I get this right?'

'Of course. Here we go: Others always want to pull a fast one on me; others want to harm me; I must not attract attention; money makes you arrogant; men cannot be faithful; women cannot remain matter-of-fact; I mustn't contradict my partner; I am not likeable; I am only average; what would others say; that's how we have been doing this always. You see?'

Caleb showed relief. 'Yes, very clear. It's interesting that many of these wrong belief patterns seem to be generalisations. But they need not be accurate in this way for everyone?'

'No, not at all.'

Caleb looked so curious that Kaya felt encouraged to expand further: 'Belief patterns form our innermost convictions, and these influence our thinking and action in a major way. We begin getting used to belief patterns in early childhood: our upbringing unconsciously makes girls believe that they must be well-behaved and must not stand out. As adults, such women will be extremely adaptable, but also prone to put their own interests last.'

Caleb tried to think this further, interrupting with: 'And boys have to be brave and must not have, or at least show, fear, otherwise they will be seen as milksops and expelled from their circle of friends.'

Kaya nodded: 'Great, yes! Other belief patterns accumulate through life experiences—if the colleague gets the dream-job more than once, this leads to the belief pattern "I am just not good enough". In some cases, wrong belief patterns may well have helped us. Patterns such as "I must not make any mistakes", or "I must be perfect in everything I do" may have brought us to the track of success we are on now, but suddenly such belief patterns turn from 'right' to 'wrong,' or their nature reveals itself as having been wrong all along, and they turn from guarantor of success to dead weight.'

Kaya stopped for a moment. She knew that this information could easily become too much to take in, and she did not want that to happen, especially today at their first meeting. It was extraordinary how their conversation had developed. But it had felt so right to share what she had said so far.

Caleb noticed her pause and sensed her reason for it. 'You have more on this, don't you? Out with it!' he coaxed.

'OK,' she grinned, 'you asked for it! Belief patterns give us a feeling of security, especially if they are well engrained in mass consciousness. We become part of an enormous energy field and feel supported by that field. However, in fact an energy field whose energy is no longer in line with natural law does no longer sustain its own energy, it needs energy from outside, from those engaging with the energy field, and thus we are drained of our own energy to support the energy field of the wrong belief pattern. We make our own lives miserable by adhering to such wrong belief patterns, because we close ourselves up to engaging in different, more rewarding experiences. Especially if we believe very strongly in a wrong belief pattern, we feed that pattern with a lot of our own energy, and if many people on earth have the same pattern, it gets very big and very strong, and forms a massive energy field. It takes a lot of effort and courage not only to find out that belief patterns are wrong, but even more so to free oneself from such energy fields.'

Kaya stopped again, almost out of breath. Caleb found her arguments very convincing and sought to apply them to his own life—maybe later, or drama.

He offered: 'I have been thinking about something like this, only in different terms, in my work. There are so many assumptions about drama and theatre, and opera, that are taken for granted. Nobody in their right mind would doubt them. Would those be belief patterns, and could they be wrong?'

'For example?'

'Well, that drama can only "function" on the basis of conflict.'

Kaya thought for a moment, then her eyes twinkled: 'Do you realise that you have now combined two of the areas we talked about this afternoon?' Without waiting for his response, she went on: 'Functionality and belief patterns. When drama, and I assume that also relates to theatre, only function, they are devoid of their essence, of the heart, anyway. And I then believe full well that drama and theatre can only function on the basis of conflict; and yes, it must be a wrong belief pattern, and I agree that it is probably the hardest of them all to crack!'

Caleb continued Kaya's line of thinking: 'So, the development of any kind of new knowledge implies, or goes along with, the cracking open of old, wrong belief patterns. That takes a lot of courage and effort and time and can be exhausting.'

Kaya concluded: 'But when you have done it, the result is so simple and straightforward, you wonder why nobody has thought of this long before.'

Caleb raised his right hand up in the air: 'High five!'

Kaya raised hers, and their hands met on her own cheerful 'High five.'

They paused their conversation for a moment, each caught in their own thoughts, and allowing the other their space for this. Kaya was surprised how what they talked about, reflecting their thinking and their lives, added up, and how much Caleb understood of her philosophical approach that was too deep for some. Caleb, in turn, wondered at the way in which Kaya was able to put his hunches into explicit, meaningful contexts.

'Family?' Kaya ended the silence.

Caleb had dreaded this question. Now that Kaya had asked it, now that it was in the air, he felt even more insecure and vulnerable than he had expected.

Kaya sensed this immediately: 'Oh, you went quite pale there—sorry, raw nerve, is it? Please leave it if you like?'

'No, I might as well.' Caleb sounded determined but added: 'Please be patient and gentle with me.' He cleared his throat—always a sign for him of nerves. 'I am divorced. I loved my wife, very much, and found out, one day, by chance, that she was having an affair. I caught them in bed together, coming home unexpectedly, meant as a surprise. I knew him as a distant acquaintance, whom I had never paid much attention to, and I wondered what she might have seen in him, might still see in him. And what she saw in me, saw me as, had seen me as ever, that she could now prefer him to me. I doubted myself, for the first time in my life. My ex-wife asked me whether I could forgive her, she had made a mistake, she wanted us to come, and be, together again. Sounded great, as in the movies, but I was just not able to forgive her, and I have not been able to forgive myself for not being able to forgive her.' His voice choked over the last few words, and he had to strain not to allow tears into his eyes.

Kaya took all this in, also Caleb's obvious and visible reaction. Very gently and slowly she extended her hands and took his into hers, ready to withdraw at any moment if she sensed any discomfort on his part at her touch, but there was none—in fact, he seemed to welcome it.

'You were deeply hurt, Caleb, and forgiving is the hardest test for anyone. It was like the Falling Tower in the Tarot pack of cards. Are you familiar with that?'

'No, not at all,' Caleb admitted.

Kaya explained: 'In the *Tarot*, there is the card of the *Falling Tower*. According to one interpretation of the spiritual dimension of the card, it represents a major insight, or cross-roads, in human spiritual development in which the majority of, or at least the major, pillars of the beliefs and belief patterns that we have established for ourselves across our lives, are subjected to a major challenge. The carpet of those beliefs is almost literally pulled from underneath one's feet, leaving the personality, hitherto soundly founded on those very belief patterns, in near-complete limbo. Absolute certainties, lived, supported, confirmed, expressed, and believed in for decades, crumble, like images of large buildings being blown up intentionally in the course of demolition. Such explosions, or implosions, leave a heap of ruins, where close examination of more superficial false truths gradually leads to the collapse of deeper and deeper, well-hidden foundations of what we had assumed to have been the certainties of our lives. Or we realise that we in fact did see the symptoms of the ruins that are only too obvious, but we were unable to accept them, unable to face them, to acknowledge them, and so we pushed them aside, buried them in our unconscious, aware, on some level, that we would not be ready, strong enough, capable, of facing the facts and taking action to address whatever was amiss.

There are different phases of the reaction to this, of different duration and intensity, sometimes several at a time—shock, disbelief, doubt, despair, insecurity, laughter, tears, bitterness. Many mistakes were made, involuntarily and unknowingly, much hurt suffered at the hands of, and inflicted on people who are invariably the most loved ones, in our lives. Increasingly, as time after the initial revelation moves on, we realise the need to forgive (never forget!), ourselves and those who hurt us, and seek forgiveness from those whom we hurt.

We come together with partners to resolve karma, or to deal with tasks. Working together is easier than doing things on one's own. With a partner we can develop such a high level of trust and understanding that we can then mirror, unconsciously, to each other the points that we need to work on most. Did you notice that with your ex-wife, that you were pushing each other's buttons, saying something to each other that hit a sore spot, again and again, until you had been able to realise it and sort it out?'

Caleb was amazed: 'Yes, that certainly happened. I could not give examples if pressed right now, but that certainly describes our relationship!'

Kaya was pleased, but serious. 'You see. And in the past centuries it was probably the case that most couples needed a lifetime together to work out all the things they had planned to sort out...'

'Between incarnations, you mean,' Caleb interposed.

'Yes. But time is working so much faster now, in many cases a whole lifetime in not needed, so you get together, fully, with one partner to work out whatever karma or tasks are on the cards for that partnership. Then those partners leave each other, to allow for some period of being alone— not lonely—in between, and then perhaps the next partnership to deal with a different set of issues. When partners leave, of course there is a period where it hurts, and then it is so important to let go, to forgive, and not to feel guilty.'

Caleb had been listening closely. 'Because feeling guilty is again related to old belief patterns, that you should be together for a lifetime and that it must be your fault, somehow, if it ends before that?'

'Exactly,' Kaya reinforced. 'Getting over such a belief pattern, and forgiving, are necessary before you can start afresh.'

'And how do you forgive? Can you learn it?' Caleb wondered aloud.

'You can practice it, at least,' Kaya assured him. 'You can create time, sit in front of a lit candle, if you like, achieve some inner calm, and then, from and with all your heart, ask whoever for forgiveness, and forgive whoever has hurt you. It helps, probably, to be aware that you are forgiving the person who hurt you...'

'You mean I am not forgiving the actual injury, as inflicted by the person who hurt you, because that is there, that will never go away, and pretending it did not happen would just push it under the carpet?' Caleb interrupted.

'Precisely,' Kaya continued, 'you forgive the person, also from the awareness that yes, they said or did what was genuinely hurtful, but they did so also to help you.'

Caleb frowned, but did not interrupt, allowing Kaya to carry on: 'The other person was the carrier of the injury, the means. But if it had not been that specific person to hurt you, it would have been someone else. You see, you carried within you the resonator for the injury, the energy field that attracted the injury. From this life, or past lives, it is not necessary to find out in detail. You had some issue within yourself, unknown to you, not consciously, probably well-hidden so as not to obstruct your life, but festering under the surface and screaming to be noticed and taken care of and reintegrated into your Self. A little child that has been lost and wants to return into the hugging arms of its mother. This hidden part of the soul sends out signals from its place of hiding, and in this way, you attract actions from others that respond to that signal. If you did not have a resonator in some area, you would not attract attention in that area either.' Kaya paused because she realised that Caleb needed another moment to allow this to sink in.

Caleb caught on: 'So I had some relationship issues buried inside myself, and the best person to bring these to my attention was my ex-wife, because of how close I felt to her, and how much I loved her and how much I was open to her?' he asked, hesitantly.

'It is amazing how quickly and fully you understand what I am trying to say.' Kaya's voice showed her surprise and admiration.

'It's because you explain it so well—grounded in your own experience, I dare say?'

'Thank you.' Kaya said simply, 'and, yes, much of what I am talking about is not my own thinking, originally, but I have experienced a lot of it in my own life.'

'Let me see if I got this right then, about forgiving,' Caleb picked up where they had left, 'My ex-wife, then, mirrored to me—am I using something you said earlier correctly now?'

Kaya nodded quickly.

'My ex-wife mirrored to me, in her betrayal, some partnership issues of mine that have been suppressed for ages but that want to be resolved. When I sit with the candle, I can forgive her, as the carrier of that stimulus to start thinking about these issues, without pretending not to have been, perhaps still be, hurt by what happened?' Caleb continued his thoughts in silence for a moment, then chuckled: 'I might in due course even come to thank her for it?'

Kaya joined the chuckle: 'It's great you can smile about it already—and yes, probably. Has happened to me!'

In the long silence that followed, Caleb came to rest in gazing at Kaya's face. *Some faces are random, they come and go, they are perceived and forgotten. This statement is devoid of judgment, an observation of fact, others will see more in those faces, for whatever reason, but I do not, and I do not feel guilty about it. Some faces are interesting, would be good for such and such a character in drama, would give their owners, or wearers, a valuable bonus to their chances as actors. Some faces, more than others, tell me: 'this person has lived her life to the full,' and I am not sure I want to know more... Some faces change very quickly to reflect the owner's or wearer's current mood or general state of being, which I can read in the face at a glance; familiarity with the face may help, but some faces have that quality even without having looked at them closely and often. There can be distant beauty in faces, impersonal, beauty that is not meant for me but for the general public—a paradox, because after all, am I not also a member of the general public? The beauty of the face is meant for me but remains impersonal to me. Others fall in love with such beauty, it enhances their well-being. For me it serves as a reminder of live beauty. The faces of actors who are rather plain in daily life can become radiantly beautiful on stage when they play 'being in love,' either happily or even unhappily. Love will make any face beautiful. Most faces on paintings lack the life of life. Leonardo is the exception: the faces on his paintings live, more so than many real faces. How he achieved this will remain an eternal mystery. Some living human faces are genuinely exceptional. Kaya's face. Solely to me, the living, loving beholder, because I project my love onto the face? Or do I detect, sense, draw in, reflect, become the beauty that is there in the face, God-made, God-given, for her to express, to relish, to honour, for me, at this moment, in this present, to realise, to marvel at, to respond to with a series of deep breaths, gut reactions to the power of the perception of yet a further nuance of the face, revealed in a new angle of the head, a new arrangement of hair around it, a new interplay of the light in the room or the outdoors environment and the features of her face? God as sculptor, because no human sculptor, or painter, not even Leonardo or Michelangelo, could have created such an infinitely finely chiselled countenance, with so many, infinitely delicate yet robust, infinitely nuanced features and shapes, gentle, flowing, sweet, but not too, all in just the perfect proportions on their own and to each other, and each individual feature with its own infinity of further layers just as perfectly proportioned and relating to each other. I could spend an hour looking at a minute section of the face in depth, and that would not suffice to grasp the dimensions of structure and form that represent and create the beauty of that section. All those aspects of beauty come together in the overall beauty of her face. By looking at it I gradually become the face. I feel her face on, or in, or through, or with my own face. I see through and with her eyes, I breathe through and with her nose, I sense her cheeks with or in or through mine, feel her hair as my own hair around her, which becomes my, face. I sense the joy of those parts of the air, down to subatomic particles, that she inhales, joy at being chosen to make their way towards her face, and in through her nostrils, and the joy of that same air when it leaves the body on the outbreath, joy at having contributed to the life of such beauty, an act of worship in gratitude to God to have become part of it.*

Kaya allowed Caleb all the time he needed. They had finished their lunch, and paid, splitting the bill half and half. When Caleb indicated to Kaya, by returning his gaze to her directly, that he was back in this world, they agreed to take a walk together on the promenade by the sea shore. They walked, holding hands again.

'There is much more I could say about myself,' he said, and added, with a wink: 'but maybe you give me a break and tell me something about yourself.'

'Of course,' Kaya smiled. 'I studied dentistry at King's College, did my Dental Foundation Training in Kent, and have been employed as a dentist in a practice here for the past six years.'

'Dentist,' Caleb repeated, pensively.

'Many people are so surprised when they hear that I am a dentist, I really wonder why,' Kaya said, mock-reproachfully.

Caleb laughed: 'You don't look like a dentist, you don't have the macho face for it that comes from so many dentists' websites.'

'Is that mainly the male dentists, though?'

'Perhaps,' Caleb admitted, 'but many female dentists have that as well. After all, you have to have some guts to pull teeth, don't you? Are you a good dentist?'

Kaya did enjoy her job, it was a calling for her as well, even if that may be difficult for patients to understand, and she told him so, full of obvious conviction.

'Yes, I think I am a "good dentist", as you put it. I have developed my physical skills very well, and always from the patient's perspective, as much as possible. I make sure for the regular check-ups that I do not cause pain by unnecessarily poking the gums with my instruments. I make sure the lips are not caught in between my fingers and instruments. I establish whether a patient can open their mouth wide, as needed for check-up or treatment, without feeling discomfort or pain, even for very short periods of time, and give them comfort breaks in line with their needs, or I use bite blocks. I am aware of the areas of the mouth where pressure could cause vomiting reflexes, and I have trained my dental nurse to use the suction devices in such a way that they do not cause discomfort and that she is aware when saliva accumulates in the areas close to where they cause the need to swallow. I never prepare cavities (I think you might call that "drilling") without local anaesthetic, and for that I have tested many products to come up with one that I find has the least side effects such as nausea. I have refined my syringe technique so that the sites of my injections are not painful after the numbness has worn off. I am very good with patients who are afraid of dentists—usually from poor experience in the past. I know that visits to the dentist are not at the top of anyone's list for having a good time, but at least I think I have found ways of making it not too much of a dreadful experience either, especially where it is possible, through some additional practice and effort and attention to detail, to definitely avoid unnecessary discomfort and pain.'

Kaya paused, then added: 'And yes, it takes determination to do all this, especially extractions, but for those again it is a question of knowing what to do in the context that presents itself to you in the moment of the treatment. A tooth that needs extracting may be more decayed underneath the surface than obvious to the eye or the x-ray, so it might break off under the pressure of the extracting forceps. This is, first of all, not really the dentist's fault: even the best use of the most sophisticated technology does not allow you to predict everything. I just have to think quickly and proceed to excavate all the parts of the tooth that are still in the mouth, using different tools and related skills.'

Caleb was clearly interested and impressed. 'I have been thinking that I seem to feel, to perceive, my teeth in my mouth, with the tongue, as much larger than they are in real life: I am always quite surprised when I see how tiny an extracted tooth is, when I see it on the dental tray, in comparison to what it feels like in my mouth. I wonder whether that is only my experience, or whether it is a common human experience. And, taking it further, do dentists develop the ability of seeing the teeth in their patients' mouths somehow larger than non-dentists, even when they are not working with the special glasses?'

'I have never thought about that, to be honest. I will think about it when I am back in the surgery on Monday, and check the literature,' Kaya promised.

'Are you planning on opening your own practice at some point?'

'I don't think so. I see my boss putting in so many more hours on the admin and management of the practice. OK, she earns a good deal more than I do, I guess, but she has not much free time at all over the week and the weekends. I work on a less than full time contract, the equivalent of four days a week: I am at work 8-5 Monday, Tuesday and Thursday, and 8-12 Wednesday and Friday. While I work, I am fully committed to it, and I love it, but I don't have to think about work outside of those hours, and I don't do it, either, and I like it that way, and I cannot imagine wanting to have the extra money for all those extra hours where the job becomes your life without space for anything else.'

Caleb changed the subject: 'Family?'

'No, not yet,' Kaya responded.

'Oh.' Caleb's voice was a hilarious mixture of joy for himself and sadness for her, and Kaya had to laugh out loud, and Caleb joined that laughter, adding: 'How come?'

'I just didn't meet you earlier,' she started, for the sake of the witty expression, but, with a very quick glance at Caleb, only half-jokingly, 'and I was very much overshadowed by my mother.'

'Which allows us to segue elegantly from husbands and wives, past, present and future, to parents and wider family. So, what is (was?) your mother like? I hope you don't mind my asking?'

'Not at all,' Kaya said, adding with a cheeky twinkle: 'it will be your turn on that soon anyway, and you started off talking about your ex-wife, so I might as well make a start here, talking about my mother, Grace. She *is* a journalist, and she has been a formidable presence all her life, brushing everyone aside with her sheer energy, and for decades not even aware of her impact. Very well-meaning, good-natured, with very strong ethical principles, but oblivious that other people just did not have the same joie de vivre as her and actually could come to feel quite oppressed and stifled in their own lives and expression by her verve, vitality, dynamism, dash and spirit.'

'She sounds like a very dramatic character, in a colloquial sense of the word,' Caleb mused.

'Melodramatic, rather, yes,' Kaya agreed.

'Was your career choice influenced by your mother's personality?'

Kaya did not have to think for long: 'It definitely was. I needed something very practical, physical, embodied, and scientific to balance what came across as her somewhat aimless exuberance. At some point in my years of study I realised that I had lived all my life just as my mother wanted me to, and that had both given me a lot of advantages that others do not have but had also deprived me of being myself. I arranged a long weekend to talk this through with her, very tough, but also very helpful. We have been able to build up a new relationship since then, more distant in a way, but also closer, but not mutually obstructive.'

Caleb's attention had been caught particularly by one word. He repeated it: 'Mutually?'

'Yes: it turned out in our two-day talk that she had felt under pressure as well with regard to me. She was a single mum, you see...'

'I had been wondering why you had not mentioned your father so far...' Caleb observed.

'He had the choice of leaving when he felt overpowered by my mother,' Kaya explained, 'and he left soon after I had turned ten. I have seen him on a regular basis, we are on good terms, but never really developed a "proper" daughter-father relationship, and at home it was always mum, never a full family, and no siblings either. My mother never said so, to this day, but I think she was very lonely without a partner and threw all her abundant energy into her job and me, to equal parts. That meant that I had to comply with all her expectations, which were OK for someone of her drive, but I just don't have her vivacity. I mean I'm not lethargic, far from it, but hardly anyone can get close to mum. At all levels of her life, she was always the best, right from primary school onwards, and I had to be at least as good. I still remember when I came home with good to average marks, she would despair and tell me that I would end up as a bank clerk—always the epitome of the most undesirable profession on the planet.'

They both laughed at this, and Caleb added: 'You were under a lot of pressure all your life, and your mother put herself under that pressure as well. Did your two-day talk resolve this?'

'Yes, it did. Our relationship came to breaking point several times across those two days, but we had promised each other at the outset never to give up and not to leave mid-way. We stuck to that, just about. And then we built up our relationship from scratch, over a few months, and it's been brilliant since without the need to dwell too much on what we discussed over those two days.' Kayas voice sounded convincing.

'What about your parents,' she asked Caleb.

'My mother died in a car crash a few years ago, she had been on a day excursion to a posh country house with friends, and on the way back a tyre burst on the truck in front of them, the trailer jack-knifed, spinning the truck around at full speed and straight into the car she was in. They were all killed on the spot, immediately, the medical people told us later. The truck driver remained uninjured; the investigation found that the tyre had ruptured through debris on the road, not the driver's fault.

'Oh no, how terrible,' was all Kaya could think of.

'It was just such a shock, gone from one moment to the next. My parents had been together for 35 years at the time, they taught at the same grammar school, she Science, he English. They were both much loved by their students, and by their colleagues alike. They taught from the heart. After the accident, my father took the first ever leave, for bereavement, and he never went back to teaching, he just couldn't face going back to the school, with all the memories of my mum there. He took early retirement, sold the family house, most of his possessions, and has been travelling the world since, I keep getting emails and we skype occasionally, he's been all over Europe, Africa, Australia and New Zealand, and is now doing the Americas. It distracts him, but it still does not make him happy.'

Caleb paused, and Kaya wondered aloud: 'What a story. At least he is doing something, rather than just sitting at home watching television and crying, though?' she offered.

Caleb considered this position. 'I see what you mean,' he mused, 'and I think you are right, in a way. He is certainly going through experiences on his travels that not many other people in the world can have, but the cost is so high, not to have a home any more, really.'

Kaya was still thoughtful: 'He is making his home truly within himself, so that he is genuinely at home wherever he is, independent of the ever-changing outside environment, and also independent of the conventional notion of home.'

Caleb picked up some of the ideas they had been talking about earlier: 'Could it be that the conventional idea of home had become an old, wrong belief pattern for him? In other words, what constitutes a right or wrong belief pattern depends on the person—for one person the same belief could be right, but wrong for a different person?'

'Yes, I think so,' Kaya agreed, 'although I had not thought about it in this way. I should double-check that with my mother, but it would make sense. How long has he been travelling by now?'

'Four years.'

'What's his name,' Kaya wondered.

'Quite conservative, Henry.'

Kaya had a sudden idea and frowned. Of course, Caleb noticed immediately, and asked: 'What is it?'

Kaya hesitated a little: 'I hope you won't find this in any way offensive, Caleb, but knowing my mother, she would be so keen to interview him for her series in the *Guardian*. And she'd be happy to travel to the US to meet with him there—do you think he might be open to that?'

Caleb liked the idea: 'Not offensive at all, Kaya, I assure you. I think he would be thrilled to be interviewed, and from what you told me about your mum, I think she would allow his voice to come through. He has been thinking so much about loss, about grieving, and I am sure he would now want to share his thoughts with others. And to tell his overall story and share the extraordinary situations he found himself in during his travels. I guess I will meet your mum at some point, and then we can discuss further?'

Kaya nodded, smiling at Caleb's expectation to meet her mum.

For the next few minutes, they just walked, hand in hand, silently, occasionally looking at each other, smiling. They returned to their cars.

Caleb broke the silence: 'Would you like to come over to my place, for some more conversation, and later I could make us some simple dinner? I mean, do you have time and…'—he hesitated.

'I'd love to,' said Kaya.

'I have not quite finished unpacking and arranging the new place yet, though. So be warned,' Caleb laughed.

'OK, I'll try to be generous and will overlook any mess,' Kaya promised.

'You better take your car over there as well, it's not too far, and there's plenty of parking available, and you might not want to walk back to your car later on.'

Caleb gave her the address and the postcode for the Satnav, just in case they got separated on the way, and his mobile number. They had no problems reaching his block of flats, parked their cars and Kaya helped Caleb carry some of his shopping up to his top floor flat. It was generously sized, with cloak room, living room, dining kitchen, en suite double bedroom, study, and en suite guest double bedroom. It was neutrally decorated, with new beige pure wool carpet flooring in the rooms and light blue linoleum flooring in the cloakroom, bathrooms and kitchen. The boxes still in need of unpacking were all in the guest bedroom, leaving the rest of the flat free of any sign that the owner had moved in only recently. Caleb showed Kaya around, and she caught herself out, with a surprised and happy smile, thinking about where to place some of her own furniture.

After packing away the shopping, Caleb offered Kaya a choice of drinks. She looked around curiously at what was on offer, and her eyes came to rest on a bag labelled "Monsooned Malabar".

'What on earth is "Monsooned Malabar"?' Kaya asked.

'It's coffee,' Caleb explained, 'from India. The coffee beans are soaked in monsoon rain for a day or two, and then aired in monsoon-humid fresh air for up to a few weeks, depending on the producer. In this way the beans are quite different from beans not undergoing that special process. Then they are roasted in the same way that other beans are. Want to try some?'

'Sounds fascinating, I had never heard of it before, yes, please, I'd like some, with lots of sugar and milk, even cream, please.' Kaya sounded really excited and watched closely as Caleb prepared the coffee. His movements showed calm and experience. For their coffee, they sat down in the armchairs of the living room around a chrome side table that Caleb had quickly placed there. Kaya relished the coffee's unusual flavour.

During her quick tour of the flat, Kaya had seen the fairly sizable vinyl record collection in the living-room, and in his study an impressive treasure of books. Caleb alertly followed her eyes as they now wandered over to the records again.

'Surprised to see all the old vinyl records?' he asked.

'I have quite a number as well,' she explained. 'May I have a closer look?'

'Yes, of course.'

Kaya went over to the shelf and browsed. 'Mainly classical, lots of violin and opera,' she remarked after she sat down again, sipping her coffee.

'Well observed.' Caleb was pleased. 'I played the violin for seven or eight years, when I was very young. I think, with hindsight, I was never a good pupil, I wasn't even taught vibrato, but the teachers were never able to explain to me how to hold the instrument properly with the left hand, the mechanics of weight and counter-weight, and even in current instructions on websites I have not found the answer. You have to put pressure on the fingers where they touch the string, you see, but how can you apply that pressure without the violin losing its horizontal position, where does the counter-pressure come from? From the point where you hold the violin with your cheek and collar bone, or from the wrist that is placed underneath the neck, and if the latter, how do you achieve a rounded wrist without resting the wrist against the violin neck? I still loved the instrument, and my own playing allowed me to appreciate it being played by the masters. I quickly developed my A-list of favourites, just from listening to records, or the radio, with Heifetz quickly taking first position. I would listen to my favourite pieces from the violin concerto repertory and compare the same movements played by different violinists. I saw some performers live where I grew up, but not in London, so we got only the 2nd league among the great ones who toured the provinces. But in the years of my undergraduate studies, I was in London almost every day, in the theatre, the Barbican, the Royal Festival Hall, English National Opera, Royal Opera Covent Garden, sometimes, on matinee days, two or three shows a day. Do you like classical music and opera?'

Kaya had been listening closely. 'Those years in London must have been extraordinary. Yes, I like them both. My mother has conducted interviews with many leading conductors, soloists and singers, and on some very memorable occasions I was allowed to be present, quietly in the background. It was interesting to see these stars of the classical music and opera scene off-stage, as more ordinary people. Mum always managed to get close to their cores and was then able to make them much more appealing to her readers than they might well have been before. Real people, you see, with their own problems and issues that we can all feel with.'

'Jarvis,' Caleb pondered. 'Does she write under that name?'

'Yes, Grace Jarvis,' Kaya confirmed. 'Why?'

'I'm sure I must have read some of her pieces,' Caleb explained. I have to google that some time. Did she meet all these celebrities in London?'

'Some of them, when their schedules brought them there. But on some occasions my mum had to travel to them to fit into their tight schedules. She got a few business trips to some quite exotic locations that way.'

'Did you join her on those trips?' Caleb enquired.

Kaya came alive with her memories. 'She took me to one trip to Verona, where she had been able to get an interview with Domingo while he had a guest appearance at the Arena. We stayed for a week and went to see opera every evening. Some productions more than once. You must have been?!'

Caleb had indeed: 'It was very impressive, to be one of an audience of 10,000 people. I didn't know what to expect, and I found that the sheer size of the auditorium and the number of spectators made me feel isolated, rather than part of something. Can you relate to that?' he wondered.

'Let me see,' Kaya considered this, 'in a space like the arena, the stage is so far away from the spectators even in the front row. Distance is part of the experience, somehow?'

Caleb agreed, taking this further: 'When I was at the Verona Arena, I thought of ancient Greek theatre, where the special relations were similar, with a lot of space between the stage and the spectators. The texts of the plays also come across as distant, or distancing. They train the spectators to see the events of the play as observers, involved but not attached, and that in turn might help them in their daily lives to observe their lives as if they are observing a play. In our times, the analogy of film might work better: watching our lives as if we were watching a film, allowing us to take an observer position. Or in terms of ancient Indian, Vedic texts: developing consciousness to a point where pure consciousness, without any content when on its own, co-exists with the waking state of consciousness and observes what is happening in the waking state of consciousness.'

Kaya picked this up: 'And I guess that in that observer position you can see clearly which of the ideas that influence your life are old, wrong belief patterns, which we talked about earlier.'

Caleb immediately saw her point. 'You're right. And, in relation to forgiving that we talked about earlier as well, if you can manage to achieve the observer position in relation to past trauma, then it is easier to forgive.' And he added after a moment: 'I had not made that link yet.'

'Maybe the observer position is also helpful in us realising and then overcoming functionality?' Kaya wondered.

'It's fascinating how all these areas and concepts relate to each other, isn't it?' Caleb added.

'Because they are precisely not intellectual "concepts", they are part of human experience, which may include, but goes so far beyond concepts,' Kaya concluded.

Caleb paused. 'How did we get here?'

'Verona, distance,' Kaya reminded him.

Caleb remembered. 'Excuse me for a moment, I just want to get something from the study.' Kaya heard him rummaging, and he was back quickly with a slim folder. 'When I travelled to Verona, I kept a kind of diary on that trip, I'd like to read you something from that. Here we go. *In past centuries, rich and sophisticated people sought to enhance their education through a journey to the major cultural centres of Italy. A group of Americans were emulating such a journey towards the end of August, where I encountered them on the train from Verona (had they been to see a performance at the Arena?) to Milano. Their accents, and the enormous quantity of their luggage, and the enormous size of the duffle bags and suitcases, identified them as Americans. Their conversation identified them as college or university professors. There were probably two or three couples of late middle age, grey-haired, taking both their specialist and their general knowledge for granted and manoeuvring comfortably within its admittedly wide intellectual boundaries. Closest to me, and therefore even more audible than those other two or three couples, were a slightly younger couple with a teenage boy who turned out not to be their son, but possibly a nephew, less likely a son of friends or acquaintances—from my cultural background, the familiarity with which they talked to the boy was such that it seemed too direct, intimate, and close for less than some kind of family tie. The boy seemed to be on the brink of his voice breaking, and struggling to cope with a recent growth spurt, sometimes not quite sure what to do with all those long arms and legs. His uncle at some point examined his braces, robustly taking hold of the boy's cheeks with thumb and middle finger of his right hand, squeezing to create indents on the cheeks, and in the process squishing the lips into a weird shape: 'Yes, you can see good improvement already,' and, pointing out the areas thus identified to his wife with the indicator finger of his left hand 'See, here, and here, and here, and there, yes, good,' so close to the teeth that he had to wipe his hand on his shirt after he had completed the examination and demonstration. The boy was admonished, by the uncle, not to scratch (I assume this related to a rash on his legs). At another point, the uncle demanded reproachfully for the boy to tell him what that meant, and the boy dutifully incanted: 'When you tell me to be ready with cases packed at 10am then I will be ready, next time, at 10 am with cases packed.' The tone of voice, not only the contents, was very close to the words of Thumper in the film of Bambi, 'If I have nothing nice to say then I should not say anything at all.' The uncle did most of the audible talking, his wife's voice was heard only occasionally, and much more softly. The uncle held forth, sharing his opinions about all kinds of subjects, mainly moaning and complaining. An interesting pattern emerged in the conversation between husband and wife: he would offer some thought, apparently every-day and harmless; the wife would respond. The husband's answer to that response, however, would reveal the initial thoughts as a subtle (unconscious?) trap—the wife's answer would trigger a sharp put-down from the husband, shutting his wife up once and for all on that opinion of hers regarding that subject—and on to the next topic: awkward segue, setting the trap, and relishing in the put-down.'*

Caleb finished his reading. Kaya found it very well observed and entertaining.

'How would you feel about some dinner, now,' Caleb asked.

Kaya was enthusiastic: 'I'd love some, I'm hungry again after the lunch and coffee—all our talking.' She added: 'Should we cook something together? Your kitchen looks very inviting and large enough for two.'

'It's such a long time that someone has cooked with me,' Caleb mused. Seeing disappointment on Kaya's face before it had quite manifested, he added quickly: 'I mean that I would be very happy for us to cook together, it can be very special.'

'Oh, lovely. You know, you sensed within less than seconds that I was about to misunderstand you as saying that it had been a long time since someone cooked with you as implying some reluctance on your part. You are very quick to read people.'

Caleb agreed, pleased: 'It's a nice combination of nature and nurture. It is probably one of my strengths, but I have refined it through my work in drama, sensing a character's subtle feelings, imitating, in acting, real-life people in their nuances, and, in directing, guiding actors to pick up and project those nuances, and then teaching actors and directors in just these skills.'

'So, what are we having to eat?' Kaya reminded him.

'Completely forgot,' Caleb laughed. 'Thanks for reminding me. Let's go and see what's in the fridge and the cupboards.' They walked across to the kitchen and rummaged for a while, at leisure, deciding in the end to make a grated carrot salad (with a dressing of sunflower oil, lemon and sugar), and a cream of asparagus soup. It was the season for thick, white asparagus in Germany, and Caleb had some left that he had purchased in an online shop specialising in German products. Kaya found the kitchen utensil drawer, took out a peeler, and went to work on the asparagus. Caleb glanced over at her quickly and liked what he saw.

Kaya noticed this, and commented: 'Am I passing the test?'

Caleb laughed: 'You are so attentive, you notice everything, too, don't you? And yes, you are very good at peeling the asparagus. But I was not really looking to judge you, to assess you. I remember from cooking with others, even though it was a long time ago, how surprised I had been to see how different some people do the same things in the kitchen from the way I am used to doing them, so I was curious to see how you work.' He was meanwhile peeling asparagus as well.

Kaya thought for a moment, without pausing her peeling: 'Come to think of it, you are right. Now I see you peeling the asparagus, I do it in a similar way, but my mother has always done it differently.'

Caleb added salt and butter to the water for boiling the asparagus, Kaya gently put the peeled asparagus into the boiling water and proceeded to peel the carrots for the salad. Caleb created the salad dressing and then went on to grate the carrots. They worked quietly.

'Don't you use an electric chopper for this?' Kaya asked, 'it must be straining to do all this by hand.'

Caleb carried on grating. 'The texture is different, it's rougher with the chopper, as if you end up with ever so many little beads. When you grate them, they get much softer, you'll see,' he promised, and gave Kaya a small spoon full to taste, without dressing.

'Wow,' she agreed, 'it's just melting on the tongue. I could start laying the table, where are the plates and cutlery?'

Caleb showed her, and Kaya laid the table. In a while he pureed the asparagus and added spices and cream, asking Kaya to confirm when the soup had reached the texture she liked. He had left some of the asparagus tips to add to the soup for additional nuance. They started with the fresh carrot salad, and then relished the rich soup. Kaya made a mental note to get some white asparagus as well, and to recommend it to friends and family. She also found herself imagining a large family gathering in her home with a rich meal cooked by Caleb and herself. Meanwhile, Caleb admired how "at home", relaxed and poised Kaya had been while cooking, and how naturally elegant she ate—something he had already noticed earlier, in the restaurant.

After dinner, they placed their cutlery and crockery and pots and pans into the dishwasher, added the detergent and Caleb started it.

'Now, Dr Jarvis,' Caleb said cheekily, 'that is, assuming you did your doctorate in dentistry. Do we need to go to the bathroom now to brush our teeth?'

Kaya laughed. 'Yes to both, factually and ideally. I am Dr Jarvis, thank you, and I would be a hypocrite if I tell my patients to brush their teeth after meals, and not do this myself.'

'Congratulations on the doctorate, you can tell me what it was about later. I have at least one spare toothbrush in the bathroom, still fully packaged. I take them for travelling and leave them behind, so that I can tell myself that my luggage on the way home will be a little lighter as a result. You can then also comment on my toothpaste. You go first.'

After their exercise in dental hygiene, they went back to the living room. Kaya cheerfully approved of both the toothpaste and the toothbrush and was amused by Caleb's reaction of infinite mock-relief. They put on a record of Mendelssohn's Violin Concerto, played by Heifetz, to be heard gently and unobtrusively in the background.

They talked more for a long time, until Kaya hesitated, before she said what she felt might not be easy to say or easy for Caleb to take. 'This afternoon and evening have been so special, like nothing ever before in my life. It's been so much to take in, I think, for both of us. I'm getting tired, and I'd like to be on my own for a while, so, I…'

Caleb sensed her hesitation and continued: 'I feel this same, this whole time was out of this world, catching up on at least one lifetime with a totally familiar stranger. I would so much love you to stay, but I also feel I need some space to digest it all, to think it through.'

Kaya was relieved: 'So you are not disappointed or angry if I leave now?'

'No, Kaya, not angry at all; disappointed perhaps, because once you're gone I'll miss you terribly, but I know you need space, and I need it as well.'

Kaya responded quickly: 'That's good. I'll miss you, too. Will you come to my place tomorrow morning for breakfast, maybe at 10?'

'Wonderful idea,' Caleb beamed. She gave him her address, Satnav details, and mobile number. She put on her coat, they hugged tightly without kissing, looked deeply into each other's eyes, and she left.

Chapter 2

Back at home, Kaya wondered whether all of the past few hours had really happened, or whether she had fallen asleep and dreamt it all, but it was real. She packed away her shopping, then considered watching television before going to bed, but decided against it so as not to spoil the thoughtfully elated mood she was in. She put on a record and sat in her comfortable armchair, closed her eyes, allowing herself to become absorbed in the music. Then she pulled her phone over and pressed one of the speed dial buttons. After a few rings she heard the beloved and familiar 'Hello' at the other end of the line.

'Hi, mum, it's me. How are you?'

'Well,' said her mother, surprised and just a little worried, 'and you? Calling so late on a Friday evening?'

Now Kaya was concerned: 'Is it late?'

'It's 10.30, dear!' said her mother.

'Oh, dear indeed, so late, I had no idea, did I wake you up?'

'No, don't worry,' her mother reassured her with a slight chuckle, 'I was still up. I just couldn't go to sleep yet: my head is still buzzing from the interview I did this afternoon. And I was probably expecting your call, I had been thinking about you a lot today, actually—happy thoughts. So, what's up?'

'Kaya grinned: 'You first. You and your interviews. Whom did you dig up now!?'

She could feel her mother's enthusiasm from her voice: 'A life that is so tragic, on a small scale, that you can hardly put it into fiction, let alone into a biographical piece, it's so difficult to keep a straight face and to capture the realism…'

Kaya interrupted: 'And those, of course, are your very strengths!'

'Thank you,' her mother sighed, adding cheerfully: 'but I think you may be right! Anyway. A woman, early forties, very pretty, tall, slim, looks after herself well, good home. Fairy tale romance and marriage when she was in her early twenties. Her boyfriend, then husband, was a fellow student, undergraduate, postgraduate MA and PhD. Then he went abroad for a year on a scholarship and she had to stay behind. They missed each other terribly, and towards the end of the year she started a relationship with someone else. He found out, and was so hurt, she cried when she told me, now, more than a decade later. She wanted to get back with him, but he was unable to forgive her. They were divorced at his request very quickly, he threw himself into his career, she into hers, she moved away from where they were together. She changed her name, reinvented her looks, they did not talk in person for more than fifteen years, ever since he left the house. She made her career in fine art, painting, and that's what my portrait of her will be about, pun intended, mainly, and she is joining the university where you are in a few days on a part-time basis as a practitioner in residence. Just imagine, not talking for fifteen years, carrying all that guilt, whether it is justified or not, for all that time without any chance of closure.'

Grace paused. 'Hello? … Are you still there?'

Kaya's voice sounded hoarse: 'Wow. I think I may have to add something to the unlikely nature of all this. This is really weird, spooky, out of this world.'

'Nice build-up, Kaya,' her mother urged her on.

'The ex-husband's name would not happen to be Caleb White?'

Now it was Grace's turn to be silent, stunned. Then she gave a big sigh. 'Of course, it is. He's a senior lecturer in drama at Brunel.'

'Ahem,' Kaya set up the humdinger: 'Not any more, he isn't. He is starting a professorship at the university where I am, as you just put it. Next week. That would be the same department where his ex-wife will be working.'

'And you know this because…?' Grace's curiosity was audibly at bursting point.

'Because, mum, and here we segue ever so elegantly into why *I* called *you* in the first place: because I met Caleb at lunchtime today in the supermarket car park, it was love at first sight for both of us, and we spent the rest of the day together, restaurant, walk at the promenade, hand in hand, then coffee and dinner at his place, talked non-stop, shared probably most memories of our lives, and yes, his ex featured prominently, and I just got back home.' Kaya was out of breath.

Grace added: 'And you'll have breakfast at yours tomorrow morning?'

'Mmmm,' Kaya confirmed, 'and in due course you can have an exclusive on the reunion of Caleb and his ex!'

'Her name is Sophia Hockley.'

'*The* Sophia Hockley? She's the most talked about British artist in years—which would be, of course, why you interviewed her, mum.'

'Right again, sweetie!' Grace's voice sounded cheerful. 'So, tell him, your Caleb, all about this tomorrow morning. If you like, I'll come over on Sunday and break the news to Sophia, and I can also facilitate a meeting between her and your Caleb.'

'And you'd love to bring all of that into your article as well, ever so delicately?' Kaya enquired with a broad smile on her face, audible in her voice.

'If ever possible, yes. But I'd do it all without that, just for her and you…'

'And *my* Caleb?'

'Yes, sweetie.'

'Great, mum, I'll talk to *my* Caleb tomorrow, and will call you then. Good night, sleep well!'

'Good night, sweetie,' Grace replied, and hung up.

***

When Caleb had closed the door, he let out a deep sigh. So many years ago, his love had been shattered, as he had thought about it to this day, or, with the new wisdom gained today, Kaya's wisdom, that chapter of his life and love had come to an end. He had buried himself in his work, and his fast rise had been bought at the cost of his denying himself any further relationship. And now, within a few hours, there was Kaya and with her the hope of something new.

He needed something to do, to start with, and quickly tidied the flat and emptied the dishwasher, all the while re-playing in his mind bits of their conversation. What partners came together for, that relationships need not be for a lifetime, the ideas of "wrong belief patterns" and "functionality", the big issue of "guilt" which were all, in in its own way, unnecessary, and blocked so many beautiful feelings and expressions of life. He got ready for bed, brought a candle to his bed-side table, lit the candle, sat on his bed, and began the forgiveness procedure Kaya has talked about. It was not difficult for him to recall the moment he had returned from abroad early, as a surprise for his ex-wife. He forced himself to think of her with her name, Olivia. He had opened the front door to their house, and called out Olivia's name, giddy with the expectation of seeing her delight and surprise of him being back early, and for good. Not having found her in the living room, dining room or kitchen, as he would have expected given the time of day of his arrival, he had worried she might be ill in bed—he was certain she was at home on the basis of some other clues. So, he had walked quietly up to their bedroom, opened the door gently, and had seen Olivia naked in bed with Timothy Bates, a distant acquaintance. They had woken up from him opening the door and stared at him, Tim with his usual dull expression, Olivia with total horror, embarrassment and the deepest sadness Caleb had ever seen, obviously realising the extent of the damage done. Caleb had snapped into a mode of extreme calm, as always in extreme situations. He had said, in a very calm, firm voice, addressed to Olivia and completely ignoring Tim: 'Oh, I am sorry to have interrupted you. You will hear from my solicitors about the divorce. I will ask some of *my* friends to collect my things in due course. Please do not contact me directly, I do not wish to have any communication directly with you any more from this day until I die. I hope Timothy is worth it. Good bye.'

With those words he had left, spent some days in a hotel, then arranged for somewhere permanent to live, and instructed a solicitor friend with the divorce proceedings. He had not given in to so many friends and family to reconcile with Olivia, to at least talk to her to hear from her what had happened. He had asked to be left alone on this front and ended some former friendships where their insistence on communication between him and Olivia had become too strong and tedious to have to deal with.

Sitting on his bed in front of the lit candle this evening, Caleb realised that he had never once, even for a moment, snapped out of that icy calm in relation to that moment of seeing Olivia in bed with Tim. In terms of what he had talked about with Kaya, this must have become a part of his soul that had separated itself from the soul's core, an aspect of his life that he had completely suppressed, but not from laziness, but for sheer survival: he just would not have been able to cope any other way. Therefore, he was sure that he should not feel guilty about the way he had behaved: he had had no alternative. But he had felt guilty, so the first thing he did now was to forgive himself for his hardness, for not having been able to communicate at all with Olivia after the incident, let alone consider the possibility of reconciliation, despite her pleas through friends and even through her solicitor. Then he proceeded to think about forgiving Olivia for what she had done to him, for all the feelings of inferiority and disgust and hatred and anger and so many, many other thoroughly unpleasant feelings she had caused him. But as he went through all these memories of the range of feelings of the hurt she had inflicted, he realised that he had never allowed those feelings the space they had demanded, keeping them rather well-managed under the coldness and calm that had characterised his first response after he had snapped. He had been aware of something under the surface, boiling and bubbling away, but he had never allowed it out. And now it did come out. Tears formed in his eyes, and he realised he had never once cried over the past fifteen years, since "the incident". His breathing got faster and irregular, choking sensations gripped his throat. He was afraid of the intensity of what was about to erupt, not sure he would be able to cope, wishing Kaya could be with him now, and glad at the same time that she wasn't, suppressing the tears, the crying, the ancient sadness, the mountain of guilt, the tons of weight he felt on his chest, the massive lump in his throat, all like a volcano about to erupt after decades, possibly centuries of inactivity. He was not able to suppress all this anymore, even if he would have tried to, and he decided not to try, to let it out, come what may. And then he had just the split second of time to throw himself on the pillow face down before the tears came in full floods. He roared and howled into the pillow as if possessed, screaming and sobbing all the pain, oh, so much pain that seemed to have filled him up entirely, leaving no space in his feelings, only in his thinking, for anything pleasant. He kicked his legs and beat his fists hard on the mattress from arms raised as high in the air as possible, all the while continuing his shrieking, shouting, wailing and roaring across the whole range of his voice in pitch and volume. He did not reflect any more on what he did, he just did, allowing all feelings that wanted to come out to express themselves fully, without inhibition, only hoping occasionally, in a rare pause, that his neighbours would not hear him and send an ambulance or the police, or both, in concern. He calmed down only after what seemed to him have been a very long time. His pillow was wet from tears, and he was sweating profusely, but he was too exhausted to do anything about that. He blew out the candle and fell asleep quickly.

Chapter 3

While usually he slept soundly for some eight hours every night, meeting Kaya, their intensive conversation, and his major release later on, had left Caleb so alert, and so much had gone through his mind, that he did not slept too much, but those few hours of sleep had been particularly sound and refreshing. He made sure he woke up well in time for their 10am breakfast at her place. He changed the sheet, duvet cover and pillowcase of his bed, had a long shower, washed and dried his hair, and selected a casually elegant outfit to wear. He left early, drove into town to do some last-minute shopping—he had had an idea for it in the middle of the night—and reached Kaya's block of flats in time to be able to ring her doorbell at exactly 10am. The buzzer sounded literally a second later, Caleb noted with a broad smile—she must have been standing right next to the door in expectation. Caleb took the lift to the top floor (Kaya also had a top floor flat, just like him), clearing his throat a little nervously as the lift doors opened. Kaya stood in her flat, door wide open, and gave him a little wave with her right hand when he saw her. He walked briskly, holding the large bouquet of pink roses in front of him and handing it over to Kaya once they were inside the flat and she had closed the door behind them.

'Good morning, Kaya,' he said softly, 'I hope you like pink. And roses.'

Kaya nodded happily in response, whispering 'Thank you so much, Caleb,' and led him to the kitchen where she put the flowers into a simple glass vase, and brought them through to the living room, placing them in front of a picturesque fireplace.

'How are you...' they started both at the same time, laughed and carried on together, 'this morning?'

Instead of responding, they slowly walked towards each other, taking each other in with their wide-open eyes, not hesitating, sensing each other's determination, meeting in warm hug that developed into a passionate kiss, more blissful and intense that they had ever experienced, and had been able to hope for.

After a long time, Caleb asked: 'Is this crazy?' There was no hesitation in his voice.

'No.' Kaya said resolutely. 'Perhaps unusual, but wonderful, and right. Do you need breakfast now?'

Caleb responded with another kiss. Kaya gently guided him into her bedroom, from which they emerged only a few hours later, fulfilled, but definitely quite hungry by then. They had showered and dressed again. Kaya cooked some pancakes, which they ate with cream and maple syrup, served with orange juice and fresh coffee (which was not as good as the Monsooned Malabar, they both agreed). For a long time, they did not talk at all, just being still in each other's presence, full of the memories of the past few hours, their bodies tingling.

After a while, however, Caleb began: 'Dearest Kaya, that was wonderful almost beyond description.'

'Same for me, Caleb,' Kaya agreed. 'I'm always trying to be in the moment rather than in the past or future, but I think I've never achieved it more than just now, and without trying, there was not space for trying anymore.'

Caleb picked up on this: 'I think trying is intellectual, and it can lead to some success, but full achievement of being in the moment, fully in the here and now, is different. We can appreciate it intellectually afterwards, but when and while it happens, it is holistic, with the intellect having its appropriate role, but not taking over as it usually does in our world that is dominated by the rational, left brain hemisphere, and an orientation towards science.'

Kaya simply nodded, allowing them both to feel the silence.

Caleb started speaking again after a while. 'I tried the forgiveness ritual you suggested to me yesterday. I don't know whether that is how it is meant to work, but I certainly released a lot. I was literally bawling for an hour or even more, really howling, roaring into the pillows, I just hope now my neighbours didn't hear me. After that I was totally exhausted, but also very clear in my head. It may sound strange, but I want to find my ex-wife. I want to find Olivia. I just realised that I have not said her name since I left her so many years ago, after I had found out. I want us to reconcile. Only where to start looking for her?'

Kaya braced herself for the news she had to share with Caleb: 'Actually, Caleb, our meeting was not the only weird and wonderful thing yesterday. It does not stop there. I told you that my mother is a journalist who writes people's profiles for the *Guardian*? I called her last night, I wanted to tell her about us, but she was so full of an interview she had done yesterday, and she told me all about it and...'

Caleb interrupted, laughing, but tensely: 'Now you are going to tell me that her interview was with Olivia?!!'

'Yes.'

Caleb jumped to his feet and paced around the flat for a few minutes. When he sat back in his armchair, he was still quite out of breath. 'Sorry, Kaya, I needed to get that out of, or into the system! Where is she, how is she, what does she do?'

'According to mum, she's changed her name, which you might actually know, so get ready to get up and run around again...'

Caleb realised that Kay was only half-joking.

'She's now called Sophia Hockley and she will start as artist in residence here in the uni here on Monday. There you are.'

Caleb did not jump up again. He remained seated, motionless. His face went completely blank, for a good while. Then he said simply: 'Oh, I see.'

And after another few minutes, he asked to be allowed to inspect the balcony to get some fresh air. Kaya opened the door and joined him outside a moment later. Caleb was inhaling the air deeply. 'Olivia, or Sophia, would be terribly shocked to see me, if she is not prepared, as I am now, kind of. Will be difficult enough knowing what to expect. Is there any chance your mum could talk to Sophia before Monday?'

Kaya was glad he had asked: 'My mum offered this already, I only need to phone her to confirm. She even offered to come over tomorrow to facilitate, as it were, your meeting on Monday —of course hoping you would both allow her to include it in her article, very delicately, but she would do the facilitating even if you decide not to allow her to write about the reunion.'

Caleb did not have to think about this for long: 'I think I would be very grateful to your mum to talk to Sophia in advance, and to facilitate our meeting, and I would be happy for her to write about it.'

They were interrupted by the ringing of the telephone. Kaya smiled. 'That would be my mum, too impatient and curious to allow me to phone, as we had agreed.'

She went over to the phone and lifted the receiver: 'Hello?' She immediately heard her mother's voice.

'Well, it's already afternoon, and you still have not called me. Are you all right? I mean, breakfast cannot take that long?!'

'Mum, hello, yes, I am fine, and may I remind you that we agreed that I would phone you?' Kaya said, intending it to sound mock-reproachful, but she noticed a certain edge to her voice that she had not intended. She glanced at Caleb, who had turned to look at her with slightly questioning raised eyebrows, and now came over and hugged her. She was moved deeply, close to tears, to find him again so sensitive to her feelings, which she herself was only just about aware of. His reaction, the expression of his eyes, the raised eyebrows and the hug, had been so spontaneous, and not at all patronising, or placing her, let alone pushing her, into a victim role, and she nestled into his embrace.

Grace did not let on whether she had noticed the tense undertone in Kaya's response, and continued with a conciliatory, not quite apologetic 'Yes, or course, dear, but I was just too curious, you know me. So?'

Kaya, still in Caleb's embrace, which he had loosened a little, was similarly conciliatory, without giving in an inch: 'Yes, I do know, mum. Caleb would be grateful if you could initiate the mediation and meeting between him and his ex-wife. Her original name is Olivia, by the way. So, you will call her at some point, and we take it from there? And, oh, I forgot, Caleb is happy for you to include this in your article.'

'Good, Kaya, good.' Grace sounded very pleased. 'Can I stay at your place tomorrow if it works out in the way that I come over there for a meeting on Monday?'

Kaya hesitated briefly. 'Yes, that's fine, but you might find yourself alone overnight,' she said firmly.

Grace knew her daughter well enough and did not tease her on that account, no matter how tempting it was for her, and she simply confirming warmly: 'That's fine, sweetie. I'll try to phone Olivia or Sophia now, and will get back to you later to tell you about any developments.' She could not resist, however, to add a cheeky 'And if you don't answer the phone, I'll leave a Facebook message.'

***

Grace hung up. She was in her study at home, elegantly furnished, spacious and rather empty, with a functional bookshelf, a large desk with computer and phone, and a comfortable arrangement of two armchairs around a side table with sophisticated microphones on tripods. The colour scheme of the furniture was focused on a generous beige. Grace searched for the phone number of Sophia Hockley, whom she had met in her London studio only yesterday. Grace had liked adventure and excitement all her life, fearing boredom more than anything else. Meeting with, and writing about other people, all extra-ordinary and many famous, also gave her the opportunity to compensate for the root of that fear of boredom, her own loneliness. It was loneliness, rather than being alone. She was not good at being alone, feeling lonely, forsaken. She had a strong circle of acquaintances, some of whom she referred to as friends, but who were probably not really friends, and she had her daughter, Kaya. Grace wanted to have friends, she wanted to have Kaya, and she would have liked to have been able to have a husband. Friends and family featured as possessions in her way of thinking, something she felt a right to have. But her husband had left her very early in their relationship, Kaya kept her distance, and so did her friends. Grace felt that not having these people as she wanted to have them was a major injustice to her, for which she could not figure out the reason. Grace had been particularly hurt when Kaya had decided not to pursue her own arts and writing interests professionally, to follow her mother's inspiration and footsteps and benefit from her mother's vast range of important business contacts. When Kaya had declared her decision to become a dentist and had not succumbed to her varied attempts at dissuading her daughter from this decision, a world had collapsed for Grace, two decades of building Kaya's future for her. She had contemplated these circumstances occasionally, less and less over the years, and thrown herself into her work.

The challenge now in hand, arranging the meeting and reconciliation of Sophia and Caleb, was just what Grace rejoiced in and excelled at. She dialled Sophia's number, and was pleased to hear her answer the phone after only a few rings.

'Good morning, Sophia,' Grace said. 'It's Grace, Grace Jarvis calling. I hope my call does not come at an inconvenient moment?'

'Hello, Grace.' Sophia's voice sounded genuinely pleased. 'Not inconvenient at all, as a matter of fact. What can I do for you? Don't tell me the recording of our conversation didn't work and we have to do the interview again?'

Sophia's voice reminded Grace of the overall tendency in Sophia's life for her to expect the worst possible scenario and then feel relief if things turned out less awful than expected. Grace had wondered about the reason for this pattern, and only now realised that it must have been the shock of Caleb leaving.

Now Grace reassured Sophia quickly: 'Don't worry, all fine with the interview. The reason I am calling does relate to something we talked about yesterday, though. You remember that you said that you would really welcome an opportunity of reconciliation with your former husband, Caleb? In one of those weird situations that you cannot call coincidence any more, I think I may be able to facilitate that reconciliation. Would you like me to explain?'

'Yes, of course, please,' Sophia immediately urged her.

'Well, very briefly, then, Caleb has just joined the same department in the university that you will be joining on Monday, and it seems that he has also met my daughter, Kaya, I told you about her. They met for the first time only yesterday, and they have apparently spent a lot of time together talking, and Caleb is keen to see you to talk through the past, what happened all those years ago.'

'Crikey,' Sophia gasped. 'Does that mean that your daughter and Caleb are an item, kind of?'

'Knowing my daughter, the way she talked on the phone to me just now, definitely yes, Sophia,' Grace admitted.

'That's a relief, in a way, actually,' Sophia explained, 'I am happy to meet with Caleb, to get closure for the past, but I don't want to be in a position that I urge myself, or others urge me, to go back to the past and undo the last ever so many years since he left. I want that closure to finally be able to start afresh, but that new start does not have Caleb in it as a potential partner. Colleague will be quite enough, thank you very much.'

Her words had come fast, and sounded to Grace almost over-determined, almost as if she was afraid of admitting she was still in love with Caleb.

Sophia paused, and as there was no immediate response from Grace, she continued: 'How would this take place practically?'

Grace responded swiftly this time: 'It's Saturday today, I will travel over from London tomorrow, visit Kaya, meet Caleb, if she allows me, and I could then meet with Caleb and yourself on Monday, in Kaya's flat, she works over the day, or in Caleb's office, or in some public place, a restaurant perhaps. I will be driving, and I could give you a lift over, at least tomorrow.'

After a while, Sophia responded. Her voice sounded tired. 'I think I'd like to travel on my own, if you don't mind, both ways, but many thanks for offering the lift,' she started. 'I will be staying in London for the months of my residence, but and commute when I am needed there.'

'No problem at all, I understand,' Grace reassured her quickly, making a special effort for her voice not to come across as motherly or patronising, but matter-of-fact.

'Thank you, Grace. I'll find somewhere to stay tomorrow night. I think a public place, as you put it, would be best for the first meeting. I appreciate you offering your daughter's place, but the idea of seeing Caleb again for the first time after so many years in his new girlfriend's place is a bit much after the last time we saw each other was with me in another man's arms.'

'Of course, Sophia, it was rather thoughtless of me to even suggest it, I'm very sorry,' Grace apologised, genuinely embarrassed. 'Kaya always tells me that in my drive to be practical I can be terribly insensitive,' she added.

Sophia was generous enough to be able to smile when she said: 'It's OK, Grace, apology accepted. Caleb and you can decide when and where to meet on Monday. I just checked my diary, I believe we have a staff meeting at 2pm, so some time in the morning would be best.' After a brief pause she added: 'And thank you very much for phoning me about this and making the effort of coming over and arranging the meeting.'

'You're most welcome, Sophia,' Grace responded.

'One further thought,' Sophia added, 'would you want to include this in your article about me?'

''I would love to have your and Caleb's permission to do this, yes. And I might even have to ask my own daughter's permission if I decide to include her in the article. I would of course she you the full text for your approval beforehand. And please, you should know that I am doing all this not only to improve my article.' Grace's voice conveyed her both her professional eagerness and her genuine concern.

'Thank you for being so open about it. We'll see how it all develops.'

Grace and Sophia exchanged their mobile phone numbers, having talked only on their landlines so far, and agreed for Sophia to get in touch once she had arrived from London.

Chapter 4

Just like Caleb, Sophia had worked hard at suppressing the events of fifteen years ago. At first, she had replayed the moments leading up to Caleb leaving, and the second she had seen Caleb for the last time, thousands of time every day. The situation he had caught her in had been unambiguous, and he had had every right to be offended and hurt. Sophia had not meant her affair with Tim to be serious, and neither had he. It was to have been over before Caleb returned from abroad, a nice time for her and Tim, no more, at a time when they both needed it. Close analysis had also allowed her to realise and admit that, at least unconsciously at the time, she had started the affair to punish Caleb for his absence. They had not dealt with their long separation well, had not talked about their feelings of loss and loneliness, of the pain every new separation had caused when he had visited and left, or when she had visited him and left. In due course, each had come to assume that the other one did not really mind their separation all that much, half admiring their toughness and half wondering whether she still loved him and whether he still loved her, or what kind of love it was that did not feel the separation as painful and undesirable. Sophia had also realised that she had blamed Caleb for having to be separated in the first place, given that he chose to take the post abroad for the year, over and above them being together, as it were—it had not occurred to her at the time and for many years that the decision was not as one-sided as she saw it, because she might have joined him if she had chosen to do so. More recently, Sophia had come to wonder whether Caleb had been disappointed that she chose not to join him.

These thoughts had developed over the years, every now and then, caused by unforeseen triggers that had caught her unawares. But for the majority of time she had managed to keep these thoughts at bay by redefining herself, with a new name. Most importantly, she had made a conscious decision about her focus and emphasis in terms of her profession, making a living through her painting. She had used money from the inheritance after her father's relatively early and unexpected death to buy an affordable flat in London that came with a large, airy room she could use as a studio, and had, over the years, developed her style, created her brand, and become a well-liked, much-talked-about contemporary artist. She made a comfortable living from her art. All this, however, had come at the expense of any private or social life worth talking about. She had a range of acquaintances from her professional circle, she would be invited to parties and events, and have the occasional "do" at her place. She had tried to form some deeper relationships with men she thought herself in love with, but had always backed away, or found an excuse to withdraw, when things had started to get too serious.

Yesterday's conversation with Grace had brought all those memories and thoughts back to the forefront of Sophia's mind; she had been genuine when she expressed her wish to see Caleb again—that wish had never left her since the day Caleb had slammed the door behind him. The prospect of meeting with him in a little more than a day, and to be seeing him possibly on a daily basis after that, the fact that he had a new girlfriend, now made her head spin. Would she even recognise him, would he recognise her, would she be able to contain her feelings, what were those feelings going to be, what was reconciliation, would she still love him—all these thoughts were milling around in her head wildly just after Grace's phone-call. She needed more clarity, though, and knew how to achieve it.

She went into her studio, arranged the blinds and curtains to allow in natural daylight, adding from the array of artificial light sources until she had created the ambience she wanted. She put a fresh canvas on the easel, helped herself to a large ceramic tumbler full of water from the dispenser, and embarked on drawing Caleb's face as she remembered it, quite spontaneously, and found herself ending up with the expression of shock on his face when he had seen her and Tim in bed together. She used the drawing as the source for a full-scale water colour painting, feeling calmer when she had completed that in a few hours' time. She decided to take the drawing and the painting with her tomorrow, to show Caleb if it made sense on the day. She walked over to her desk in the studio and checked her diary. She had planned to travel to work on Monday in time for the staff meeting, returning to London that same evening. She now booked a journey for Sunday and reserved a room in her favourite hotel. She packed her travel bag, selecting her outfits for the journey on Sunday, Sunday evening, and the day on Monday. She stuck with her plan to return to London on Monday evening. She was clearer about the position she wanted to start out with in her conversation with Caleb, and issues she wanted to raise, and she was confident she could allow some spontaneity to govern the meeting on that basis, which she considered to be firm on her part. Sophia then prepared some food, ate it quickly, and went for a long walk in the nearby park, an activity she had come to love and appreciate over the years.

***

Grace, meanwhile, felt satisfied with her conversation with Sophia. The artist's obvious polite distance, she realised, was characteristic of so many of her interview partners—there was always distance, for them she was always only a side-show, they never allowed her fully into their lives, no matter how much she might imagine herself to be getting genuine access. This left her with some sadness on occasion, which she usually brushed aside. However, today Grace wondered why she was feeling slightly upset by the reluctance of her interviewees to relate to her as if they were close acquaintances or friends, and not the relative strangers they actually were. On the one hand, she concluded, it must be because she herself did of course not open up fully to those strangers either—she did not even open up fully to Kaya, her own daughter, who was closer to her than any other person in the world. Her expectations were misguided, and her own unknowingly distancing behaviour attracted the distancing response of her interviewees. But she still got more out of them than many other interviewers, which had been her road to success, and she felt justified to be proud of this achievement.

At the same time, she reconsidered her intention to include the reunion of Caleb and Olivia/Sophia in her article about Sophia and decided against it in the interest of the standard of her writing—her niche and strength was subtle reflection, not the crass revelation of investigative journalism, nor the sensationalism of the popular media. She phoned Kaya, told her briefly about the conversation with Sophia, efficiently discussed and agreed the best venue for the meeting on Monday, and arranged to meet with Kaya and Caleb for dinner in a restaurant on Sunday evening. Not having had much of a lunch, she now cooked herself a delicious early dinner, wondering briefly whether she would cook for someone else, someone special, ever again.

***

When the phone conversation with Grace had ended, Kaya was still in Caleb's embrace. 'Thank you so much for comforting me, I needed that,' Kaya smiled.

'I just followed my instinct, there was something in your voice,' Caleb explained.

'It is so amazing how well you pick things up about me and how you know how to respond to what you pick up,' Kaya admired.

Caleb was modest: 'Thank you. We seem to have known each other for a long time already, perhaps in previous lives.'

'Reincarnation?' Kaya mused, 'We have to talk about that as well, but not now.'

At that moment, the phone rang. 'Perfect timing, as ever, from my dear mother,' Kaya sighed with a grin, and picked up with her usual 'Hello?'

It was indeed Grace, as Kaya had predicted. Kaya listened to her carefully for a while, making a few notes on the notepad next to the phone, and interjecting a few instances of 'OK,' and 'I see.' Then she turned to Caleb and summarised: 'Sophia is fine to meet with you. Mum suggested you meet at the café inside the Odeon, it's spacious, and open and not too crowded in the mornings. 10.30 am might be a good time, not too early, and in time for the staff meeting to get some lunch in between, wherever. Alright with you?' she asked Caleb.

'Yes, sound great to me. Can't imagine it will be really happening. But the logistics are fine.'

'You heard that, mum?' Kaya asked into the phone.

'I sure did, honey,' Grace answered. 'Very lovely voice, your Caleb's got, and very loving,' she added, very warmly.

'I agree,' Kaya said happily. 'When are you coming over tomorrow?'

'I am planning on leaving here around 2pm, so I should reach your place around 5pm at the latest, what with Sunday afternoon traffic. Maybe we can all have coffee, and then go out for dinner together,' Grace suggested.

'Yes, that's fine, mum, good idea,' Kaya confirmed.

Grace just could not resist adding cheekily: 'And then I can go back to yours, and you to Caleb's for the night—wasn't that the plan?'

'Honestly, mum!' Kaya protested. 'But yes, that's the plan,' she insisted, 'see you tomorrow, have a good time until then, and a good trip.' After a few moments, Kaya hung up.

'You really have to be very alert around your mum, it seems, or she succeeds in her attempts at dominating you,' Caleb observed, also noticing that on this occasion Kaya had been better prepared than earlier and did now not need his hug to reinforce her own position.

Kaya nodded, noticing herself that Caleb had not come over for a hug this time, and quietly appreciating the alertness they afforded each other. 'You'll meet her tomorrow, she's coming here around 5 for some coffee— could we please have some Monsooned Malabar for her? And later we can go for dinner,' she summarised the plans, and added softly: 'And then she can stay in my place and I would love to spend the night at yours?!'

'All fine with me,' Caleb stated. 'Meeting your mum might be a bit daunting, but the night at mine will be plenty of compensation, or a victory celebration, depending,' he added with a broad smile.

Kaya punched his ribs happily with her elbow: 'Cheeky! Oh, I forgot, mum decided that she does not want the whole thing between you and Sophia and the meeting as part of her article about Sophia. It's the last thing you need to have the whole world, and especially your new colleagues, gossip about you, and it won't help our relationship either, she figured.'

'I'm relieved, to be honest, I had almost regretted my earlier consent, but I would not have withdrawn it. Very self-effacing and mature from your mum.' Caleb's voice reflected both his relief and his appreciation of Grace's decision.

They spent the rest of the afternoon in further conversation, freely and comfortably alternating between casual, cheerful and deep moods. In the early evening, they had a light dinner of tomato and cheese on toast. When they both felt they were getting tired, they agreed to spend the night together in Caleb's flat, because Caleb had suggested that they should rise very early the next day because he wanted to take Kaya to a very special place for the sunrise.

Their night was even more blissful, apart from affording some rest as well, than their few hours in Kaya's bed earlier that day. They rose early, and Caleb led Kaya to a secluded bench off the main promenade walk.

The view across the bay, from this elevated position, was impressive at any time of day or night, but the current sunrise rendered it astonishingly breath-taking. The blood-red sun made its first appearance on the horizon almost shyly, as if in awe of the night, of the dew that had formed in the air and on the plants, roads, houses, and cars, and tentative to break the magic spell of that nightly peace and calm. The sun also knew that its rise was part of nature, part of creation, and that therefore those moments of hesitance would not last long. Nevertheless, or precisely because those moments were so brief, the sun relished the gentle, loving feelings they triggered on a daily basis. Unconditional, infinite, unbounded, universal love thus re-established, and re-confirmed itself anew, each morning, as the sun's innermost core and essence, informing and permeating, and thus decisively shaping, all life on Planet Earth.

While the first glimmers of the blood-red sun were therefore hesitant, the remainder of the sunrise was a spectacle of determined splendour. The colour of the sun itself, through the increase in light behind it, mutated through a rich palette of deep red, and this radiated through shades of dark, deep red via lighter red and orange all the way towards golden and yellow, at times mixed with a hint of blue. Those colours spread out from the sun into its vast surroundings of the morning sky in ripples and intricate patterns of undulations. Some of the hues resembled that of an animated salt lamp, or, among precious stones: agate, blood jasper, garnet, red coral and red ruby. The air was crisp and fresh, the kind of cool that foreshadows higher temperatures during the day. Caleb sensed a minute hint of the acerbic fragrance of cedar oil—or was it the slightly sweeter clove?

'Did I promise too much?' he asked. His voice revealed his quietly excited anticipation.

'No. It is really truly beautiful!' The answer came from the heart, deeply felt, and resonated with Caleb's heart. 'I wonder whether you could have asked that question differently, though?' Kaya added.

Caleb thought for a moment. 'You mean—not with a negative implication that you implicitly ask me to deny.'

Kaya smiled: 'Yes, exactly—although that is not so easy, actually: many questions, also rhetorical ones, seem to have a negative phrase in it, such as the "isn't it" in "beautiful, isn't it?"'

Caleb continued this train of thought: 'Will a simple question, "Beautiful?" do the trick?'

Kaya nodded: 'Yes, perfect, it is much more open, do you (not don't you!!) see?'

Having agreed on this, they were silent for a while, until the sunrise was complete, the sun had risen, and the new day had begun.

***

Later that day, in Kaya's flat, the doorbell rang. This was the moment of truth, both Caleb and Kaya thought, at the same time. Kaya pressed the buzzer and Grace was upstairs in a few minutes. Caleb had decided to wait in the living room. He heard Kaya welcoming her mother, and they made their way to the guest bedroom where Grace would stay on all of her visits. Kaya came back to the living room, while Grace settled in as quickly as she could. She had googled Caleb, of course, so she knew what he looked like, and remembered the stages of his academic profile, but she burned to see and meet him in person, possibly the first real serious boyfriend her daughter had ever had, in all those years. Grace took a final look into the mirror, was pleased with what she saw, and made her way into the living room. Kaya and Caleb were sitting on the sofa together, with both armchairs free for her to choose from. When she entered, they got up.

Blushing, Kaya introduced Caleb and her mother to each other: 'Mum, this is Caleb. Caleb, this is my mother, Grace.'

'I am very pleased to meet you, Caleb,' Grace started, extending her hand.

'The pleasure in mine, Grace,' Caleb responded, gentleman through and through, with an open smile, and taking Grace's hand for a warm handshake.

'Shall we sit down,' Kaya suggested, motioning Grace to her choice of armchairs and Caleb to the sofa, taking the seat next to Caleb she had been in when Grace had joined them.

They sat down, Caleb and Grace smiling at each other comfortably.

'Did you have a good journey, Grace?' Caleb asked, adding quickly: 'I bet you told Kaya already, though.'

Grace smiled at his consideration: 'Yes, the journey was uneventful, which is good, and no, I hadn't told Kaya already.' She thought for a moment: 'I like the way you say her name, by the way.'

'Oh, thank you,' Caleb said, surprised. 'It is a beautiful name. What made you choose it, if I may ask?'

Kaya had to pull herself together not let out a squeak of joy at that question. They had not rehearsed the conversation with Grace, but Caleb's question was the best trigger for the launch of a conversation she could imagine. Her parents had apparently spent a very, very long time indeed on the choice of Kaya's name, were very proud of that choice, and always annoyed when people casually mispronounced the name.

Grace beamed: 'The name has different meanings in different languages, but our choice was influenced by its meaning in the Native American Hopi language, where it means "my wise elder sister". We liked the spelling, the pronunciation and the meaning.'

'I like them, too, and I love Kaya,' Caleb smiled.

They continued their conversation with ease now that the ice had been broken so quickly and warmly. Caleb talked about his work, his love for drama and theatre, and some of his teaching and research, making sure to catch the signals from both Grace and Kaya when they had heard enough, and it was time for someone else to take over the conversation. Kaya talked about her daily routine as a dentist, and Grace shared some of the insights from her interviews.

This was an appropriate moment for Kaya to launch a new idea. 'We were wondering whether you might be interested in doing an interview with Caleb's father, mum,' she announced.

'Really?' Grace sounded interested. 'Tell me about him, Caleb.'

'Right, here's the pitch,' he smiled, and Grace smiled back encouragingly. 'Four years ago, when he was sixty years old, my mother died in a car crash. She had been a teacher of Science at the same school where he taught English. He retired from his job, sold the family house, gave me my part of the inheritance, and has been travelling the world since. He had seen him in person about once year since then, and we skype occasionally when he feels like it.'

'That sounds fascinating, Caleb,' Grace agreed. 'I'd love to interview him. You said you are not in touch regularly, so we play it by ear. Call me when he's been in touch and if he's interested, and then we can arrange something at short notice.'

'I told you that mum is always very practical,' Kaya beamed.

'I like practical, and your suggestion works well,' Caleb confirmed. Now it was just seizing the moment when Henry would get in touch again.

For the rest of the day, Caleb, Kaya and Grace had coffee, and Grace loved the Monsooned Malabar. Later they decided against dinner in a restaurant. Instead, Grace cooked a self-made cream of mushroom soup with toasted croutons, and not too long after that, they double-checked the arrangements for Caleb's meeting with Sophia, Kaya packed a few things for the night and the next day, and then left with Caleb to spend the night at his place while Grace had Kaya's flat all to herself. They all agreed that it had been a very happy first encounter between Caleb and Grace.

Chapter 5

The next morning, Kaya and Caleb had to be woken up by their alarm clocks, not being able to sleep in due to the demands of daily life, working life. They still managed to have a relaxed, long and lovely shower and then breakfast together. They agreed to meet back at Kaya's place after their work, so that Caleb could share how his meeting with Sophia, and his first staff meeting, had been. Grace would also be there, briefly, before heading back to London.

Grace and Caleb met at the Café as planned, ready for their encounter with Sophia. Finally, she arrived. Caleb recognised her immediately, and she him, although they had not seen each other face to face for the last fifteen years. Sophia walked over and said hello to Grace. That seemed easier and was straightforward. Grace gave her an encouraging hug, making sure at the same time that it was a distant hug. Then Sophia turned to Caleb.

'Hello, Caleb.' Her voice sounded dull, distant, forced.

'Hello,' Caleb hesitated, and decided: 'Sophia.'

They shook hands, and for both touching the other's hand brought back the memory of physicality in their marriage. Although fifteen years had passed, that touch was still familiar.

Grace motioned them to sit down and motioned the waitress over to take their order. Caleb had a hot chocolate, Sophia as well, and Grace a café latte. They spent the minutes until their drinks were served engaging in small-talk, about the weather and the coincidence of Caleb and Sophia working in the same department at the same university. Once the drinks had been served, Grace took hers to a separate table further off. Caleb and Sophia were on their own.

'This is not easy for either of us, I guess,' Caleb broke the silence. 'I wanted to start off by thanking you for agreeing for us to have this meeting.'

'Nothing since "that day" has been easy for me,' Sophia said bitterly, 'and I am relieved we can meet today.'

They were silent again for a while. Caleb started again. 'I wanted to apologise that I was so hard on you at the time, and that I was unable to forgive. I was not happy with that inability, but there was at the time nothing I could do to get over it. You know that I met Kaya, Grace's daughter, and she talked to me about forgiving, and what to do to achieve it, and I think that I have been able to forgive you, and I hope you can find a way of forgiving me.' And Caleb told Sophia in detail about the purification and release process he had gone through in the night after the first meeting with Kaya.

Sophia listened quietly, without interrupting Caleb a single time. 'You have not lost your ability of being so very clear and precise, I always admired that,' she said, with a hint of smile, with a hint of warmth, in her eyes, if not her face. 'I would have told you in person, if you had allowed me, and I told you through the solicitors that my affair with Tim was meant to have ended before you were back, and that I still loved you despite the affair. I had not realised that my affair, if you did find out, would hit you so badly, that it would make you shut down and off so completely.'

'I guess you can never predict the impact it may have on the partner who is the victim of the betrayal. The victim role is of course quite easy to sustain, it certainly was in my case. I felt sorry for myself, more than angry with you. The moment of insight was like being punched in the stomach with a wrecking ball, I think I doubled over first. Then total coldness and shutting off all emotions, for sheer survival. Probably you were unable to cope with our separation in any different way, and I not with seeing you in bed with Tim.'

'I have felt guilty about this all my life since then,' Sophia informed him. 'I never had a proper partnership since, always ran away when it got serious. I think I will try the approach to forgiving that Kaya taught you, and then I hope I might be as lucky as you and find my own new partner. I certainly wish you luck with Kaya, and, to be clear, I am under no illusion that I might get you back. We cannot undo what happened.'

'I am very happy with Kaya, although we have known each other only for three days. I will always cherish the good memories of our life together, and I hope that our meeting today can make it possible for us to dwell more on those good memories than on the separation and its circumstances and aftermath. I hope you can forgive me, and forgive yourself, and that you find another partner.' With those words, Caleb briefly placed his hands on Sophia's. She turned her hands and took hold of Caleb's, squeezing them, equally briefly but firmly, and then let them go.

They had reconciled, it had not been too difficult, they both realised, and it felt better. Sophia knew she still had to start the inner forgiveness process, and Caleb realised that there were still remnants of unforgiven material left over that he had to address. They could now, however, move on to more practical matters.

Sophia started. 'I think we should leave the past to itself, Caleb, and not reveal to anyone at work that we were married to each other once. I took on a different name to distance myself from the past. Do you agree?'

Caleb was relieved. 'Yes, absolutely, just imagine having to tell everybody what happened. It would make us very unhappy, and for what? For a few party conversations? We are too precious for that!'

'Good, we are agreed on this.' Sophia was relieved as well. She added: 'I'd like to meet Kaya, but not yet, in due course, when your relationship has firmed up.'

'And I'd like you to meet her, and I hope I will be able to meet, very soon indeed, someone who is then as dear to you as Kaya is for me,' Caleb said with genuine warmth in his voice.

Sophia swallowed. 'Part of this meeting today, for me, is to realise even more how much I lost, seeing what I could have been part of, you and your life, and I will need time to work through that, with the forgiveness thing and all.'

'I understand that, Sophia. In a way, it is the same for me, despite me having found Kaya. It's the "if only" scenario, in so many ways. If only you hadn't had the affair, if only we had handled our separation during my year abroad better, talked more openly about how we felt, if only I hadn't come back early unannounced, if only I had been able to forgive you, all of these, at random, not in any specific order.

'But we are both agreed that we cannot go back in time, and do not want to, either. We have both suffered a lot and are still in the process of coming to terms with what happened, getting over it properly,' Sophia concluded.

'Yes, very well put,' Caleb agreed, 'we are now in the process of transforming it, of healing. And this meeting and our conversation helped a great deal in this process, and we will be able to co-exist peacefully in the same department.'

Sophia and Caleb had had both looked forward to the meeting as something very necessary but had also been apprehensive about the meeting. They were relieved that the meeting had been so amicable and productive. Neither of them felt inclined to engage in small-talk, and without hesitation they thanked each other again for the conversation, and Sophia left. Caleb saw her walking over to Grace, who got up. They talked briefly, gave each other a friendly but distant hug, and Sophia left the café, waving at Caleb casually through the window as the passed his table outside. Caleb waved casually back and finished his drink.

Grace came over and joined Caleb at his table. She looked incredibly curious, so much so that Caleb could not help but bursting out laughing. Grace looked confused.

Caleb explained: 'Sorry for laughing Grace, but your face is one big question mark of curiosity, and at the same time polite hesitation not to ask immediately what has happened between Sophia and me.'

Knowing how her face tended to be a very accurate mirror of her soul, Grace joined Caleb's laughter. Then Caleb told her what had happened, briefly, to the extent that he felt she should know, in some cases, Grace felt, a little short on the personal, emotional side of things which of course was most interesting to her, but she respected this as part of his private sphere. She had noticed already in her conversation with him earlier and the day before, and from his exchanges with Kaya she had overheard, that he was firm in demarcating and retaining his private sphere, without being uncomfortable about it, pushy, or impolite—merely gently firm, if that existed. Caleb expressed his genuine gratitude to Grace for having arranged the meeting, and Grace was pleased it had worked out so well. Grace then went back to Kaya's flat, while Caleb walked across to his office. They would meet again later in the day after work at Kaya's.

***

Kaya, meanwhile, had gone to her surgery, prepared for the day and started seeing patients. She had a number of routine check-ups scheduled, as well as some routine fillings, and an extraction of two teeth in a young teenager at the request of the orthodontist, prior to starting orthodontic treatment. The 12-year-old girl came with her mother, who had taken half a day off work so that she could be with her daughter. Kaya could see that the girl was quite frightened. Kaya motioned the girl to sit in the dental patient chair and moved a visitor chair to a position where her mother could be as close as possible, also holding her daughter's hand, without obstructing her own work. Then she asked the girl whether she would like her to explain to her what she was going to do. The girl nodded to her mum, who confirmed to Kaya that knowing what was going to happen, and then what was happening, would help her daughter a lot. Kaya got out some models to help her explain what the purpose of the injection was, and how she would work to extract the teeth. The girl understood and seemed to relax a little. Kaya then adjusted the chair backrest and prepared the syringe for the injection, showing it to the girl before the started, and talking her through her movements just as the girl had seen them with the model a little before. Kaya was very pleased and the girl rather surprised when the injection had been set without her feeling much pain. Kaya then took an elevator to loosen the tooth, followed by the extraction forceps to remove the tooth. The procedure was straightforward and successful, for both teeth that had to be removed. The dental nurse then gave the girl instructions on how long to keep biting the gauze to stop the bleeding, and further information to her and her mother about what to expect and what to do, including the possible need for pain killers, and reminded them to phone the surgery during office hours, and to call the NHS on 111 after hours if needed. Kaya led the girl and her mother out to the reception, where the girl hugged her, thanking her for the treatment, for having made it so bearable. Moments like this were always wonderful for Kaya, confirming how right she had been with her career choice.

After that patient, the dentists and nurses had a scheduled break which they used to have their packed in between snacks. Caleb had brewed some Monsooned Malabar for Kaya to take with her, and her colleagues noticed the striking aroma and asked her about the coffee. Kaya explained, they all had a little to try, and loved it very much indeed.

Emily Smithson, who owned the surgery, had known Kaya for the past six years, ever since she started working in her surgery. She looked at her curiously now: 'I say, Kaya, you seem to be in exceptionally great spirits today, and that cannot just be the new coffee?'

Kaya grinned. 'Well observed, Em. The coffee is not the only thing
that's new in my life, although what's also new is not really a think either,'
she giggled jauntily.

'OK,' Emily investigated further, taking up Kaya's mood: could it be a
fish?'

'What?' Kaya gasped.

'Not a fish, I conclude,' Emily stated.

'I know, a doggie,' ventured Emily's nurse.

Kaya just raised her eyebrows.

'A man, it must be a man. The man in her life, the man of her dreams,
Mr Right,' squealed Kaya's nurse.

Kaya nodded shyly. 'I didn't expect it to be so obvious already on the
first day back to work,' she remarked.

'Transparency is a motto of this surgery, you just can't escape that, it
moulds you for life,' Emily joked.

Kaya told them about Caleb, and Emily hoped he would become a
patient at their surgery, so that they could get to know him quickly. Emily
also thought about arranging an in-between social to which partners would
be invited—she was just too curious to meet Kaya's new man.

When Kay's office hours had ended, she phoned Caleb in his office so
that he knew he could come over to her flat in line with his own
commitments. Then she walked to her car and drove home.

***

After the conversation with Sophia, Caleb walked across to the university
and had a light lunch in the refectory. Then he proceeded to his office and
worked through some emails, before making his way to the staff meeting
in one of the studios of the performing arts building. He greeted those
colleagues he knew already, and was introduced to some additional ones,
including Sophia, and neither let on that they had known each other
before. When the meeting started, the Head of Department welcomed his
staff, formally introduced Caleb and Sophia as new staff members and
invited all others to briefly introduce themselves. For Caleb, it was
interesting to match photos on the staff web-pages, which he had read
closely, to real faces. The Head of Department then moved refreshingly
swiftly and efficiently through a lengthy agenda, and in much less time
than anticipated, Caleb found himself sharing a coffee with some
colleagues in the Performing Arts Centre's posh and expensive Café.
When he returned to his office, he had time for some more emails, then
Kaya phoned him to tell him she was on her way back home.

Although he was, he did not want to come across as desperate, and waited for another ten minutes or so before he shut down his computer, left the office, and walked swiftly, faster and faster, he noticed, to Kaya's flat. Grace was with Kaya, of course, and they reminisced briefly about the successful meeting of Caleb and Sophia, earlier that day, although it now already seems like in the distant past. Grace said her good-byes soon, wanting to be able to return to London in at least near-daylight. Caleb then told Kaya in more detail about his day, the meeting with Sophia, the staff meeting, and coffee with new colleagues, and Kaya shared some of her day's impressions, her work and her colleagues' curiosity about him.

Over the next two or three weeks, Kaya and Caleb got to know each other even more, shared many stories from their lives with each other, the first times they had been in love, their parents, memories from school, classmates, teachers, and their professional lives. They alternated where they would spend the night, they cooked together and had the occasional meal in a restaurant. One Friday night, at Caleb's place, the phone rang, and Caleb answered it with his version of 'Hello?' He gave a little gasp when he had heard who was calling. 'Dad! Such a surprise! Where are you calling from?' He paused for a moment. 'Of course, we can skype! I just need to turn on the computer. You call me?' Another pause. 'Great, so looking forward. Bye.'

'Your father?', Kaya enquired. 'You sounded very happy to hear him.'

'I certainly am,' Caleb confirmed, 'sometimes it takes weeks for him to get in touch. He sounded as if he had exciting news to share. And I can tell him about us and about your mum being interested in interviewing him.' He walked over to the study, Kaya joining him, put on his computer and launched skype. His father's call came as soon as the programme was open. The connection worked well.

'Such a lovely surprise to see you, dad,' Caleb said happily. 'It's been a particularly long time.' He looked at the background of the space where his father was sitting—clearly a hotel room, but no clue as to where. 'Where are you skyping from?'

'You can't find a clue in the picture, can you,' Henry joked, having noticed Caleb's searching glance. I'm in Germany. I got back here from New York only yesterday, and I am planning on travelling over to the UK tomorrow morning, and I'd love to come over for tea tomorrow afternoon. I should reach the station at 3.30pm and will take a taxi to your place. What do you say now?'

'Wonderful!' Caleb said. 'In that case, I will leave all my surprises for when you get here,' he teased.

'You never have surprises, Caleb,' Henry White said to his son, only half-joking.

'You're right, I am very predictable, but this time I'm making up for the last decade at least' Caleb smiled. Then he added more formally: 'You haven't seen my new place yet—do you want to stay here with me, or would you like to keep your independence by staying in a hotel?'

Henry hesitated, but not for long. 'Always independence if I have a choice. I'm very curious about all your news. Connection's getting a bit wonky, see you tomorrow!' And with that he hung up.

Henry was still a little jet-lagged from his travel. He had been in New York for a couple of days, to fit in a few Broadway shows and a night at the Metropolitan Opera. Now he was in Munich, for another night at the opera, and an early morning flight to London the next day. He had now been travelling for the past four years, and while he was busy, relentlessly so, he had realised a few weeks ago that he was not getting the distraction from his suppressed grief any more—even the travelling, the constant barrage of new impressions, had become routine. On the flight over from New York he had made the decision to finally come to terms with his wife's death, by whatever means, even if that meant counselling—a thought he had found abhorrent so far. He would settle down again somewhere in the UK because that was his home after all, and he realised that he did need a physical space to call home again, after four years of all but formal homelessness—for legal reasons, he had had his place of residence with Caleb.

'He's very brief and to the point,' Kaya observed after Caleb had closed down the skype software and his computer. They went back to the living room.

Kaya had been thinking while Caleb skyped: 'From what you told me about him, he might not be here all that long. Should we check with my mum whether she is free the day after tomorrow to come over and meet and interview him?'

That's what they did. Grace was free on the specified day and sounded very keen to come over and meet and interview Harry. For her it was a completely new way of trying to cope with bereavement, and she was certain it would make for a fascinating article for her to compose.

Chapter 6

For Henry's visit, Kaya and Caleb had agreed for Caleb to be on his own when Henry arrived, and for Kaya to join them an hour or so later. Henry's train had been on time, and he reached Caleb's flat around 3.45 in the afternoon. Caleb found Henry looking tired and weary, showing his age of by now sixty-four for the first time, as far as Caleb could recall. It was more, Caleb also realised, than mere jet-lag or travel-fatigue. Henry seemed to have arrived at a crossroads, Caleb felt.

Henry, in turn, was not too absorbed with his own thoughts to realise the change in Caleb since he had last seen him. There was so much life in him, warmth, and love, as he had not remembered from him ever since his divorce. He also saw Caleb's concern when he had seen him.

'I look old and tired, don't I,' Henry asked, briskly interrupting Caleb's attempt at a response 'No need to comment, Caleb, right now. I saw your concern when you saw me. Your face is still so familiar to me, even if I don't see you on a daily basis any more. But you do look great, so please, do tell me your surprises, right away!' he urged.

After Caleb had shown his father around the flat, and Henry had made use of the guest bathroom, they sat down together in the living room. Henry had had some coffee on the journey and now really wanted to hear the news before having tea.

'There's a lovely fragrance of perfume in the flat here, Caleb, and it isn't yours, and it is not so stale that it could have been left from the people who lived here before you moved in,' Henry observed. 'Would one of your surprises be that you have a girlfriend?'

'Good guess, dad, and spot on,' Caleb beamed. And he proceeded to tell Henry all about Kaya, how they had met, that she was a dentist, and many other details. Henry had many questions to ask, and Caleb was happy to answer them. He told his father also about his meeting with Sophia and their reconciliation. Then he came to mention Grace, and that she was keen do to interview him. 'Grace would be able to come over here tomorrow and talk to you then. I mean I don't know your plans, but you might be far away again soon?'

'So that's your surprises done, Caleb, is it?' Henry asked, and when Caleb nodded, he continued: 'They were wonderful surprises, all of them. I am very happy for you that you have found Kaya, and that you are reconciling with Olivia. Sorry, I know that she is called Sophia now, but for me she is still Olivia. I admire you for admitting that you had problems forgiving her. I always fully understood why you were unable to set eyes on her again. You know how upset I was at the time, and how furious with her: I could easily have killed her myself, and I need some help in dealing with that whole chapter of your life, and also mine and that of your mother. All in due course. And I am grateful to Kaya and you to think of me a suitable subject for Grace's interview series. I am very touched and honoured by that, believe me. And I would be very happy to be interviewed.'

Henry paused and got up, as he now came to his surprise, which had firmed up further overnight. Caleb made a move to get up as well, but Henry motioned him gently to remain seated. 'Here's my surprise,' he started, clearing his throat. 'I have now been running away from the grief about your mother's death for the past four years. I have given up my home and travelled the world. Financially, I could go on like this until I die, literally. But even travelling has become a routine that does not stop me from thinking of Imogen...' he hesitated because he had not said that name aloud for a long time, 'of Imogen. So, I want to settle back in the UK, I don't yet know where exactly, I'll make up my mind over the next week, and then I want to get grief counselling to help me cope better with my loss.'

Caleb was very happy for his father and told him so immediately. He proceeded to make coffee, and had even baked, at very short notice, his father's favourite cake. Just when they were ready, the doorbell rang, and Kaya joined them. She had heard much about Henry, and he about her, from Caleb, and so they met for the first time as if they had known each other already well. Kaya was keen to see Caleb and his father together. They were very relaxed and cheerful with each other, which made her happy for Caleb and Henry, but she noticed feeling a little sad herself because she did not have that kind of relationship with her mother, let alone her father. Henry, in turn, was pleased to see how relaxed and cheerful Caleb and Kaya were together. He liked Kaya from the moment he first saw her. She was so different from Olivia, Henry thought, even if he tried to be objective and dismiss his antipathy towards Olivia, which he had held even before Caleb had left her. Kaya was right for Caleb, Henry felt, and Caleb for her, they were right for each other. He had high hopes for their future. Which would include him, and perhaps even see him become a grandfather, in due course.

They continued their pleasant conversation, with Henry relishing the opportunity of sharing memories of his years of travel, Caleb and Kaya made dinner for them all, and some time after dinner they took Henry to his hotel. He would come back some time in the later morning for breakfast together, they would go out for lunch and then leave Henry to meet with and be interviewed by Grace.

***

Time passed quickly and congenially, and Grace arrived at Caleb's place as arranged. Kaya introduced her to Henry, and Henry and Grace looked at each other attentively as they shook hands. They had coffee together, then Caleb and Kaya went for a walk, leaving Henry and Grace to their interview—Grace would call Kaya when it was time for them to return. Grace took out her recording equipment and arranged it in relation to where Henry and Grace had decided to sit for their conversation. Then she put on the recorder and launched her questions. As usual, she had prepared as much as possible, based on information from Caleb and Kaya, but there was no public material available on google about Henry. As a result, she had to start with some questions that filled in the facts, his life up to his travels, and some detail of the travels themselves. Henry's responses allowed Grace to form some feeling for him and guided the direction of her later questions. She found, as Caleb and Kaya had already over the last day or so, that Henry felt a strong urge to share his life experiences, and that, as a teacher of English, he was very erudite and expressed himself very eloquently and poetically. He was able to draw her into his world, which, during his years of travel, had been a world of adventure. In terms of its route, it may well have been similar to a young person's travels in the gap year between school and university. But it came across as so much richer than that because Henry's experiences were those of four years of travelling, not one, it was not a time in between one very specific set of circumstances and another one, school and university, or university and life in employment, and, even more importantly, he was able to bring some forty years of a rich adult life to the travels, which afford many more nuances and points of comparison than twenty years of infancy, childhood, adolescence and very young adulthood.

Grace was impressed by his life and his narration. All she had to do was provide an occasional nudge to steer him into a direction she had become particularly interested in, and she was certain she would gain so much material in transcript of the recording that there would be plenty to go with for an article in two parts over two weeks. Henry was aware that in Grace he had a very interested listener, and he was glad to be able to tell his stories to someone who would not consider him off because of their contents.

They spent quite a long time on their conversation. Kaya and Caleb had meanwhile returned to Kaya's place and waited there for Grace to phone them. In the end they had even made their own dinner there, and Grace and Henry had made their own dinner at Caleb's place, interrupting the recording for that hour. After dinner, Henry and Grace tidied the kitchen and placed used cutlery and crockery into the dishwasher and carried on with their recorded conversation. When this had drawn to a close, they continued their conversation without recording, even though the recording had not felt too formal for either of them. Henry suddenly remembered that only two days ago he had wondered if he would ever cook for, or with someone again. Now he had, and he felt that it had been with someone special. They talked about the formalities of Grace having the recording transcribed and then composing the article, and then she would send it to Henry for approval, and then it would be published.

Henry sat up a little straighter in his comfortable armchair. 'I have enjoyed talking very much and enjoyed talking to *you*. Look, we are both a little advanced in years. You must have realised that I don't like wasting time. What I am trying to say is that I would not want our next meeting to be left to chance, and not be occupied by a formal interview either, although I hasten to add that you made me feel very comfortable throughout. Oh, I'm not good at this, at all, am I? It's been a long time,' he faltered.

'I know what you mean. And you have said it very beautifully, Henry! I also enjoyed our meeting and conversation, and the cooking and eating together, more than many other formal interviews that I have been doing over the years,' Grace reassured him. 'I would like to invite you to come to my place in London, whenever it suits you with your plans, sooner rather than later please, and we can talk, can cook and do whatever else we like,' and with the last words she placed her left hand on his right one and squeezed it firmly.

Henry then phoned Caleb and because it was late in the evening by then, they arranged for Henry to go to his hotel, while Grace would stay in Kaya's flat and Kaya and Caleb in Caleb's. They laughed a lot working out these logistics, but in due course everyone ended up where they were meant to and had a restful night. They met for breakfast at Caleb's, then Grace returned to London in time for an early afternoon interview with Simon Callow.

Henry had vacated his hotel room and asked to stay at Caleb's for a few days. He had been thinking hard over night and raised some of his thoughts with Kaya and Caleb. 'I hope you don't mind if I confide in you,' he started, 'but I am quite smitten with your mum, Kaya, even though I only met her for a few hours yesterday. I told her, quite clumsily, I think, that I would not like to leave seeing her again to chance. She assured me that she would like to see me again as well, and invited me to have tea with her, even at her place. I just don't know whether she was just being polite to an old fool and secretly hoping he'd not take her up on the invitation.'

Kaya smiled warmly when Henry had finished, aware that all eyes were on her. 'It seems we don't waste time courting in this family,' she commented. 'My mum would never play with someone's feelings—her own have been hurt more than enough for that. She would have found a very clear and kind way of turning you down on the spot, Henry, if that had been the way she felt. If she invites you, then you are in there with a big, fat chance. And don't feel you need to be polite about timing. If you feel like travelling over to her today or tomorrow, do it.'

Chapter 7

Henry felt good to have asked and pleased with the information and assurance he had received. He phoned Grace the next day, and they arranged to meet, initially for lunch at a new Indian restaurant Grace had found, tucked away in Soho, two days later. Before that, Grace had to finish writing up the interview with Callow and arrange another one. They were both very excited about the prospect of meeting relatively soon, though, and their excitement was amply reflected in their voices on the phone. Henry immediately told Caleb and Kaya, who shared his joy, and Grace phoned Kaya as well to tell her the news, although she then realised that Kaya must have heard, and had indeed heard, from Henry herself. But she simply had to tell someone how happy and excited she felt, almost like a giddy teenager awaiting her first prom.

On the day, they met at the restaurant. Henry was curious, because Grace had praised the cooking so highly. The fragrance of the spices was already prominent when they studied the menu. The combination of ingredients struck Henry as imaginative, and mouth-watering, to an extent he had not expected and known from any other restaurant he had been over his many years of travel. They ordered, and Grace shared some of the insights from her recent interviews, which went beyond the material she would then publish officially. It took a long while for the food to be served, confirming the chef's claim to prepare the majority of items on the menu fresh to order, rather than having many dishes pre-cooked and only re-heated, or, worst of all, microwaved, on order. When their food arrived, its arrangement in the metal bowls was a feast for the eye, almost too precious to disturb by tucking into it. The meal proved a feast for the taste buds as well. The combination of flavours of the meat and the vegetables and the combination of spices was so intricate and varied, so adventurous and simply right, so multi-layered without the layers dissolving in the mouth to an anonymous mass. And the flavours in their infinitely subtle and still rich textures and blends remained in their mouths and their

memories for a long time after they had finished their three courses—
another experience Grace had only encountered at her previous meals at
this restaurant, and Henry never before in his life. They ate mainly in
silence, focusing fully on their experience of relishing the food. Unlike
many restaurant experiences, their stomachs felt pleasantly filled rather
than stuffed to the brim (independent of the quantity of food they had
actually eaten). After lunch, they took a taxi and went for a leisurely walk
in Hyde Park.

After a while, Henry realised he did not know where in London Grace
lived, and he asked her.

'Around the corner, in Mayfair,' Grace answered. Seeing that Henry
fell silent and went pale, she added quickly: 'Don't worry, I am not
earning enough to be able to afford this. It was left to me a few years ago
by my favourite teacher in school, with whom I had kept in touch after
leaving school. She had inherited it herself from an uncle, had lived there
for her long retirement, but she did not have family, and I was very
surprised when I had the summons from a London solicitor one day. I
went there, and he read her will to me. I was the only one of her many
pupils over the years who had kept faithfully and genuinely in touch. It's
of course a great privilege. The will stipulated I had to live here myself
and leave it in my will to family or friends to live in—it must never be
sold to a stranger on the open market.'

They reached the flat after a short walk, ready for a coffee, and Grace
had in the meantime bought the family's new favourite, Monsooned
Malabar. They exchanged further memories, of Henry's travels, of his life
with Imogen, of Henry's childhood, and Kaya's childhood, of Julian, of
Grace's interviews. Time passed very quickly for both, and Grace
prepared some light dinner. Henry had arranged to spend the night in a
Travelodge near King's Cross station, and returned there quite late at
night, returning to Grace's flat for breakfast the next morning.

'Good morning, Henry,' Grace welcome him in. 'Did you sleep well?'

'Yes, fortunately I can sleep well in most places,' Henry told her,
'otherwise travelling as much as I have done would not be possible.' He
sniffed the air. 'Smells delicious—pancakes?'

'Yes,' Grace confirmed, 'with maple syrup.'

'Wonderful! Let's go,' Henry urged.

They had a rich breakfast, then moved on to the living room to sit
comfortably in the armchairs. Henry cleared his throat, but before he could
start to say what he wanted to say, Grace laughed: 'You have this
particular way of clearing your throat which always means you want to say

something important. You did that after the interview when you said you didn't want to leave our next meeting to chance.'

Henry giggled. 'Guilty as charged, your honour,' he said, and cleared his throat again. 'Look, I may be rushing things, or may be jumping the gun, or whatever other appropriate phrase you can think of. Meeting you, for me, was love at first sight, and yesterday and today have only confirmed this for me. I never thought it would be possible, after having lost Imogen, but I love you, with all my heart, and…'

Grace interrupted him, gently 'I love you too, Henry, for me it was love at first sight as well, I think, the way I feel, it is the first time I really love someone, and it's you I love.'

They got up from their armchairs for a warm and tight embrace. Then they sat down on the sofa net to each other, holding hands. Grace picked up the important conversation they were having. 'We said before that we are not ones to waste time. You love me, and I love you, we are certain about it, and we have told each other, and I will tell you at least a thousand times every day. You are making a fresh start anyway after all your years of travelling. Please move in with me, right away of you like. I think given our years of independence, I would like us to be in separate bedrooms, to have our personal space if we need it, also if we find that we snore. I would of course like to sleep with you, but I have not had that pleasure, of sleeping with anyone, I mean, for a very long time, possibly even longer that the four years you have been without Imogen, so I am out of practice and a little anxious and shy about that. So that's my position, in a nutshell.'

Henry closed his eyes. He thought of Imogen, and that he was not betraying her in being here with Grace, whom he loved so dearly, even if very differently from the way he had loved Imogen. Feeling Grace squeeze his hands, he opened his eyes again and looked into Grace's. 'I would love to move in with you, I will just need to get my things from Caleb's flat. I like the separate bedrooms arrangement, and both beds are double beds, so we can always visit one way or another. We will take making love to each other as it happens, and it will be wonderful.'

Kaya and Caleb were both surprised, and at the same time not surprised when Grace and Henry told them about the development. Henry picked up his things, the contents of one very large suitcase, from Caleb's flat and moved in with Grace less than a week from the day he had first set eyes on her. They now gave each other all the space and freedom they wanted or needed, and found their life together was thoroughly enjoyable, and it included making love.

Chapter 8

A few weeks had passed since then, and altogether three months since Caleb and Kaya had first met. They had decided, at quite short notice, to travel to Edinburgh for the weekend, where they had found a deal for a last-minute two nights in a flat close to Waverley station. After an uneventful train journey, Kaya and Caleb arrived into Edinburgh station. They took their sparse luggage and left the train, walked through the station to the exit, and walked across to the flat they had rented for the weekend, self-catering. They needed to collect the keys from the owner, so they rang the doorbell as instructed in the email they received when they had paid the 2nd rate of the rent due. The owner, a feisty woman probably in her late sixties, welcomed them, showed the around efficiently, was open to their questions, and then wished them a wonderful weekend and left to go back to her own home somewhere else in the city. The flat was as lovely as they had hoped, the photos on the website were not too photoshopped, and they made themselves at home quickly. They had seen a food store on their way from the station and walked back there to do some basic shopping. They left that in the flat and went out for another, longer walk before it was getting dark. Back in the flat, they prepared dinner in the small kitchen and ate at the dining table in the living/ dining room, then lit some of the candles that were spread around the room, dimmed the electric light, and relaxed in the comfortable arm-chairs. At some point in their conversation, Caleb paused.

'Kaya,' he said.

Kaya laughed. 'Whenever you have said my name in this way, it always means you have something special to say.'

Caleb laughed as well. 'And you always notice in advance. Yes, you are right. I have been thinking: we have been together now for the past three months, and we have spent only few nights not together, when one of us was ill, or when I was away at a conference or you at an advanced training residential. I wanted to suggest that we move in together, and if you agree in principle, then we can discuss whether to move into my flat or yours, or whether we find a new place to live in together.'

Kaya had come over to sit on Caleb's lap already while he was talking. 'This is a wonderful idea, Caleb. Yes, I agree in principle, and I have actually already been thinking about whether your flat or mine or somewhere else.'

They hugged and kissed happily, and then Kaya continued: 'I own my flat, yours is rented. Yours is bigger overall. I have talked to someone in the university, without commitment: they would be interested to rent my flat, for as long as I like, with the option for me to move back in at a six-month notice period. They want to use the flat as a facility to house guest academics. They would offer a regular rental payment, would add furniture as needed once I have left, and take care of thorough cleaning after each visitor has left, and I would be invited to inspect the flat after each changeover of visitors. They would be prepared to start the contract at any time, with a week's notice. I would like to bring some furniture with me, but by far not all. We could have your current bedroom as our bedroom, and have the current guest bedroom as guest bedroom for visitors, or if one of us needs to have more space, when we start snoring too much as we get older, perhaps, or if one of us is ill? What do you think?'

'I like the idea very much indeed,' Caleb beamed. When we get back we can walk through my or rather our, flat to see which furniture to add, or to swap, or which of the current ones can go to the British Heart foundation to be replaced by yours. And what we want to add that isn't there yet in my or your flat. That will be fun.'

'And we can work out the finances, sharing the rent and the insurances and utility bills and council tax and all that,' Kaya continued.

'Yes,' Caleb agreed.

They enjoyed their weekend in Edinburgh, doing a lot of sightseeing together, Holyrood Palace and Park, the Castle, the Royal Mile, among others, and before they knew it, it was time to return home. They agreed which furniture to move, which to leave in Kaya's flat, and which to pass on to the British Heart Foundation to collect. Within a few days, Kaya had moved in and they began to create their lives really together, without having to arrange short notice over-night arrangements any more.

Grace and Henry were very happy to hear about the development, especially since they had moved in together even earlier and had not regretted that remarkable shift in their lives for a moment. Caleb and Kaya visited them in London a few weeks later, and each couple found the other exuberant with their new-found happiness. They reminisced about their first few moments with each other, not too long ago, and Grace wondered aloud whether it was possible for so much happiness to last.

'You mean that it is scary to be so happy, and something bad must happen when there is so much happiness?' Caleb asked.

'Yes, there is often a feeling of guilt attached to being happy, as if one has not deserved so much of it,' Henry agreed.

Kaya was adamant: 'I think this is an old, belief pattern, one that is very well established, but also very, very wrong. There so much potential in life for gratitude, adventure, positive thinking, candour, cooperation, imagination, purpose, patience, flexibility, generosity, clarity, charity, wealth, laughter, joy, beauty, and goodness. We are so focused on negative emotions and negative experiences that we feel guilty when we have any of those wonderful things in our lives. But the purpose of all life is just those positive things, otherwise there would be no point, no point at all. So, let's be happy, let's be beautiful, and all of those other things, as much as possible, and rejoice in those positive experience, modestly, from the heart, I mean without excess, but without feeling guilty.'

Henry was amazed. 'Hear, hear. Quite a speech, Kaya, thank you. I think you are right. We must not feel guilty about our happiness, we should rejoice in each other's happiness, and make the most of it.'

'And not from an "while it lasts" perspective either, which allows the old fear that happiness cannot last back in through a side door,' Caleb added.

Chapter 9

The weeks passed. Grace involved Henry in her interviews, discussing the subjects with him beforehand, and establishing which questions he would find of interest. He would, however, not be present at the interviews themselves, and not meet the VIP interviewees in person either. In turn, Henry took Grace to his favourite places across the world every few weeks, and thus they travelled to Italy, Greece, the USA and Japan together.

To the great satisfaction of Emily Smithson, and of course, Kaya herself, Caleb enrolled in the Smithson surgery and soon had his first check-up as Kaya's patient. As a special treat for him, and as a surprise for Kaya, all practice staff were assembled in the treatment room for the occasion, bursting into a round of spontaneous applause when Kaya had completed the examination without finding any signs for concern.

Caleb's Head of Department asked him to represent the Department, on his behalf, at a major conference for the subject, taking place in London, at relatively short notice because he was unable to attend himself. Caleb discussed the logistic with Kaya.

'You remember your mum offered me to stay at her place when I needed to be in London?' Caleb asked.

'Yes, of course.'

'Well, now that my dad is with her, that won't work anymore, but I would still like to visit her.'

Kaya supported this, and Caleb phoned her. Grace was indeed very happy, and so was Henry. On the day, he reached Grace's apartment in the late afternoon. After the welcome, with a cup of Monsooned Malabar, what else, in the kitchen-diner, Caleb sensed some tension in Grace, which he hoped was not to do with his presence in principle. Henry must have noticed it as well because he raised his eyebrows at some stage and glanced over at Caleb. They engaged in some small-talk for a while, then moved to the living room and made themselves comfortable in the elegant armchairs.

Grace cleared her throat, bringing Caleb's level of alertness to a new high point. 'Caleb, I have not known you for a long time yet, but I believe you and Kaya are serious. This is why I have been thinking long and hard whether to share with you some very delicate information. I have not told Henry about this yet either. I have decided that I must share it with you, as it is fact that will have an impact whether you know it or not, and if you do know it, you have a better chance of dealing with it.' Grace paused. 'This is not really coming out making much sense, is it?'

'Perhaps more than you think,' Caleb reassured her. 'I am tempted to take up some of the ideas Kaya and I have talked about, and that I expect you are also familiar with—I think some of them come originally from, or through, you. Are you talking about something in Kaya's life that she has suppressed, that she may not even remember, or want to remember herself, but that is always there under the surface? And perhaps something that also explains a certain tendency of yours to be very protective regarding your daughter?'

Grace had to take a deep breath and blink away some tears that her eyes had spontaneously filled with. Henry took one of her hands in his, and she gave him a grateful smile. 'Kaya said to me more than once that she was stunned by your exceptionally high level of sensitivity and of reading other people,' she said. 'Spot-on, again, Caleb. Brace yourself.'

'Ready,' Caleb said.

'I don't know how much background info I need to provide,' Grace started. 'How familiar are you with the debate around child sexual abuse— I mean, over and above what is in the media all the time?'

Caleb shook his head in disbelief and then put his head in his hands: 'So that's why I had to...'he almost stammered. 'Sorry, I am being incoherent. I know a lot, in fact, because I am about to finish co-writing a short book on the ways that contemporary drama, in America, England and Germany, has dealt with child sexual abuse, often conflated with the concept of paedophilia. I worked with a psychologist on the book. We are now looking for a publisher willing to take this up. It was a total coincidence, as this is usually not the area I publish in, and I was always wondering why I was drawn to this topic. It may well be for me to be prepared, as much as that is possible, now, for what you have to tell me.

Grace took this in. 'Good. Kaya must have told you about my husband, Julian.'

Caleb nodded.

'Also, that he left me after some ten years of marriage.'

Caleb nodded again.

'We stayed in touch, of course, and he had full access to Kaya and saw her a lot. After he had left, and I guess she did not tell you about that, we saw much more of his brother, Nathan, than of him. I was glad to have the company, and Kaya adored him. With hindsight, I now know that he systematically groomed Kaya, for three long years, and then...' Grace's voice choked, and she started crying.

'No need to go into too much detail, Grace. I can imagine the rest,' Caleb said, shocked but still managing for his voice to sound warm and encouraging. 'How did you find out?'

'It was almost a similar situation to Sophia and you: one day I got home earlier than planned, which never happened with me. I found them together in her own bed.' A shiver ran down Grace's spine from this memory, almost visible for Caleb. 'It is an image I will never forget, I remember it so well as if it had happened only a few moments ago now. I don't know whether anything can be described as fortunate in such a context, but fortunately this had been his first violation, he had not taken it to the intended point yet, and up to that moment it had not met with any apparent emotional or physical opposition from her, she was quite excited about it all, and even, if only for a second, disappointed that I had interrupted them.' Grace paused, overcome by her memories.

Caleb was thoughtful. 'I bet that apparent pleasure only led for her own feelings of guilt to be even stronger later on?'

Grace hesitated. She told Caleb that she had beaten Nathan up so badly he had needed lengthy hospital treatment and she escaped only narrowly from being taken to court for grievous bodily harm. Nathan had been imprisoned for a number of years and responded well to therapy, from what she had heard—she had insisted he did not seek to get back in touch with them ever, during his prison term or afterwards. Grace had always blamed herself for not having protected Kaya and had become and remained overly protective since. She had been in therapy for what it was worth, to be able to support Kaya, who had suffered a total nervous breakdown after Grace had found her. That breakdown had left her with a case of what some psychologists might call repressed memory. 'I read a lot of the literature about this over the years. I am aware how controversial the concept has been, but anyway, nothing since has given any indication that Kaya remembers anything of what happens today. She does not show any special reaction when Nathan's name is mentioned, and the repression mechanism, if you want to call it that, seems to have worked well, I have not noticed any obvious signs of all the kinds of mental illness which can arise from abuse and repressed memory. The only thing is that you are her first boyfriend after a brief relationship ten years ago by now, when she was twenty, in uni. So, to answer your question, she did not have feelings of guilt directly related to this incident because she has never remembered it.'

'Thank you for sharing this with me, Grace,' Caleb said. 'Anything could trigger a flashback at any moment, though, couldn't it, and any adverse effect of the experience could materialise in a different area of her life, or has already, without her or you knowing.'

'Yes, you are right,' Grace agreed, 'and that is indeed why I have been so protective of her, because I didn't pay enough attention at the time.'

'I guess your therapists have told you that many times already, but I think you are not to blame, and should not blame yourself. These perpetrators are so clever and cunning, they wind their victims, both Kaya and yourself, and possibly also your ex-husband, around their little fingers. And you don't expect something like this from someone close to you.'

Henry had listened quietly throughout, looking compassionately at both Grace and his son. 'This has been quite some revelation, Grace, dearest,' he finally said. 'All these repressed emotions in Kaya will come out, no doubt about it, and your work and knowing about what happened, Caleb, will allow you to be there for Kaya when she needs you.' Then he added, after a pause: 'I think I should make us all dinner now, we could do with sum sustenance after this conversation.'

Grace and Caleb agreed wholeheartedly, and soon they sat down together for dinner, allowing more inconsequential conversation to take over, which ended up focusing on the differences of comedy, and what people laughed about, in different countries. Caleb remembered that as a student he had spent some time on a rural university campus and seen a Woody Allen film. 'The American students were laughing hard, quite a lot, and I sat there thinking "Ok, I know why this is supposed to be funny, but it really isn't funny at all". A week later, there was a British film comedy, *The Wrong Box*, in which Queen Victoria accidentally beheads a man she wants to bestow a knighthood on. She is seen with sword in hand, creating knights by touching the sword on the knights' shoulders. The camera then moves to a close-up of her face when she is about to knight another man; you hear a loud thudding noise, the Queen rolls her eyes sharp left, then sharp right, and then enunciates in a perfectly calm voice: "Oh, I am soo sorry, *Sir* William". I laughed at lot at that, but nobody else in the audience did.'

Grace commented that comedy also depended on the current mood of an audience. She added some instances of comedy around dentists, where often intentional cruelty was part of the comic formula. Henry had come across the late German comedian Loriot, whose kind of comedy was still considered hilarious in Germany, while it could cause controversy as being insensitive towards minority groups in other countries. The conversation then shifted to the impact of film on audiences. Caleb shared the example of common release of emotions in the large audience that watched the launch of the film *Steel Magnolias* in London, with around a thousand people in the vast auditorium.

'There is a sequence of scenes that build up to a very intense release of pent-up emotions,' Caleb explained. I will use the actors' names, not the characters.' The film is set in one of the southern states of the USA. Dolly Parton owns a beauty parlour, her husband is Sam Shepard. Her assistant is slightly simple, very religious Darryl Hannah. Her circle of friends consists of the widow of the former mayor of the town, Olympia Dukakis. Sally field is the mother of Julia Roberts, and then there is the town oddball, Shirley MacLaine. Roberts is suffering from diabetes. She is getting married. She gets pregnant against her doctors' advice. She had kidney failure, a transplant of a kidney donated by Field is not successful. Roberts collapses when her child is a toddler. Her husband finds her, she is rushed to hospital, never regains consciousness despite her mother trying all they can to revive her. They decide to have life support machines turned off. The funeral takes place, and in the cemetery after the funeral, Dukakis, Hannah, Parton and MacLaine are together with Field, who has a big emotional outburst: she should have been the first to go, it's all so unfair, she is so angry, she wants to hit someone. All the while from Roberts's collapse onwards, spectators have desperately repressed the expression of their emotions. Now Dukakis grabs MacLaine, pushes her towards Field and says: "Here, hit this". This punch-line comes so unexpectedly, to the characters and to the audience, that it can serve as a conductor for the audience to release all their pent-up emotions in waves and waves of laughter.'

They realised that it was time to call it a day. Grace and Henry thanked Caleb for his visit, and he thanked Grace again for sharing the information about Kaya.

Chapter 10

Soon after this, Caleb was in his office on his own, working through a smallish backlog of emails. There was an urgent knock on his door, and even before he could call 'Come in,' the door burst open and, to Caleb's considerable surprise, Sophia burst in.

'That's a surprise, I didn't know it was your office day today. Come in, take a seat—or should we go and have coffee somewhere?'

'Sorry, Caleb, to be barging in. I had some additional commitment here today, and then I checked my mail, and then I just had to see you immediately.' Sophia was out of breath and sounded very agitated. 'Better here, where we have some privacy.'

'OK,' Caleb said, more curious now than concerned any more. 'What's the news in your mail?'

Sophia hesitated, then pulled an opened letter out of her elegant briefcase. 'Here, see for yourself,' she said, shaking her head as if in disbelief.

Caleb reached for the envelope and took out an A5-sized colour photograph showing—Kaya in a loving embrace with a stranger. 'What the...' Caleb muttered under his breath.

'I am so sorry, Caleb, but I thought I had to show you this at once.'

'Yes, of course, thank you,' Caleb stuttered. Then he quickly pushed his emotions to the side. 'So, you found this in the mail today?'

'Yes,' Sophia confirmed.

'Let's see,' Caleb mumbled, looking at the envelope, 'posted in London, the day before yesterday, and addressed accurately to you. I'll talk to Kaya about this, Sophia, and thank you so much for coming over with it straight away.'

Sophia was still upset: 'I am so sorry this had to come from me, Caleb, especially after what we went through all those years ago, and I have no idea why someone would have sent this to me, but I thought I had to tell you.'

Caleb reassured her again that she did the right thing, although he had to agree that coming from her made this particularly painful for him, at this moment, no matter what explanation might emerge in the future. With that he left the office and returned home, thinking hard about what had happened and what "home" could still mean.

Kaya was already at home when he reached. She sensed that something was wrong as soon as Caleb entered the flat. He quickly disappeared into his study and came out to the kitchen after a while.

'Kaya,' he said, trying to sound casual, 'can we talk for a moment?'

'Yes, of course, Caleb, what's wrong? You look completely shaken,' she said with genuine concern in her voice.

Without a word, Caleb passed the photo to Kaya. She looked at it, shook her head in disbelief, looked at Caleb, and then looked again very closely at the photo. Then she let out a laugh of relief, and, overcome with emotions to the point that tears filled her eyes, she sighed: 'Oh Caleb, how awful for you. How did you get this?' she asked, pointing to the photo?

'It was sent anonymously to Sophia, posted in London, and she gave it to me. Why did you laugh?'

'It is clearly a fake, poorly photoshopped, and I laughed with relief when I found the evidence. To get that from Sophia, after all you had been through together, must have been awful.'

'Well, not exactly fun,' Caleb agreed bitterly. 'I never doubted you, but it was still alarming. What's the evidence?' He was genuinely curious and beginning to get angry at whoever might have played at best a very poor practical joke on them.

Kaya took Caleb's hands in hers and squeezed them tightly. Then she pointed to a detail of the image. 'Here,' she said, 'See this? The shape of the wall in the background bends around that man. That shows it's been photoshopped.' She jumped up, ran to the chest of drawers in the living room and came back with a magnifying glass. 'And here's another clue, actually,' she gasped. 'The picture has been taken in sunlight. But if you look closely, for me the sun comes from the right, and for that man, the sun comes from the left.'

'You cannot have been together. This is a fake. And now I recognise you in the photo, we have it on Facebook, of course, with me where that other man has been photoshopped in.' The relief in Caleb's voice was very obvious.

'So, it's clear and settled, it's a fake,' Kaya stated. 'Now I really would like to know whether this was just a very poor practical joke, or a clumsy but serious attempt at getting us apart.'

'It came via Sophia. Nobody outside of our family knows that she was my wife,' Caleb considered. 'And I think they would not have talked about it as a party-piece, I mean your mum or my dad, or your dad, if someone told him. Sophia was genuinely worried when she gave me the envelope, I don't think it came from her. That only leaves...'

'Sophia's mother, Myrtle' Kaya interjected. 'You told me that she hated you after you did not take Sophia back.'

'But so much hatred, after so many years, that she makes this effort, that she in effect commits a crime, and that she also involved her own daughter. It's pathetic, sad.' Caleb concluded. 'And, in the end, she brought us even closer together than before if that is possible.' With those words, he took Kaya's hands and they kissed and embraced for a long time.

'Do we do anything about it?' Kaya wondered.

'I think we should not tell family unless this photo spreads. I will tell Sophia that the photo is a fake. Perhaps she sorts it out with her mother and gets her to admit it and apologise. If not, we or I could pass by Myrtle's place when we are next over in London?' Caleb suggested.

'Good ideas, on all accounts,' Kaya agreed. 'Let's keep this as low profile as possible, it does not deserve more of anyone's energies.'

Caleb told Sophia in passing when they happened to meet again at the office, pointing out the evidence that the photo had been fake, and wondering aloud, but with not too much concern, who had done this. Sophia was visibly pleased that there was no problem in Caleb's marriage, but she was also aware, quietly but very acutely, of the implications of the photo having reached Caleb through her. She made some comments to that effect, but Caleb quickly reassured her that she had done the right thing in telling him and giving him the photo.

That evening, Sophia had returned to her London studio and was due to meet with her mother anyway as they had arranged a while ago. She told Myrtle about the letter and the fake photo. 'I just hope Kaya and Caleb decide to take this to the police, because creating such a photo and sending it to a third party, me, is a criminal act, I am certain,' she finished.

Myrtle had been fidgeting in her seat all the while. Now she burst out crying. 'I didn't know it was a criminal offence, pet,' she sobbed. 'I just wanted to punish him for not forgiving you all those years, for making your life a misery, and now he's all happy again with that Kaya woman and you are not.' She was no longer able to suppress all the anger and frustration that had built up over the years, and her voice croaked, and she fought back the tears.

'My God,' Sophia exclaimed, shocked. 'It was you? Did you create that photo yourself, with Kaya's Facebook image?'

'Yes, it was me, and I do not regret I did it, and I told you why,' Myrtle almost shouted. Then she added, a little more subdued: 'I just didn't know it would be a considered crime under the law.'

'Well, is, mum,' Sophia admonished her. 'It was a very selfish and foolish thing to do, and Caleb and Kaya will be very generous indeed if they do not take this further and if they can forgive you.' She got up and phoned Caleb and told him what she had found out. Caleb listened patiently and said that he was grateful that the culprit and her motive had been identified, and that he would not pursue it further. There was nothing else left to say and they ended their phone conversation very quickly.

'Sounded like Sophia,' Kaya commented when Caleb had hung up.

'Quite,' he said. 'Myrtle confessed, and Sophia apologised on her behalf, although I don't think Myrtle is apologising. She's just afraid we are taking legal action, but I told Sophia we are not.'

'An unpleasant episode, finding oneself under attack like that,' Kaya stated. 'But we come out of it only stronger. I love you, Caleb.'

'I love you too, Kaya.'

Chapter 11

Henry and Grace had now been living together for a few months. They had spent a good amount of time travelling in between Grace's VIP interviews and were now visiting Caleb and Kaya. One very early morning on that visit, they found themselves approaching the bench overlooking the bay that Caleb and Kaya had told them so much about, and they relished the sunrise.

'This must be the bench they were talking about,' Grace said.

'Yes, indeed,' Henry agreed.

They sat down and marvelled at the view across the bay, the sight of the sunrise.

'True magic,' Grace sighed.

'Grace,' Henry said, 'I didn't prepare this, and I didn't rehearse or anything, but nature is so spectacular, and living with you has been so wonderful that I am doing something completely spontaneous now.' With those words, he moved off the bench and knelt in front of Grace. 'Will you marry me, Grace, darling?'

'Such a wonderful surprise, Henry. Yes, I will, with all my heart,' Grace responded almost immediately.

Henry scrambled up to sit next to Grace again. 'Wonderful, thank you so much,' he said happily. 'I will go and buy you an engagement ring later today. Should we get married in about three months from now? In London?'

'That would be lovely, Henry. It will be such a surprise also for Kaya and Caleb when we tell them later.'

It certainly was a surprise for them.

'Engaged?!' Kaya squealed, and everybody hugged everybody else.

Henry bought a beautiful rose quartz engagement ring for Grace, and three months later, as they had planned, they got married in one of the leading landmarks in London, the London eye, in their special wedding

capsule, and later had a reception at their flat, with catering provided by
the owner of the Indian restaurant in Soho that they had come to love so
much.

***

Caleb and Kaya had been inspired by the wedding and the party and had
embarked on taking turns in cooking a special meal each weekend. Kaya
heard Caleb from the living room: 'Don't forget to turn off the oven,
lollipop.'

"Lollipop". Kaya felt as if a bomb had exploded right in her head. She
tried to observe, like watching a film, all the layers of what followed that
explosion, to achieve some distance, necessary for her to survive, in terms
of mental well-being, and literally. The word itself echoed around her
head, distorted in volume and pitch, like the bizarre shapes distorting
mirrors could create, with their convex or concave surfaces, or
combinations of those for more sophisticated types. They were also called
funhouse mirrors, but the distortions of "lollipop" in her head were not
funny at all, not funny at all, they were expressions of a nightmare, a
living nightmare, right here, and one she was unable to get out of, only
able to distance herself from by observing it like a film. The word was also
being said in her head by different voices that she was able to recognise as
those of her mother, Caleb, her dad, her dad, some acquaintances and
friends, actor's voices she was familiar with, John Gielgud, Paul Scofield,
Benedict Cumberbatch, her dad. She heard the sound of cutlery smashing
on a floor and realised that she had dropped a plate she was handling at the
time Caleb had called her "lollipop". She also noticed that she had started
sweating profusely. She was in melt-down, she realised, and giggled. Only
that the giggle did not come out like a giggle— "lollipop" in different
voices, and different intonations went on and on during all this—but the
giggle came out as a distorted grunt, groan, deep from her belly, very low
pitch, grumbling, guttural, croaking. The voice repeating "lollipop" now
had a cooing tone, endearing, ingratiating, superficially loving but totally
cold, calculated, put on, not even acted. Kaya realised that she must have
heard that word before, spoken by someone in this cold, calculated way,
but she had not seen through the pretence, the coldness, she had admired
the speaker, had liked him, had loved him, like a child. She had been a
child, innocent, trusting, and "lollipop" had been the signature word. But
who. The voice was still modulating in her head, until it settled on one she
could not yet place, identify, put a name to. She was sweating, she felt so
hot, she felt weak. She had to find the name for the voice, otherwise all

this was in vain. Her dad kept coming into her mind, her dad, but it was not his voice. Someone close to dad? A friend? A relative? He did not have any relati… UNCLE NATHAN. She gasped and had to hold herself up on one of the chairs, grabbed its backrest, miscalculated its position in relation to her own the weight, it scraped on the floor. Uncle Nathan. Her dad's brother. It was his voice. He had called her lollipop. He had said it in this particular way. He had been her best friend after her father had left her mother. She had loved him, trusted him, told him her innermost secrets. And he had done all he could for her to do this, he had wanted her to love him, to trust him, to confide in him. And he had called her lollipop. And then… UNCLE NATHAN. The chair did not hold her up any more, it had given way too much, she was hot, her head felt hot, her knees felt weak. She needed help. She needed Caleb.

'Help, Caleb, I need help!' She wanted to shout, but she heard herself that she was able to manage only a croak, a groan, hardly able to articulate the words, but she also heard Caleb reacting immediately. Lollipop, uncle Nathan, whose coldness and calculation she had not noticed. The excitement that such a lovely man was nice to her, liked her, told her that he loved her, told her that he loved her not only as his niece, as a little girl, but as a woman, a young woman, and—Caleb was on his way. She felt herself getting weaker and weaker, if that was possible. The lights seemed to flicker.

And then a flash, and she remembered clearly the moment when her mother had come in when she was in bed with uncle Nathan. Uncle Nathan had jumped out of bed, startled, shocked. Her mother had commanded uncle Nathan out of the room and into her own bedroom in a voice that she had not heard from her mother ever before or after, total authority that would not tolerate any resistance, cold, righteous anger, but also an enormous effort to control herself, for Kaya's sake. Her mother had come over to Kaya, had embraced her so warmly and so lovingly, and had told her: "It's good, it's all good, relax. Let go! I'll be back with you in a moment". Relax. Relax. Kaya now felt tears just streaming out of her eyes. The possibility of relaxing, of letting go. Heaven.

She had heard strange, unfamiliar noises from the elsewhere in the house, had gotten up, out of bed, naked, had put her bathrobe over and followed the noises, had opened the door to her mother's bedroom, and had seen her mother very quietly, without shouting, screaming or saying a word, hitting out at uncle Nathan, again and again, with her fists, very hard, and kicking him with her feet when he had collapsed to the floor.

Her mother had stopped only when she had become aware of her daughter standing in the doorway. Kaya remembered that she had been curious about this sex thing, excited that a man she loved so much—but she was still a child, she was thirteen years old, she had had a crush on him, as children at that age can have. But he had exploited that crush, that girlish, childish feeling, triggered it, nurtured it, kindled it, and betrayed her. That a man she loved so much was interested in her in that way, but she also thought that he was not really her boyfriend, as other girls in her school had boyfriends. That should be someone at least roughly your own age, not someone who was twenty or more years older. And she also knew that sex was not allowed until a certain age. She was a child, he had insulted her love, her innocent crush, her trust, he had betrayed her, hurt her, abused her.

She had realised that when she had seen him curled up on the floor in her mother's bedroom, she had felt responsible for what had happened, she felt ashamed at what she had done, at how her mother had seen her, at what her mother now had to do to uncle Nathan. She felt anger at her mother to have allowed uncle Nathan to be with her for so much of the time, not to have realised what was happening, not to have stopped the hurt, the betrayal, the abuse, and had been grateful to her then that she was punishing uncle Nathan. He deserved to be punished. She had wanted him dead, and that had brought a new wave of guilt for wanting someone dead whom you had loved so much until a few moments ago when you had realised the cunning, conniving and cold abuse you had suffered at his hands.

The chaotic swirl in her mind, then in the door-frame to her mother's bedroom, and now, combining memory and observing reflection, were too much for Kaya's brain, and she fainted, into her mother's arms then, into Caleb's arms now. The last thing she had seen, and saw, before she lost consciousness, had been her mother's face, was Caleb's face.

***

Caleb called over to Kaya: 'Don't forget to turn off the oven, lollipop.' Then he wondered to himself that he had never given any pet name to Kaya before, and that "lollipop" was not really part of his vocabulary. He heard some strange noises from the kitchen, a piece of crockery smashing to the floor, some muffled, guttural sounds from Kaya, the scraping of the legs of a chair on the kitchen floor, and then a faint 'Help, Caleb, I need help' from Kaya. Caleb had never been aware how fast his body could move, and in no time at all he was in the kitchen, taking in the scene in a fraction of a second, and catching Kaya, who was in the process of collapsing, safely in his arms. She looked at him with wide open eyes, gave a flicker of a smile, and fainted.

Caleb managed to carry her swiftly to his bed and placed flat on her back with her legs raised with a pillow, closely following the instructions that had been part of a recent staff health and safety training session. He ran over to the kitchen to turn off the burners and oven, then to the study to get his old-fashioned index card telephone directory, and back to sit next to Kaya. She was still unconscious, breathing normally, and with a regular, normal pulse, as far as he could tell. He looked up and found the phone number of a former school mate of his, now a GP, with whom he kept in regular touch. He dialled the number, very relieved when Peter Small answered the phone. 'Hi, Peter, it's Caleb. Sorry for cutting out the small talk, this is business, my new girlfriend, Kaya, thirty, healthy as far as I know, has just collapsed and fainted. No injuries from the fall, because I caught her just in time, she is lying flat on her back with a pillow under her legs. No vomiting as far as I can tell, breathing regular, pulse regular. What do I do?'

Peter giggled: 'You have seen so many episodes of *Casualty*, my dear friend. But you forgot to mention what medication you have given her, and the BP values,' he joked, briefly, to lighten the tension that was clear in Caleb's voice.

'I knew you'd say something funny, Peter,' Caleb acknowledged. 'So'?

'How long has she been unconscious?' Peter asked.

'About thirty seconds, probably,' Caleb responded.

'OK. Is the window open?'

'No. It isn't.' Caleb jumped up and quickly opened the window wide. 'It is now.' He looked closely at Kaya and saw her eyelids flickering. He reported this observation to Peter.

'Good sign, Caleb,' Peter reassured him calmly, 'and well observed.'

'She has opened her eyes, Peter,' Caleb said in the exhalation of tremendous relief.

'OK, Caleb. You should now reassure her, comfort her, and then after while she might try sitting up, then getting up. Call me again after five, ten minutes, if you like. OK?'

'OK, Peter, will do, thanks so much,' Caleb said gratefully and hung up.

Kaya had not yet been able to find her orientation. She had heard Caleb's voice, though, and now his face came into view. He looked at her with very big, warm, loving eyes, and much relief. She blinked, as if to get some haze was obstructing her view and frowned.

'Where am I? I thought I was in the kitchen…' she wondered.

'You are in our bedroom, on the bed,' Caleb explained. 'You were in the kitchen, making funny noises, smashing a plate, and called for help. I just caught you before you would have fallen to the floor.'

Kaya tried to get raise herself but was not quite yet able to: 'The burners.'

Caleb reassured her: 'Don't worry, I put them off.'

Kaya was relieved. 'And you talked to someone when I came round just now. To yourself?'

Caleb smiled: 'No, I had phoned a GP friend of mine about what to do. I seem to have got the most important things right, apart from opening the window. I hung up when you came round but I can call him back in a few minutes to give him an update to see whether we need to do anything else.'

'It was so strange. Something had happened, and then my head was just spinning, so much going on, total overload, and then I felt my legs giving in, and then the last thing I remember is looking into my mum's face.'

Kaya stopped suddenly, turned pale as a sheet and continued: 'into your face, Caleb.'

'But now you've remembered what the thoughts spinning in your head were all about?'

'Yes, I have. Can I try sitting up?'

'Yes, of course.' Caleb supported her gently, but Kaya had regained much of her strength anyway.

'You calling me lollipop triggered it all,' Kaya remembered. 'It was an odd thing for you to call me that.'

'I know,' Caleb agreed, 'I never use pet names, and lollipop is not really part of my vocabulary. I was quite surprised myself when I had said it, but then you already called me, and I ran over.'

'It was only a few seconds, wasn't it?' Kaya mused, 'but the amount of thoughts was enough for a year. I guess that's what caused me to faint. Just as I had fainted so many years ago, into my mother's arms, when I was thirteen years old. I think, to put it bluntly, I had been groomed and was just about to be harvested, pardon the crude phrase, by my uncle, Nathan, my dad's brother, when my mum came home early and found us together, just before "the act". She sent him to another room and beat him up, I think, and then I fainted and had forgotten about all of this until a few moments ago, when your 'lollipop' triggered the memory, because that's what he called me.'

Kaya was red in the face from the memory, and from talking so fast. 'You are taking this in your stride, aren't you,' she wondered.

'Your mom told me about this soon after we had met,' Caleb explained, 'the time I stayed in London and visited my dad and her at her place. She was convinced that it would come up, out of hiding, at some point, she was hoping it might come sooner rather than later, and that you would feel free and confident enough of my love to be able to release this, I mean not worried what I might think of you, afraid that I might judge you or something like that.'

'Oh, how sweet of mum,' Kaya said, very moved and touched. 'And you have been carrying this knowledge for all this time? Weren't you tempted to simply tell me and trigger my memory in that way?'

'I thought about it, but once when we talked about your dad, and you said explicitly that he was an only child. I then felt that it must come from within you, rather than being provoked explicitly for that purpose from anyone else, your mom or me. I simply let go, asked nature to take its course, and asked nature to allow me to be alert and present when it happened. You and your mum had done so much to help me cope with the circumstances of my divorce, and to reconcile with Sophia, and to cope with the major test of Myrtle's attack on our relationship, I was hoping I would be able to be there for you to deal with this revelation of that part of your life that you had hidden away for so long and so successfully.'

Caleb now quickly phoned Peter, reported Kaya's recovery, and asked for advice on what to do now.

'Plenty of water, and something to eat whenever she feels like it. Better no coffee or other caffeine-products for the rest of day. And plenty of rest for a day or two. If you need a medical note, take her to your local surgery and tell them what happened. They can contact me if you like.'

'Thank you so much, Peter,' Caleb said. 'I owe you. I'll invite you over for a visit soon, if you like, to catch up.'

'That would be lovely, and always happy to help, Caleb,' Peter said, 'Bye.'

They hung up. 'According to Peter, you need water, and something to eat when you like, and rest for the next few days.'

'At least with the need for rest I would not have needed a doctor's advice,' Kaya laughed.

Caleb joined her laughter. 'I'll bring you some water, though, and then you can tell me what you would like to eat.' When Caleb came back with the water within a very short while, he found Kaya lying on the bed again, fast asleep, snoring gently. He closed the window and the blinds and curtains, and put a blanket over Kaya, not wanting to wake her up by trying to get her under the duvet. He tucked her in and gently kissed her forehead. He put off the light but left the door open so that he could hear her if needed. Then he went to the living room, leaving that door open as well, and speed-dialled Grace's number.

When she answered the phone, Caleb spoke in a hushed voice: 'Hello, Grace, it's Caleb. I wanted to tell you right away that Kaya remembered the events with Nathan earlier this evening. She is sleeping now, I have the doors open, therefore my slightly subdued voice.' He proceeded to give her the details of what had happened.

Grace was glad and thanked Caleb for having phoned her right away. 'I had been thinking of this possibility for the last few months, really, hoping for it to happen. She may want and need to talk about it all a lot when she has recovered from the first shock and has had the rest she needs. And I will be happy to share in the effort of helping her work it all through— after all, I was part of it at the time,' she said.

'Thank you for the offer, Grace,' Caleb answered, 'I will let her know, and she will be in touch if and when she is ready to.'

Over the next few days, Kaya took sick leave, and Caleb was at home with as much as his work commitments, mainly teaching, allowed. Kaya felt the need to talk much about the events she had so successfully repressed, and Caleb reminded her of the forgiveness procedure she had told him about in their memorable first meeting. In the course of their conversations, Kaya realised that she had been very angry with her mother, and even her father, for not having protected her, and she started forgiving her mother for that, and asking her mother, mentally, to forgive her if she had behaved inappropriately towards her mother, unknowingly, from this repressed anger. Then she turned to Nathan, the abuser, the paedophile, the child sex offender. She read the material Caleb had gathered in his research for his book, she read the plays about child sex abuse from the English, American and German repertory, and the comments about those plays in the book, and found all this very informative and helpful. She realised the complexity of the issues, and the knowledge empowered her, made it possible for her to think through what had happened, and provided the basis for the possibility of forgiveness, although she realised early on that it would take a lot of tenacity and determined effort on her part to forgive. She was glad that the material she read never suggested that forgiveness should go ahead with forgetting, because that was just not possible. The memory of the events was now very fresh in her mind, and she felt they would stay like that forever. Over time, the memory might recede to the background and not demand front stage attention most of the time and would not come back to the forefront of her thoughts and dreams uninvited, triggered by any arbitrary stimulus, it seemed. Over time, that memory would come into the forefront of her mind only if she wanted it to, for whatever reason, but even then, it would remain as fresh and clear as if it had all happened only moments ago. Forgiving was hard enough, forgetting was impossible.

Chapter 12

For the anniversary of their very first meeting, Kaya and Caleb decided to have a very early morning watching the sunrise again. The weather was on their side, with the early morning providing the kind of cool air that is refreshing in a heat wave but still carries the ambience of that heat. Caleb took a bag with him and was a little secretive about its contents. They found their favourite bench, not overlooked from anywhere, and offering a gorgeous view across the bay. They sat close together, in silence. The sun had not yet made its appearance on the horizon but was about to make its glorious entrance any moment now.

'Kaya,' he said.

Kaya laughed. 'Whenever you have said my name in this way, it always means you have something special to say.'

Caleb laughed as well. 'I do.' He placed the bag on the ground next to the bench and took out a large bunch of red roses. 'This is a very special day for us, and it has been a very special last few months, meeting you, falling in love with you, moving in with you, living with you, and I want this to continue, and to continue to be as special every single day.' He glanced at the horizon. 'Look, the sun is rising. It has the colour of these roses, Kaya.' With those words, he took the roses from their wrapping paper and passed them gently to Kaya. 'I have removed the thorns,' he informed her. As the sun rose further, he took a small jewellery box from the bag, knelt on one knee in front of Kaya, opened the box, revealed the beautiful aquamarine ring, and said: 'Will you marry me, Kaya, please?'

At that moment, the sun had released its first full ray of sunshine for that day. Caleb held the box with the ring towards Kaya, with the happiest smile on his face, manly, determined and shy and modest at the same time. Kaya did not have to think about her answer. 'Yes, Caleb, yes, with all my heart,' she cried, taking the ring, putting it into Caleb's hands to put on her finger. It fitted perfectly. Caleb got up, they hugged tightly and kissed, then sat down again on the bench, relishing the moment and the sunrise.

Kaya was the first to speak again. 'How long should our engagement last before we get married?'

'I think not too long, perhaps three, four months, also depending on the kind of wedding we want, and how long it will take to plan for it,' Caleb suggested.

'I like that idea,' Kaya agreed. 'I was thinking of a registry wedding with just you and me and closest family, and then an official celebration somewhere, with the speeches and a sit-down meal, at some place in the area that offers such events.'

And this is what they had, three months later, with fabulous weather of an Indian summer. They had scouted all the possible venues in the area, and decided on one located quite centrally, and thus accessible easily by those guests coming by train. They had selected around one hundred guests, with their secret reserve list in case some of the chosen hundred was unable to attend. Henry and Grace had of course had their wedding half a year ago and were able to support Caleb and Kaya with their advice. They all thoroughly enjoyed preparing for the event, and the wedding day itself, with the small ceremony at the registry, followed by a few hours to go back home and change and get ready for the celebration. The food was delicious, the ambience and environment, created in coordination with Kaya and Caleb's requests magical, and the speeches were brief and moving, or very funny and witty where appropriate, including someone dressed up as a decayed tooth that became miraculously healthy again at Kaya's mere touch—dentistry of the future, which of course none else than Kaya would invent soon. So as not to disappoint Caleb, he was promised the Nobel prize for drama.

At the end of the day, Kaya, Caleb had had a very good time indeed, had been able to have many interesting conversations, and they had even been able to show off their skills at dancing which they had newly acquired for this event. Their guests had enjoyed the day as well, as many later emails and phone calls and social media messages amply confirmed. A few days later they embarked on their honeymoon, for which they had decided on a one-week whirl-wind trip across Italy.

They flew from London to Venice, the main Marco Polo airport, and took a Vaporetto to Lido, where they had booked a nice little hotel. They changed from their travel clothes and walked across the island for about ten minutes until they reached the beautiful public beach. They took a locker, stripped to their swimsuits and went straight into the pleasantly warm water, spending a good hour splashing about. By then they were quite hungry, so they changed back into their leisure wear, carrying their wet swim-suits in a plastic bag, and walked slowly over to the restaurant half-way back to their hotel that they had already selected for their dinner on the way to the beach. The restaurant had a large space outside, in the shade, under Mediterranean-looking trees. It was not too crowded, and the waiter came over quickly with their menus. The range of food to choose from was considerable, all looked and sounded very delicious. They decided on a large plate of caprese salad as starter, with mozzarella slices, tomato slices and avocado slices with black pepper, olive oil and basil, and two pizzas to share, one with grilled chicken, one with cherry tomato, artichoke and mushrooms. They had orange juice with their meal, and selected panna cotta and semifreddo for their deserts, also sharing. The food was delicious.

'All this tastes so different in Italy than even the best food in Italian restaurants back home in the UK,' Caleb observed when they had finished and were waiting for the bill.

Kaya agreed. 'Maybe the atmosphere of the environment has an impact on the food. You cannot get the Italian atmosphere anywhere else than in Italy, even if the chefs are Italian. '

They returned to their hotel after another leisurely walk. The next day they crossed by Vaporetto to the main part of Venice, near St Mark's, and spent several hours walking around the streets and bridges of this inspiring city, then made their way to Santa Lucia train station to get a Frecciarossa train to Florence, where they changed to a Regionale Veloce train to Chiusi-Chianciano Terme. From there it was only a five-minute taxi ride to their second destination, picturesque Città della Pieve. Here they saw that year's production of the Philadelphia-based International Opera Theater and had a long post-show dinner with its artistic director. After a long sleep-in and delicious lunch, they travelled on up north again, to Verona, where they followed the trail of the characters in the film *Letters to Juliet* before taking their seats in the arena for a performance of *Carmen*. They criss-crossed to Rome, then to Naples, to Capri, and back up to Milan, where they spent a few hours before catching their flight back to London.

'It was striking,' Caleb mused on the plane, 'how different the atmosphere is in each of the cities we just visited. Did you feel that too?' he asked Kaya.

'Yes, come to think of it,' Kaya agreed. 'Venice felt very vibrant, full of rough but pleasant energy. Verona is really a city of the heart. Milan is very tense, finance-driven, with lots of conmen in the streets and at the station.'

Back at home, they converted their hundreds of photos into a film and created a DVD, which they sent to Grace and Henry. Occasionally, they would watch the DVD themselves, getting all nostalgic about their honeymoon. They also created a much smaller collection which they could show their colleagues at work.

Chapter 13

On their return from their honeymoon, they finally managed to invite Peter and Monica over for a weekend. They had been at their wedding, of course, but after Peter's consultation over the phone about Kaya's health, they had not yet honoured that promise of an invitation. Peter and Monica lived further north and came over after work on a Friday evening. Peter ran a small country surgery with one partner, a nurse and a receptionist, while Monica worked in the local library. They were not able to have children, which was a permanent cause for sadness for both of them, on an off, but they seemed to comfort each other. On their visit, they spent Saturday morning talking, had a relaxed lunch, then went out for a walk and returned for more talk. On Sunday, Peter and Monica came for a late and long breakfast, and then it was time for them to head home again.

Over the course of the weekend, Caleb became more and more concerned about some observations of very subtle interactions between Peter and Monica, which they perhaps were not even aware of themselves. He became ever more alert to them and noticed more and more instances as the days progressed. At suitable moments on Sunday, when he knew himself alone with one of them, and definitely not in earshot of the other, he turned the conversation to allow him to slip in a casual "if ever the need arises, you can always get in touch and talk to us, confidentially, and trust us". Kaya had been with him in those moments and had not let on any surprise—rather, she had quietly and calmly confirmed Caleb's assurance.

When Peter and Monica had left, after what for all four of them had otherwise been a cheerful social occasion with much laughter, and after clearing up what was necessary, Kaya and Caleb sat down next to each other on the sofa.

'Now, finally, out with it,' Kaya urged. 'I have been on tenterhooks all day. You are a wonderful actor, so they won't have noticed anything, but I know you well enough: you were on edge, incredibly alert for something particular, all weekend, and then you kept telling them they could come to us with any problems.'

'Well, you are a great actress yourself, Kaya.' Caleb's voice was full of loving admiration, but it also showed the strong surge of emotions he had been forced to keep under control, hiding them all weekend. 'You just went along with me, and reassured them when I said that, it must have sounded crazy to you, but they knew, deep down, what I was talking about.'

'Thank you,' Kaya said, now getting really impatient. 'Please!'

'I think, to put it bluntly, that Peter beats Monica.'

'No way,' Kaya gasped, 'he is so poised, so confident, so charming.'

'He is, outwardly. But there are subtle hints. He is prone to making sudden movements, very unexpected ones, jerky. And she responds immediately, with her whole body, to each of them, terrified, although she has learnt to camouflage her terror well—over time. Makes him feel powerful, to have her live in fear of him every moment.'

'But how did you notice?'

'When I was in A&E some years ago, I observed a woman with a major bruise on her face, waiting for an x-ray, probably to see whether any bones were broken, and her husband or partner was sitting next to her with a very smug face, and whenever he moved an inch, she almost jumped out of her wheel-chair with fear. It was obvious that he must have beaten her up and was now calmly accompanying her to hospital. That was such a striking impression that I have never forgotten it.'

Kaya thought about this explanation and sighed: 'You may well be right. I'd hope you are not, but you probably are. How awful for people to have to be attracted to each other under such circumstances.'

'A police officer came into one of my lectures once,' Caleb remembered, 'to talk to the students about the presence of police on campus, ready to help when needed. The officer talked to me a little before the lecture. He had been in the unit that deals with domestic violence, but he had asked for a transfer because he just could no longer deal with the tragedies he was confronted with on a daily basis. He also talked about the men beaten up by their wives, they were particularly difficult cases to deal with because often they would not want to admit that as men they were abuse victims.'

Kaya shook her head: 'I can well imagine that police officers and other who deal with such cases need lots of support to deal with all of this and can't do it forever. They'd just break down. Let's hope, for Peter and Monica, they will come to us for support if they need it, and we should find out where we can point them, even at short notice, if we can't cope ourselves with what they bring to us.'

Caleb did the necessary research and shared the results with Kaya. Quietly they hoped that they might never need to make use of it, but at least they would be somewhat prepared.

***

Although Kaya and Caleb had been talking about their childhood experiences of being taken to the zoo by their parents, they had never been to one together. On their trip to Vienna, on the occasion of their first wedding anniversary, they decided to change this and went to the Tierpark Schönbrunn, the first ever zoo in Europe. They were lucky with the weather, it was mild but a little overcast, not too hot, sunny or humid. They paid at the entrance and took a first look at the map of the zoo.

'This is huge,' was Kaya's first observation.

They went to the giraffe enclosure first. Two giraffes were in the indoors, daintily nibbling at some green leaves that had been placed appropriately high up for them, looking with apparent curiosity at the visitors, and flicking their ears in response to the noises they heard.

'It's always such a shame that we don't really know what goes on in animals, isn't it,' Caleb observed.

'I know that animal behaviourists always make the point that we must not superimpose our human ideas on what we observe in animals. But I find that difficult,' Kaya mused. 'When that giraffe looks at us, I sense that it is curious, or at least interested, because it would not be looking at us if it were not bothered, and I expect we will come across plenty of animals like that as well today.'

One of the giraffes now walked slowly to an area further back in the indoors area, which probably led to their overnight cages. Caleb and Kaya walked over to the wallabies. Three were outside, foraging on the ground and feeding the occasional item. One came close to another with its snout, rubbing it on the other's back, and uttering some sounds with it. The other wallaby stopped what it was doing, obviously noticing the activity of the first one, but initially unperturbed by it. The first wallaby let go of the other, hopped away, but returned shortly afterwards. Now the second wallaby seemed unhappy with that approach and in no time, both were on their hind legs, heads held high and tilted slightly backwards, and attempting to hit the other with the front legs. They were dishing out punches to the other animal like boxers, clearly aiming for the other's head, and when one of them was shaky from a punch, the attacker would kick with the hind leg and if possible even jump on top of an opponent that had fallen to the ground. The punches and the bodies hitting the ground caused loud whacking noises. The third wallaby in the enclosure first remained uninvolved, but then joined in the fight. After a few minutes, when no end to the fight seemed in sight, and it was getting more and more fierce, a zoo keeper came in to the enclosure and immediately the wallabies stopped fighting. The zoo keeper crouched near the wallabies and talked to them in a soft voice. Her movements were slow and calm as well.

'They are all like children having been told off by their mother,' Kaya observed.

'See how they react differently to her, though,' Caleb prompted Kaya. 'One of them is genuinely contrite and apologetic. The other one is just waiting for her to disappear to be able to go on fighting, its front legs are still poised, see. And the third one is fed up with the fun fight being interrupted again. It's the stroppy teenager using swear words behind mum's back.'

At that moment, they heard loud roaring somewhere further inside the zoo. They looked at each other.

'An elephant?' Caleb wondered.

'More like a big cat,' Kaya ventured.

'I got it: a polar bear,' Caleb smiled.

'Yes, that's most likely.'

The zoo keeper had now left the wallaby enclosure, and the three brawlers were peaceful for a moment, but the fight flared up again soon enough and they were even joined by two further wallabies who came running from the indoor area. Now it was five animals fighting, and the whacking sounds attracted further visitors to come over, look in surprise, laugh, and comment. The zoo keeper had to come back and tell the animals off again.

Caleb and Kaya walked further to the big cats, leopards, tigers and lions. The leopard was in an old and old-fashioned enclosure separated from the visitors by metal bars. The leopard in view was clearly suffering from his incarceration, displaying stereotypic behaviour of pacing back and forth near the metal fence. When it reached the perimeter of the wall, it jumped up the wall and turned its body around in the air on bounding back from the wall, doing a weird mixture of backflip and somersault in the process, opening its mouth wide in the moment of the twist. On reaching the ground, it paced forwards again. In all of this is never looked at a visitor once.

The lions had just been fed and were chewing away at meat and bones, some very close to the thick glass walls that allowed very close observation. One of the tigers was having a long walk in its enclosure—Caleb and Kaya were not too sure whether the path it had clearly trodden into the grass, and that it was not deviating from, represented a more hidden form of stereotypic movement. The tiger then jumped around several of the platforms that were part of the enclosure, and sat down on one of them, facing the visitors and looking very impressive and regal.

Kaya remembered something she had read about these big cats. She nudged Caleb. 'Look at my eyes, Caleb, and the tiger's,' she said, excitedly. She made sure she was not staring at the tiger with wide open eyes, because that would come across to the tiger as aggressive, but with half-closed eyes. To their surprise, the tiger mirrored this, and looked at Kaya with similarly half-closed eyes.

Chapter 14

Later that summer, Kaya and Caleb were on a long Sunday afternoon walk, and Kaya had suggested, towards the end of it, to walk past their special spot with the special view across the bay. When they reached, and sat down on their special bench, Kaya felt that it was now the best time to share some thoughts she had harboured for a while.

'Caleb,' she started, and they burst out laughing both at the same time, 'Was that my special announcement "Caleb" again, so obviously?'

'Yes,' was all Caleb could manage, having to struggle not to snort with laughter. 'Out with it!'

'I would like to have a baby, I mean us, to start a family.'

'And, knowing you, you have been thinking about this for at least a little while, kind of since yesterday morning, and made all kinds of calculations and considerations and plans, haven't you?' he responded warmly.

'Well, yes or no,' Kaya insisted.

'Of course, yes, no question, yes, wonderful, yes. Right away, yes!' Caleb was clearly enthusiastic about the idea. 'So, what are your thoughts?'

'I think we could do with a bigger place. The current arrangement is perfect for us now, with the shared study, the share bedroom, the spare bedroom for guests or snoring, but for a baby we would need a nursery. Of course, a baby would first of all be in our bedroom for a long time. So, we could move when our child is old enough to get his or her own room, or we could move before I give birth. And I have been doing some fertility calculations, and I have read about how to prepare for a baby, and I have thought about names.'

Kaya shared all those thoughts with Caleb, and they decided to stay put for now, and to move in due course when they felt like it.

A month or two after this conversation, Caleb and Kaya woke up on what was supposed to have been a regular day, with her due in her surgery, while he had a lecture to deliver, and a seminar to teach in the university. Kaya felt poorly, with a headache, but decided to struggle through, without taking sick leave. Caleb noticed that she was a little "under the weather" and comforted her accordingly before they both left. When Caleb returned from work, he was surprised to find Kaya already at home, and in bed, clearly in considerable discomfort. She had had to leave work in the early afternoon. While headache had receded into the background, she had developed what she could describe and explain to herself only as the most severe period pain she had ever experienced, together with the deepest sadness. She had left work early after having asked the nurse to rearrange routine check-up appointments. At home, had cried a lot, gone to bed, and managed to sleep intermittently. She had a high temperature but had not felt like taking any medication against it.

Kaya was glad when Caleb came home, she needed comforting.

'Oh, dear, what's wrong,' Caleb cried when he saw Kaya in bed, tears puffy from crying, and obviously unwell. Kaya explained her symptoms, the excruciating stomach pains, the deep sadness with tears, and the temperature. Having established that Kaya did not feel it was necessary to get their GP's advice, let alone to attend the hospital's accident and emergency department, Caleb prepared a hot water bottle for Kaya to put on her stomach, he aired her room, cooked her some oat porridge, and made lots of boiled water for her to drink. She ate and drank, and he sat with her and read to her from her favourite novel. He also made an appointment for Kaya to see her GP the next day, which they had considered best under the circumstances.

The next morning, Kaya's pain had subsided only a little, but the temperature was back to normal, and she had a good appetite for her breakfast. At the surgery, the nurse took a urine sample and a blood sample, and a little later, Kaya told the GP, Dr Sharma, about her symptoms. Dr Sharma looked at the notes the nurse had passed him, and raised his eyebrows, then frowned.

'Are you here with your husband, Kaya?'

'Yes,' Kaya confirmed, surprised. 'Would you like me to get him in?'

'Don't worry,' Dr Sharma answered reassuringly. Then he pressed the intercom and asked the receptionist to bring Caleb over. Caleb was leafing through some magazines in the waiting room, unable to concentrate enough to read any of the articles. He was startled and concerned when asked to join Kaya in the doctor's office.

'Take a seat, Caleb,' Dr Sharma welcomed him. 'It was a good decision to come and see me, Kaya,' he continued. 'Nothing to worry about, long-term, but sad news right now. The tests show that you were pregnant, Kaya and had a miscarriage. Very early on in the pregnancy, a few days, at maximum a week after conception. That would explain the severe pain, and the other physical symptoms you mentioned. It also explains that sadness you talked about. I am so very sorry to have to tell you this. The good news is that this happens in many pregnancies, and it does not affect future pregnancies.'

Kaya and Caleb looked at Dr Sharma, speechless, and then at each other. Tears welled up in their eyes.

'You should take this opportunity to mourn together, because even though the miscarriage happened within days of conception, new life had formed and has now left,' Dr Sharma said, taking the cue from their tears. 'It may help,' he continued, 'to imagine that you gave this opportunity of life to a soul that needed this experience, and hopefully now you are ready to conceive a child to be born and raised, rather than miscarried.'

'This reminds me of the *Mahabharata*,' Caleb said, blinking away tears. 'The great Indian epic. The goddess Ganga comes to Earth in human form to be married to King Shantanu of Hastinapur. He had agreed never to query her actions—if he did, she would immediately leave him and never return to him. He never questioned her actions, even though she drowned seven of her new-born sons. He only asked the question when she was about to drown their eighth son. She revealed that the babies were all celestial beings who had been cursed to be born as humans, but the curse had been softened so as to allow Ganga to bear them and to drown them soon after they had been born. In this case there was a reason for the apparent murder. In a similar way, I guess there is a reason for that life to have come and gone so quickly. It may help to cope, but the grief is still real.'

'A sad and strong story, Caleb. You may be familiar with it from your religion, Dr Sharma?' Kaya asked.

'Yes,' Dr Sharma agreed. It is a most popular story from the great Epic.' He collected some papers in a folder, and Kaya and Caleb took the hint that his ten minutes of NHS time with them was coming to an end.

Thank you, Dr Sharma,' Kaya said. They got up, left the surgery and headed home. They would need to find their individual ways of grieving, and of grieving together.

A few months later, they found themselves back at the surgery. A home pregnancy test had shown positive, and they came to have that result verified. Dr Sharma was happy to be able to confirm Kaya's pregnancy, and the NHS process for pregnancy set in, with regular check-ups at the surgery, scans at the hospital, advice from the hospital's consultants, and any number of advertisements coming through email and mail, with loads of free samples of all kinds of products for pregnancy, birth and infancy, in addition to maternity clinics, and paternity classes. There was a lot to take in, and it was all incredibly exciting for Kaya and Caleb, especially for Kaya to note the changes in her body from day to day, and to share them with Caleb. The pregnancy went well, without complications, and their daughter, whom they decided to call Leah, was born precisely on the predicted day, in hospital. Because of the time that elapsed after Kaya's waters broke, she had to be induced to go into full labour and made good use of the pain relief methods on offer, gas and air, and an injection of pethidine. She became pleasantly groggy from that medication, hallucinating about a cherry tree in full blossom outside the window where there was none. After nine hours of labour (she was promised a much shorter time for subsequent babies, but that did not help her now!), Leah was born, happy and healthy.

They went through all the usual (so they were told, it was all completely, excitingly, sometimes frighteningly new, and thus far from "usual" for them!) ups and downs, exhausting nights, the first tears of teething, the insight that what Kaya ate for lunch or dinner had an impact, through the breast milk, on Leah's own digestion, including uncomfortable wind. There were Leah's first utterances of sound, and the gradual development of speech and control of her movements. Caleb shared fully in all the related chores, especially changing nappies at night-time. Kaya went back to two afternoons of three hours each at work after her maternity leave.

When Leah was at the appropriate age, she joined kindergarten, and with that came six months to a year of constant bouts of flu and tummy problems that Leah brought home, and which then made the round to Kaya and Caleb. It was a good time for them all to boost their immune systems with all kinds of natural remedies and ingredients, and they assured themselves that it was working well. In due course, Leah was ready for infant school, and it was around that time that Caleb and Kaya decided to have a second child. They moved house to be able to create additional space needed for the new arrival. When Dr Sharma had confirmed Kaya's pregnancy and the NHS machine set in, they took the opportunity of a leisurely weekend to break the exciting news to Leah that she was going to have a baby brother or sister in a couple of months' time. Leah was shaking with happiness when she heard, and from then on wanted to know all there was to know about pregnancy, how it worked, and what could go wrong, and what to do if something went wrong. Kaya and Caleb made the effort of telling her as much as she wanted to know, in as much detail as requested, and more than once in those months they wondered whether with Leah they were looking at a budding scientist, given the nature of her questions.

Chapter 15

He still felt the cool, clear water of the brook against the back of his throat, a feeling that had not been much stronger when he had swallowed. It was refreshing, clear, purifying, subtle. He could taste and feel nature in it. Then he had leaned back a little too much, lost his balance, and fallen over, going into slow motion, not noticing any more how his body had made harsh contact with the ground. He had been surprised, that was all he could remember. Pleasant, bright orange light now engulfed him, the sensations of the body receded, became nothing more than memory. The dimensions of space and time became vague concepts, no longer applicable to his current state of existence. He merely was, and the question of where he was seemed no longer relevant, or appropriate, let alone important. He was. His body had made him who he had been, but that identifier did not apply any more either. Wherever he was now, he was as a holistic being, not either man or woman, but holistic existence.

He was not alone either. As soon as he had become aware, in the first instance, to his new form of existence, and begun to adjust to it, he became aware of others, some like him, some not. They equally existed as such, not in the context of space and time, and therefore their presence was different from the presence of other people in life on earth. Their presence for him, and probably his presence for them, was without impact on, or consequence for each other, and it was up to him to want to perceive the others—he did not have to, and there was no automatic perception as in human life on earth. He realised that some other forms of existence had not emanated from, or lived on earth, but from and on other planets, and there were also forms of existence that had lived on earth as plants or animals.

Two individuals seemed to be regarding him more closely than others. He sensed them, as he sensed the other forms of existence, but did not perceive them as he had perceived through his human eyes, or with his other human senses. All forms of existence he encountered, and those two individuals, did not have the kinds of characteristics he had come to associate with fellow-humans. They were neutral, in a neutral way, neither pleasant or unpleasant. He could sense both his and their form of existence as pure being. Those two individuals approached him, not in space but in consciousness, and communicated with him, not through human organs of vocalisation, not in human words, but abstractly, differently from what he had been used to in his life on earth, and yet so very lucid, clear, transparent, and completely without even the slightest potential of ambiguity. The writing here, with its recourse to conventions of human dialogue, can only hint at their mode of communication.

'Welcome,' one of the individuals said.

'I feel like I am nowhere, at least nowhere in particular, and I have also lost any sense of what I was used to as "time".'

'We know,' the individual said. 'To make the transition easier for you, we will call you by the name you had in the life you just left, "Oliver". You have left your life as Oliver. Those with whom you lived will come to know of you having died, passed away. You are now in a different form of existence, beyond space and time, to reflect on your past life, and to prepare for your next one, to choose your parents, and the tasks you will have an opportunity to tackle and master in your next life. We are here to guide you in this reassessment and planning. We are your spirit guides. We are souls, like you, and we have taken on the task, in the bigger scheme of existence, to support you, and many others like you, between lives.

'I have so many questions, and at the same time I seem to know all the answers,' Oliver said. 'How do I address you?' he asked the individuals.

'I am Ananda,' one of them said.

'I am Satya,' said the other one.

Oliver smiled—or rather, he would have smiled if he still had had his body—so he felt like smiling when he commented: 'Bliss and truthfulness in Sanskrit.' After a pause, he added: 'Will I get a Sanskrit name for my in-between existence?'

'No, not on this occasion,' Satya responded. 'You will remain "Oliver", but you will also come to remember other identities, each with its own name.'

'We will now begin a process of reviewing your life, what you had taken on as tasks before you came to earth as Oliver, how you addressed those tasks, and where you might want to go for your next life, and which tasks you will address then,' Ananda expanded. 'I think fear may have been central to the life you just left behind?'

'Yes,' Oliver confirmed, 'fear has been a major part of my life. Many children seem to want to be train drivers, it's a cliché. When I told teachers and careers advisors in school that I wanted to be a train driver, the most common response included reference to the chance that I might involuntarily kill some people intent on suicide, and for that reason alone I should reconsider. When I applied for the training, this danger was a major aspect of the interview—I was asked how I proposed coping with the fear of such incidents. The teacher's warnings had prepared me for that question. I said that I would make use of any counselling on offer from the employer, and that I had to live with the knowledge that in terms of statistics, there was a likelihood I would encounter at least one occasion in my career where someone would throw themselves in front of the train I was driving, and I would be unable to stop that person being at best seriously injured, or most probably killed. I was aware of that risk, but my wish to pursue this career was stronger than the fear. I got the trainee position, and then progressed quickly to the top of the profession, and I was lucky that I never had a person under my train throughout my career. But the fear was always there, it was always on my mind. I came across colleagues who had had incidents. Every time when there was news about train delays because of a person under the train, I was grateful that I was not the driver on that occasion, and I was afraid that it might happen to me. I think I prayed before each journey, please let this not happen.

A good friend of mine has an incident, very early on in our careers, and it completely destroyed him, he had to leave his job, he never quite recovered. It was then that I realised I need to deal with this fear. Otherwise it would destroy me as well. So, I took a few days off work, went away for a few days from the family, and thought all this through, very thoroughly. The chance of such an incident was part of the job. I loved the job, I loved it so much that I wanted to find a way of dealing with that risk and the fear of something happening. If it happened, it was not my fault. There was nothing I could have done any differently to prevent it from happening. I was not to blame. That was the starting point. I was not in a position to know the person who would have chosen my train to commit suicide and finding out about them afterwards would not be of any use either. I would deal with the situation as best as I could if it occurred. To be afraid that it might happen was of no use either, it was a waste of energy, it only made my life a misery now, where nothing had actually happened. I really confronted that fear. I imagined it being another person trying to threaten me, and I said to that other person: "Fear, what do you want from me? You are no longer real for me, I am no longer afraid of you. You are only a fata morgana, an illusion, and from now on you have no more power over me". The fear dissolved like fog in the sun. Whenever I felt fear coming back, I sent it away in that manner.'

Ananda and Satya had listened to Oliver's words intently. The equivalent of full concentration was the norm in this mode of existence, anyway.

Ananda now observed: 'Imagine you enter a dark room. Giving yourself over to fear means that you try to get rid of darkness by fighting it. That is futile. You did the right thing: you faced your fear, and you dissolved it. You got rid of darkness by switching on the light.'

Satya complemented: 'Dealing with fear was a major challenge and task you had selected for your life as Oliver.'

'You did quite well, overall,' Ananda concluded. Then he added: 'Can you sense why this was such a critical issue for you?'

Oliver hesitated only very briefly. 'On this level of existence, a mere hint is enough for many long-lost memories to come to the foreground as if the events had happened only yesterday. I always loved gladiator movies, and now I know why. I was a gladiator once, many lives back, and I was very good at it. I was then far too involved with the daily fight for survival for me to have any time to think about being afraid, but it was there in the background. I survived because I was so successful, and I built my reputation on my ability to survive. That of course implied others died, many of them, and prospective opponents were terrified of me. I did not have any personal issues with any of them, but my survival meant someone else's death, on a daily basis. I could sense, smell, their fear. But I had to push it aside if I wanted to have the clear head I needed to survive.'

'This is a good connection you are making, Oliver,' Satya praised. 'We have to confront our fears. Not fight them but address them. Fighting them would only keep them alive. Addressing them dissolves them, as you said earlier. Suppressing them, as you did in the gladiator life, or waiting for them to disappear on their own accord, is like waiting for Father Christmas.'

'I noticed another challenge or task of yours, both in your life as Oliver and the one as gladiator,' Ananda remarked. 'You mentioned in both contexts that you were "good at it". Is there an issue with perfectionism?'

Again, Oliver did not need long to confirm: 'Yes, of course there is. I perfected my mode of killing as a gladiator and was very proud of it. As a train driver, I was obsessed with accelerating and braking smoothly, without the train going into jerky movements. I was really harsh with myself in both contexts. The slightest perceived mistake and I considered myself a failure. I had to function at 100% all the time, otherwise I was unable to accept myself and I feared (fear again!) that others would think badly of me or think that I am a loser. I judged others along the same lines: those who were not perfect were losers. I thought that others could love me only if I was perfect, and I found it difficult to love others if I saw them not being perfect. I was constantly trying to find mistakes and weaknesses in others.'

'Nothing wrong with being perfect, or with striving to be perfect,' Satya explained. 'As long as this does not deteriorate into perfectionism.'

'This is an area for further development in the future', Ananda concluded.

'Let's turn to your private life, your parents, and partnerships.' Satya added.

As if observing a movie he was watching, and therefore safely and securely distanced from the events, Oliver first allowed himself to consider his parents.

'My father was a teacher, and he was very disappointed that I was not very strong intellectually, that I was not at least a teacher as well, but ended up (as he put it) as a train driver. I felt under constant pressure from him, and no matter how much effort I put into something, he never seemed to appreciate it, always finding fault, always shrugging his shoulders, almost desperate, almost close to tears, when he had to realise yet another aspect of my perceived shortcomings. He made me feel inferior all my life, right from the beginning when I was slow to learn to speak, and I never spoke very elegantly. He made me very unhappy. I never thought that he loved me. I realise now that he did, in his own way, but his expectations always got the better of him. My mother realised, at some level, what was happening, and tried to provide some balance. She had realised early on that she would not be able to change my father, but she tried to soften the blows and comfort me when he had hurt me again. This constant tension between my father and me, and through that between herself and her husband, wore her down in the end. She died quite young, when I was only ten years old. My father of course blamed me, although he never said this explicitly, at least. I internalised that blame and made feeling guilty the centre of my life from then on.'

Oliver paused, and Ananda took the opportunity to come in. 'Children, in particular, are very open to developing feelings of guilt. They go along with fear and insecurity, they take away our energy and make us weak, and they take away any joy of life we might otherwise experience. Feelings of guilt often relate to us believing we are responsible for someone else's fate. If I had behaved in this way, such and such would not have happened. You should realise several things in this context, Oliver. First, it may well be that we are being employed, by our creator, as tools to enable others to encounter an experience that is necessary for them.'

Oliver interrupted: 'You mean that I had to be as I was to enable the tension between my mother and my father because that represented a task for them to work out?'

'Yes, precisely,' Satya confirmed.

Ananda carried on: 'Feelings of guilt are like strange, dark clouds that suddenly come up and dampen our mood. They are not really feelings either. They are thoughts that we pick up and internalise, deeply inside, allowing them to gain the impact of an avalanche and the speed of an electric shock.'

'This is clearly an area to revisit in a future life,' Satya concluded.

'When my mother died, I was devastated,' Oliver further remembered. I was angry and desperate. I did not want it to be true that she was gone, nor that I had to live on without her.'

'Your "no" caused pain and fear,' Satya explained. 'A response of "yes" would have allowed for sadness and fear to wash away in the flow of life. When someone dies, it is always the right thing to happen, it is part of that person's divine plan, and also in the divine plans of those left behind. Life tells you: one era is at an end; please accept it, because it is the best for everyone: it is part of the divine plan, even if we cannot intellectually tell why, because we can never comprehend the entire divine plan in its multitude of layers of complexity.'

'You can move on to partnerships now, if you like, Oliver?' Ananda suggested.

'Yes, sure,' Oliver agreed. 'I had lots of very short-lived relationships throughout my teens. I think I introduced a new girlfriend to my father every few weeks, driving him crazy. I had lots of fun. When I had been with the railway for a couple of years, I met Abigail, a maintenance controller, and we hit it off right away, and got married within a year. I was very happy in my marriage—I mean there were ups and downs, of course, but overall... We didn't quarrel much, especially not in front of the children. I had a good income, we could afford things, a nice car, and holidays to Mallorca.'

'Was Abigail happy?' Satya asked.

Oliver was thoughtful. 'Now that you ask me,' he responded, 'I don't really know. I never asked her, we never talked about it, I simply assumed she must be because I loved her, and I was able to provide well for her. She did not have to work, she didn't want to, she said, and could focus on the home and on bringing up the children.'

'A little one-sided, perhaps,' Ananda observed.

'Affairs, escapades, infidelity?' Satya asked.

'There were two women I had developed a crush on while I was married to Abigail,' Oliver admitted. 'I felt guilt about it then, but I am not feeling guilty talking about it now'.

'Your current level of existence is beyond guilt,' Satya assured him. 'Go on.'

'I was rather calm and laid-back, and the crushes were not strong enough to make me actually act on them. I was just drawn to these two women, as if by some magnetic power. Abigail must have noticed, but she was generous and did not tell me off. On each occasion, it did not last too long, and it may even have triggered Abigail to make extra effort to keep me interested in her. I also remember that she seemed to have a crush on another man every now and then, and when that happened I made a special effort for her as well.'

'You still had karma from previous lives with these women, and Abigail with these men,' Ananda elucidated.

'You mean I had known them, in a previous life, or even more than one, and that's what made me feel attracted to them this time round?'

'Precisely', Ananda confirmed. 'Such karma is often the reason why we like or dislike people right away, at first sight, without knowing why. You did the right thing, on these occasions, not following your impulse of attraction. In other cases, not in yours, it would have been the right thing to follow that instinct, because what seems like a chance meeting is never chance, and a change or partner may be on the cards as the right development in line with your divine plan.'

'So much depends on intuition, doesn't it?' Oliver mused.

'You are right, Oliver', Satya said. 'Intuition means that we are open to higher truths, believing in ourselves, and allowing intuition the appropriate space to unfold. Intuition reveals completely new perspectives to us. It can never be forced or conjured up—it is always a godsend. We must become aware of, and get rid of, old, mistaken belief patterns. Intuition functions through the sixth of the energy centres, or chakras. It is called Ajna-chakra, forehead chakra, also called third eye, eye of wisdom, inner eye or command- chakra. It is located a finger's width above the root of the nose in the middle of the forehead. It opens to the front. The colour of the third eye is indigo blue, also yellow and violet. The forehead chakra is associated with all senses, also in the form of extra-sensory perception. It is called 96-leaved lotus.'

Satya and Ananda discussed many other issues of Oliver's life. Then Ananda concluded: 'It may now be time to consider which aspects you want to work on, as tasks, in your next life.'

'How exciting,' Oliver beamed. 'And then you match what I need with what others need, and slot me in accordingly?'

'Not us personally, no,' Satya smiled, explaining: 'That's for the creator, too much for us.'

'We will inform you of the result, though,' Ananda added.

'As Oliver, I was an only child,' Oliver mused, 'and we came across the need to work out some issues with sibling rivalry—perhaps I could get a chance for that next time round?'

'I'll make a note of that,' Ananda confirmed.

'That may go nicely hand in hand with addressing perfectionism again,' Satya suggested.

'Good idea', Ananda and Oliver agreed, almost at the same time.

'You could also consider getting rid of what is left of fear and guilt?' Ananda asked.

'Because you dealt well with your father's disapproval, you might this time get a break on that front with very approving and supportive parents', Satya suggested.

'That would be wonderful', Oliver concurred. 'And I should learn to be more aware of others from their own perspectives, rather than merely assuming their feelings.'

'Indeed,' Ananda said. 'There will also be some people in your next life who have some karma with you to resolve, even though you may not have karma with them, and you may become a tool to teach them lessons. Those situations will train you further in remaining in the observer position.'

'Sounds good, but can you please remind me what "being in the observer position" means, precisely? You have mentioned it in passing several times, so it must be quite important', Oliver pleaded.

'No problem,' Ananda assured him. 'The idea is that you should not get overshadowed by your daily experiences. You achieve a healthy distance if you observe everything that happens to you, in relation to you, and around you, as if you were watching a movie.'

Meanwhile, Satya had closed his eyes, and opened them again now. 'We have a family for you, Oliver. You will be born as the second child, a boy, of Kaya and Caleb White, and brother of Leah, who will be four years old when you are born. Your family lives in England, your mother is a dentist, your father teaches drama at the university.'

Chapter 16

This was so care-free and relaxing. In a warm, not-too-bright environment, cosy, comfortable, he felt very much at home. At first, changing status from a body-free spirit in infinity to relocate to the constrictions of the body of a human being had seemed strange. The spirit resides in infinity, beyond space and time in between incarnations. His parents were very much in love with each other, and with the full approval and goodwill of their families. He was their second child, and he had been with them since his conception in a wonderfully cool August night which had followed a particularly hot July. He could still recall some events of previous incarnations at will, but they did not crowd his thoughts unwanted. This was just as well, because ever since his new incarnation had taken place, he was preoccupied with observing the growth of his own body in his mother's womb. Witnessing the division of cells, and the formation of specialised tissues, organs and structures brought ever new blissful waves of joy and wonder at the workings of creation. He could observe not only his own development but also his entire immediate environment, as well as that of his parents. He loved the house they were living in, the space they had allowed for their arrangement of practical but elegant furniture, and the large windows providing ample sunlight which had to be dimmed occasionally by drawing exquisitely shaped and patterned silk blinds of various tasteful colours. He was fascinated by the harmonious blend of natural candle-light and ordinary electrical light from various sources intricately distributed over the rooms in the evenings. His aesthetic intuition found a rich source of enjoyment in the imaginative juxtaposition of colours used in the rooms, together with round or angular shapes of the walls, and ample use of distinct types of wood carved to astonishing finish. All this, however, would have been only half as pleasing for him without his parents, who had created this house and filled it with their souls, with life.

Something was happening. He had been feeling too tight in his environment for a while. He sensed the presence of Ananda and Satya, sensed the great trust he could have in them, but had already lost the full awareness of their nature, their role in his existence, and much detail of what he had learnt from them. He knew there was more, but he did not have access to it any longer. Their presence still assured him. He glided through a very narrow passage, then came into an altogether new and unfamiliar environment. He inhaled, quite automatically. A strange feeling, liberating and restricting at the same time: restricting because it was more of an effort, but liberating because now he was independent of his mother's body. He felt comfortable, and explored breathing, quietly and calmly. His eyes were still closed. Then he suddenly, unexpectedly felt a painful sensation on his buttocks, and both the shock and the pain caused another unfamiliar reaction of his body in this new environment. He expressed both pain and dismay in a sound that came spontaneously from his throat: he cried, in two angry, determined bursts. And he opened his eyes. The lights were bright, very bright, and it took him a while to adjust his eyes to this—everything so new and unfamiliar. His body felt cool, first comfortably so, and gradually too cold. But then he felt something warm and soft being wrapped around him, took a look, and saw a beige flannel   around his body. He felt being lifted in the air, and then placed on a soft surface. He heard comforting words from the voice he knew from his time in the warm, cosy, homely environment. This was his mother's voice, he realised, and his eyes searched from where the voice came. He saw her face, her eyes, full of love, and he felt snug and secure, drinking in his mother's love with his eyes and all his body. His eyes shifted to locate the person associated with the other voice that was coming his way, a deeper, darker voice, which he was familiar with as well, although not as much as his mother's. That must be his father—his face came into view now, equally full of love. Both his mother and father kept repeating a word, "Evan", and that, he realised, must be his new name.

A new sensation then made itself known—so many things happening, how exciting. It was hunger, and he instinctively latched on with his mouth to the part of the flannel that had moved over his mouth. He noticed that his mother reacted to this movement, her eyes sparkled, her throat created a lovely sound, laughter, and he noticed that she took the flannel out of his mouth, very gently. Then he was being moved around again, and his mouth was guided to latch on to something else, and when he now repeated the movements with his mouth that he had tried with the flannel, he felt his mouth fill with the most delicious liquid he could imagine, and by reflex he swallowed it down, moved his mouth again, his mouth filled up, and he swallowed. The feeling of hunger disappeared, making way for a warm and comfortable feeling in his stomach. He thought about the voices he had heard, and remembered the sound of his own voice, when he had cried, briefly. He had to work this one out, he promised himself. He became sleepy, forgot to swallow after some gulps, noticed the liquid dribbling out of his mouth, and he choked when he inhaled again, with his mouth still half-full. His mother lifted him up gently, and patted his back, which helped getting the sequence of breathing and swallowing right—it was not advisable to do both at the same time. He then drank a little more, then wriggled around to get a look at his mother face, followed his instinct to move his face in response to the joy he felt, and love, and gratitude, and fell fast asleep to the sounds of the voices of his mother and his father, recognising his name, Evan, in what they were saying, and the much-repeated word "smile".

When he woke up again, he realised that the surroundings were different. Gone were the bright lights and the strange smell. The light was comfortable now, pleasant, and the smell was that mainly of his mother and father. He moved his body, his arms and legs, and felt decidedly uncomfortable in the middle, kind of wet and sticky. He was also hungry again. Neither his mother nor his father was in sight. He recalled that he had heard their voices when they were talking to him, and he had heard his own voice when he had cried out in pain. He had not had a chance yet to practice his voice further; now he repeated the body movements that he remembered from the crying, and after some unsuccessful attempts, he burst out with a series of well-defined wails that resounded in the room. He enjoyed this new-found ability, and, getting the hang of it, continued for a while for its own sake, almost forgetting how uncomfortable he was and that that was why he had started crying in the first place. In a pause between wails, he heard a noise and then his mother's voice, softly calling his name, Evan. She came into view, smiled at him, wrinkled her nose, smiled again, and said some more soothing words. She went out of sight, he heard more noises besides her voice, a little further off. Then his mother came into view again, lifted him up gently in her arms and carried him a short distance and put him down again, flat on his back, on a soft surface. He felt the presence of Ananda and Satya, not really localised. His mother talked to him gently, lovingly, he looked at her, into her face, into her eyes. She moved her hands around his body, and he realised that he was not wearing the same flannel that he had been wrapped in earlier. Whatever it was he was wearing now was removed by his mother, and he felt a little uncomfortable with his body exposed to the air in the room and not protected by the soft fabric any more. He expressed his discomfort by a short wail. His mother touched his body gently and comfortingly. He felt that the wetness around his middle was gone and felt another soft material in his mother's hands remove what had felt sticky. She then put his clothes on again, and his body felt fresh and comfortable. But he was still hungry and made this known through a brief cry. His mother laughed—how he loved that sound. He tried to remember the movement of his own face when he had felt happy some time ago, and in response felt the touch of his mother's lips on his cheeks. He then felt himself lifted up again, placed in his mother's arms, and found the source of the delicious liquid to latch on to. He was alert, and thus able to both remember and apply the lesson he had learnt about the sequence of sucking, swallowing and breathing, and he did well. After a while he did not feel hungry any more and was surprised not to feel ready to sleep again either. He was quite widely awake, in fact. His mother held him closely, upright, and gently patted his back. After a while, he felt a new sensation, something coming up inside him and then releasing through his mouth with a little sound. His mother said something that sounded like "burp". She then placed him on his back again and looked at him. Time to work on this sound thing. He was able to cry, and did that well, but the sounds he heard from his mother and father were different. Before he could start focusing on this, however, the were noises, similar to those when his mother had come after his first crying, and he could hear other voices, which he also remembered. It was not his father, or his mother. One voice was similar to that of his mother, but higher in pitch. Now the face that belonged to that voice came into view. His mother and father were in some way similar, he realised, but this face was different altogether. His mother and the new person kept repeating the word "Leah". Evan remembered from Ananda and Satya that he would have an older sister, Leah. The way that her face was different from that of his mother and father was because she was a child, she was younger, whereas his parents were older, of a similar older age. Leah looked lovingly at him as well, but in a different way from his mother and his father. With the sensitivity of a new-born, which is highly refined but deteriorates in the course of days and weeks, he sensed some worry, concern, or even alarm, behind, underneath and mixed in with the love that dominated in Leah's eyes and in her voice. Almost ready to cry, Evan noticed that Ananda's presence had become more distinct, and he picked up a communication from Ananda, not to worry about Leah, and that working on sibling interaction was on the cards for him in this life. This allowed Evan to smile at Leah instead of crying in response to her presence.

Another voice and face now came into view, and his mother handed him over for that new person to hold him. It was different again in the same way that Leah and his mother and father were different—only this time the new person was older than his parents, and much older than Leah. He remembered the voice also from the time he had developed in the womb. The new person was like Leah and his mother, in some ways, not like his father. She was apparently "grandma", and he also noticed the name Grace in relation to her, just as his sister was Leah and his mother, or mama, was Kaya, and his father, or dada, was Caleb. Grandma talked animatedly at Evan, and he smiled at her, causing much laughter. Then he was passed by grandma to the final stranger that day, more like his father, but also similar to grandma. He was grandpa, and, looking at him closely, Evan could see the happy smile on his face, but something else, which he was not yet able to place, and he saw that grandpa's eyes were quite red and wet. He remembered his own eyes feeling wet when he was crying with pain earlier on. This grandpa, however, was not in pain, to judge by his face. The name associated with him seemed to be Henry.

But now it was really time to work on his voice, and his father, who had meanwhile joined them, and his mother and Leah talking animatedly with their different, distinctive voices, gave him opportunity enough to observe and then to try for himself to create a sound through his throat that was similar to what he heard from them, and different from his crying. He realised that the production of sound was related to breathing, so he first tried to produce sound on breathing in. It did not really work, sometimes resulting in choking, and his mother or father sat him up and patted his back. After a while, his mother seemed to understand what he was trying to achieve, however, and placed one his hands in front of her mouth when she talked, so that he could feel her breath on his hand. She also placed his hand on her throat, so that he could feel the vibrations of the voice. On this day, he did not quite succeed. He got tired and frustrated and let out some crying sounds, both to vent his feelings and to check whether at least those sounds still worked. Then he fell asleep.

***

The next time he woke up, he did not feel particularly hungry, and not wet either. He spent some time exercising his arms and hands to make more coordinated movements, as he wanted them to move, not as they seemed to want to move on their own. Remembering his unsuccessful attempts at producing sounds with his voice that were not crying, he tried again, and managed to produce some very clear sounds, shaking all over with joy at this success. Then he alerted his mother, or father, to the fact that he was awake by a few determined bursts of crying, followed by some of the newly-found, clear sounds. It worked again, his mother came in, checked whether he was wet, and offered him something to drink, but he was not interested. He repeated his other sounds, and his mother shared his joy. His mother then took him to a different area which he did not yet recognise, and he subjected his environment to careful and critical inspection. The smell was again different, and there were many quite bright and shiny surfaces. He heard a new sound, his mother removed his clothes, then she took him gently up and placed him in pleasantly warm water, holding him safely.

A certain kind of routine seemed to develop—at least there were recognisable phases of sleeping, waking up wet and sticky, being cleaned, having a bath, feeling hungry or not, drinking, working on the movement of his arms and legs, and working on his voice. He learnt the meaning of the words his mother and father and sister uttered, both from association with objects they pointed at when saying the words, and from memory of some other time—it grew more and more hazy, distant and indistinct. He was still aware of Ananda and Satya, but no longer remembered details of what they had told him. They helped him sense them by appearing as beautiful patterns of colour within his field of vision, and when this happened, Evan felt particularly joyful and loving, and smiled and laughed. His parents' and sister's reactions on those occasions suggested to him that they did not sense the presence of Ananda and Satya and did not see their expressed form of colourful patterns, but that they nevertheless shared his joy at whatever he apparently saw. Thus, ever new experiences came Evan's way.

He found that the delicious liquid he received from his mother was milk; it tasted slightly differently every day, and he liked some of the flavours decidedly more than others. There was also a link between the flavour of the milk and how he felt in his stomach—particularly unwelcome were occasions when felt his belly rumbling uncomfortably. His parents and Leah, and grandma and grandpa, when they happened to be around, could hear it as well, and they commented with reference to "wind". On those occasions, his father would usually rub his belly with his big, warm hands. This eased the discomfort, and he showed his appreciation through grateful smiles.

He particularly liked laughter, that of others, and his own. It was even better than smiling. Quite often, his mother and father, sometimes grandpa and grandma, and on occasion even Leah, would do something that made him laugh. Often, he could sense that it was intentional, when they pulled funny faces or told stories that had funny sounds or showed pictures that were amusing. Some things worked only once to make him laugh, others made him laugh again and again, just as much each time as the time before. Some wore off after a while, some sooner, others later. He loved those occasions most where the cause for laughter came unexpectedly. Being tickled also caused laughter, he realised with delight, but it could get a bit much after a while.

One day, he was placed in a new chair, not the one that would bounce in line with his movements or those of the others, but one where he sat quite upright, resting his back against a comfortably padded but firm surface, and with a horizontal board in front of him. His mother placed a bowl on that board, similar to the ones he had seen the others eating from. It was smaller, however, and displayed a range of bright, cheerful colours. A lovely smell came from the bowl, and he was curious to see what would happen with it. He saw his mother place a spoon into the bowl, take out some of the food from the bowl onto the spoon, and move it gently towards his mouth. He instinctively opened his mouth, even though some apprehension mixed in with the excitement. He felt the food in his mouth and closed his lips over the spoon—his mother gently removed the spoon from his mouth and used a soft cloth to wipe his mouth. He used his tongue to get a feel for the food in his mouth. The texture was pleasant, and the flavour delicious. He realised he was able to breathe through his nose, though not through his mouth, while he worked on the food. Eventually he swallowed the food down and opened his mouth in the hope of receiving another spoon-full of the food. In this way, he ate quite a lot, until he felt really full in his belly, and did not open his mouth for a further spoon-full, and kept his mouth shut when his mother offered another spoon-full. His mother then took him away from the new seat, and placed him over her shoulder, tenderly patting his back until he burped.

He now had some milk from his mother, and some food from the spoon, whenever he felt hungry. The spoon-food seemed to come at quite set times, the milk mainly when he asked for it by crying, and this seemed to be at less regular intervals, and often when it was dark outside. The milk was always the same, only with very subtly different flavours, while the spoon-food was very different one time from the next, both concerning texture and flavour. There were some foods that he did not like at all, and on those occasions, he would not take more than one spoonful, and his mother, or whoever gave him the food on the spoon (sometimes his father, sometimes grandpa or grandma, but never Leah), would smile and sigh and return with food he liked after a while. Usually they did not try to offer him food again that he had not liked.

He learnt much of what he had to learn by closely observing and then imitating others. In the context of food, he realised that the others would take food into their mouths with a spoon, or something else, and then they would move their jaws up and down with mouth closed. He tried this out. With open mouth, he realised, the food would come out of the mouth and need to be wiped off. The others did not do this, so he tried to avoid it, too. He could move his mouth as he saw the others doing, but he saw no point in this for his eating, there was no difference to him whether he did this or not. He then saw that the others had something white showing when their mouths were open, a row of little white pieces close to each other. When he felt his own mouth with his lips or fingers, he could not find any such things in his mouth. He sought to touch these things in the others' mouths, but only his mother would allow him, and only once. She explained that they had teeth, and he would have some soon.

He forgot about all this, but remembered when one day he felt a sharp, stinging pain in his mouth, and started crying immediately. He also noticed that he had much more spit in his mouth, which had soaked his sleeper quite considerably. His mother came, but he was neither wet, nor hungry. He continued crying. She noticed the wet sleepsuit, changed him, and checked his mouth. His mother walked away and came back with a bright green thing she gave him to put into his mouth. He tried, and soon bit heartily on it in the area that the pain was. His mother pointed to her teeth, and then to his mouth, and said that he was teething.

At certain times of the day, his father or mother, sometimes grandpa or grandma, would take what they called a book, and sit with him and read to him. Often there were interesting pictures in the book as well, and often the language was funny because of its distinct rhythm. These books helped him develop his ways with words. He had been able to understand much from very early on; now was the time to develop that understanding from grasping the gist of what was being said to achieve attention to detail; it also meant further training his mouth, tongue and voice to comply with his wishes to express himself towards his parents, grandparents and sister.

Chapter 17

Over time, Evan's skills relating to his body became more and more sophisticated, and his parents and grandparents took every opportunity of praising both his efforts and achievements. Early on in his life, they had observed a particular pattern in this regard.

'Did you observe Evan moving his arms and legs today?' his mother, Kaya, asked his father, Caleb, one evening after Evan had fallen asleep after a meal.

'Yes', Caleb responded, 'he is trying so hard, and when it does not go to plan, he gets very angry with himself, red in the face with it.'

'I think he's a little perfectionist,' Kaya observed. 'Otherwise he wouldn't get so frustrated and be more playful about the exercise itself— he seems to be working almost according to a planned programme in his little head.'

'That is quite possible,' Caleb confirmed. Then he wondered: 'Is there anything we can do to support him with this?'

'We could join him in moving, give him a clear model to imitate, to make it more playful, and of course praise him a lot when he has achieved something, and be very loving and perhaps distract him a little when he takes it too seriously or does not get right away to where he wants to be.'

'Good idea,' Caleb agreed, 'and we could also talk to Grace and Henry about this'.

Kaya interrupted with a smile: 'Grandma and grandpa, as they now like to be referred to. They have been so happy to be grandparents.'

'Yes, grandma and grandpa,' Caleb smiled as well.

'Not to forget Leah, I guess sibling imitation is a key factor in Evan's development,' Kaya concluded. 'But let's try it out in practice ourselves first, whether it works for us?'

Caleb shared this view, and they took the next opportunity of testing their ideas with Evan. On that day, sitting in his high-chair, he had decided to work on moving both his arms together, rather than at random. Kaya and Caleb observed him closely, and soon figured out his intention.

'Do you think we should try to show him how to clap, so that he can then try to imitate us?' Kaya suggested.

'Hmm,' Caleb considered this, 'clever idea.'

They clapped their hands, with slightly exaggerated movements. The sound of the clapping caught Evan's attention, and he responded with a smile and laughter.

'See how closely he is watching us,' Kaya quietly said to Caleb.

He nodded, and they continued clapping. Soon Evan tried to imitate them, at first missing the hands or not creating a sound when they met because the palms were not flat. Soon he was showing first signs of frustration. After exchanging a glance, Caleb and Kaya took up Evan's way of clapping as if they were inspired by it and were imitating him. They moved their hands towards each other, but missed, or almost missed, or avoided the sound effect. They laughed and giggled all the while, showing Evan how much fun they were having. Their enthusiasm and playful mood caught on, and Evan laughed and joined them in light-hearted movements. At Caleb's signal, Kaya and he moved on to seeking to touch not only their hands in an attempt at clapping, but each other's, and soon they sought to integrate Evan in his, holding out one of their hands for him to touch. Squeals of laughter from Evan accompanied every successful hit he achieved, and there was so much going on that he did not have the space to get frustrated and grumpy. During their playing, they noticed that Evan was getting better at the more purposeful movements he had tried to achieve at first, having his palms straight for impact with his own hands, or with those of one of his parents. He would also become better at hitting the target and not missing it, and even managed to produce some clapping sounds in the end. In a while, he was happy and got tired, losing interest in the game without frustration, and then beginning to stare hard at his mother, and smiling happily when she understood that he wanted a feed.

While drinking, he sensed Ananda and Satya's presence, and he had a brief phase in which he could reflect calmly, even though not in words he had learnt as if anew in this life, but in terms of more abstract processes of consciousness, about what had just happened. He realised that he had had fun, he had been playing, had had a wonderful time with his parents, and he had practised and progressed a lot with the movements of his arms. This was so much better than previous occasions when he has tried so hard. The fun just now had not been hard at all. And working hard made him tired much sooner, and he was not happy when he worked hard. Just now he had been happy with himself—when he worked hard he was mainly frustrated with himself. Satisfied both with the experience, and his insights about it, he snuggled up to his mother to allow himself to fall asleep.

Ananda and Satya were satisfied as well, as this had been Evan's first, and successful, encounter with the task of addressing perfectionism. Kaya and Caleb, too, were happy with the way this had gone.

'I think our idea was right, and what we did worked out great,' Kaya said after she had placed fast-asleep Evan into his crib for a well-deserved rest.

'Yes,' Caleb confirmed. 'We should tell Grace, Henry and Leah when we get a moment'.

They did so, and particularly Grace and Henry expressed their surprise at this insight and how well Evan seemed to have taken to it. They tried themselves in due course and found it a very uplifting experience. They initiated the game of clapping themselves, and as expected, Evan joined in, already familiar with the game, and still keen on playing it. Grace and Henry pretended not to be able to hit their own and each other's hands, while Evan was successful right from the start, making him visibly happy. For a moment, he seemed to be teaching his grandparents rather than the other way around.

On one occasion, Kaya observed Leah playing the game with Evan, at first in line with their instructions, but then she did her own clapping very fast and loudly, and Evan had no chance of imitating his sister successfully. He frowned and started crying—to Kaya it seemed he was in fact angrier with his sister than with himself. Sticking to their number one parenting principle not to react right away and without consideration to unexpected events unless there was immediate danger, Kaya did not interfere at this point, but discussed the observation with Caleb later that day.

'It seemed to me that Leah was winding him up intentionally, and he cried because he was angry at that,' Kaya concluded her narration of what had happened.

'Sometimes Leah has this tendency to be a bit nasty to Evan, very sweetly and lovingly so, but still,' Caleb responded. 'I bet Evan senses it, just as we do, but he can't defend himself properly yet—all he can do is start crying. Usually that then brings one of us on the scene, at least popping our heads around the corner to see what's up, and even if we don't interfere, our presence gives him reassurance.'

'You think it's sibling rivalry from Leah's perspective?' Kaya ventured.

'Must be,' Caleb agreed. 'She was happy when we told her that you were pregnant with Evan, and when he was born, and we came home with him from hospital. She really loves him, deeply. But there is still something there in the background that bubbles up to the surface every now and then. Sometimes I get the feeling that Leah does not quite know herself what's hitting her on those occasions.'

'I think talking to her directly about this would not be the best way forward,' Kaya developed this train of discussion further.

'I agree,' Caleb said.

'It would foreground the issue too much, take away the innocence and intuitive level which this is currently on,' Kaya went on.

Caleb picked up from there: 'We should make sure we have time with her on her own, and when we are with both of them, not to give our attention only to Evan, and arrange for situations where we have reason to praise her in his presence, not only the other way 'round.'

'It is so easy to take all the things Leah can do already for granted, because she is four years older than Evan, after all,' Kaya added.

His parents had interpreted his behaviour quite well. He enjoyed Leah's company, he really did, but he had sensed, right from the moment he had first set eyes on her, that there was some tension, which they seemed both aware of, in distinctly different ways. Evan felt very close to Leah, and he sensed that she felt the same way about him. That feeling formed the foundation and core of their relationship. But there were moments, very brief but also very poignant, when Leah slipped into hostility—very subtle, possibly not perceptible for the others, but he most certainly noticed, and felt hurt. Sometimes he was strong enough to outwardly ignore the attack—although he was sure that Leah, somewhere deep down, realised and knew that her attack had hit home. Sometimes he simply had to react immediately, to get the shock and hurt and anger out of his body—and the only way he could react at that point in his relatively new life was to shout out his feelings by crying.

The days, weeks and months passed. Evan was by now a little more than a year old. He had come to feel pain when he moved his arms, hands, legs or feet. He became reluctant to move, to crawl, and engage in all those things that he had enjoyed so much until a while back when this pain had started, and it was getting worse. His parents seemed to notice, looking at him with concern, comforting him, but unable to help, for some reason. One evening he felt particularly weak, there was a lot of pain, and he also felt very hot. While he had developed a satisfactory level of control over the movements of his arms and legs, suddenly he felt his whole body shaking violently, all jerky, and he did not have any control over it. Fortunately, his mother was close by and immediately lifted him up on her shoulder. Food came up from his belly and out of his mouth, spreading all over his mother's back. Then everything went completely black and quiet. When he could see again, the shaking had stopped, fortunately, he was lying on his bed, his parents looking at him with great concern. He was changed, he heard his father talking to someone, but could not hear the person he was talking to. He was placed in the car, into the car seat he liked so much, and they drove off quickly. After a while they took him out of the seat and into a large building where he had never been before. Bright lights made him wince, and there were unfamiliar sounds and smells as well. Normally he would have been excited, but he was merely tired and weary. Several people looked at him, poked him here and there, felt his arms and legs, made him move them this way or that way. He felt a sharp sting on his arm, cried out briefly, and was comforted by his mother. He was given something to eat and drink, which did not taste either familiar or nice, but, judging by his mother's expression, it seemed necessary that he accepted it. Soon he fell asleep, and felt a little better when he woke up, at least not as hot any more. He was not at home again yet. He had something tasty to eat and drink, and soon some people, some he had seen before, and some others, again looked at him closely. His mother was there, always providing reassurance when he needed it, and his father and Leah were there as well. Leah seemed very concerned, and their father had to reassure her a lot. There was not enough peace and quiet in that environment for him to sense or see Satya and Ananda, and he hoped he would be home again soon. There were several more occasions when he felt a sharp, stinging pain, but his mother's reassurance was enough to comfort him.

At long last, they were at home again. His mother talked to him for a long time, and he understood that normally he was healthy, but he had just been very ill, and was now getting better again. Being ill meant having pain and not feeling well, feeling hot, shaking, not being able to see anything anymore for a while, and much more. The place they had taken him to was a hospital, and the people who had looked at him so carefully again and again were doctors. He was now taking medicine with his food to help him get better.

Chapter 18

Leah proceeded to primary school, then secondary school, Evan to kindergarten, then infant and primary school. Caleb and Kaya had organised a big family party for Evan's eighths birthday, which Grace and Henry, who were very involved with their grandchildren, had of course also attended. They had returned to London later that evening, still full of both the buzz and the emotional current of the special event. At home, Grace and Henry had a glass of wine, and an early night.

The next morning, Grace woke up with a mild headache, which she was not usually prone to. At first, she did not pay much attention to it, but after showering it got worse, and in the kitchen, while she was preparing breakfast, she noticed that she was also feeling dizzy, with everything in her vision suddenly spinning anti-clockwise. She just about managed to sit down, because the dizziness was making it difficult for her to sit straight with her eyes open, let alone stand or walk. She got worried, and called out for Henry, who was still fast asleep in bed when she had last looked. Fortunately, Henry was just about waking up and therefore able to hear a strange, gurgling sound from the kitchen—this was all Grace could utter, although she was certain she had called Henry's name. He rushed to the kitchen and found Grace slumped over the kitchen table, still making unintelligible sounds. He established that she was conscious, but his attempts at making her sit up or talk were futile. She needed medical help. Henry dialled 999 and gave information and instructions to the emergency services operators as prompted. Within ten further minutes, an ambulance had arrived, the paramedics efficiently and professionally assessed the situation and then strapped Grace on a stretcher and carried her to the ambulance. They told him briefly that they suspected Grace had suffered a stroke, and she needed to be treated in hospital urgently. Henry joined them on their way to the nearest available hospital. He phoned Caleb, who answered the phone quickly.

'Good morning,' Henry said.

'Oh, good morning, dad.' Caleb sounded surprised. 'I tried phoning you at home a moment ago, but you didn't answer. And this is clearly your mobile phone you are calling from, and a lot of noise in the background, an ambulance very close by,' he observed.

'Caleb, listen,' Henry said, his voice reflecting the urgency of the situation, 'I am in an ambulance with Grace, on the way to the hyper acute stroke unit at King's College Hospital, Grace seems to have had a stroke.'

'Oh my God, no,' Caleb exclaimed, and called out for Kaya to come over to the phone. 'Please call again when you know more, use Kaya's mobile number to be on the safe side, I think we'll make arrangements to come over right away. Yes, bye.' Then he turned to Kaya. 'That was Henry,' he said to her, 'it seems your mum's had a stroke. They are one the way to the hospital now.'

Kaya was of course very upset and started crying. Leah and Evan had woken up from the phone ringing and the excited talking, and came down the stairs sleepily, to ask what was going on. Kaya explained to them. They decided to have breakfast first. They needed that, whatever happened and whatever they would be doing next.

'I suggest,' Caleb said, 'that I stay behind with Leah and Evan, and you take the next train down to London to be with your mum, Kaya.'

They agreed that this was the best solution for the moment. Kaya quickly packed a few things and they booked a taxi to take her to the station—she reached just in time for the next possible train and was in London within three hours of first hearing about the stroke. She took a taxi from the station to the hospital and enquired about the whereabouts of her mother at the reception. She was given directions to the relatives' waiting area, where she found Henry. They hugged.

'It's great that you were able to come over so quickly, Kaya,' Henry said. 'Did Caleb stay with the children?'

'There was no alternative to me coming over immediately,' Kaya stated. 'Yes, Caleb is with Leah and Evan. What is the latest you have on mum?'

'They are doing all kinds of checks on her now. I think that includes an MRI scan. She is stable in terms of heart and other vital functions. She was awake during the trip to the hospital, in the ambulance, but not able to talk properly. But I am certain that she did recognise me, and her environment. The paramedics checked on that as well and said it was a good sign. So now it's a question of waiting.'

Kaya and Henry helped themselves to a coffee from the machine provided in the waiting area, and remained quiet for a while, caught in their own thoughts.

Caleb at home tried to distract the children as much as possible, but that was not so easy any more, given that they were now twelve and eight years old, respectively.

'What exactly is a stroke, dad?' Leah asked.

Before he could start on his response, Evan took over: 'It's when a blood vessel in the brain bursts. Then lots of blood comes out of the vessel, and puts pressure on the brain, and the brain goes dead in those areas where the pressure is too much.' He looked proudly, but also quizzically at Caleb.

'Yes, well explained, Evan,' Caleb praised his son. 'This is one type of stroke, bleeding in the brain. There is another type, where the blood vessels do not burst, but get blocked, and blood does not reach important parts of the brain. Does it make sense to you, Leah?'

'I think so,' she considered. 'What makes a blood vessel burst?'

Evan did not know the answer, and Caleb stepped in: 'It is probably, in granny's case, a question of age. The walls of the blood vessels just get thinner with age. So much blood flows through them all their lives, it's wear and tear. It's the same in the body as it is with clothes. Remember your favourite shirt, how sad you were when it got so thin from all the times it had been in the washing machine that it tore?'

Leah nodded. 'And what do the doctors do?'

'They try to stop the bleeding, or they try to unblock the blood vessels. They try to do this with medicines, but if necessary they have to operate,' Caleb explained.

The answer was enough for Leah.

'Which kind of stroke did granny have?' Evan asked.

'We don't know yet,' Caleb responded. At that moment, his mobile phone rang. It was Kaya, who gave him an update on the situation at the hospital.

'That was mum,' Caleb said, she sends her love. 'Granny is in hospital having some tests and treatment, but the doctors have not yet told them what they found.'

'Is granny in a lot of pain?' asked Leah, concerned.

Caleb thought for a moment. 'Grandad said this morning that nanny had had a headache when she woke up. I think the doctors will take pain relief into account when they work with granny,' he tried to reassure her.

'I see,' Leah said. 'Am I asking too many questions?'

'No, not at all,' Caleb smiled at her warmly. 'Ask as many questions as you like, please.'

Encouraged. Leah went on: 'And if the doctors cannot help granny, will she die?'

Evan was clearly uncomfortable with that question, which had been genuine and open from Leah's perspective. He swallowed, and complained: 'That's a bit much, Leah!'

Caleb caught the atmosphere. 'No, it's alright. Stroke can always lead to a person dying, depending how strong it is. But in granny's case, the paramedics were quite hopeful that she will get through it alright.'

'And if she does die, what is that like?' Evan now asked.

'We don't really know, because nobody who has died is able to tell us later what it was like,' Caleb said, in a very matter-of-fact voice.

Still Evan had to laugh at the logic.

His laughter was not quite free, though, Caleb realised, and therefore he added: 'There are some people who were considered dead by the doctors, but who came back to life, after a very short while. They often write about their experiences, and psychologists try to study those "near-death experiences", as they are called. Many of those experiences have in common that people are quite surprised how pleasant they seem to be. Death is the aspect of life we know least about, and because we don't know much we could get afraid of it, but it seems not to be frightful at all, but in fact somehow a pleasant experience.' Caleb paused to let this sink in.

Leah considered this for a while, and then added: 'I would be afraid of death because I don't know what happens afterwards.'

'Very good point, Leah,' Caleb praised her. Different religions tell us different things about us. For example, our soul goes to God, or it goes to a space where it reflects on the life just ended and prepares for a next life. And people who do not believe in God, no matter what religion, think that it simply all ends at death, nothing happens afterwards.'

'That's rather sad, to have to be thinking that. What's the point of life in that case?'

'Can we stop all this philosophy now, please, my head is hurting,' Leah complained at this point. 'I'm hungry from all this talking.'

'That's good,' Caleb said, 'let's stop talking for now, but if you do have any further questions, always ask me,' he encouraged them.

At the hospital, Kaya and Henry were pulled out of their silence when they saw a doctor approaching. He looked at the notes on his clipboard, puzzled.

'Mr and, ahem, Mrs White?'

'Yes, and yes,' Kaya confirmed, and managed a smile. 'Confusing, isn't it? I met my future husband, Caleb White, and our respective parents, Grace, your patient, my mother, and Henry, here, my father-in-law, met as well, fell in love and got married. Make sense?

The doctor tried to solve the puzzle by mumbling and pointing to imaginary objects with his hands. Having succeeded, or given up, Kaya was not sure, he introduced himself:

'Sorry, it is rather complicated at first sight. I am Mr Anand, I am consultant neurologist in the hyper acute stroke unit here. Mrs, ahem, White had what we call a TIA, a transient ischaemic attack, caused by a temporary blood clot in one of her brain vessels. The lay term is mini-stroke. We did MRI and CT scans, and can rule out any other kind of event. All the symptoms that you will have noticed, or that your wife mentioned, Mr., ahem, White, are consistent with that diagnosis, headache, dizziness, and the problems with speaking. We call that dysphasia. We have treated this with aspirin in the first instance. The symptoms have gone back, she is now resting, as such attacks can be quite draining, in addition to the tension of having to go to and be in hospital. We are monitoring her closely and would like to do so for another day or so. You can go in and see her now if you like. Do you have any questions for me?'

'What is the prognosis?' Kaya asked.

'A fellow medic?' Mr Anand smiled.

'Dentist,' Kaya corrected him.

'Really?' Mr Anand sounded surprised. 'You…'

'Now don't say that I don't look macho enough for a dentist,' Kaya protested.

'You hear that a lot, do you?' Mr Anand apologised.

'Far too often. Prognosis?' she reminded him.

'Oh, sorry,' Mr Anand remembered. 'She should make a full recovery, it will just take time to regain her strength.'

'Thank you,' Kaya replied, and turned to Henry. 'Henry?'

'Nothing at the moment. Presumably we will get some advice when she is being discharged?'

'Yes,' Mr Anand confirmed, 'lots of leaflets with all the info you need.'

He called a nurse and she led Kaya and Henry across to the room where Grace was resting.

'Hello there,' Henry said gently, and Kaya said: 'Hi mum.'

Grace looked at them, tired but relieved. Many thoughts had gone through her mind after she had realised that she needed help, and called, as she remembered, for Henry. She was aware that she had been on her way to the hospital, and that lots of people had made a lot of fuss around her, and now she saw both Henry and Kaya. She had wondered what had happened. Someone had told her something, at some point, but she had forgotten again. Grace smiled: 'Hello. You too look very concerned, is anything wrong?'

To mainly Henry's relief, because he still remembered the disjointed sounds Grace had made in the early morning, Grace's words now had come out clearly and cogently. He told Grace briefly what had happened, and that they were so happy she was feeling better.

'Tired, now, mostly. I'd like some water to drink, and then I'd like to have a long beauty sleep.'

The nurse advised them that Grace might be sleeping for quite a long time, possibly through until the next day, and she would not be woken up by hospital staff. She took down Kaya's and Henry's mobile phone numbers and promised to call them if there were any changes. Henry and Kaya left the hospital and made their way back to Henry and Grace's flat, stopping on the way to buy some food. Then they called Caleb and set up a skype session with him and the children. Henry and Kaya explained in detail what had happened, the diagnosis and the treatment.

Grace was discharged from hospital two days later, Caleb had travelled over to London with Leah and Evan for the occasion, and they were all given many information leaflets about life after a mini-stroke, as well as details of websites and support groups—enough to keep all six of them busy for a long while. Caleb, Kaya and their children returned home again soon, leaving Henry to take care of Grace in the weeks she had to take it a bit easy.

The children went back to school, and only occasionally came back in their conversations with each other, and with their parents, to the events around Grace's stroke. Grace recovered apparently very well and quickly, but she did heed the advice and for a few months at least, she held back on too strenuous activities. They cancelled all their planned travels as well, with the insurance paying out after a sharp letter from their solicitor.

Chapter 19

The events around Grace's stroke did have another, unexpected, effect on Kaya and Caleb. Reflecting about the events, Kaya realised with considerable surprise that Mr Anand, the consultant, had openly flirted with her, and that she had felt flattered by his interest. She also remembered her irritation at the way Caleb had behaved with the nurse that had discharged Grace. Come to think of it, he had been flirting. She had never attracted flirtatious behaviour from any man since she had met Caleb, fourteen years ago, and had never been flattered by any man's behaviour in the way that she was flattered by Mr Anand's behaviour. She had never seen Caleb behave the way he had with the nurse in the hospital with any other female. Alarm bells were ringing for her.

She took the next opportunity of talking privately with Caleb, a few days later, when he came home from work after the children had gone to bed already. Kaya had prepared some light dinner, and afterwards, on their way to the living room, she said: 'Caleb, I need to talk to you.'

'That sounds serious,' Caleb responded. 'Is Grace alright?'

'Yes, all fine there, children as well,' Kaya reassured him. They sat down.

'I noticed something the other day that makes me concerned. When the consultant told us the news about Grace, he flirted with me, and I liked it. And you flirted with the nurse, and you liked it, and I didn't,' Kaya said.

Caleb was quiet for a moment. 'Yes, I did flirt with the nurse, and I did like it,' Caleb admitted. 'Was it the same for you and the consultant?'

'Yes, it was,' Kaya confirmed. 'I realised later that this was the first time I flirted with someone else, and that I saw you flirting with someone else, since we met. That made me sad, and made me think, and that's why I am raising it now.'

'In other words, what is happening, has been happing, to our relationship, to our marriage?' Caleb concluded.

'I have no doubt in my mind, for myself, that I love you, with all my heart, Caleb,' Kaya stated.

'I have no doubt in my mind that I love you, with all my heart, Kaya,' Caleb assured her.

'And yet there is something wrong, and we have to find out together what it is, and do something about it,' Kaya insisted.

'I agree,' Caleb admitted.

They followed their own thoughts for a while.

'We have worked out our lives so well together, Kaya,' Caleb began again.

Kaya stopped him right there. 'That's it. That's precisely it. It all works perfectly, doesn't it? We have a plan A for everything and plans B and C and D and in many cases even plan E of plan A does not work and so on. We just need to shift from one to the other, without thinking.'

Caleb looked puzzled. 'And you mean there is a problem with that?'

Kaya took this thought further: 'Not in its own right. But all this becomes functional. We talked about being functional in our first meeting, remember?'

Caleb smiled: 'I will never forget our first meeting, Kaya. Yes, I remember us talking about functionality. Everything has become routine, nothing is spontaneous any more, everything is automated, there is, as you say, a plan for every situation in life, at least for everyday life. No immediacy, nothing new, as it was when we had met and got to know each other, nothing new as it was when we had Leah,'

Kaya interrupted: 'And with Evan's birth and his infancy and early childhood we already had routines we could rely on. For example, we know exactly what to do when one of the children gets ill, and we follow that routine without fail. We have much of our daily lives planned-out, day by day.'

'Our love for each other is falling victim to this routine,' Caleb concluded.

Caleb and Kaya decided that it was absolutely worth making a major effort of reviving their marriage. They started with each of them spending a good amount of time writing down the things they loved about each other, and their marriage, and then they shared the lists. They were very long, and only some of the points were on both lists. They made copies of the lists, so that they both had both. They made the effort of setting time aside for each of them to be able to be on their own, and for them to be together on their own also during the day, not only in the evenings when the children were in bed and they were too exhausted to do much anyway and went to bed soon as well. They planned more visits to Grace and Henry, and would invite them more often, and not only them, but other friends and colleagues. Each of them thought about surprises for the other, which needed some effort on their own part. They were also able to foreground and pay special attention to some items on the list of what they liked about each other and their marriage. For example, they made an effort to look smart and sexy, as defined by the other, also when relaxed at home. They went back to their special bench on the promenade more often, after realising with some alarm that they had not been there for several years. They promised not to take each other for granted any more, and they agreed that they would check up on their progress of reviving their marriage, and then ultimately of keeping their marriage lively, on a regular basis, initially once a month, and then, in due course, perhaps three to four times a year.

'I am very glad you noticed this happening and that you did something about it right away,' Caleb thanked Kaya.

They stuck to their plan, and it worked out. They were able to stop the downward spiral they had found themselves in.

Chapter 20

Some years later, when they had said goodnight to the children and they were fast asleep, Caleb and Kaya were just about to settle down for some music when the door-bell rang repeatedly.

'Who this can be,' Kaya wondered, 'so late, and so urgent.'

Caleb went to open the door.

'Open it with the chain on, just in case,' Kaya called after him.

He did so and saw Monica. She was shaking, shivering, pale, her face puffed up from crying, and there were several fresh bruises in her face as well. Seeing the state Monica was in, Caleb called to Kaya: 'Come over here, please Kaya. I think you better help her.' He released the chain and opened the door, Kaya caught Monica, who was swaying with fatigue, and helped her inside, into the kitchen to start with, and eased her on to a chair. Caleb locked the front door and joined them, dimming the light in the kitchen, hoping to make it more comfortable for Monica. He filled a jug with water and poured some into a plastic tumbler, passing it over to Kaya. She offered it to Monica, who drank all of it in almost a single gulp. Caleb refilled the tumbler. None of them had said a word so far.

Now Monica spoke, stifling sobs in between; 'You said I could come if I needed help. It's a long time ago, several years, but I never forgot it. I always thought that things might improve, but they have not. I'm now really fearing for my life, and my sanity, and Peter's life, because if we carry on like this, either he is going to kill me, or I am going to kill him, or one or both of us will be committing suicide.'

'Yes, we, actually, mainly Caleb, feared, at the time, that something like this might be happening, and we did mean it and do mean it that you are welcome here for help,' Kaya assured her. 'Does Peter know you have left, where you have gone?

Monica hesitated. 'I left when he was in his surgery, but he will have found out when he got back in the late afternoon. I did not leave any indication of where I am, and I don't think Peter would be phoning or driving around all the places I could be.'

'OK,' Caleb took over, 'do you think he might become aggressive and violent to us if he found you here?'

'I don't think he would,' Monica sighed, after stifling another wave of sobbing and drinking her third glass of water. 'With others he is really shy, and careful, and afraid, and he has been violent only with me.'

'I think, then,' Kaya continued, looking at Caleb for confirmation, 'that you can stay here for the time being. Caleb, would you mind getting the spare bedroom ready, while I stay with Monica?'

'I agree, and I'll get the room ready for you,' Caleb said. 'You didn't bring any clothes or anything else with you?' With that he went over to the guest bedroom.

'No,' Monica said apologetically.

'No problem,' Kaya comforted her, 'you can have some of my things, they should fit you quite well. Now,' she added, 'let's take a look at your face. Are there any other injuries on your body that you are aware of?

Monica was deeply embarrassed. 'Only old bruises, nothing fresh,' she said very quietly. Kaya looked at her face—from her dentist's medical training, she could establish that while the bruising was considerable, nothing seemed to require immediate medical attention in the hospital's

A&E. She also checked the inside of Monica's mouth and could not find any damage. She would take Monica to her local GP tomorrow for a closer look, but all that was needed for now was to get Monica settled in for as much sleep as possible. Monica has a sandwich to eat, drank some more water, and by that time Caleb had finished preparing the guest bedroom. Kaya found some suitable pyjamas and a set of fresh clothes for Monica to wear the next day, and Monica withdrew for the night. Kaya and Caleb could hear her sobbing for a little while longer, but then she seemed to have fallen asleep. They checked on the children, who had remained undisturbed during all that had happened, and then went to bed themselves, rather quiet and withdrawn, each enclosed in their own thoughts.

A few days later, after they had delivered Monica to the local branch of Refuge and returned home, Caleb phoned Peter, as they had agreed with the counsellor from Respect, the charity helping perpetrators. Fortunately, Peter answered the phone right away. He was surprised to hear Caleb's voice. 'What's up, old friend,' he asked, jovially, 'another medical emergency?'

Caleb's voice sounded pressed and hoarse. 'No actually, Peter, it's about you, actually, and Monica.'

'Oh, I see,' Peter said, dumbfounded. 'How, I mean, what? Why?' he stammered.

'Monica came here a few days ago, after you had beaten her up again. She is now somewhere safe, not with us anymore.' Caleb had to clear his throat repeatedly. 'I don't find this easy, to talk to you at all, I mean,' he explained, 'but I promised Monica to do this. You need help, Peter. I don't know whether your marriage to Monica can be salvaged, but you need help anyway, you cannot go on living with whatever leads you into acts of domestic violence, makes you a wife-beater.'

There was a pause at the other end of the line. Caleb was by now wiping the sweat off his forehead. Kaya, who had been with him, nodded encouragingly.

'I am so sorry, so sorry.' Peter's voice sounded hollow and empty. 'I love Monica, but so many things about her just make me lose my temper, so badly I hit out at her. I don't know what's wrong with me, it's not much fun, I can tell you. Is there help for people like me, or only contempt and prison?' He sounded genuine, not self-pitying.

'You should get in touch with RESPECT, a charity that can get you in touch with local support services. See how you respond to their approach. If that does not do the trick, there are other approaches, and they can guide you there.

After these dramatic events, Kaya and Caleb withdrew from the forefront of the further development of Peter and Monica's relationship—after all, they were not trained counsellors or therapists. Peter and Monica realised that and did not impose themselves on Caleb and Kaya—they were grateful for the help they had offered and kept them informed about developments as a matter of courtesy: they reconciled, but decided, each encouraged by their respective support group, that too much had occurred for them to try to re-establish genuine love and live together again. They divorced, and sought to rebuild their lives independent of each other, with continuing support from the relevant charities and organisations.

Chapter 21

In bringing up their children, Kaya and Caleb placed much emphasis on a balance of arts and science, combined with physical activity. They realised and supported Leah's potential for science, but also nurtured her interest in the arts, taking the children to see live classical music, opera and theatre, and talking about it at home. They realised Evan's strength in drama, but also nurtured his interest in science, by ensuring Evan knew all about, and was able to talk to Leah about her science projects, while also supporting Leah to communicate meaningfully with Evan about all his drama projects.

After completing her secondary education, Leah had left home to study Neuroscience at Cardiff University for a B.Sc., had followed this with a Masters at King's College, and was now embarking on a PhD scholarship at University College London. Evan was just starting his undergraduate studies in Drama at Canterbury Christ Church University. With both children out of the house, Kaya and Caleb took the considerable change in their home life as an opportunity to take stock of their lives, their careers, their relationship and marriage. This happened initially in private, for each in their own thoughts, in their own time, which they had made sure they had available, after Grace's stroke many years ago by now. They noticed this desire for reflection not only in themselves, but also in the other, and were curious about the joint outcome that would reveal itself in due course.

One evening, Caleb had come to a point where he was ready to talk, and what he had to say would be of considerable impact for both. It was a genuine crossroads. 'I would like us to go to our bench tomorrow morning for sunrise, Kaya,' he said, 'would you like that?'

There was no surprise in Kaya's voice when she answered: 'Yes, I'd like that. It might become a long conversation, right? So, we should bring enough to eat and drink to make us comfortable.'

They prepared some provisions that night, then went to bed for the early rise, packed a bag and left in time to reach the bench before sunrise. It was still chilly that early, but they had brought warm clothes to see them through the time until the sunlight brought natural warmth—the weather forecast had been favourable.

'It is strange, the house so empty without the children, even more so now that both have gone than when only Leah had left for her studies,' Kaya started.

'I feel the same,' Caleb agreed. 'It made me think a lot, about me, about my career, about us, about the children. About my parents and yours.'

'I noticed that about you, and I was doing the same,' Kaya mused. 'I have come to a set of far-reaching decisions, Caleb,' she added, 'which will be quite monumental for all of us, I think. And I bet you have arranged this meeting here today because it is the same for you?' Her voice here combined question with statement.

'You are right, or course,' Caleb smiled. 'I think we have been blessed with each other, right from the start and throughout. We have had much happiness and joy together, with our relationship, with our parents and in-laws, respectively, and our wonderful children. There were ups and downs, naturally, we had a lot to work through from our respective pasts, with Sophia and Nathan, but we were always there to support each other. We picked up quickly, after the scare with your mum's stroke, on a low point in our relationship, and we worked hard and together to avert the danger of getting stuck in routine.'

'I agree,' Kaya nodded. 'We were brought together, if you like, to learn those things, how to cope with what Nathan did to me, what you suffered with regard to Sophia, to be there for each other the way we were, to develop a wonderful relationship with our parents and in-laws, and to be given the great honour of bringing up Leah and Evan.'

Caleb took over again but hesitated a little in what he had to say. 'We made mistakes along the way, of course, but where we realised those mistakes, we owned up to them, and put a lot of effort into making up for mistakes and not making them again. We always did the best we could, at all times. Without wanting to doubt, or question, or in any other way reduce the validity and memory of any of this happiness and joy and luck we had, I think, somehow, we have come to the end of what we were meant to do, to tackle, to achieve together.' Caleb ended with a big sigh. The cat was out of the bag.

Kaya sighed as well, not with sadness, but with relief. 'I have been thinking along the same lines as you about all this, over the last few weeks, since Evan left,' she said. 'We said this when we first met: in the past, marriages were probably meant for life, until death do us part, but time is moving much faster, we have, as you said, achieved what we were brought together to achieve, what we, before this incarnation, decided to achieve together. It will be sad to part but staying together now that we have achieved all we wanted to achieve together, would mean blocking our own further spiritual development, blocking us and the other from achieving whatever else we planned to do before we chose this incarnation. It would also block the spiritual development of family members affected by this decision we are about to make, or have made on our own already and are now discussing with the partner, because Leah and Evan, in particular, would also have come to us to be able to address these issues in this life that our separation will mean for them'.

'What we are talking about, then,' Caleb summarised, 'is that we have realised that we have achieved what brought us together as husband and wife, and that we now want to separate to make way for whatever else is due for us?'

'In very sober terms, yes,' Kaya confirmed. 'I said earlier that I have also thought about my career. I want to do a three-year full-time training to become an orthodontist, while carrying on as a regular dentist here with Em, then open an orthodontic wing at Em's practice, or join one of the local orthodontic specialist practices.'

'That sounds like an exciting development of your career, Kaya,' Caleb said warmly. 'In a way, it is a shame that I will not be part of that development as closely as I would have been, were we to have remained husband and wife. But even after we have separated, I guess we will remain very fondly interested in each other's well-being and progress, and will visit, and the children will be visiting, and so on?'

'Yes, of course,' Kaya agreed, and took this further. 'There will be sadness, grief even, at first, even though we both want this turn of events. That is inevitable because we have been together for so long, and so closely. We may also feel at times, at first, or even in years to come, that this development is not fair, but there is, I think, no viable alternative. Staying together for the sake of the past, to perpetuate the past, would only make us unhappy in the long run.'

'I have also had thoughts about my career,' Caleb now told her. 'I feel my professorship, my teaching in higher education, and my research in more and more restricted frameworks, have all run their course. I have had my say. I have been able to have an impact, hopefully a good one, on two to three thousand or more students across the years. I have established a new field within research, developing it from its infancy to a prominent, mainstream place in the research landscape. I can leave that to the next generation to develop further, if they like, or leave it to become an episode of the past. I have had all the administrative or managerial experience I want—I have never aspired to be a full-time Head of Department, or, even higher up, Dean (or assistant or associate Dean), let alone Pro Vice Chancellor or Vice Chancellor—and I have not developed any such aspirations now.'

Kaya had listened intently. 'What do you want to do, then?' she asked.

'I think I will take early retirement, once we have worked out all the logistics of the separation and see what comes my way then.'

At that moment, the sunrise was in its fullest glory, and Kaya and Caleb paused, remembering their first, and their many important visits to this special place, and realising, with a mixture of nostalgia, melancholy, sadness and—excitement that this was likely to be their last visit together, as a couple, to their special bench to experience the sunrise with the view across the bay.

Chapter 22

The announcement of their separation, at the time, had caused quite a stir with Grace and Henry, and with Leah and Evan. They were surprised, stunned, and, above all, had many, many questions, which Kaya and Caleb answered patiently over the weeks. They sold their home, split all the proceeds, agreed on how to divide their joint possessions, and found their own places to live. Kaya enrolled in her studies of orthodontics, while continuing her work in the surgery on a part-time basis. While Kaya was thus busier than ever in terms of her professional life, Caleb went through with his plan to take early retirement and found himself with much more time on his hands than ever before.

Kaya never regretted her decision to embark, quite late in life, relatively speaking, on the new career path of orthodontics. She threw herself into her studies with full energy, juggling her part-time role as conventional dentist in Emily Smithson's surgery with her study commitments in London. Initially, she used her car for the commutes, but found driving in London too straining, and driving to a tube station on the outskirts of London did not save much time, either. After a while, she relied on public transport, becoming quite expert at the intricacies, devoid of any logic, of the advance booking systems. When her graduation approached, Emily added orthodontics to her surgery's official profile, with Kaya initially as the only orthodontist, and relevant technical and nursing support. The new orthodontic branch of the surgery was thus well advertised and marketed. Because of a shortage of orthodontists in her area, which had meant many patients had to travel far to be treated at over-subscribed orthodontic practices, they received plenty of registrations. The investment for new equipment, the dentist to replace Kaya, a new technician, paying for Kaya's tuition fees, and the fees for additional training of existing nurses, was recovered in full already in the first year and returned profit in the years after that. Kaya was very happy with her new role and was very popular with her patients—especially the young ones were keen to get her smiling approval of, and praise for, their efforts at wearing their removable braces, or properly cleaning their teeth underneath permanent braces.

***

Yellow, or better even, golden, had always been Sophia's favourite colour. From an early age, she had loved her mother's amber jewellery, and later discovered tiger's eye. When it was her turn to buy flowers, they were always yellow, and she asked for yellow bedlinen and pyjamas. On a family holiday in Italy, she almost burst into tears, so moved was she when they travelled by train through a beautiful landscape and came across their first vast field of sunflowers in full bloom. Yellow and golden continued to be her favourite colours for clothes, for her cars, for her stationary. In her paintings, yellow and golden dominated, and she was renowned for her skill in depicting even dark topics and themes with an ever-increasing range of shades of yellow and gold, thus adding a dimension of hope where many would not be able to consider the possibility of hope at all.

In moments of despair in her private life, looking at the patterns in the core of the sunflower blossom helped her without fail. The pattern resembled mandalas as she had come across in India, and she realised that the pattern, carried by the colour, combined stillness and unity with purposeful, orderly, dancing activity and movement that radiates powerful, joyful and at the same time gentle and full beauty.

Since Sophia's mother had interfered in her life and tried to bring disharmony into the life of her ex-husband, Caleb, and his then new girlfriend, Kaya, Sophia had withdrawn from Caleb and Kaya's life almost completely. She had resigned her artist-in-residence post at the university department where Caleb taught, returning full-time to her career as a painter, which was thriving then, and had developed to further heights since. She did stay in touch with Kaya's mother, Grace, however, at her own request, and they would meet every two or three years at a convenient café in London, catching up with the latest news about themselves and Caleb and Kaya. In this way, Sophia learnt about the births of Leah and Evan, about their progress in life, about various health scares such as Evan's rickets, or Grace's stroke.

In turn, Grace found out that Sophia got married, but had no children of her own, because she felt that, by approaching her 40s, some years younger than Caleb, she was too old. However, her husband, Lucas, brought two daughters from his first marriage into their new home—he was a widower. After initial problems, because the girls were still grieving for their mother, and not quite ready to accept their father's new wife, Sophia had been able to develop a very strong bond between herself and her new step-daughters, coming to love them like she thought she would have loved her own children. She was happy with her husband, he appreciated her work and supported it fully, allowing, in particular, the freedom and time she needed in her particularly creative phases. Sophia's step-daughters, Charlotte and Jasmine, who had been twelve and fifteen years of age when she got married to their father, completed their school and left home to study: Charlotte was an avid historian, interested especially in the middle ages, and went to study Medieval History at Queen Mary, University of London, followed by an MA in the same field at University of East Anglia. She completed her PhD at Durham University and joined the University of Birmingham as a lecturer. Jasmine, on the other hand, was not as academically minded as her sister. She studied criminology at Loughborough University and moved straight into a career with the police from there, rising to the rank of Detective Superintendent.

Sophia's next meeting with Grace was coming up, almost twenty-four years after they had first met. Grace invited Sophia to her flat, because, by now in her mis-80s, she found it too difficult to walk, or travel by taxi, to a café. Sophia had brought a large bunch of flowers with her, which she presented to Grace as Grace welcomed her in.

'Oh, such nice flowers,' Grace admired, 'Of course yellow, as I expected,' she added with a broad smile. 'Make yourself comfortable in the living room.'

'It's always so good to see you, Grace,' Sophia said. Grace noticed how genuine and open Sophia's voice sounded and was curious to detect the cause for this in the events of Sophia's past few years. On the other hand, she could hardly wait herself to reveal all the news of her own family.

Sophia settled down in a comfortable armchair. 'Is Henry well?' she asked.

'Yes, he is, thank you, Sophia,' Grace responded, having chosen the other armchair opposite Sophia. 'It's quite early in the afternoon, is it all right with you if we wait a little before tea?'

'Yes, of course, Grace,' Sophia smiled. 'So, tell me straight away, what are your news since we last met?'

'OK, it's me to start, as always,' Grace beamed. 'Let's see. Leah started on a PhD at University College London, and Evan started to study drama at Canterbury Christ Church University.'

'They have both left their home, then?' Sophia enquired.

'Yes, they have,' Grace confirmed. 'In more ways than one actually. Because the home they left does not exist anymore.'

'That sounds very mysterious, Grace. You were always great at creating suspense,' Sophia mock-admonished her. 'Come on, then, out with it.'

'Kaya and Caleb separated, they are divorced,' Grace said simply. Seeing Sophia's reaction, she added quickly: 'You turned quite pale, Sophia, dear, are you all right?'

'That was quite a shock, Grace! What happened?'

'Nothing specific, really, as far as I understood from them', Grace explained. 'They felt they had done together what they were brought together to achieve in this life. Now they are free to move on. Kaya did a degree in Orthodontics, and Caleb took early retirement. They separated amicably, they were both hurting in the process, they are still good friends, regularly in touch with each other, and with me. But they sold their house, got rid of loads of stuff through auctions, and have their own, smaller places now. That's it, in a nutshell.'

'Very unexpected. Poor Caleb with his second divorce and left his job. Talking about new beginnings.' After that, Sophia was quiet for a while.

'What are your news then, Sophia,' Grace nudged her gently after a while.

'Quite momentous events as well, I'm afraid.' Sophia paused again. 'And so very sad. Lucas died, quite soon after we last met. A very short illness, pancreatic cancer. He was quite a bit older than me, of course, but still…' Sophia hesitated, trying to stifle her tears.

'Oh no, Sophia,' Grace comforted her, got up and sat in the armchair next to her, taking her hand in hers. 'I am so sorry, I cannot imagine what it feels like. How are you coping, and how are your step-daughters?'

Sophia was clearly moved by Grace's expression of sympathy, and gratefully accepted the love extended to her. 'Settling Lucas's estate, with the help of some solicitors, took a while, and kept me busy. I got very close to Charlotte and Jasmine, as you know, and we have supported each other a lot over the weeks after his passing. But then came the time that is probably worst, when the bustle in the immediate aftermath disappears, and you begin to realise the loss, and the real grief sets in. As you know, I have been prone to be miserable, especially in the years between Caleb and Lucas, and I was, and still am, to be honest, afraid of relapsing into full blast depression, and that because I am older and weaker, I might not be able to pull myself out of that swamp by my own hair, not even through my art practice.'

'I can understand your concerns, Sophia', Grace said warmly. 'At my age, I think occasionally what might happen if Henry died, and believe me, so many of my and his friends and acquaintances are leaving us, I can't avoid thinking about this. At least you have your step-daughters to comfort you.'

'Lucas was sixty-six, not very old for our current times, Grace,' Sophia said, with more than a clear hint of bitterness in her voice. 'And I need to comfort Charlotte and Jasmine possibly much more than I can hope to be comforted by them—after all, Lucas was their father, I was only his second wife.'

Grace was about to interject, but Sophia carried on after a determined glance: 'In a way you are right, though, I have to remain calm and collected for them, and that gives me strength.'

'Good,' Grace assured her. She had developed some further thoughts and was not sure whether to share them with Sophia. Then she decided to do so, if only not to be left with the eternal "what if". She spoke slowly all the same when she addressed Sophia: 'You have known me for the past twenty years or so, Sophia, and there have been several occasions when you were surprised at how adventurous I was. I think I still am'.

Sophia could not help but smile. 'I saw that you were hatching one of your ideas, Grace. Well?'

'It was not too late for Henry and me when we were in our early sixties, and it may not be too late for yourself and Caleb either,' Grace said, bluntly but from the heart.

'You are not one to beat around the bush, are you,' Sophia gasped. 'To be honest, something like that was the first thing I thought earlier when you told me that Caleb and Kaya had separated. I have lived much of my life from the head, not enough from the guts, not enough from intuition, as I probably should have. I channelled all my heart and my intuition into my painting. Getting together with Caleb, and later Lucas, came initially from the head as well, the heart followed suit only in due course, and perhaps not enough in Caleb's case, otherwise I could not have betrayed him. Maybe it's time to at least try to do what is completely devoid of reason or logic, and follow my initial reaction?'

***

After returning home from visiting Grace, Sophia prepared a light dinner for herself, because it was still quite early in the evening, and thought about the unexpected developments of that afternoon, and the important decisions she now had to make. Should she follow her instinct, her intuition, her gut feeling, and explore a future with Caleb? The example of Grace and Henry was promising. The worst-case scenario she could imagine was that Caleb turned her down at the first opportunity. Even if a relationship did not develop from initially rekindling acquaintance, nothing much would be lost, for either of them. How to go about it? Just to turn up at his doorstep was probably too much. Sophia decided to go with a brief, honest email. Their communication before and while they were married had been like that. In an instant, she also decided that in an attempt at a new relationship with Caleb, she would abandon her post-divorce name, Sophia, and re-create herself as Olivia. Olivia searched and found Caleb's email address, and quickly wrote to him, signing "Olivia", then pressed the "send" button, all within a few minutes. Then she took a deep breath, sighed, and left the rest to fate, destiny, God, whatever.

On this day, Caleb woke up early, and, rather than turning around in an attempt to go back to sleep (which was often very successful), he had decided instead to get up. He put on his bathrobe and headed straight to his study and turned on the computer, smiling at his curiosity, burning as ever, to check emails. Usually there was nothing exciting or worth getting up early for, since his retirement, but he was still curious. Today he was therefore quite surprised to find, among messages from the e-lists he still subscribed to, an email from "Olivia", no last name. He opened this email first and was very surprised by its contents.

'Dear Caleb', it read, 'I had tea with your mother this afternoon. She told me that Kaya and you had separated and that you are divorced. I told her that my husband, Lucas, passed away after a short illness about three years ago. Remembering the candour that was key to our relationship in our marriage, I wanted to tell you that I would like to meet with you, to see whether there is the potential for us to make a fresh start with each other. Please let me know what you think. Olivia.'

Not only was Caleb surprised to receive an email from Olivia, and to find out about her husband's death—he was even more surprised when he observed his immediate reaction that she wanted to meet him, and why she wanted to meet him: he felt joy and excitement, and those feelings were like the feelings he remembered he had for, and regarding, Olivia when he had first met her and when they were married. Of course, so many years had passed since, he had been on his own after the divorce first, then had the wonderful years with Kaya, they had Evan and Leah, and even though he and Kaya were now divorced, he still felt very close to her. But although the feelings he realised he still had for Olivia had been sculpted by those experiences, their core was the same as it had been so many years ago. He wrote back immediately, then headed for the bathroom to have his morning shower, followed by breakfast.

After sending the email to Caleb, Olivia found herself quite restless. It was early evening, but she turned off the computer, not ready to read any response from Caleb now, should he send one this evening. She tried to calm herself with music and a favourite film but gave each up quickly. The only respite came from painting. Olivia rushed across to her studio, created a soulful arrangement of light in the large, airy, very uncluttered studio space, and, for the first time in months, selected watercolours to paint with, rather than her usual oils. She painted a sunflower blossom, from memory, starting with the central core, and working her way to the periphery and the blossom's aura. More settled, and well after midnight, she went to bed, and woke up in the late morning, refreshed. Breaking with custom, she did go to her computer and her heart missed a beat or two when she found Caleb's email in the inbox.

'Dear Olivia,' it read, 'Your email surprised me no end. I am so sorry to hear that Lucas passed away. I did not meet him often, but you looked happy with him, and Grace confirmed this impression occasionally over the years. Please accept my most heartfelt condolences. I was sad, in a way, that we did not see more of each other over the past 20 or so years since our memorable reconciliation facilitated by Grace. I also understand the reason why we needed distance. That said, I agree we should find out whether we can indeed, as you put it, make a fresh start. Now retired, I am quite flexible with my time and will be happy to meet. Please suggest date, time and venue. Caleb.'

***

Caleb and Olivia arranged to meet, and after their first meeting, many further meetings followed. In comparison with their own whirl-wind romance when they had first met, so many years ago, and in contrast to the fast pace of the relationships between Caleb and Kaya, and Grace and Henry, Caleb and Olivia now took their time, all the while keeping their eyes open for a different partner. Eventually, however, they made the decision to take their new relationship further—explicitly not as a compromise because they could not find anyone else, let alone better. Their meetings became romantic dates. After many of those, they decided to move in together. Both relished the opportunity of a fresh start, together again, possibly with the prospect of marriage on the horizon. That fresh start was to include "a change of scenery", as they put it, and they leisurely decided, in the end, to move to the seaside on Anglesey. They sold their respective houses and selected one that offered ample opportunity for Olivia to set up her studio without compromise in comparison with the gorgeous London facility she had become used to.

Chapter 23

Caleb and Olivia's Anglesey home also offered several guest bedrooms for a constant stream of visitors. Over the years, Leah and Evan started their own families, as did Olivia's step-daughters, Charlotte and Jasmine, and had children of their own in due course. Kaya got married again, and her husband, Adam, had two sons from his first marriage. Grace and Henry loved visiting their many children and grandchildren or inviting them to their London flat. Soon after returning from a trip to Anglesey, on a beautiful spring morning, Grace and Henry settled comfortably in their living room after breakfast. Grace had noticed that Henry was unusually withdrawn and quiet that morning. Now she looked at him quizzically, and asked: 'What's up'?

'I've been somewhat quiet, haven't I?' Henry responded. He knew very well why, but found it difficult, for once, to share it with Grace—he was afraid of seeing her worried or upset. But now that she had asked, there was no way out—he would not start now to tell her anything but the truth. That had been his principle all his life, with Imogen, and with Grace, and with Caleb. 'I was awake a lot during the night. I hope I didn't wake you up, I was probably quite restless, moving around?'

'Not at all, dear,' Grace assured him.

'Anyway, I was thinking about my life, childhood, my time with Imogen, my time after that, our time together. I thought that I was blessed, really, with this life, and that I tried to give back for that blessing, to all my pupils, colleagues, Imogen, Caleb, you, and the grandchildren. I have done so much, been so happy, really, for most of my life, seen so much. And now...' he hesitated.

'Now you have come to a natural ending point, is that what you are trying to say?' Grace's words came very spontaneously, and she was surprised at them herself after she had uttered them. Surprised and a little shocked, in the aftermath of the utterance, at its meaning and implication.

Henry stared at her, equally surprised, and relieved. 'Yes, Grace, I feel, in a very strange way, that I have come to near the end of a very long arch, and that I am ready, for the final time in this life, to let go.'

'To let go of this life, you mean,' Grace prompted again.

'Yes,' Henry said, simply.

'No wonder you were so quiet this morning,' Grace sighed. She took Henry's hands in hers. 'I have been thinking about age, and dying, on a number of occasions over the last few years myself, of course, although we have never talked about it together. I had always hoped that I would not be the first one to have to go, so that you could be spared having to go through again what you had to endure after Imogen's death. At the same time, I dreaded, naturally, losing you. Then I left it all to the creator, fate, whatever you want to call it. It's just too much for me to be thinking about, it's beyond our control. Whenever you feel that it is time for you to move on, please do not try to stop that from happening because of me. Nothing ever happens in our lives that we cannot cope with, ultimately, and even if only just about.'

'You are amazing and wonderful, Grace,' Henry said, looking at her very warmly, 'and I love you so very, very much'.

After that, they were quiet, holding hands, looking at each other lovingly. After a while, Grace noticed that Henry's grip got less firm. He turned his head to look straight ahead. A deep sigh of satisfaction raised and lowered his chest. His face seemed to lose many of its familiar wrinkles in a broad smile in response to something he seemed to be seeing at some distance in the room. The expression on Henry's face reminded Grace of the expression on Evan's face, in particular, when he was a baby. Briefly, his grasp of her hand firmed, then relaxed again. Briefly, he turned his head back to her, and regarded her with an expression of total, unconditional love, then his gaze returned to his vision at the other side of the room. His breathing had become shallow. He inhaled deeply, freely, one last time, then life had left his body.

Grace remained with him, in silence, for a long time. She felt the peace that had been characteristic of the moments before, and the moment of, his death. She was no longer afraid of death, anyone's death, her own death. Eventually, she took her hand away from his, and closed his eyes. She realised then that she was quite shaky after all. The telephone was in reach, and she dialled Kaya's number. When she heard her daughter's voice, she had to pause.

'Hello, darling, it's mum,' she said. 'I hope I am not disturbing?'

'Never, mum!', Kaya laughed, but stopped herself quickly. 'You sound strange—are you alright?'

'I am, yes, or rather, no, I'm not—I really don't know anything anymore at the moment.'

She paused again, and Kaya knew her well enough not to interrupt her at that point.

'No other way of saying it, love: Henry just died.'

When Grace phoned Kaya, she was assuming she was on her own at home. Nothing was further from the truth, however. Unexpectedly, and for a whole range of different reasons, Caleb, their children and Olivia had all come for an impromptu breakfast. When Kaya had answered the phone, they continued their conversations at slightly reduced volume, both to allow Kaya to hear the caller properly, and to be able to eavesdrop out of curiosity. Thus, they were all aware, and immediately stopped their conversations in alarm when Kaya had suddenly turned very pale and slumped into the chair by the phone.

'Oh my God', they heard her say. 'Oh my God! Oh no! So suddenly. Oh mum, I am so sorry, so sorry, that's awful. How are you? Silly question, sorry, but still.'

They saw that Kaya was too involved in her conversation to be able to share any news with them now.

After a while, Kaya said: 'I see, thank you. Leah and Evan, Caleb and Olivia are all here, as it happens. I will briefly tell them all, then you can talk to Caleb and the others, and then we will get ready to come over to help you with all the formalities. Hold on.'

Kaya put the receiver to one side and turned to the others. Having had her back to them so far, she now saw their concerned faces. 'Very, very sad news for the family, I'm afraid', she said, 'That was Grace. Henry died this morning, peacefully, sitting in the armchair next to her, they held hands, and he was smiling at something in the distance, just like Leah and Evan did when they were babies.' She moved over and hugged Caleb first: 'I am so sorry, Caleb'. Then she moved on to hug all the others as well.

Caleb, then Leah and Evan, then Olivia, took turns to talk to Grace, who repeated the details of Henry's last moments to each in turn—doing so, she realised, comforted her. Caleb and Kaya travelled to London to take care of the formalities, while the others joined them only for the funeral a week later. At Henry's request, he was cremated and Grace, accompanied by the rest of the family, scattered the ashes into the ocean near the bench with the view across the bay where he had proposed to Grace so many years ago, and which also held such special memories for Kaya and Caleb.

THE END

BIBLIOGRAPHY

American Psychiatric Association: Diagnostic and Statistical Manual of Mental Disorders, Fifth Edition 2013. Arlington VA, American Psychiatric Association.

Anders, Sonja. 2008. Mitte – Rampe – vorn: Jedem sein Regietheater. Über Zuschauerreaktionen auf Thalheimer-Inszenierungen. In *Regietheater! Wie sich über Inszenierungen streiten last*, edited by Ortrud Gutjahr, 115-124. Würzburg: Königshausen.

Anderson, Rosemarie. 1998. Intuitive inquiry: A transpersonal approach. In *Transpersonal research methods for the social sciences: Honoring human experience*, edited by William Braud & Rpsemarie Anderson, 69 - 94. Thousand Oaks, CA: Sage Publications.

Anderson, Rosemarie & William Braud. 2011. *Transforming Self and Others Through Research: Transpersonal Research Methods and Skills for the Human Sciences and Humanities*. Albany: SUNY Press.

Apostolopoulos, John G., Philip A. Chou, Bruce Culbertson, Ton Kalker, Mitchell D. Trott, and Susie Wee. 2012. The Road to Immersive Communication. *Proceedings of the IEEE* 100 (4): 974-990.

Ardelt, Monika. 2009. How Similar are Wise Men and Women? A Comparison Across Two Age Cohort's. *Research in Human Development* 6 (1): 9-26.

Ardelt, Monika, Scott D. Landes, Kathryn R. Gerlach, and Leah Polkowski Fox. 2013. Rediscovering internal strengths of the aged: the beneficial impact of wisdom, mastery, purpose in life, and spirituality on ageing well. In *Positive psychology: advances in understanding adult motivation*, edited by Jan Sinnott, 97-119. New York: Springer.

Arlin, P.K. 1990. Wisdom: The art of problem finding. In *Wisdom: its nature, origins, and development*, edited by Robert J. Sternberg, 230-243. Cambridge: Cambridge University Press.

Arseneault, Michel. 2007. Solidarity of the Shaken. *The Walrus.* December/ January. Accessed July 5, 2016. http://www.walrusmagazine.com/articles/2007.01-art-wadji-mouawad-solidarity-of-the shaken/1/.

Atkinson, Paul, Richard Watermeyer & Sara Delamont. 2013. Expertise, authority and embodied pedagogy: operatic masterclasses. *British Journal of Sociology of Education* 34 (4): 487-503.

Auslander, Philip. 2008. *Liveness: Performance in a Mediatized Culture*, 2nd edition. London: Routledge.

—. 2012. Digital Liveness: A Historico-Philosophical Perspective. *PAJ: A Journal of Performance and Art* 34 (3): 6.

Bachelard, Gaston. 1983. *Water and Dreams: An Essay on the Imagination of Matter*. Dallas: The Pegasus Foundation.

—. 1994. *The Poetics of Space*. Boston: Beacon Press.

Bærenholdt, Jørgen Ole, Jonathan Everts, Brynhild Granås, Nicky Gregson & Ruth L. Healey. 2010. Performing Academic Practice: Using the Master Class to Build Postgraduate Discursive Competences. Journal of Geography in Higher Education 34 (2): 283-298. Accessed February 21, 2018.
http://dro.dur.ac.uk/10408/1/10408.pdf

Bakker, Arnold B. 2005. Flow among teachers and their students: The crossover of peak experiences. *Journal of Vocational Behaviour* 66: 26-44.

Bakhshi, Hasan and David Throsby. 2014. Digital complements or substitutes? A quasi-field experiment from the Royal National Theatre *Journal of Cultural Economics* 38: 1–8.

Balme, Christopher. 2008. Werktreue. Aufstieg und Niedergang eines fundamentalistischen Begriffs. In *Regietheater! Wie sich über Inszenierungen streiten last*, edited by Gertrud Gutjahr, 43-52. Würzburg: Königshausen.

Baltes, Paul, and Jacqui Smith. 1990. Toward a psychology of wisdom and its ontogenesis. In *Wisdom: its nature, origins, and development*, edited by Robert J. Sternberg, 87-120. Cambridge: Cambridge University Press.

Banks, Martin S, Jenny C.A. Read, Robert S. Allinson, and Simon J. Watt. 2012. *Stereoscopy* and the Human Visual System. *SMPTE Motion Imaging Journal* 121 (4): 24-43.

Barker, Martin. *Crash*, theatre audiences, and the idea of 'liveness,'. *Studies in Theatre and Performance* 23 (1).

—. 2013. *Live at Your Local Cinema: The Remarkable Rise of Livecasting*. Basingstoke: Palgrave Pivot.

Baumgartner, Aurelia. 2013. Interview by Daniel Meyer-Dinkgräfe, 14 December, Starnberg, in person.

—. 2016. 'Catch me if you can!' –Eurydice 2012 Reloaded: Notes on the Performance. In *Consciousness, Theatre, Literature and the Arts 2015*, edited by Daniel Meyer-Dinkgräfe, 1-16. Newcastle: Cambridge Scholars Publishing.

Benedict, David. 2013. London Legit Review: 'Much Ado about Nothing'. *Variety*, September 20. Accessed August 7, 2016.
http://variety.com/2013/legit/reviews/london-legit-reviewmuch-ado-about-nothing-1200654547/

Berendt, Joachim-Ernst. 1987. *Nada Brahma: Music and the Landscape of Consciousness*. Rochester: Destiny.

Beyer, Barbara (ed.) 2007. *Warum Oper? Gespräche mit Opernregisseuren*. Berlin: Alexander.

Biasutti, Michele. 2012. Orchestra rehearsal strategies: Conductor and performer views; *Musicae Scientiae* 17(1): 57-71.

Billington, Michael. 1983. Review of *Not About* Heroes. *The* Guardian, reprinted in *London Theatre Record* III:7, 242.

—. 2008. Review of *Scarborough*. *The Guardian*, 13 February. Accessed August 16, 2015.
http://www.theguardian.com/stage/2008/feb/13/theatre.

—. 2013. Review, *Much Ado About Nothing*. In *The Guardian*, September 20. Accessed August 7, 2016.
https://www.theguardian.com/culture/2013/sep/20/much-ado-about-nothingreview-rylance.

Binder, Hans. 2012. Personal communication, Email.

Bordo, Susan. 2003 *Unbearable Weight: Feminism, Western Culture and the Body*. Berkeley: University of California Press.

Boyko-Head, Christine. 2015. Email correspondence with the author, 3 February.

Brandt, Keri. 2004. A language of their own. An interactionist approach to human-horse communication. *Society and Animals* 12(4): 299–316.

Brask, Per. 2015. Email correspondence with the author, 2 February.

Braud, William. & Anderson, Rosemarie. 1998. *Transpersonal Research Methods for the Social Sciences*. London: Sage.

Briegleb, Till. Wer anständiges Theater will, soll ins Kino gehen. Ein Plädoyer für die komplexe Narration. In *Regietheater! Wie sich über Inszenierungen streiten last*, edited by Ortrud Gutjahr, 81-92. Würzburg: Königshausen.

Britain's Got Talent (2014, United Kingdom: ITV)

Brockmann, Sigi. 2012. Minden: Tristan und Isolde—Premiere. *Der neue Merker*. Accessed September 16, 2012.
http://www.der-neue-merker.eu/minden-tristan-und-isolde-premiere

Brook, Peter. 1972. *The Empty Space*. Harmondsworth: Penguin.

Brown, Peter. 2013. Review, *Much Ado About Nothing. London Theatre*, September 19. Accessed August 7, 2016
https://www.londontheatre.co.uk/reviews/much-ado-about-nothing-5

Brug, Manfred. 2012. Liebestod im Lippischen. *Die Welt*. 12 September. Accessed September 16, 2012. http://www.welt.de/kultur/musik/article109156791/Liebestod-im-Lippischen.html.

Büning, Eleonore. 2012. Hier weht Bayreuths Fahne auf dem Dach. *Frankfurter Allgemeine Zeitung* 11 September. Accessed September 16, 2012. http://www.faz.net/aktuell/feuilleton/buehne-und-konzert/richard-wagner-in-minden-hier-weht-bayreuths-fahne-auf-dem-dach-11885449.html

Bundy, Penny, Kate Donelan, Robyn Ewing, Josephine Fleming, Madonna Stinson, and Meg Upton. 2012. Talking about Liveness: Responses of Young People in the Theatrespace Project. *NJ: DramaAustralia Journal* 36.

Burton-Hill, Clemncy. 2014. What does a conductor actually do?" BBC Culture, 31 October. Accessed September 13, 2014. http://www.bbc.co.uk/culture/story/20141029-what-do-conductors-actually-do

Care Services Improvement Partnership (CSIP), Royal College of Psychiatrists (RCPsych) and Social Care Institute for Excellence (SCIE), 2007. Accessed September 13, 2014. http://www.scie.org.uk/publications/positionpapers/pp08.pdf,

Carlson, Marvin (2007), "I am not an animal". Jan Fabre's *Parrots and Guinea Pigs*, *The Drama Review*, 51(1): 166–69.

Chalmers, David. 1996. *The Conscious Mind: In Search of a Fundamental Theory*. Oxford: OUP.

Chalquist, Craig. N.d. A Glossary of Jungian Terms. Accessed September 13, 2014. http://www.terrapsych.com/jungdefs.html.

Chaudhuri, Una. 2003. Animal geographies, zooesis and the space of modern drama. *Modern Drama*, 46 (4): 646–62.

—. 2007. (De-) facing the animals, zooesis and performance. *The Drama Review* 51 (1): 8–20.

Clapp, Susannah. 2015. The Hard Problem review — Tom Stoppard dodges the big question. *Observer,* 1 February. Accessed July 24, 2015. https://www.theguardian.com/stage/2015/feb/01/the-hard-problem-tom-stoppard-review-dodges-big-question

Clements, Jennifer. 2004. Organic inquiry: toward research in partnership with spirit. *Journal of Transpersonal Psychology* 36 (1): 26-49.

Coghlan, Alexandra. 2013. Review, *Much Ado About Nothing*. In *The arts desk.com*, September 20. A accessed August 7, 2016. http://www.theartsdesk.com/theatre/much-ado-about-nothing-oldvic.

Cook, Nicholas. 1998. *Analysing Musical Multimedia*. Oxford: Oxford University Press.

Coveney, Michael. 2013. Review, *Much Ado About Nothing*. In *The Stage*, September 20. Accessed August 7, 2016. https://www.thestage.co.uk/reviews/2013/much-ado-about-nothing-review-atold-vic-london/.

Creech, Andrea, Helena Gaunt, Sue Hallam, Linnhe Robertson. 2009. Conservatoire students' Perceptions of Masterclasses. *British Journal of Music Education* 26 (3): 315-331. http://eprints.ioe.ac.uk/6276/1/Creech2009Conservatoire315.pdf

Csikzentmihalyi, Mihaly. 1993. *The evolving self: A psychology for the third millennium*. New York: Harper Collins.

Darwin, Charles. 1859. *On the Origin of Species*. London: John Murray.

Davis, Andrew. 2010. *Il Trittico, Turandot, and Puccini's Late Style*. Bloomington: Indiana University Press.

Dawkins, Richard. (1976) 2006. *The Selfish Gene*. Oxford: OUP.

de Waal, Frans. 1999. Anthropomorphism and Anthropodenial: Consistency in our Thinking aboutHumans and Other Animals. *Philosophical Topics* 27(1): 255-280.

—. 2013. *The Bonobo and the Atheist: In Search of Humanism Among the Primates*. New York: Norton.

Dewey, John. 1934. Art as Experience. New York: Pedigree.

Dittmann-Kohli, Freya and Paul Baltes. 1990. Toward a neofunctionalist conception of adult intellectual development: wisdom as a prototypical case of intellectual growth. In *Higher stages of human development. Perspectives on adult growth,* eds. Charles N. Alexander and Ellen J Langer. New York: Oxford University Press.

Dixon, Steve. 2007. *Digital Performance*. Cambridge, Mass.: MIT Press.

Dixson, B.J., A.F. Dixson, B. Morgan, and M.J. Anderson. 2007. Human physique and sexual attractiveness: sexual preferences of men and women in Bakossiland, Cameroon. *Archives of Sexual Behaviour* 36 (3): 369-375.

Dolan, Jill. 2005. *Utopia and Performance: Finding Hope at the Theater*. Ann Arbor: University of Michigan Press

Dombek, Kristin.(2007. Murder in the theme park: Evangelical animals and the end of the world. *The Drama Review*, 51 (1): 138–53.

Duffie, Bruce. 2002. Conversation Piece: Conductor Yakov Kreizberg. *Opera Journal* 35 (2-3): 29-46.

—. 2008. Conversation Piece: Conductor Antonio Pappano. *Opera Journal* 41 (3-4): 27-45.

Edge, Simon. 2013. Review, *Much Ado about Nothing*. In *Sunday Express*, September 19. Accessed August 7, 2016. http://www.express.co.uk/entertainment/theatre/430755/Theatre-review-MuchAdo-About-Nothing-Old-Vic-Theatre-London.

Evans, Fiona. 2008. *Scarborough*, London: Nick Hern.

Euripides. 2008. *The Trojan Women and other Plays*, Oxford: Oxford University Press.

Farrelly, Nicholas. 2016. Being Thai: A Narrow Identity in a Wide World. *Southeast Asian Affairs*: 331-343.

Fischer-Lichte, Erika. 1989. Das Theater auf der Suche nach einer Universalsprache. Forum Modernes Theater 4(2):115-21.

Fisher, Ronald A. 1930. *The Genetical Theory of Natural Selection*. Oxford: Clarendon Press.

Flack, Jessica C. and Frans de Waal. 2002. Any Animal Whatever: Darwinian Building Blocks of Morality in Monkeys and Apes. In *Evolutionary Origins of Morality: Cross-Disciplinary Perspectives*. Edited by Leonard D. Katz, 1-29. Thorverton: Imprint Academic

Gabrielsson, Alf. 2010. Strong Experiences with Music. In *Handbook of Music and Emotion. Theory, Research, Applications*, edited by Patrick N Juslin and John A Sloboda, 547-574. Oxford: Oxford University Press.

Galtsin, Dmitry. 2015. The Divine Feminine in the Silver Age of Russian Culture and Beyond: Vladimir Soloviev, Vasily Rozanov and Dmitry Merezhkovsky. *The Pomegranate* 17 (1-2): 14-50.

Ghosh, Manomohan. editor and translator, 1950. *The Natyasastra. A Treatise on Hindu Dramaturgy and Histrionics*. Calcutta: The Royal Asiatic Society of Bengal.

Goodall, Jane. 1986. *The Chimpanzees of Gombe: Patterns of Behavior*. Cambridge: Harvard UP.

Gorny, Christine. 2015. Theater Bremen: Verbrennungen. *Radio Bremen, 2*8 September. Accessed July 5, 2016. http://www.radiobremen.de/kultur/theater/verbrennungen104.html

Grassby, Paul. 2013. Interviewed by Daniel Meyer-Dinkgräfe, unpublished, 14 October.

Griglio, Gianmaria. 2013. Interview by author, e-mail, July 14.

Groenewold, Anke. 2012. Ekstatische Reise: Ein Erlebnis: Richard Wagners "Tristan und Isolde" in Stadttheater Minden. *Neue Westfälische Zeitung*, 10 September. Accessed 8 November 2012 http://www.nw-news.de/owl/kultur/7022790_Ekstatische_Reise.html.

Gründgens, Gustaf. 1963. *Wirklichkeit des Theaters*. Frankfurt/Main: Suhrkamp.

Gutjahr, Ortrud (ed). 2008. *Regietheater! Wie sich über Inszenierungen streiten last.* Würzburg: Königshausen.

Haig, David. 1995. Prenatal Power Plays. *Natural History* 104 (12): 39.

Haldane, J.B.S. 1932. *The Causes of Evolution.* Longmans, Green & Co.

Hamilton, W.D. 1964. The Genetic Evolution of Social Behavior II. *Journal of Theoretical Biology* 7: 17-52.

Hammer, Anita. 2007. Exploring Ritual Dynamics by Means of Fiction: The Non-Ethics of the Inbetween. In *Consciousness, Literature and the Arts 2007,* edited by Daniel Meyer-Dinkgräfe, 134-155. Newcastle: Cambridge Scholars Publishing.

—. 2008. Theatre as Event of Material Imagination Materialized. *Consciousness, Literature and the Arts* 9 (3).

—. 2010. *Between Play and Prayer: The Variety of Theatricals in Spiritual Performance.* Amsterdam: Rodopi.

James, William. 2002. *The Varieties of Religious Experience.* London: Routledge.

Hanken, Ingrid Maria and Marion Long. *Master classes – What do they offer?* Oslo: NMH-publikasjoner 2012:8. https://brage.bibsys.no/xmlui/bitstream/handle/11250/172653/Hanken_Long_2012.pdf?sequence=1&isAllowed=y

Hatten, Robert. 1990. Pluralism of Theatrical Genre and Musical Style in Henze's We Come to the River. *Perspectives of New Music* 28 (2): 292–311.

Healey, Jennifer. 2014. *The Nether,* London: Faber and Faber.

Heeg, Günther. Die Zeitgenossenschaft des Theaters. In *Regietheater! Wie sich über Inszenierungen streiten last,* edited by Ortrud Gutjahr, 29-42. Würzburg: Königshausen.

Heibach, Christiane. 2012. Einleitung. In *Atmosphären: Dimensionen eines diffusen Phänomens,* edited by Christiane Heibach, 9-24. München: Wilhelm Fink.

Helming, Christian. 2012. Premiere für 'Tristan und Isolde': Kammerspiel und Sinnenrausch. *Mindener Tageblatt.* 10 September. Accessed 16 September 2012. http://www.mt-online.de/start/video/lokale_videos/7031059_Premiere_fuer_Tristan_und_Isolde_Kammerspiel_und_Sinnenrausch.html.

Hemming, Sarah. 2013. Review, *Much Ado About Nothing.* In *Financial Times,* September 22. Accessed August 7, 2016. http://www.ft.com/cms/s/2/2fc5a128-21ea-11e3-bb64-00144feab7de.html#axzz2fv84qFf7.

Hiß, Guido. 2005. *Synthetische Visionen: Theater als Gesamtkunstwerk von 1800 bis 2000.* München: Epodium.

Hofmann, Gert and Snježana Zorić (eds.). 2017. *Presence of the Body: Awareness in and beyond Experience.* Leiden: Brill, 2017.

Howard, Kathryn M. 2009. 'When meeting *Khun* teacher, each time we should pay respect': Standardizing respect in a Northern Thai classroom., *Linguistics and Education* 20 (3): 254-272.

Hytner, Nicholas. 2015. Tom Stoppard and Nicholas Hytner on *The Hard Problem.* Video. Accessed July 24. http://www.nationaltheatre.org.uk/video/tom-stoppard-and-nicholas-hytner-on-the-hard-problem.

Istel, John. 2005. Minor Offenses. *American Theatre* 22 (8):114-120.

Julien, Martin. 2015. Email correspondence with the author, 2 February.

Jung, Carl Gustav. 1969. *Psykens Verden.* Oslo: Cappelen.

—. 1964a. *Man and His Symbols.* London: Aldus Books.

—. 1964b. *The Archetypes and the Collective Unconscious.* Bollingen Series XX. Princeton: Princeton University Press.

Kaiser, Joachim, Ulrich Khuon, Peter Kümmel, Lars-Ole Walburg, Manfred Osten. 2010. *Regietheater – Theaterregie. Zur Lage des deutschen Theaters.* Berlin: Theater der Zeit.

Kallio, Eeva. 2015. From causal thinking to wisdom and spirituality. *Approaching Religion* 5 (2): 27-39.

Kauffmann, Bernd. 2010. *Regietheater—Theaterregie: Zur Lage des deutschen Theaters.* Berlin: Theater der Zeit.

Khodyakov, Dmitry. 2014. Getting in tune: A qualitative analysis of guest conductor–musicians relationships in symphony orchestras. *Poetics* 44: 64-83.

Khuon, Ulrich. 2008. Abhängigkeiten im Regietheater: Über Regisseure, Schauspieler und theatralische Lügen. In *Regietheater! Wie sich über Inszenierungen streiten last,* edited by Ortrud Gutjahr, 53-60. Würzburg: Königshausen.

Kitajenko, Dimitrij. 2015. There is always part of a mystery. ICMA, Interviews. 9 March. Accessed February 21, 2018. http://www.icma-info.com/dmitrij-kitajenko-always-part-mystery/.

Klonovsky, Michael. N.d. Herunter, Herunter. Accessed 8 November 2012 http://www.michael-klonovsky.de/content/view/104/42/.

Koch, Ursula. 2012a. Zuschauer sollen mitleben und mitleiden. *Mindener Tageblatt.* 21 April, 21. Accessed September 16, 2012. http://www.mt-online.de/lokales/kultur/6621513_Tristan_und_Isolde_-_Zuschauer_sollen_mitleben_und_mitleiden.html

—. 2012b. Erste Tuchfühlung mit der Mindener Bühne. *Mindener Tageblatt* 4 August 2012, p. 27. Accessed September 16, 2012.

http://www.mt-online.de/lokales/kultur/6930162_Proben_zu_der_
Eigenproduktion_Tristan_und_Isolde_starten.html.

Königsdorf, Jörg. 2008. Quotendenken und Entdeckerlust – Im Gespräch
mit Kirsten Harms. *Classic-Card.* November. Accessed September 15,
2012). http://www.classiccard.de/de_DE/home/interview/78422/5.

Koivunen, Niina, and Grete Wennes. 2011. Show us the sound! Aesthetic
leadership of symphony orchestra conductors. *Leadership* 71 (1): 51-
71.

Konwitschny, Peter. 2007. Wir bauen die Katastrophen nach. In 2007.
Warum Oper? Gespräche mit Opernregisseuren, edited by Barbara
Beyer, 21-40. Berlin: Alexander.

Kropotkin, Peter. 1902. *Mutual Aid.* London: William Heinemann.

Ladkin, Donna. 2008. Leading beautifully: How mastery, congruence and
form create the aesthetic of embodied leadership practice. *Leadership
Quarterly* 19(1): 31–41.

Lalli, Richard. 2004. Master Plan. *Opera News* 69(1): 24-26.

Lappin, Graham. 2013. Interviewed by Daniel Meyer-Dinkgräfe,
unpublished, 14 October..

Law, K.S., Wong, C.S., & Song, L.J. 2004. The construct and criterion
validity of emotional intelligence and its potential utility for
management studies. *Journal of Applied Psychology* 89 (3): 483-496.

Lee, Sulim, Soyoung Choun, Carolyn M. Aldwin, Michael R. Levenson.
2015. CrossCultural Comparison of Self-Transcendent Wisdom
Between the United States and Korea. *J Cross Cult Gerontol* 30:143–
161.

Letts, Quentin. 2013. Review, *Much Ado About Nothing.* In *Daily Mail*,
September 20. Accessed August 7, 2016.
http://www.dailymail.co.uk/tvshowbiz/article-2426161/QUENTIN-
LETTS-Firstnight-review-Much-Ado-About-Nothing.html

Long, Marion, Susan Hallam, Andrea Creech, Helena Gaunt, Linnhe
Robertson. 2011. Do prior experience, gender, or level of study
influence music students' perspectives on master classes? *Psychology
of Music* 40(6): 683 – 699.

Long, Marion, Andrea Creech, Helena Gaunt, Susan Hallam, Linnhe
Robertson. 2012. Blast from the past: Conservatoire students'
experiences and perceptions of public master classes. *Musicae
Scientiae* 16 (3): 286 – 306.

MacDonald, Heather. 2007. The Abduction of Opera. *City Journal.*
Summer. Accessed September 16, 2012.
http://www.city-journal.org/html/17_3_urbanities-regietheater.html.

—. 2011. Regietheater Takes Another Scalp. *City Journal*. 24 August. Accessed September 16, 2012. http://www.city-journal.org/2011/bc0824hm.html.

MacDonald, Stephen. 1983. *Not about Heroes*. London: Faber and Faber.

Macfadden, Wayne. 2013. Interviewed by Daniel Meyer-Dinkgräfe, unpublished, 17 October.

Malekin, Peter and Yarrow, Ralph. 1997. *Consciousness, Literature and Theatre: Theory and Beyond*. London/New York: Macmillan/St. Martin's Press.

Mangan, Michael. 2015. Email correspondence with the author, 5 February.

Mangan, Timothy. 2010. Ambushed by Regietheater 'Fidelio', St.Clair quits Berlin. *The Orange County Register*. 13 May. Accessed September 15, 2012. http://artsblog.ocregister.com/2010/05/13/ambushed-by-regietheater-fidelio-st-clair-quits-berlin/29309/.

Mangelsdorf, Marion. 2013. 'Liebesgeflüster' zwischen Menschen und Pferden – Möglichkeiten und Grenzen speziesüberschreitender Emotionalität', *Tierstudien*, 3, n.p.

Marcus, Paul and Gabriela Marcus. 2011.. *Theater as life: practical wisdom drawn from great acting teachers, actors and actresses*. Milwaukee, WI: Marquette University Press.

Marjanic, Suzana. 2010. The zoo stage as another ethical misfiring: The spectacle of the animal victim in the name of art. *Performance Research* 15 (2): 74–79.

Marotto, Mark, Johan Roos and Bart Victor. 2007. Collective Virtuosity in Organizations: A Study of Peak Performance in an Orchestra. *Journal of Management Studies* 44 (3): 388-413.

Maslow, Abraham. 1968. *Towards a Psychology of Being*. New York: Van Nostrand.

The Masterclass Media Foundation. 2015. Haitink: Conducting And The Importance of Eye-contact. Youtube, 22 July. Accessed February 21, 2018. https://www.youtube.com/watch?v=idnY8DOCpTw.

McCannon, John. 2004. Passageways to Wisdom: Nicholas Roerich, the Dramas of Maurice Maeterlinck, and Symbols of Spiritual Enlightenment. *The Russian Review* 64 (July): 449-78

McConachie, Bruce and F. Elizabeth Hart, eds. 2006. *Performance and Cognition: Theatre Studies and the Cognitive Turn*. London: Routledge.

McDonagh, Martin. 2003. *The Pillowman*, London: Faber and Faber.

McGinn, Colin. 1999. Consciousness and Space. In *Explaining Consciousness: The Hard Problem*, edited by Jonathan Shear. Cambridge, Mass: MIT Press.

McNiff, S. 1998. *Art-based Research*. London & Philadelphia: Jessica Kingsley.

Meacham, J.A. 1990. The loss of wisdom. In *Wisdom: its nature, origins, and development*, edited by Robert J. Sternberg, 181-211. Cambridge: Cambridge University Press.

Melrose, Susan. 2013. Email to e-list of SCUDD (Standing conference of university drama departments). 21 March.

Mental Health Foundation, 2014. Accessed September 13, 2014. http://www.mentalhealth.org.uk/help-information/mental-health-a-z/R/recovery/,

Meyer, Leonard B. 1989. *Style and Music: Theory, History, Ideology*. Philadelphia: University of Pennsylvania Press.

Meyer-Dinkgräfe, Daniel. 2005. *Theatre and Consciousness: Explanatory Scope and Future Potential*. Bristol: Intellect.

—. 2006a. The Spaces of Consciousness: New Possibilities for Contemporary Theatre. In *Mapping Uncertain Territories: Space and Place in Contemporary Theatre and Drama*, edited by Thomas Rommel and Mark Schreiber, 149-158. Trier: Wissenschaftlicher Verlag Trier.

—. 2006b. Cold Dark Soft Matter Research and Atmosphere in the Theatre. *Body Space Technology* 6. Accessed August 7, 2016. http://people.brunel.ac.u k/bst/vol0601/home.html.

—. 2013a. *Theatre, Opera and Consciousness: History and Current Debates*. Amsterdam: Rodopi.

—. 2013b. *Observing Theatre: Spirituality and Subjectivity in the Performing Arts*. Amsterdam: Rodopi.

—. 2014. Dancing horses and reflecting humans. *Choreographic Practices*, 5 (2): 241–57.

—. 2016. Holistic experience of opera and the International Opera Theater (IOT). *Studies in Spirituality* 26: 373-392.

—. 2017. Towards a Theatre of the Heart. *Annals of the University of Bucharest: Philosophy Series* 66 (1): 199-221.

Mills, Daniel. 2013. Conversation with Daniel Meyer-Dinkgräfe and Aurelia Baumgartner, Skype, 29 August.

Moss, Jane. 2001. The Drama of Survival: Staging Post-traumatic Memory in Plays by Lebanese-Québecois Dramatists. *Theatre Research in Canada* 22 (2): 173-90.

Mouawad, Wajdi. 2009. *Le Sang des promesses*. Montreal: Leméac.

—. 2005. *Scorched*. Trans. Gaboriau, Linda. Toronto: Playwrights Canada.

Moustakas, C. 1990. *Heuristic Research: Design, Methodology and Applications*. London: Sage.

Myskja, Audun. 2014-16. A series of lectures and exercises at Senter for livshjelp, Ski, Norway.

Nelson, Robin. 2013. *Practice as Research in the Arts, Principles, Protocols, Pedagogies, Resistances*. Basingstoke: Palgrave MacMillan.

Newton, Anne. 2015. Email correspondence with the author, 2 February.

nmzMedia. 2015. Meisterkurs Dirigieren Youtube, 13 March. Accessed February 21, 2018. https://www.youtube.com/watch?v=5k0VvShijk0

Norrington, Nigel. 2013. Review, *Much Ado About Nothing. London Evening Standard*, September 20. Accessed August 7, 2016 http://www.standard.co.uk/goingout/theatre/much-ado-about-not hing-old-vic-theatre-review-8828894.html.

Norris, Bruce. 2007. *The Pain and the Itch*, London: Nick Hern.

nuevamusicologia. 2012. The Art of Conducting: Great Conductors of the Past. Youtube, 29 July. Accessed February 21, 2018. https://www.youtube.com/watch?v=LYnqU4AJvtA

Orozco, Lourdes. 2013. *Theatre & Animals*, Basingstoke: Palgrave Macmillan.

Orwoll, L., and Achenbaum, W.A. 1993. Gender and the development of wisdom. *Human Development* 36: 274-296.

Ostermeier, Thomas. 2008. ...die Selbstbefeiung des Regietheaters von Moden. Ein Interview. In *Regietheater! Wie sich über Inszenierungen streiten last*, edited by Ortrud Gutjahr, 155-170. Würzburg: Königshausen.

Ott, Meredith C. 2009. *Child Actor Ethics: Children in Plays with Adult Themes*, MA thesis, University of Oregon. Accessed 16 August 2015. https://www.google.co.uk/search?q=ott+child+actor+ethics&ie=utf-8&oe=utf-8&channel=fs&gws_rd=cr,ssl&ei=TWbQVbzSI8X1aMG-gpgB.

Otto, Rudolf. 1959. *The Idea of the Holy*. London: Penguin Books.

Paterson, Eddie and Lara Stevens. 2013. From Shakespeare to the Super Bowl: Theatre and Global Liveness. *Australasian Drama Studies* 62: 147.

Pfabigan, Sieglinde. 2012. Minden: Tristan und Isolde. *Der Neue Merker*. October. Accessed September 21, 2012. http://www.der-neue-merker.eu/minden-tristan-und-isolde.

Phelan, Peggy. 1993. *Unmarked: The Politics of Performance*. London: Routledge.

Pinchbeck, Michael. 2014. Interview with the author, tape, 18 February.

Pirandello, Luigi. 2008. *Six Characters in Search of an Author*. In a new version by Rupert Goold and Ben Power. London: Nick Hern.

Polkinghorne, D. 1983. *Methodology for the human sciences: Systems of inquiry*. Albany: SUNY Press;

Popp, Fritz Albert. 2006. *Biophotonen—Neue Horizonte in der Medizin: Von den Grundlagen zur Biophotonik*. Stuttgart: Haug.

Poppiti, Kimberley. 2005. Galloping horses: Treadmills and other theatre appliances in hippodramas. *Theatre Design and Technology*, 41 (4): 46–59.

Power, Cormac. 2008. *Presence in Play: A Critique of Theories of Presence in the Theatre*, Amsterdam: Rodopi.

Prebble, Lucy. 2012. *The Effect*. London: Methuen Drama.

Punt, Michael. 2015. Email correspondence with the author, 2 February.

Putnam, Walter. 2007. Captive audiences, a concert for the elephants in the Jardin Des Plantes. *The Drama Review* 51 (1):154–60.

Reason, Matthew. 2006. *Documentation, Disappearance and the Representation of Live Performance*. Basingstoke: Palgrave Macmillan.

—. 2006. Young audiences and live theatre, Part 2: Perceptions of liveness in performance. *Studies in Theatre and Performance* 26 (3).

Ridley, Philip. 2005. *Mercury Fur,* London: Bloomsbury.

Roesner, David. 2013. Dancing in the twilight: on the borders of music and the scenic. In *The Legacy of Opera: Reading Music Theatre as Experience and Performance*, edited by Dominic Symonds and Pamela Karantonis, 165-183. Amsterdam: Rodopi.

Rosch, Paul J. 2009. Bioelectromagnetic and Subtle Energy Medicine: The Interface between Mind and Matter. *Annals of the New York Academy of Science* 1172.

Rosenthal, Rachel. 2007. Animals Love Theatre. *The Drama Review* 51 (1): 5-7.

Running, Donald J. 2011. Charisma, Conductors, and the Affective Communication Test. *Journal of Band Research* 47(1): 18-27.

Rushdie, Salman. 1997. *Shame*. Toronto: Vintage Canada.

Ryan, Robert S. and Jonathan W. Schooler. 1998. Whom Do Words Hurt? Individual Differences in Susceptibility to Verbal Overshadowing. *Applied Cognitive Psychology* 12: S105-S125.

Sadler, Veronica (2013). Review, *Much Ado About Nothing*. In *The Huffington Post*, September 17. Accessed August 7, 2016. http://www.huffingtonpost.co.uk/victoria-sadler/much-ado-aboutnothing-old-vic-review_b_3926023.html.

Saillant, Karen. 2013. Interview by author, Skype,

—. 2015a. Interview for *Turning Points for Children*, Philadelphia. Accessed February 21, 2018. https://www.youtube.com/watch?v=guZRWiYX_wU

—. 2015b Plenary talk at the 6th International Conference on Consciousness, Theatre, Literature and the Arts, St Francis College, Brooklyn Heights, New York, 10 June.

—. 2015c. Facebook statement, 8 February.

Saint Germain. 2004. *Das Tor zum Goldenen Zeitalter*/'The gate to the golden age', Seeon: ChFalk.

Sakteera, Maneephan. 2010. *The Study of the Dhammas on Beauty in Theravada Buddhist Scripture*. (Master of Arts (Buddhist Studies)), Mahachulalongkornrajavidyalaya University, Bangkok, Thailand. Accessed March 16, 2017. http://www.mcu.ac.th/userfiles/file/library1/Thesis/845.pdf

Schiller, F. 1789/1972. *The Nature and Value of Universal History: An Inaugural Lecture*. *History and Theory* 11 (3): 321-334.

Schmidt, Christopher. 2008. Geist, der stets bejaht. Regietheater in der Konsensfalle. In *Regietheater! Wie sich über Inszenierungen streiten last*, edited by Ortrud Gutjahr, 71-80. Würzburg: Königshausen.

Schröter, Regula. 2015. "Wo beginnt die Geschichte? / Where does history (the story) begin?" Programme notes on *Scorched*. Bremen: Theater Bremen.

Schubert, Friederike. 2015. Interview with Daniel Meyer-Dinkgräfe, 20 November.

Schubert, Friederike and Simone Sterr. 2015. Interview with Daniel Meyer-Dinkgräfe, 20 November.

Shaffer, Peter. 1980. *Amadeus*. London: Deutsch.

Shafiri, Azadeh. 2014. Postmigrantisches Theater: Eine neue Agenda für die deutschen Bühnen. In *Theater und Migration. Herausforderungen für Kulturpolitik und Theaterpraxis,* edited by Woldfang Schneider, 35-45. Bielefeld: Transkript.

Sheets-Johnstone, Maxine. 2009. *The Corporeal Turn. An Interdisciplinary Reader*. Exeter: Imprint Academic.

Shepherd, Philip. 2015. Email correspondence with the author, 3 February.

Shepherd-Barr, Kirsten. 2012. *Science of Stage. From Doctor Faustus to Copenhagen*. Princeton: Princxeton University Press.

Shook, Estelle. 2008. Making theatre with horses. *Canadian Theatre Review* 135: 55–57.

Sicchio, Kate. 2014. Interview with the author, tape, 13 February.

Simoncic, Tara. 2013. I'm an orchestra conductor. What do you want to know? *The Guardian*, 22 July. Accessed 21 february 2018.

https://www.theguardian.com/commentisfree/2013/jul/22/female-orchestra-conductor-life-of-music

Skjoldager Nielsen, Kim. 2016. Über die Schwelle, in die Welt hinein. Das spirituelle Potential der Performance. double – magazin für puppen-figuren- und objekttheater No. 33 and https://www.youtube.com/watch?v=JhQqtNUlITY

Skramstad, Per-Eric and Kathrine Holte. 2009. Peter Konwitschny: I do not consider myself a representative of the *Regietheater*. *Wagneropera.net*. Accessed September 15, 2012. http://www.wagneropera.net/Interviews/Peter-Konwitschny-Interview-2009.htm

Sloterdijk, Peter. 2012. Anthropisches Klima. In *Atmosphären: Dimensionen eines diffusen Phänomens*, edited by Christiane Heibach, 27-38. München: Wilhelm Fink.

Spencer, Charles. 2014. Review, *The Nether. The Telegraph*, 14 July. Accessed August 16, 2015. http://www.telegraph.co.uk/culture/theatre/theatre-reviews/10991160/The-Nether-Royal-Court-review-haunting.html.

—. 2013. Review, *Much Ado About Nothing. The Telegraph*, September 20. Accessed August 7, 2016. http://www.telegraph.co.uk/culture/theatre/theatre-reviews/10321616/Much-AdoAbout-Nothing-The-Old-Vic-review.html.

Steier, Lydia. 2004. Shock and awe in the German capitol. Online draft. 24 July. Accessed September 16, 2012. http://www.striporama.com/steier_kids/Eine_Schande.htm ().

Steinbach, Ludwig. 2011. In Bayreuth wird die Erinnerung geweckt. *Musenblätter*. 27 July. Accessed September 16, 2012. http://www.musenblaetter.de/artikel.php?aid=8981&suche=.

Stoppard, Tom. 2015. *The Hard Problem*. London: Faber and Faber.

Suleiman, Susan. 2002. The 1.5 Generation: Thinking About Child Survivors and the Holocaust. *American Imago*, 59 (3): 277-295.

Tait, Peta. 2009. Trained performances of love and cruelty between species. *Performance Research* 14 (2): 67–73.

Tart, Charles T. 1972. States of consciousness and state-specific sciences. *Science* 176: 1203 -1210.

Tesch, R. 1990. *Qualitative research: Analysis types and software tools*. Bristol, PA: Falmer.

Thalheimer, Michael. 2008. ...diese Arbeit am pulsierenden Zentrum des Stückes. Ein Interview. In *Regietheater! Wie sich über Inszenierungen streiten last*, edited by Ortrud Gutjahr, 189-202. Würzburg: Königshausen.

This is a world of dew. Kristina Gjems. Premiere: 1 9.5.201 5, Danses Hus, Oslo. http://www.dansenshus.com/forestillinger/this-is-a-world-of-dew/

Thomas, Stefanie and Ute Kunzmann. 2013. Age differences in wisdom-related knowledge: does the age relevance of the task matter? *Journals of Gerontology, Series B: Psychological Sciences and Social Sciences* 69(6): 897-905.

Tomlinson, Lee. 2013. Review, *Much Ado about Nothing*. *TimeOut London*, September 20. Accessed August 7, 2016. http://www.telegraph.co.uk/culture/theatre/theatre-reviews/10321616/Much-AdoAbout-Nothing-The-Old-Vic-review.html.

Travis, F.T., T. Olsen, T. Egenes and H.K.Gupta. 2001. Physiological patterns during practice of Transcendental Meditation Technique compared with patterns while reading Sanskrit and a modern language. *International Journal of Neuroscience* 109: 71-80

Travis, Frederick and Craig Pearson. 2000. Pure Consciousness: Distinct Phenomenological and Physiological Correlates of 'Consciousness Itself'. *International Journal of Neuroscience* 100 (1-4): 77-89.

Trivers, Robert. 1971. The Evolution of Reciprocal Altruism. *The Quarterly Review of Biology* 46(1): 35-57.

—. 2006. Reciprocal Altruism: 30 years later. *Cooperation in Primates and Humans: Mechanisms and Evolution*, edited by Peter M. Kappeler and Carel P. van Schaik, 67-83. Berlin: Springer.

Turner, Victor. 1982. *From Ritual to Theatre*. New York: PAJ Publications.

Varela. Francisco J. and Jonathan Shear (1999). First-person methodologies: What, why, how. *Journal of Consciousness Studies* 6 (2-3): 1-14.

Watson, Ian. 1993. *Towards a Third Theatre: Eugenio Barba and the Odin Teatret*. London and New York: Routledge.

Webster, Jeffrey Dean, Gerben J. Westerhof, and Ernst T. Bohlmeijer. 2014. Wisdom and mental health across the lifespan. *Journals of Gerontology, Series B: Psychological Sciences and Social Sciences* 69(2): 209-218.

Wedekind, Frank. 1980, *Spring Awakening*. Trans. Edward Bond, London: Methuen.

Werner, Hendrik. 2015. "Dunkle Familiengeheimnisse." *Weser Kurier*, September 28. Accessed on July 6, 2016. http://www.weser-kurier.de/startseite_artikel,-Dunkle-Familiengeheimnisse-_arid,1217863.html

Westerside, Andrew. 2014. Interview with the author, tape, 3 February.

Williams, David. 2007. Inappropriate/de others or the difficulty of being a dog. *The Drama Review* 51 (1): 92–118.

Wright, Sewall. 1931. Evolution in Mendelian Populations. *Genetics* 16: 97-159.

Yarrow, Ralph. 2015. Email correspondence with the author, 2 February.

Zacher, Hannes, Bernard McKenna, David Rooney. 2013. Effects of Self-Reported Wisdom on Happiness: Not Much More Than Emotional Intelligence? *J Happiness Stud* 14: 1697-1716.

Zorn, Christa. 2015. Email correspondence with the author, 2 February

CONTRIBUTORS

Anita S Hammer
Anita S. Hammer studied Theatre, Literature and Nordic Language at the Universities of Trondheim and Bergen. She has worked with mythology, creative writing, acting and storytelling in Norway and New Zealand. Her Ph. D, in Theatre Studies was obtained from the Norwegian University of Science and Technology in 2001 . She was a Professor/associate Professor of Theatre Studies at the University of Oslo from 2002 to 201 1 . Since 201 1 she has been a Professor at the Queen Maud University College in Trondheim. She works actively to combine aesthetic academic approaches with holistic practices. She has published books and articles on the topic of theatre and spirituality, and has a special interest in ritual practice and theory, and performance theory. She has been connected to the network of Consciousness, Literature and the Arts since 2006.

Tanatchaporn Kittikong trained as an actress in Russia and holds a PhD from the Western Australian Academy of Performing Arts (WAAPA). She is a lecturer in the Performing Arts Department at Khon Kaen University, Thailand. Inspired by her practice of Buddhist Vipassana meditation, she seeks to understand what lies beyond a performer's consciousness.

Dr. Yana Meerzon teaches for the University of Ottawa. Her research interests are in the areas of drama and performance theory, theatre of exile and immigration, and Michael Chekhov acting theory. Her recent publications include *Performing Exile – Performing Self: Drama, Theatre, Film* (Palgrave 2012); *History/Memory/Performance*, co-edited with Kathryn Prince and David Dean, (Palgrave 2015); and a special issue of the journal Theatre Research in Canada (Vol. 36. No.2, Fall 2015) on Theatre and Immigration in Canada.

Barbara Sellers-Young is a professor emerita in the Dance Department at York University. Her research on transcultural body has been supported by grants from the American Council of Learned Societies, Davis Humanities Center and the Center for RISK at Charles Sturt University. She is the past president of the Congress on Research in Dance and has taught at institutions in the United States, Australia, China and England. Her books include two single authored books: *Teaching Personality with Gracefulness* and *Breathing, Movement, Exploration* and three edited volumes *Embodied Consciousness: Technologies of Performance, Belly Dance: Orientalism, Transnationalism and Harem Fantasy* and *Belly Dance Around the World*.

Gregory F. Tague, Ph.D. is Professor of English at St. Francis College, N.Y. Generally, his work examines the intersection of ethics/evolution/arts. More specifically, he studies the notion of character, moral sense, consciousness, and the evolution of culture. Go to his site to learn about publications and such: https://sites.google.com/site/gftague/

INDEX